Alan Lomax, Assistant in Charge

ALAN LOMAX
ASSISTANT IN CHARGE

The Library of Congress Letters, 1935–1945

Edited by Ronald D. Cohen

University Press of Mississippi / Jackson

AMERICAN MADE MUSIC SERIES
Advisory Board

www.upress.state.ms.us

The University Press of Mississippi is a member of
the Association of American University Presses.

page ii: Alan Lomax and Jerome Weisner transcribing folk
songs and documenting records in the Library of Congress.
(Photo by Bernard Hoffman/Time Life Pictures/Getty Images)

First printing 2010
∞
Library of Congress Cataloging-in-Publication Data

Lomax, Alan, 1915–2002.
Alan Lomax, assistant in charge : the Library of Congress letters, 1935–1945
/ edited by Ronald D. Cohen.
p. cm. — (American made music series)
Includes bibliographical references and index.
ISBN 978-1-60473-800-1 (cloth : alk. paper) — ISBN 978-1-60473-801-8
(ebook) 1. Lomax, Alan, 1915–2002—Correspondence. 2. Ethnomusicolo-
gists—United States—Correspondence. I. Cohen, Ronald D., 1940– II. Title.
ML423.L6347A4 2010
781.620092—dc22   2010027833

British Library Cataloging-in-Publication Data available

To Bess Lomax Hawes

(January 21, 1921–November 27, 2009)

Contents

1935
FLORIDA
1. Belle Glade
2. Chosen
3. Eatonville

GEORGIA
(with Zora Neale Hurston and Mary Elizabeth Barnicle)
4. Frederica

NEW YORK
5. New York City
   Aunt Molly Jackson

1936
TEXAS
(with John A. Lomax)
6. Austin – includes first recordings of the Soul Stirrers gospel group

1937
KENTUCKY
(with Elizabeth Lyttleton Lomax)
7. Arjay
8. Big Creek
9. Billy's Branch
10. Cody
11. Dalesburg
12. Floress
13. Fort Thomas
14. Goose Rock
15. Hazard
16. Horse Creek
17. Hyden
18. Lakeville
19. Manchester
20. Martin's Creek
21. Middlefork
22. Middlesboro
23. Paintsville
24. Pine Mountain
25. Providence
26. Salyersville
27. Webb Branch
28. West Liberty
29. Wooten

MARYLAND
30. Chevy Chase
   Songs played and sung by Alan Lomax, Bess Brown Lomax, Margaret Valiant, and the "Resettlement Folk Singers." Recorded by Lomax.

NEW YORK
5. New York City
   Jim Garland
   Mr. and Mrs. Joe Gelder
   Sarah Ogan Gunning
   Aunt Molly Jackson

OHIO
31. Akron

WASHINGTON, D.C.
32. Library of Congress
   Charles J. Finger
   Myra E. Hull

1938
ILLINOIS
33. Chicago

INDIANA
(with Elizabeth Lyttleton Lomax)
34. Bloomington
35. Brown County
36. Crawford County
37. Deuchars
38. Evansville
39. Goshen
40. New Harmony
41. Princeton
42. Vincennes

MICHIGAN
43. Beaver Island
44. Calumet
45. Champion
46. Charles
47. Detroit
48. Grandville
49. Greenland
50. Marinesco
51. Mt. Pleasant
52. Munising
53. Newberry
54. Ontonagon
55. St. Ignace
56. Traverse City

NEW JERSEY
(with Kay Dealy)
57. Gloucester

OHIO
(with Elizabeth Lyttleton Lomax)
31. Akron
58. Cincinnati
59. Hamilton

PENNSYLVANIA
60. Bryn Mawr

WASHINGTON, D.C.
32. Library of Congress
   Barbara Bell
   Ernest Bourne
   Jelly Roll Morton
   Judge Learned Hand
   W. C. Handy
   James P. Johnson
   Pete Johnson
   Huddie Ledbetter (Lead Belly)
   Rindlisbacher Lumberjack Group
   Johnnie Robertson
   Gertrude Smartts
   Blaine Stubblefield
   Minnie Swearingen

WISCONSIN
61. Odonah

1939
NEW HAMPSHIRE
(with Helen Hartness Flanders)
62. Orford
63. Walpole

NEW YORK
5. New York City
   Albert Ammons
   Aunt Molly Jackson
   James P. Johnson
   Pete Johnson
   Meade Lux Lewis
   Captain Richard Maitlin
   Saunders Terrell (Sonny Terry)

VERMONT
(with Helen Hartness Flanders)
64. Bennington
65. Chelsea
66. East Calais
67. Quebec *(location unknown)*
68. Springfield

VIRGINIA
(with Pete Seeger)
69. Galax
70. Roanoke

WASHINGTON, D.C.
32. Library of Congress
   Blaine Stubblefield

1940
WASHINGTON, D.C.
32. Library of Congress
   Woody Guthrie
   Herbert Smoke

1941
MISSISSIPPI
71. Lula
72. Clarksdale

73. Senatobia
74. Stovall Plantation
   (first recordings of Muddy Wa

NORTH CAROLINA
75. Asheville (with Jerome Wiesn and Robert Liss)
76. Swannanoa

VIRGINIA
77. Fort Myer, Arlington
69. Galax
78. Rugby
79. Salem
80. Winchester

WASHINGTON, D.C.
32. Library of Congress

1942
ALABAMA
81. Birmingham (Sacred Harp Convention, with George Pullen Jackson)

ARKANSAS
82. Sadie Beck's plantation, near Robinsonville, Mississip

MISSISSIPPI
72. Clarksdale
83. Robinsonville
73. Senatobia

VIRGINIA
84. Saltville

1944
FLORIDA
85. Tampa

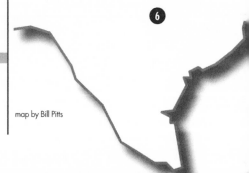

ALAN LOMAX RECORDING SESSIONS IN THE UNITED STATES 1935-1944

6

map by Bill Pitts

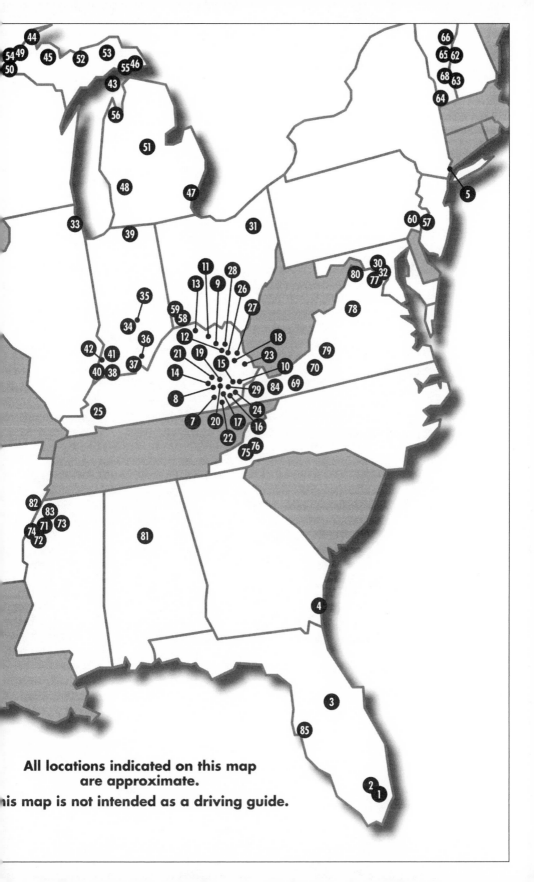

All locations indicated on this map
are approximate.

his map is not intended as a driving guide.

Alan Lomax and Jerome Weisner of the Archive of American Folk Songs (Photo by Bernard Hoffman/Time Life Pictures/Getty Images)

Introduction

Alan Lomax's life spanned much of the twentieth century (1915–2002), and during most of this time he was an active folk song collector and scholar. He has been both praised and criticized. The Rounder Records Alan Lomax Collection, with at least 100 CDs, is only one example of his incredible musical output. He was not only active in making field recordings, he was also a prolific writer, as demonstrated in Ronald D. Cohen, ed., *Alan Lomax: Selected Writings 1934–1997* (New York: Routledge, 2003), which also includes biographical information, analyses of his musical theories, and a complete bibliography. He was also a busy correspondent, particularly during his time with the Library of Congress, demonstrating a complex individual, far more interesting and expansive than the folklorist/ethnomusicologist, even radio personality, who has been written about and feted. Fortunately, John Szwed has now covered much of his amazing story in *Alan Lomax: A Biography* (New York: Viking, 2010).

A reading and examination of his letters reveals not only someone who led an extremely complex, fascinating, creative life. He also had great love for his family and extensive relationships with hundreds of friends and others. Most of the letters published here are located in various collections in the American Folklife Center of the Library of Congress; others are from smaller, scattered repositories. Lomax was a prolific correspondent with his family, even when young, but I have had to begin in 1935, when he initiated his formal relationship with the Library of Congress. I have included all of the available letters that are in the public domain through 1945, when Lomax was mostly working for the government. I have also occasionally cited pertinent letters to Alan in the notes. There are certainly others that will eventually be indexed in the American Folklife Center correspondence files, both to and from Alan. I do not have permission to quote from those letters that are part of the Lomax Papers at the Center for American History at the University of Texas, which vividly indicate Alan's intimate, and occasionally feisty, relationship with his father. Some of these letters, including details missing from his professional letters, are referred to in the endnotes.

Lomax had a complex relationship with his elderly father, John. They shared many experiences and personal moments, but also disagreed about politics and music. He also confided in his brother Johnny and younger sister Bess. He did field collecting with his father and particularly with Elizabeth, his wife. Lomax's life was full of triumphs, but also many hardships, criticisms, health problems, and financial difficulties. He was skilled at luring plain folks before his microphone, and continued to correspond with them in order to maintain contact. He was also involved with the mechanics of recording in the field, often with primitive, troublesome equipment. As an employee of the federal government he had to continually deal with bureaucratic hurdles and financial matters and constraints; during this period he was always short of personal funds. His radical politics surfaced in various ways, sometimes giving him trouble, but also meant the excitement of meeting and working with politically active musicians such as Woody Guthrie, Pete Seeger, Lead Belly, Burl Ives, Josh White, and the Golden Gate Quartet.

He recorded extensively in the South, which is commonly known, but also in Haiti, the Bahamas, Michigan, Indiana, Ohio, Wisconsin, Washington, D.C., and Vermont during the years covered in these letters (and, of course, in Great Britain, Spain, and Italy in the 1950s, and other places in the United States in the 1950s and 1960s). He was an omnivorous reader and collector, always bubbling over with fresh ideas and projects, many of which never went much further than his fervent, creative imagination. He was as much at home behind a microphone in a dusty field as before it in a radio or recording studio.

Alan Lomax was born in Austin, Texas, January 31, 1915, the third child of John Avery and Bess Brown Lomax, after Shirley and then John Jr. Their fourth child, Bess, followed six years later. Following a year at the University of Texas (1930–1931), then a year at Harvard College (1931–1932), he returned to the University of Texas, and finally graduated in 1936. During 1933 he accompanied his father on a recording trip through the South, and he continued occasionally to travel with his father while at the University of Texas. He helped his father with the publication of *American Ballads and Folk Songs* (1934), and the same year published his first article, "'Sinful' Songs of the Southern Negro," in the winter 1934 issue of the *Southwest Review*. Father and son also worked together on *Negro Folk Songs as Sung by Lead Belly* (1936) and *Our Singing Country: A Second Volume of American Ballads & Folk Songs* (1941).

In mid-1935, accompanied by the folklorists Zora Neale Hurston and Mary Elizabeth Barnicle, Lomax participated in a collecting trip through Georgia, Florida, and the Bahamas, having gotten some Library of Congress support. Alan began working for the Archive of American Folk Song at the Library of Congress in 1936, first as a special and temporary assistant, then as the permanent Assistant in Charge starting in June 1937, until he left in late 1942 to work for the Office of War Information, where he stayed into mid-April 1943. He joined the army on April 4, 1944, and remained in the military into early 1946, continually stationed within the States. This means that his government letters wound down in 1943, although there were a few into 1945. While in the army he continued broadcasting a variety of radio shows.

Alan's interest in folk music and radical politics sprang from a combination of his father's aesthetic influences and his own experiences at Harvard during the nadir of the

Depression. While John remained a political conservative, Alan connected vernacular music with a strong populist sensibility, infused with a belief in racial justice, that would carry throughout his life. He was anxious to spread these messages through his numerous publications, radio shows, promotional activities, collecting trips, and so much more. While his health at times appeared rather fragile, he nonetheless kept up an amazing, and seemingly tireless, creative and physical agenda. He was prickly and sensitive, and his single-minded focus on his work sometimes made him appear ruthless and uncaring. However, despite occasional outbursts of temper or frustration, he focused not on the negative but on the tasks ahead.

There were some controversial issues, such as his collecting trips in Mississippi connected with John Work and other researches from Fisk University in 1941–1942. Alan's letters help present his side of this rather complex story. He tried, more or less successfully, to document and present folk music in all sorts of formats and venues. His recording sessions with Woody Guthrie, Lead Belly, and Jelly Roll Morton are major achievements. Through his early radio programs he presented Woody, Lead Belly, Pete Seeger, Burl Ives, Josh White, Sonny Terry, and Brownie McGhee to a broad public, and in the process was vital in shaping their commercial successes. He corresponded with most of the folk song and ballad collectors of the day, both major and minor, while cultivating grassroots informants throughout much of the country.

While Lomax is most noted for his field recordings, the letters make clear that he was also very interested in the commercial hillbilly, race, and even popular recordings of the 1920s and after. Indeed, Alan eagerly collected thousands for the Library of Congress, and he followed his father's reissue collection, *Smoky Mountain Ballads* (Victor, 1941) in compiling two Brunswick 78 rpm albums of early country songs, *Mountain Frolic* and *Listen to Our Story* (1947). Moreover, while his role in recording and promoting African American music has often been emphasized—partly stimulated by his late publication of *Land Where the Blues Began* (1993)—throughout his life his musical tastes were truly, even increasingly, eclectic.

During his last months in the army he was living in New York with his family. After his discharge in the spring of 1946, he plunged back into the worlds of folk music and radical politics, through his radio shows on the Mutual network, as well as through his work with People's Songs, an organization formed by Pete Seeger and others in late 1945 to promote a singing Left. Alan organized musical shows for Henry Wallace's Progressive Party presidential campaign in 1948, for example; but, feeling the heat of the growing Red Scare beginning to sweep the country, he moved to England in 1950. During much of the 1950s he promoted folk music through his BBC radio shows, while conducting collecting trips through the British Isles, Spain, and Italy. Lomax returned to the United States in 1958 and immediately began a recording trip to the South, while connecting with the developing folk music revival. His writings now took a more theoretical turn, first with Cantometrics, his ideas about singing styles based an international comparative perspective, resulting in *Folk Song Style and Culture* (1968), followed by Choreometrics, a similar study of the world's dance and movement styles. He published his final songbook, *The Folk Songs of North America*, in 1960, followed by the award-winning *Land Where the Blues Began*. Up to his death in 2002, Alan continued to promote his ideas about cultural equality—the notion that all cultures were equally valuable and relevant—through various publications and activities.

Until a full biography of Alan Lomax appears, these letters will serve as a way of understanding his fascinating life, both public and private, at least through the end of World War II. Unfortunately, some topics are barely touched upon, if at all. For example, there is little overt discussion of his left-wing political views, his wife Elizabeth's role in their various collecting trips, or his radio shows. Alan Lomax was one of the most stimulating and influential cultural workers of the twentieth century, and it is time to allow him to speak for himself through his voluminous correspondence. His work for the Library of Congress was particularly important: he greatly expanded its collection of field and commercial recordings, and promoted the positive role and image of the federal government throughout the country. He quickly became recognized as perhaps the preeminent folklorist in the country.

I had a brief exchange of letters with Lomax in 1993 and have cherished his two responses; I believe I have taken all of his information and advice to heart. I feel privileged that he took the time to write, and I hope this volume is another step toward acknowledging his helping "a younger colleague."

Since Alan was a most prolific writer, and was often in a hurry, I have found it necessary to correct any obvious misspellings and punctuation errors in order to smooth things out (and avoid numerous uses of [*sic*]). I have attempted to retain his occasionally idiosyncratic style, and have tried to preserve his paragraph breaks as much as possible (while grouping together shorter paragraphs to enhance the flow). He was, fortunately, an excellent typist, but his handwriting could be problematic. He usually dated his official correspondence, but with undated letters I have made an educated guess, and I have omitted some for which the dating is too problematic. The letters are in basic chronological order, in a narrative format, allowing Alan to tell his story as it unfolded. I have included background information as headnotes to the letters, where appropriate, and also in the numerous endnotes; but until a full biography of Alan appears, it will be necessary to assume that the reader has some general knowledge about him, or at least access to the numerous secondary works I have cited. I have also tried to identify as many of the individuals mentioned as possible, along with supplying detailed information for many, but certainly not all. Moreover, I have not referred to Alan's detailed field notebooks and documentary films now available in the American Folklife Center at the Library of Congress, which add significant information about his collecting trips.

I want to thank Nancy-Jean Ballard for the Helen Hartness Flanders letters; the Center for American History at the University of Texas for the Lomax and John Henry Faulk correspondence; the Woody Guthrie Archives for Alan's letters to Woody; Steve Weiss of the Southern Folklife Collection at the University of North Carolina for his letters to Annabel Morris Buchanan; the Wisconsin Music Archives, Mills Music Library at the University of

Wisconsin–Madison for the Helene Stratman-Thomas letters; Matt Barton; and so many others. I have had the extraordinary assistance of Todd Harvey at the American Folklife Center, who is the keeper of the Lomax collection and so much else. Without Todd's help there would be no book. I particularly want to thank David Evans for his exacting editorial skills and keen insights, Jim Leary of the University of Wisconsin for his assistance, as well as Anna Lomax Wood, Don Fleming, and Ellen Harold of the Association for Cultural Equity for their most helpful comments. Craig Gill of the University Press of Mississippi has been most supportive as this project has proceeded to publication.

Following are the manuscript collections I have drawn upon, with the abbreviations used in the text sources:

ALC:	The John A. and Alan Lomax Manuscript Collection, American Folklife Center, Library of Congress (AFC 1933/001 and 2004/004)
AMB, SFC:	Annabel Morris Buchanan Collection, Southern Folklife Collection, University of North Carolina-Chapel Hill, North Carolina
CBS:	Alan Lomax CBS Radio Series Collection, American Folklife Center, Library of Congress (AFC 1939/002)
F-LC:	The Library of Congress Fisk University Mississippi Delta Collection, American Folklife Center, Library of Congress (AFC 1941/002)
FVMF:	"'Now What a Time': Blues, Gospel, and the Fort Valley Music Festivals, 1938–1943" (online presentation), American Folklife Center, Library of Congress
HS-T:	Helene Stratman-Thomas Collection, Wisconsin Music Archives, Mills Music Library, University of Wisconsin-Madison
JHFP:	John Henry Faulk Papers, Center for American History, University of Texas at Austin
N-JB:	Nancy-Jean Ballard Collection, Bethesda, Maryland
LP:	Lomax Family Papers, Center for American History, University of Texas at Austin
Lomax FBI file:	Alan Lomax file, Federal Bureau of Investigation, U.S. Department of Justice, Washington, D.C.
RRP:	Radio Research Project Manuscript Collection, American Folklife Center, Library of Congress (AFC 1941/005)
VFDB:	"Voices From the Dust Bowl: The Charles L. Todd and Robert Sonkin Migrant Worker Collection, 1940–1941" (online presentation), American Folklife Center, Library of Congress
WGA:	Woody Guthrie Archives, Mount Kisco, New York

WGC: "Woody Guthrie and the Archive of American Folk Song
            Correspondence, 1940–1950" (online presentation), American
            Folklife Center, Library of Congress
WMC: Willie McTell Correspondence File, Archive of Folk Culture
            General Correspondence, American Folklife Center, Library
            of Congress

Alan Lomax, Assistant in Charge

A PROGRAM OF
AMERICAN SONGS
FOR
AMERICAN SOLDIERS

arranged entirely on
THE DAVY CROCKETT
or
go ahead PRINCIPLE

1846. CROCKETT ALMANAC. 1846.

GO AHEAD

CROCKETT, BEN HARDIN, AND DEATH HUG, GOING AHEAD OF A STEAMER.

The White House
Monday, February Seventeenth
Nine P. M.

Program cover to "A Program of American Songs for American Soldiers," a concert at the White House, 1941, produced by Alan Lomax. (Alan Lomax Recordings of Rehearsals for White House Program, AFC 1941/006, fol. 302, American Folklife Center, Library of Congress)

LETTERS, 1935–1938

1935

In May 1933, at the tender age of eighteen already a fast learner, Alan began traveling and collecting folk songs through the South with his father, John A. Lomax; this was also the start of his connection with the Archive of American Folk Song at the Library of Congress.[1] John Lomax would become Honorary Conservator of the Archive in September 1933. Alan assisted his father with the publication of their pathbreaking compilation *American Ballads and Folk Songs* in 1934, and the same year published his first article, "'Sinful' Songs of the Southern Negro," in the winter 1934 issue of the *Southwest Review*.[2] In 1936 father and son would again collaborate with the publication of *Negro Folk Songs as Sung by Lead Belly*, whom they had met at the Angola State Prison Farm in Louisiana during their 1933 trip. In 1935, while still in college, accompanied by the somewhat older Zora Neale Hurston and Mary Elizabeth Barnicle, Alan launched another collecting trip to Georgia and Florida; he then went with Barnicle on a similar journey to the Bahamas, after having obtained the loan of a recording machine from the Library of Congress. Hurston (1891–1960) was already an established folklorist and novelist of African American life, while Barnicle (1891–1978) taught English and folklore at New York University.[3]

During his trip with Hurston and Barnicle, he composed a lengthy letter from Miami, Florida, on July 1, 1935, to his father at the Library of Congress. The message demonstrates his sharp eye and ear for detail, fascination with and knowledge of vernacular music, and a felicitous writing style, but also evinces some of the racial stereotyping so common in that era:

I have just completed a count of our records. So far we have made seventy-five double-faced records consisting of the following types of recordings: Spirituals, chanteys, ring-shouts, folk-tales, jumping dances, work songs, ballads, guitar picking, minstrel songs, praying, sermons. The chanteys are of two sorts. 1) Chanteys sung by the longshoremen at Savannah and Brunswick to help them load cotton and turpentine aboard ship. 2) Chanteys sung by Bahaman Negro sailors, some traditional, some indigenous. The ring shouts are the oldest spirituals we have yet recorded, date back to slavery times, are sung to the accompaniment of dancing and hand-clapping. They are closely linked up by their rhythm and their melodies to the Bahaman jumping dances, which are sung with a drum accompaniment, in which the dancing is a direct descendant of African dancing. The folk-tales we have recorded have to do with a Negro heroic character called John who is the strongest and most cunning man who ever lived. They are wonderful stories and, since so common and so important, I am sure you won't regret a few records devoted to them. Our narrator was at least as good a story teller, if not a better, than [Mose] Clear Rock [Platt] on that occasion we both so pleasantly remember [at Imperial Prison near Sugarland, Texas]. This same John Davis, the man who told the John stories for us, staged an argument about the nature of the world in which he drew in a whole crowd of Negroes and worked them up to a high pitch of excitement. I couldn't resist the chance to turn on the recording machine and get down this garrulous, aimless discussion, so full of Negro wit and Negro illogic.

You will love the records. The prayers and sermons I have recorded have not been particularly good. I am quite disappointed in them, but they are important, perhaps, if only they show what the Negro does even when he copies the white man word for word, even when he reads a white sermon, as one old fool of a preacher did, when I asked him to record. This incident was both ridiculous and tragic. Picture to yourself a huge, lazy, ignorant black preacher in a high stiff white collar and a long grey frock coat—the whole topped by a black stetson hat—picture this man in a big Methodist church with a congregation of fifteen assembled for the Sunday afternoon service, this old fool who had been told carefully that we wanted one of his rousing, revival sermons, rising and roaring and mumbling out, stumbling as he read a wordy discussion of the relation between special and general providence in which "we may clearly see Mr. Bushnell was well established in his position." Not a single amen did the old man get out of his congregation, not a single song to rest him when his voice and eyes were tired. But even after an hour of roaring at a stone faced audience, the old fool was still pleased with himself and rocked back and forth from heel to toe, thumbs in his vest and said; "In this first sermon I give out to the world, I want to let them know that I'm a man of learning and education." The records were painfully accurate and the congregation stood around the machine and shrieked with laughter as they listened until the poor old man realized what a fool he'd made himself and went away talking to himself into his own house and shut the door on the laughter of the young people.

This was in Eatonville [Florida] on a Sunday, Eatonville being the town where Miss Hurston was born and raised, the town about which she wrote her first novel. Her first novel, by the way, was about her father—a very successful, spell-binding preacher and a regular devil among the women. The day before on Saturday Miss Barnicle [and] Miss Hurston had gone over to a neighboring city, Orlando, to get Miss Barnicle's camera fixed. I was very dirty and needed a haircut, so I stepped into a little barber shop where it was advertised you could take a shower for a dime. I got my haircut, took my shower, and was walking across the sidewalk when a policeman accosted me, asked me where I was from, what I was doing in town and etc. I told him. He didn't like my story, so I was loaded into a police car and with Miss Barnicle bringing up the rear with a trailer of motorcycle cops we made a nice little parade down to the police station. There I was booked, my pockets ransacked, carefully searched and put into a cell in the city jail, too stiff with amazement to protest. In about an hour, during which I slept most of the time and recovered somewhat from the shock, I was taken up to the chief detective's office, carefully questioned and finally released. At the time I couldn't understand why I was picked up, but I now do. Police all over Florida were on the lookout for suspicious characters and bums. They are making every effort to keep this beautiful place from being overrun with criminals and hoboes. We were stopped on our way into Miami, Miss Barnicle and I, after we had dropped Miss Hurston with some [of] her friends, and we were stopped and our license was inspected.

Because of the experience we had in Orlando, I have decided to go around and see the police when we work a small town. In Belle Glade, the town in the Everglades we have just come away from, this is what I did. I called first on the mayor, then on the chief, explained what I was doing, showed them my letter to Governor Sholtz. They were very nice and even sent around a special officer to the tourist camp where I worked to help keep order. Belle Glade I have found to be the most interesting town I have visited in a long time. It lies in the center of a huge tract of drained swampland. The sun boils down with tropical intensity. The air is humid. It rains almost every day. The soil is black muck, so rich that it stings one's flesh slightly. It is a new development and a new town, swarming with new cars, laborers, rich in money and opportunity. It is the center of a great bean and cabbage industry which feeds the Northern markets. And in season, which lasts from the fifteenth of September until the last of May, the town is overrun with ten to fifteen thousand laborers, who earn from a dollar and a half to four dollars a day, who come from all over the South, white and black, who sleep in their own cars or in the filthy rooming houses or in the hovels that the plantation owners have erected for them. In the four days we were there we ran into a great deal of material and the most interesting set of Negroes I have seen in a long time. In town during the season the streets are so crowded with Negroes that it is impossible to drive a car through certain sections at night. The barrel houses and gambling joints run all night long every night, for the men are paid off every day. Out in the country, where the Bahaman Negroes live, the drum goes all night long and the Negroes dance just as they used to in Africa and in the fire dance they strip off all their clothes and the men leap over the fire to get to the women. We left there only because we were utterly worn out with the day-long grind of contact with swarms of people who wanted to sing but were suspicious. You know how this can weary one. Now, after two days of doing nothing here in Miami, I am just beginning to feel myself again. But you and I must come back to Belle Glade together during the season; it is the richest place in material I have ever been out of season and when those fifteen thousand poor whites and blacks from all over the South are about it must be marvelous. If I can't come back, I have left introductions all over the place for you, these along with glowing descriptions.

I think you can see why I would feel safer with some more letters of identification. I wish you would try to get something of the sort together for me and send them to me here—a letter on Library of Congress stationary that mentions us both along with a personal letter from yourself, mentioning Miss Barnicle and Miss Hurston and what we are doing. I will need these in the next few days because of two plans that are on foot. 1) To visit Mr. Hansen, Commissioner to the Seminole Indians at Fort Myers, to record Indian songs. 2) To sail over to Nassau, which is only overnight from here and which costs $19.50 roundtrip, to get the chanteys, the jumping dances and the African songs which Miss Hurston says are so thick there. From my contact with the Bahaman Negro I should judge that he has more songs than any other variety of Negro we have so far encountered—English Ballads, English Sea Chanteys, indigenous sea chanteys, indigenous ballads, African songs, jumping dances, etc. You see in the Bahaman, cut off completely as he is from his white associates by the British colonists' attitude, you have the mixing of the English and the African cultures in the earliest stage—a condition probably duplicated in America at the end of the eighteenth and beginning of the nineteenth century. In Bahama we can get at the root stuff and since it is such a short distance away from us here it seems a pity not to go after it. Miss Hurston tells us that on one island of the group—Cat Island, the plantations have been deserted for fifty years and the Negroes have lived in isolation and have dropped back into their way of living in Africa. They practice juju openly and sing many African songs. I think the records and pictures I can get there will make a sensation in Washington and will make up for whatever they have against us there. There, where they dance every night, where every sailor knows the chanteys and the ballads, I could probably get seventy-five records in a week.

I figure that I have spent of the Library's money in the month I have been away from home $117 and some cents. I think it would not be too unreasonable, since I have done such good work and so much wo[r]k in that time that you allow me a hundred dollars more to spend between this time and the day we will meet in Northern Florida toward the end of the month. Miss Barnicle and I can carry on with that sum, by living inexpensively for fifteen or twenty days and then we could go on to Nassau or down to Key West, where the French, Spanish, and English Negroes meet, just as we see fit at the time. Right now we are all a little too weary to decide exactly what to do and we shall spend the next two or three days writing letters and working the records.

I want to add that I have appreciated and enjoyed your frequent letters and your encouragement and I want to apologize for not having written more often. But I have worked harder and learned more in the past two weeks than I have ever done since I have been in the field. I have lived pretty hard as well and the combinations of all these things has left me too tired to write or do anything but flop to bed. This is the richest state, besides Texas that I have ever worked. You and I must come back together some day and take our time at it.

I am happy for your and Miss Terrill's sakes that she got her appointment for another year, but in some ways I almost wish it hadn't happened, so much did I want to see you gracing an official desk in Washington this year. Well, anyway, love to you and Miss Terrill and don't forget to give my felicitations to Elnora. Keep well and happy and please send me some letters of introduction and one hundred dollars in cash by airmail return, because until it comes we are pretty well tied down here. I have consulted bankers here and they tell me the best way to get money in a country where you're not known is to send it cash, by registered letter.

P. S. It may console you to know that I wrote you a letter three days ago in Belle Glade, lost it in the rush of leaving when a tube went bad, found it here, but decided it was too far out of date to send it. By the way, I have made two sets of recordings of children's game songs and some hollers of Negro boys which latter remind me of Lead Belly's Hoday. Which further reminds me that I have the Lead Belly material, shall get in the mail at least by tomorrow and shall get an airmail to Dr. [George] Herzog tonight. You were very considerate to give me the details of Dr. Herzog's letter, but I am glad you didn't send his musical introduction along. I have no mind left to give it. As I read it, this reminds me a little of Lead Belly's letters but perhaps my good intentions can make up for my lack of coherence. [ALC][4]

On August 3 he informed Oliver Strunk,[5] chief of the Music Division of the Library of
Congress, of his current situation, now that he was in Nassau, the Bahamas:

The department's recording machine has had an interesting time this summer and I should like to give you some account of it before you leave for
Europe. In many ways this has been the most exciting field trip I have made
and, really, can only be told in a long, rambling novel, but I shall confine
myself to a catalogue of records which, while exciting enough, is by no means
adequate for the whole story. Miss Mary Elizabeth Barnicle, professor of the
ballad at New York University, Miss Zora Hurston, Columbia anthropologist
and probably the best informed person today on Western Negro folk-lore,
and myself met in Brunswick, Ga. on June the fifteenth and began our search
for folk-songs there. Through Miss Hurston's influence we were soon living,
in an isolated community on St. Simon's island, on such friendly terms with
the Negroes as I had never experienced before. This community is a settlement of Negroes that has remained practically static since the days of slavery.
We rented a little Negro shantey and sent out the call for folk-singers. The
first evening our front yard was crowded.

In a week's time we had made about forty records. 1) Children's game
songs, both traditional and indigenous. 2) The shrill, strange cries that these
children use to signal to each other across the fields. 3) Chanties of the sort
that the Negroes sing in loading the ships in Charlestown, Savannah and
Brunswick, songs of the like that the white sailors heard in the days of clipper ships and turned to their own use—probably the earliest type of Negro
work-song. 4) Ring-shouts, probably the earliest form of the Negro spiritual,
widely current in the days of slavery, but now all but forgotten except in a
few isolated communities. These songs are for dancing. 5) Records of what
is called "jooking" on the guitar. The "jook" is the saloon and dance hall of
this part of the South and "jook" music furnishes the rhythm of the one-
step, the slowdrag and the other dances of whiskey filled Saturday nights.
At St. Simons island we were lucky enough to find still current and popular an early and primitive type of guitar playing, in which the drum rhythm
is predominant, that was forerunner of the more highly developed and
sophisticated "blues" accompaniments so popular over the South today. 6)
A miscellaneous set of spirituals, ragtime songs, ballads, and a few stories
completed this group of records. We felt when we left St. Simons island that
we had turned back time forty or fifty years and heard and recorded some
genuine Afro-American folk-music of the middle of the nineteenth century.
Our next stop was in Eatonville, Florida, where Miss Hurston was born and
brought up. Miss Hurston introduced us there to the finest Negro guitarist I
have heard so far, better even than Lead Belly although of a slightly different

breed. His records along with a more usual group of spirituals, work-songs, and children's games were made up and we moved on to Belle Glade on Lake Okeechobee in the Everglades.

About ten or fifteen years ago the Government drained this section of the Everglades and opened it up for farming. The soil is rich, black muck, so acid that it burns a sensitive skin, and out of this soil you can almost see the plants as they grow. In the bean-picking season, for let it be known that this section of the world furnishes most of the beans and cabbages for the Northern markets in the winter, Belle Glade, a town of two or three thousand inhabitants, swarms with from ten to fifteen thousand workers from all over the South. Most of these are Negroes—and folk-songs are as thick as marsh mosquitoes. For the first three or four days we recorded work-songs, ballads, spirituals of the usual sort, then Miss Hurston introduced us into a small community of Bahaman Negroes. We then heard our first fire-dances and for the first time, although we and other collectors had searched the South, the heavy, exciting rhythm of a drum. The dances and the songs were the closest to African I had ever heard in America. These, along with a set of spirituals and chanties new to me, we recorded and then moved on to Miami for a little rest. Up to this time we had made ninety records. We decided that the only thing for us to do was to make a visit, however brief, to the Bahamas where we could hear the fire dances in their own country. Here we came and here we have remained ever since, bewitched by these fairy islands and busy recording the liveliest and most varied folk-culture we had yet run into. Miss Hurston, who had been, so to speak, our guide and interpreter in Georgia and Florida, who had led us into fields we might never had found alone, who had generously helped us to record songs & singers she had herself discovered, could not, for various reasons, come with us to Nassau; but we felt that up until the time she left us, she had been almost entirely responsible for the great success of our trip and for our going into the Bahamas.

Our first week in the Bahamas we stayed on Cat Island where the spirits of the dead and voo-doo men walk by day and by night the drum begins to roll for the fire-dances. Here we recorded—1) Rushing songs—a form of the holy shout where the congregation shuffles round and round the church singing, clapping, and stamping on the floor. When the Baptist church wants to raise money, it has a "rush" and the church is sure to be packed. Instead of a collection being taken, each "rusher" is supposed to drop a penny or a thruppence in the plate as he shuffles by. The boys break their shillings & sixpences up into halfpennies and distribute it among the young women. Then they all sail away. When I see you next, I'll teach you how to rush. It's great sport. The melodies are very fine & some of them quite odd. 2) Anthems—a Bahamian adaptation and elaboration of American spiritual singing. 3) Jumping dances. A ring is formed. The goat-skin drum, taut from heating over a fire of cocoanut leaves, begins its peculiar jerkey[?] thump. The girls begin to clap and raise a song that consists of an endless & timeless repetition on a simple tune of such a sentence as—"See Uncle Lou when he falls in the well." A boy leaps from the circle out into the moon-lit ring. A dramatic, angular, sensual posture & then he flings away in his dance, his own personal move, as much his property as his skin. For a minute he dances then, when the drummer by muffling his beat, has told him to leave the ring, the dancer stops his "move" short before a girl. She has her dance & then "goes for" a boy. Thus the dance goes on free, lovely, primitive, and, it seems to me completely African. There are hundreds of jumping dance songs. 4) And then there are the ring-plays, hundreds of them too, calling for a different kind of dancing, a different drum rhythm. 5) Along with this material which was so largely of Negro origin, we recorded a number of fine English ballad airs.

We left Cat Island on the bi-weekly mailboat to return to Nassau, not because we had exhausted or even begun to hear all the material, but because our batteries had discharged and something had gone wrong with the recording instrument. A day or so later in Nassau, we were recording again—jumping dances, ring play, quadrilles, anthems and the songs of the streets—a genuine, casual ballad lore that concerns itself with the latest street fight or love affair. Three weeks ago, when we came to town, I was calling Miss Barnicle "sweetie pie" as a joke. Today, out on the streets, one hears nothing but "sweetie pie" bandied back & forth and there are already two songs simply riddled with "sweetie pies." Here, you see, there is a live, flowing, vital folk culture and the collector lives in a continual state of confusion & exhilaration. A week ago we returned from another trip to the Outer Islands—this time to Andros. There we had spent another week when songs & stories & superstitions were pouring in from morning until night. On Andros, since the native dances have more or less gone out of fashion, we recorded nothing but the folk tales—variants of European fairy stories, shot through, as must have been their originals with songs & dances. Some of these songs are fragments of old English ballads & sea shanties; some African songs; some from Jamaica, Haiti & Cuba. Altogether they are the loveliest folk-melodies I have recorded and in their dramatic setting are perfect. About 20 records of this sort.

Back here again, so exhausted we could scarcely stagger, found an old lady whose mother had come from Africa. From her we recorded 35 African melodies. Then a group of Haitians strolled our way and gave us ten fine records of their singing. Songs & people pour in on us all day every day until we have to stop them in our weariness. Altogether we have made, despite trouble with the machine, lack of charging facilities for our batteries, and shortage of blank records, some ninety double-face records since we have been on the islands. With a month's experience behind us and a fair wind we can make easily a hundred more before we leave and get besides some fine movies of the native dances. The material here, besides being interesting in itself, will have great importance in the study of the Afro-American music, since it represents a mixture of African & English cultures at a much earlier stage than can now be found anywhere in America. The absorption of the Negro into white civilization has gone on very slowly on these islands and is, I should say, where it was in America about the time of the American revolution. I hope to see you face to face some time and tell you a little more clearly and in detail about this material. But for now this report is quite long enough I think. [ALC]

Once back in New York, Alan initiated some new plans, while following up on his work with his father regarding their previous recordings. He now began reaching out to the wider world with his increasingly expansive ideas and queries. He needed additional assistance from the federal government, since his recording work for the Library of Congress, through his father's position, carried few funds, and the private foundations were difficult to tap.

For instance, on September 12 he wrote to Miss Francis McFarland, Director of Music Projects for the Works Progress Administration (WPA). Here he continued his multi-pronged approach, stressing the many uses of folk music, including academic and professional. Regarding the latter, American composers, particularly Aaron Copland, were using folk songs in their compositions:

The possibility of the Works Progress Administration approving a project in American folk music has been this week suggested to me by Mr. Herbert Halpert.[6] On the basis of your interest in American culture, I should like to submit a project that will be an important contribution to the scientific study of American folk songs and to American culture. I have discussed this project with many musicians and students of folk song, and it has generally been agreed that it is vital to the study, preservation and proper presentation of American folk music. As you perhaps know, my father, John A. Lomax, has been for twenty years a collector of American Folk Songs and was the compiler of the first book of indigenous folk-songs issued in this country—"Cowboy Songs"—which still remains the authoritative book in its field. For the last two years my father has been Honorary Consultant in Folk Songs at the Library of Congress and under a grant from the Carnegie Corporation has been, by means of a high fidelity electric recording instrument, engaged in recording folk songs in the South. During this time I have been his assistant and have collaborated with him on two books, "American Ballads and Folk Songs," issued last fall by the Macmillan Company, and "The Songs of Lead Belly," to appear in the near future.

Our collection of recordings, made up of Negro folk songs from all over the South, French folk songs from Louisiana, Mexican material from Texas, songs from the mountain whites, and a large and interesting collection made by myself last summer in the Bahamas, is deposited in the Archives of the Library of Congress. But to make use of this material in furthering either the scientific study of folk songs or the composition of an American music which should be based on our extensive and beautiful folk traditions, it is first necessary that a careful musical analysis of the available recorded material be made. There are few musicians capable for this highly technical and precise work, which consists in the studies of subtleties most of which are foreign to conventional music; and yet it is these subtleties, often unnoticed or "corrected" by musicians, that make a folk-song what it is. The project I suggest is the establishment of a course, which will at the same time be a research and artistic project, in the transcription of folk music. This class should work under the supervision of some expert in the field of primitive music, most preferably Dr. Herzog of Yale University; and use as its raw material the collection of records at the Library of Congress supplemented by material from Yale, Harvard and Columbia.

The results of a yearlong project of this sort would be manifold and important. 1) There would be in this country a group of experts in the transcription of folk music whose services in the study of primitive and folk music would be invaluable. 2) An analysis of American folk music on a large scale would have been made which analysis would be basic to all other work in that field. 3) A group of young performers and composers would, perhaps, be on the track of a genuine American music—operas, symphonies and so forth based on American folk music. Fitting arrangements for American Folk Songs, that we are sorely in need of, could certainly be written by these musicians when they had become thoroughly acquainted with the style of this music. 4) Certainly a few American musicians would know how to perform American folk songs.[ALC]

Almost a week later, on September 17, he followed up to Betty Calhoun, also with the Music Projects division of the WPA, with greater details of his expansive proposal:

I have in mind a project in folk song which I believe will be an important contribution to the scientific study of folk song as well as to American culture.

Some Credentials: My credentials are mostly my father's. For three years under a Sheldon Fellowship from Harvard he, John A. Lomax, collected folk songs in the West and organized folk lore societies through the South. This research resulted in rich manuscript collections and in the publication of the first book of indigenous American folk songs—"Cowboy songs." This book, along with "Songs of the Cowcamp and Cattle Trail," are the sources for the "Lonesome Cowboys" who haunt the radio today.

A little over two years ago he and I set out to record folk songs in the South, using the first portable electric recording instruments and visiting the Southern Prison Camps where we believe the richest stores of Negro material had been preserved. In this two year period we have collaborated on two books—"American Ballads and Folk Songs," published by Macmillans last fall, and "Lead Belly and his Songs," to appear shortly. In addition we have brought to the Library of Congress a collection of over five hundred aluminum records of genuine Mexican, Mountain white, 'Cajun, Bahaman and American Negro Folk Songs. There are thousands of hitherto unknown folk tunes on these records. This collection makes up the largest part of the Library of Congress folk song archive. Of this archive my father is Honorary Curator. Our traveling and part of our collecting expenses have been paid by the Carnegie and Rockefeller foundations through the Library.

The Project: But folksongs should not be buried in Libraries, as they are in Washington and in Universities over the Country. This project, which I have talked over with folk-songists all over the country, would provide for their distribution and ready use. This plan has two main features: a) A research group in accurately transcribing folk songs into musical notation. b) A clearing house for folk songs at the Library of Congress.

a) The first project could be complete in a year or less. A group of your musicians and composers under the direction of some expert in primitive music and using as its raw material our collection of records and the additions that can easily be made to it—this research group would bring forth:

1. A group of musicians versed in the precise and difficult technique of writing down folk songs accurately. There are only four or five such experts in American today and they have more work than they can do.

2. A group of potential composers of genuinely American, or at least of competent arrangers and performers of folk songs. Musicians, because they have not carefully listened to and analyzed folk tunes, have generally neglected what is most vital to these tunes—the manner in which they are sung. This manner is characterized by features which fall outside the domain of formal music but which can be transposed into that medium. When composers have once understood the feeling of popular ballads they will be able to put this feeling into their compositions.

3. There will also be amassed during this course of training a large body of analyzed and correlated musical material which will be invaluable in the study of folk songs in this and other countries.

This research project will call for: 1. A set of duplicates of the records in the Library of Congress archive. 2. An expert in primitive music to occasionally instruct the group. 3. A small group of *young* musicians. 4. A fine reproducing machine for records. 5. And perhaps for some time my services in gathering the raw material and interpreting it.

b) A clearing house at the Library of Congress under the direction of my father and myself should, by adopting a completely generous policy in regard to the material it collected, induce folklorists and libraries throughout the country to send in the collections of songs in their possession. The aim of such an agency should be to direct the collection of new material, classify and catalogue the great body of already collected material, and make available in the form of records and mimeographed bulletins as much of this material as possible. It will call for: 1. The services of several stenographers to copy manuscripts and carry on the extensive correspondence necessary. 2. A machine to duplicate records for distribution and the funds at first to furnish raw material for this machine. 3. Technician to operate this machine. 4. Perhaps a Harvard Ph.D. to assist in the preparation of catalogues and bibliographies of records and books. 5. Covering expenses for the Library's recording machine. 6. The services of my father and myself to direct the work.

In an intensive year, the machinery for the collection and distribution of American folk songs should have been set up and the greatest part of the work should have been done. I can see no reason why the Library of Congress should not undertake the financing of this organization after it had been well started.

In General: Composers, singers, theatrical and radio producers, writers, all are searching for fresh material. By making available in the form of actual recordings the rich folk culture of America we can supply their needs in a way that will be fruitful for American civilization.

Folk song is the natural and easy introduction to both poetry and music. Insofar as the coming generations will become acquainted with our American folk songs, just so far will there grow up in this country a natural and healthy interest in literature and music. Speaking for myself, as a young person, I have found folk songs not only an open sesame to the hearts of American people, but also an incentive to my interest in the understanding of these people. They can so serve the coming generations over the whole of the United States. This project will be an unending contribution to American culture. Also, it will help greatly in the study of folk songs all over the world, because in that work the assistance of many hands is essential. [CBS]

1936

From New York Alan moved briefly to Washington, D.C., to work at the Library of Congress, then back to Austin to graduate from the University of Texas in the spring of 1936. He now

planned a research trip to Saltillo, Mexico.[7] To support this work, he received a letter of recommendation from Harold Spivacke, Assistant Chief of the Division of Music at The Library
of Congress, on September 25, 1936:

I should like to recommend Mr. Alan Lomax for the E. D. Farmer Fellowship
to be awarded by the University of Texas for the coming year. In my position at the Library of Congress, I have had several opportunities, during the
past two years, to come into close personal contact with Alan Lomax and to
observe his work. The result of this observation has convinced me that there
is probably no young man in this country better fitted for the study of American folk songs and folklore, than he is. His collaboration with his father and
his own independent work recording material for the Music Division of the
Library of Congress has given him an unusual amount of experience in this
type of work. He is also observant and has often demonstrated his ability to
report his observations in a most interesting fashion. The work he plans to
do during the coming year, the collecting of folk material in Mexico, represents a field which has hardly been studied. . . . In addition to this, I should
like to call attention to his seriousness and sincerity of purpose which combined with a very winning personality should go a long way toward success
in his chosen field of endeavor. [ALC]

After returning from Mexico, he was employed by his father working for the Archive
of American Folk Song, which covered his living expenses in the nation's capital; indeed,
he was the Archive's first paid staff member, named special and temporary assistant on
November 21, since his father received no salary. Their *Negro Folk Songs as Sung By Lead
Belly* was just published, although to little notice. But he now had a new interest, Elizabeth
Lyttleton Harold. Alan decided to do research in Haiti, where Elizabeth would join him and
where they soon were married. He would be paid $30 per month, and the Library would
cover all materials and recording expenses. On November 24 Oliver Strunk wrote to the
Haitian Minister in Washington:

This will present to you Mr Alan Lomax, son of the Honorary Curator of
our Archive of American Folk Music, who is about to make a visit to Haiti in
the interests of the Library's collection of recorded folk music. In Haiti Mr.
Lomax will be associated with Miss Zora Neale Hurston, holder of one of
this year's Guggenheim awards. Mr. Lomax has previously worked with Miss
Hurston [*sic*, actually Barnicle] in Jamaica and the Bahamas; it is confidently
expected that his present expedition will result in an important contribution
to the Archive. [ALC][8]

Hurston arrived in Haiti in mid-December, stayed until March, then returned for another
visit from May to September. Alan sailed for Port-au-Prince on December 10 and probably

arrived four days later.[9] Soon having equipment difficulties, he updated Herbert Putnam[10] at the Library of Congress on December 21:

Perhaps an explanation of the sizable bill from the Sound Specialties Company is forthcoming, since it was somewhat larger than the original estimates. I enclose my copy with each item numbered and shall forthwith explain the items one by one where explanation is called for.

1) The turntable unit (comprising the converter, the turntable motor, the cutter and mechanism, the pickup) had given a year and a half of service under trying conditions without being touched; it deserved a complete overhaul, greasing and cleaning. The amplifier formerly consisted of two parts. These were combined with considerable saving in weight and with the addition of power and better quality.

2) The new cutting head was an absolute essential if I hoped to be able to record drum music. The old cutter, as I had discovered in the Bahamas, would not serve to record drum music, and, since le tambour [tanbou or drum] is the national instrument, I thought it best to take advantage of the obvious improvement [Lincoln] Thompson[11] has made in his cutters. I might add that the records I have so far made are the best from the point of view of quality and low surface noise I have ever made, that is, considering the acoustic conditions.

3) [Missing]

4 & 5) The tubes were bought as spares in expectation of a breakdown far from any radio shop or from a shop where the necessary tubes could be bought. I have wasted days at a time in the field waiting for tubes to be sent to me.

6 & 7) [Missing]

8) The old pickup or reproducing-head was always the worst feature of the Thompson recorder because it simply would not track on aluminum records. It skipped grooves whenever the total volume in the sound track jumped suddenly and has often caused me to curse the day I ever was born.

9 & 12) The two batteries were expensive because they are not ordinary automobile batteries, which discharge in a very few hours and are otherwise generally unstable, but are capable of giving more hours of steady power. They are not essential in the United States because there one is always near a garage and charging is relatively inexpensive, but here when I am back in the mountains somewhere and my batteries go dead, it means hours on horseback and then more by automobile to the nearest generator.

I hope this explanation is satisfactory and not too long, long-winded and boring. At least I can assure you that the machine makes the highest quality aluminum records I have yet heard.

I have encountered a few unexpected difficulties here. The Haitian government, because of the yellow journalism that Seabrook[12] and other for-
eigners have indulged in, is naturally wary of visiting ethnologists and other
of that ilk. If I had gone directly to work, making records, my purpose here
might have been misunderstood and it is not impossible that I should have
been sent back home empty-handed. The President and his staff were en
voyage when I arrived and I was forced to wait four days for their return.
It has taken several days to arrange, largely through the good offices of Dr.
Roux-Léon, the head of the department of national hygiene, the issuance of a
permit to make records freely in any part of the island I may choose. I believe
that the permit will come through tomorrow. (Miss Hurston has been most
helpful in introducing me to the proper people.)

For the foregoing reason my first week in Haiti has had little material
result in the way of adding to the folk song archive. I have had very little
time to study French and Creole, but have spend most of my time in ante-
rooms and in taxiing from office to office to office to keep my white suit as
unwithered as possible. I have, however, looked about enough to be sure
that this is the richest and most virgin field I have ever worked in. I hear
fifteen or twenty different street cries from my hotel window each morning
while I dress. The men sing satirical ballads as they load coffee on the docks.
Among the upper-class families many of the old French ballads have been
preserved. The meringue, the popular dance of polite society here, is quite
unknown in America, and has its roots in the intermingling of the Spanish
and French folk-traditions. The orchestras of the peasants play marches,
bals, blues, meringues. Then mama and papa and kata tambours officiate at
as many kinds of dances—the congo, the voodoo and the mascaron. Then
there seem to be innumerable cante-fables. Each of these categories com-
prise so I am informed, literally hundreds of melodies—French, Spanish,
African, mixtures of the three. The radio and the sound movie and the phonograph record have made practically no cultural impression, so far as I
can discover, except among the petit-bourgeois of the coastal cities. Their
influence does not seem to have penetrated to the poor people, the really
poor people, at all. And American jazz is hardly known here at all except
among the rich who have visited America. Composition, by which I mean
folk composition, is still very active. And so I think I can say that unless a
piece of sky falls on my head this trip will mean some beautiful, valuable and
interesting records for the Library's collection.

I begin to boast more than is safe and besides this letter is already overly
long. Next time I will, if you like, send you a few sample records with notes
and explanations. Let me thank you again for the marvelous opportunity you
have given me. P. S. I shall send a copy of this letter to Mr. Strunk.[ALC]

Alan did write to Strunk on the same day:

Accept my humblest apologies for the bad carbon paper used in my first report to Dr. Putnam. It was the best thing I could lay my hands on at this late hour. Next time I'll report to you and send Dr. Putnam the carbon, but precedence is precedence. I am afraid the whole letter sounded a trifle enthusiastic, but, to tell the truth, I had to restrain myself to keep from banality. The machine is indeed greatly improved; all the defects of the old Thompson recorder have been done away with. And this country is, so far as my experience goes, the richest folk-song field I know. The drumming is intricate and sophisticated. Last night I listened for an hour to one of the native orchestra[s], composed of a pair of bones, a three string guitar, a pair of Cuban cha-chas (or gourds), and a manoumbas (a peculiar bass instrument)—a rectangular box, with a circular opening in the side across which are ranged in an iron bar eight inch-wide iron tongues (an octave of them I think) with one hand and beats the box with the other—; each of the instruments had a distinct rhythm which fitted into the rhythmic pattern of the whole, the guitar played the melody and the manoubas the bass, and the four players sang. It was deliciously lovely.

I have hired a trustworthy boy to teach me Creole to help me in the transcription of records, to help carry the machine, to do my haggling for me. His pay is ten dollars a month with room and board. He speaks just enough English so that he can interpret for me but so little that I prefer to use my own French patois whenever possible. He is proving invaluable and I hope to get time enough in the next few weeks to teach him to read. So far I have spent rather more than my five dollars a day and I have sent a copy of my expense account up until now to Mr. [Chief Clerk for the Library of Congress Robert A.] Voorus for his suggestions. From now on I think I shall manage on less, especially when I get back into the interior. The biggest item there will be transportation. I suppose this letter will not reach you before Christmas. Therefore a happy New Year to you. Give my best regards to Messers. Spivacke and [Edward] Waters [also at the Music Division]. P.S. Would you be kind enough to ask Miss Rogers [a secretary in the office] to send me some mailing labels. I would suggest, in case either you or Dr. Putman write, that you send the letter airmail. The plane comes in three times a week, the steamer only once.[ALC]

On the same day, December 21, he also wrote to his father:

I can't recall whether I have written you before or not since I have been here, but I know that I got the first letters I have received since leaving New York today. Two of them came from your hand and were dated the eleventh and twelfth respectively, mailed in Washington. So you see what you lose by straight mail. The airmail takes only a day and comes three times a week. The other comes once a week and takes four days. So, if you want to correspond with me, you'll have to pay some money. I'll tell you as much about my week here as I can crowd on a page and then I'm going to bed. It's late and I've worked hard and I have to be up betimes. Zora has been splendid. She has advised me constantly, introduced me as a friend to all the people I needed to know, has fed me and made me feel at home in her house, and at the same time has let me know in no uncertain terms that she wants to interfere only so far as I want her and no farther. When I came the President and all the important officials were in the South and it wasn't until three days ago that I began to see the men I must see before going to work. I discovered, you see, that a very carefully reflected upon permission was necessary before I could go to work. After the two or three days of interviews that has at last been arranged although I shall probably devote the remainder of this week too to my official devoirs here in Port-au-Prince. But now I don't feel quite so anxious as I did at first. Perhaps it is the tropics, but I believe that I have at last seen a lot of the material and know what the job is ahead of me more or less and I have tested the recorder quite exhaustively and got it in the pinkest condition that any of our recorders was ever in. So far as I can tell from a few minutes of talk here and a little bit of dancing there, there is the richest country for folk-songs I have yet hit with the possible exception of Mexico. I've ticketed twelve categories already, each comprising God doesn't know how many titles and there are certainly other types. The drumming is amazing and the stuff is all pure folk, with absolutely no radio, movie or phonograph adulterants. I have hired a boy to interpret for me and at the same time teach me Creole, which must be learned entirely by ear, and to help me with the machine and in transcription. Later when we are traveling he will also be my cook and housekeeper and laundress and etc.—all for the amazing sum of ten dollars a month. He speaks a little English when I need it, but already I am pleased to say that my part of the conversation at least is almost entirely either French or Creole or my personal patois.

I shall certainly miss Christmas with you and the family. You know it's too damn warm here to be Christmas and I shall have to overlook the date completely except to go with Mr. Polines [Révolie Polinice] to mass (Polines is the man Friday). And it will be damn lonesome, let me inform you, the sun only making it more lonely. . . . It seems to me that you are in the best position you have been in since the crash [economic depression] and you can certainly say that is it all due to your own effort and courage.[ALC][13]

1937

As the new year began and his expenses mounted, Alan explained the situation to Robert A. Voorus on January 7:

I am unable to understand why I have as yet received no reply to the letter I sent you last month, in which I enclosed a sample expense account and asked you if you thought it followed all the rules and met all the qualifications of a proper expense account. I hoped you would mail it back to me at once with a few suggestions so that I could submit the whole thing at the first of the month. My present position is somewhat awkward. I do not have the receipts, the numbers of the travel request vouchers, or another copy of the expense account and am therefore unable to submit any account at all. This would not be impossible in itself but I am running short of funds and in two or three weeks will be without money. I should, therefore, appreciate an immediate answer from you by airmail enclosing the vouchers and receipts that I sent you. With the hope of hearing from you at your very earliest convenience.

[Postscript to Harold Spivacke:] Thompson writes the records are on their way, ought to be here on the eleventh. I am about to smother under the material here and am learning for the first time just how stupid I am. I'm up against a real job—

The above is a copy of a frantic appeal addressed to Voorus. Would you, please God, see to it that it gets answered? I've only 30 dollars in the bank and I'm going to go into real debt before I get my money back as it is. Thank God for Zora. I suppose she'll lend me something. Could my salary check be sent by airmail???

When you hear my recordings you will understand at once where the Negro got his spirituals. The melodies are completely different, of course, but the voodoo chants have the same feeling as the spirituals. And my God, what drumming! Give me a month and I'll try to pretend the cold scientist, but right now everything is too new. Could you tell me how Strunk feels about the copy of the report (written to Dr. Putnam) that I sent him?[14]

Charles Seeger[15] received a detailed letter from Alan dated January 16 from Pont Beudet:

I can still see you standing in your doorway on P Street, lean and friendly, asking me to write often, and I can remember my earnest resolve to write. And so nearly a month has sifted away and my resolution has turned into a piece of wishful thinking, like most other resolutions. If I had an idea then what I was promising you, I'd never have promised, because since I have been in Haiti I have encountered my first real difficulties and my first real problems as a collector. You can imagine what they are, I suppose. The first one—in point of time the first and in point of importance the least significant—was to get permission to make records in Haiti. After Seabrook and other yellow journalists, and after the visit of a couple of purported ethnologists who turned out to be gun smugglers, the Haitian government has naturally been chary of people with little notebooks and other recording devices. It took a lot of influence to get me started here. The second problem came second, but it is still with me. I am just beginning to struggle out from beneath its cloud and do some intelligent work. The second was the sensual and significant impact of a completely new world where two new languages were spoken and where several cosmoses of folk-material whirled about my head until my poor brain whirled again. You see—this is the first place I have ever visited where there were *two* classes, each of which had its language and its culture, completely separated and distinct.

The working class, the peasants who sit flat on their buttocks on the soil, so to speak, are all informants, so far as the folklorist is concerned, especially if he has a lot of radical notions about folklore not being old, necessarily or cut to fit any special pattern, or the sole possession of a few adepts, but the property of whatever person it has by the tongue. That makes every single peasant I meet here an informant, and most of the population is peasant. So I have been buried, snowed under. I wish I had the virtue of the single-track mind, but I am interested in everything I hear. And as for songs, *mon dieu.* Tin Pan Alley thought itself fertile, but I can fill a couple of hundred discs without stirring my stump from this one little community. (I would, by the way, have stirred it a long time ago, but Thompson has delayed shipping discs to me for almost three weeks and I am to get them tomorrow—I pray God. Let last night's experience explain why I have thought for weeks that I would stifle under the crush of new material. It is typical of twenty nights out of my month here.)

Polines put his flat straw *cady* on the shelf for the first time since I have been with him. Polines is my servant and interpreter, my brother and friend, and, although he does not know it, poor fellow, is acting at present as special assistant to the folk-song archive of the Library of Congress. Polines has worked for Americans before and he wears, as the symbol of the riches of the United States and the generosity of former bosses, a graying but still shiny flat straw hat, called a *"cady"* in the Southwest. But last night he put it aside and donned the broad-brimmed, high-crowned, soft straw hat of the country people. It was the first sign of Mardi Gras. We walked between the cane

patches to Le Roux, a quarter of a mile away, listening to the drums and joining in the refrains of the songs all the way, so far do the two sounds carry in
the still night.

We found a crowd of fifty men in front of André's door, watching *baka.*
Baka is the great *tambour* of Mardi Gras, the same size as the mama drum of
the Vodou dance, that is, about three feet tall, a foot broad at the head, taper-
ing down to the base—a foot broad, but of lighter wood than mama, and
with a thinner shell, so that the sound is a metallic sort of bark, rather than a
deep woody roar like the mama. The drummer was stretching the head taut
with the ropes that pull at the crown of soft, light wood that holds down the
goatskin head of the drum; and Saul, master of the rara band, was knocking
home the crown with deft blows delivered with a great stone on a *bâton* of
mahogany. Ta-ta and bass stood by waiting for *baka* to begin. Ta-ta is a tiny
drum, not a foot high and scarcely a hand across, that hangs about the neck,
close to the heart, and is beaten with two little sticks. It has two faces. But
bass is like a tambourine, a great tambourine, and has only one head; this is
sprinkled with powdered beeswax and rubbed with a thumb. Bass growls or
roars or groans deeply, have it the way you like. Bon, *baka* is taut and begins
to bark. The general of the rara bands hold his little oil lamp high in the air
and begins to sing.

> *Moin c'est pitit papa-yoyo.*
> > *Ouvri porte-la, pou' moin entrer.*
> *("I am the child of a big prick,*
> > *Open the door and let me come in.")*

The men all about who have been arguing, shouting, cutting a few preliminary capers join in, then ta-ta, then bass, then *baka.* The rhythm is a march
rhythm, the song is gay and light-hearted, and the whole crowd begins to
shuffle and revolve its hips. The words of this rara song, as of all I have heard,
are what we call "dirty." The tunes are all merry. And the dancing is masculine
in its emphasis. The singers are men. All this is new to me, for I have only
seen Voudou dances so far, and there the woman takes the lead. She does all
the singing and most of the dancing, so that her whole body shakes or sways
or shakes her hips from side to side. But the rara dance (or at lest that part of
it that is at all comparable to the Vodou) reproduces the screwing, thrusting
movement that is the particularly male role in sex intercourse.

Rara season is spring, even though there is no spring here. It is pre-Lenten
rejoicing. Some men carry great tall poles and sincerely don't know why, but
just as sincerely do because they like to. The conventions of propriety are
thrown to the wind more and more as the season draws to a close—not, of

course, that the rara is an orgy. It is not. It is a season when people have a good time, when they show what is the most interesting thing in the world to most people, when they revolve their hips and thrust with them. Toward the end of the season the men and women dance together (and the penis thus rubs against the female's body), but now, when the bands are merely beginning to practice, only the young girls are to be seen, and they are not dancing with the men. As for the women, who took such a prominent role in the Vodou *bamboches* [parties], they are at home in bed considering more serious matters. But here we have our men and they are beginning to dance.

The drums have been going for minutes. The general with his candle has fought well and cleared a space before the drums, and suddenly, out from between the legs of the men appears a little boy about twelve years old, brown skinned and with big soft eyes. His big bare feet are set with their heels together, an arc the size of a third of a circle between his toes. The knees are slightly bent, and the space between his legs is a closed diamond, the angularity of which is further accentuated by his hunched shoulders and elbows. This creature appeared from nowhere like a great brown moth that one suddenly notices on the wall at night, softly curling and uncurling its antennae. The boy, leaping and at the same time maintaining the diamond shape between his thighs, makes a diddle-diddle-dum rhythm on the ground with his heels. Again. Then one heel is lifted and brought round before the ankle just above the instep and describes three short taut arcs and after thumps back behind the other heel. The hips and thighs shimmy slightly, not in the loose female fashion—no, the motion is lean and hard and the result of tight rather than relaxed muscles. The whole evolution is repeated several times. The boy shuffles round and round the open circle of watching men, past the drum, past me, sitting against the wall of André's *cay* [house]. The crouching posture is maintained and the same rhythm is beaten out with the heels. Then with his back to me and his narrow buttocks almost in my lap he swims forward with his shoulder. Whap, whap, whap, whap, whap, whap, whap and a shimmy of the whole back, every muscle alive and taut. After this evolution is several times repeated, he turns, repeats the first steps with his hand toward me. I give him two cents and he disappears into the crowd. Another song: "Ever since I slept with you last night I have felt strange in the pit of my stomach."

A great man pushes his hat over his eyes and shuffles out into the ring in the same posture, throws his belly forward, and, letting his arms hang loosely, kicks sidewise with one foot after the other, like a great clumsy bear. Shimmies, the swimming movement with his shoulders. He is given a package of cigarettes, which he divides with the drummers, the major, and the director of the band. Bon. André has given the rara players all that he intends to tonight, and the drums and the general, blowing his little whistle and holding his cane high into the night, begin to move away through the darkness. The crowd, grown by now into seventy-five or a hundred men and a few women, singing, capering, arguing, and rejoicing, follows. The drummers take their position before the next house, and the general leans close to the keyhole and blows and blows his little whistle, while the drums and the singers make a terrible fuss. Five minutes and the door stays obstinately shut, probably because the owners have only a little money and they are saving that for Mardi Gras week itself. So it is with the next and the next house in the Le Roux habitation, until the Mardi Gras band comes to Dodo's house. Dodo is the *gros neg'* [important individual] of Le Roux (a group of thirty or forty families and as many houses). His house has a tin roof and a front porch. He has two houses, several wives, twenty children. A woman's arm comes out through a crack between the door and the jamb and puts a cent in the hand of the major ["general" above]. The door slams and the band with the drums flickers away down the road to Vielle Pont, the crowd singing and stumbling along in the dark. I left them there to rejoin them again some four hours later [at] about midnight at Vielle Pont.

The use of the terms *rara* and *Mardi Gras* may be a little confusing. Mardi Gras season begins the middle of January and culminates in three days of steady dancing on the seventh, eighth, and ninth of February. Rara practice begins directly thereafter and culminates in Holy Week just before Easter. The same bands generally participate in both seasons, but the dances and their rhythms are different. It so happens that the first dances I saw on the night I am giving account of were rara dances. Later the dances were proper Mardi Gras.

The Mardi Gras band I am describing is organized, financed, and directed by Saul (Sael) Polines, half-brother to Revolie. Out of his yearly income of perhaps a hundred and fifty dollars, he saves enough to pay the first installment on the Mardi Gras costumes and buy food and drink for the members of the band during the season of practice and Mardi Gras proper. For these bands practice, beginning Saturday the sixteenth, drum, dance, and sing all night until eight Sunday morning. They begin again in the afternoon or perhaps after dark on Sunday and practice until twelve or one, or perhaps, if it is the week before the seventh of February, all night again on Sunday. They wander about the countryside and collect enough money to pay for their candles and the oil for their lamps, oil for their voices and souls in the form of clarin [rum made from sugar cane]. During the three days they dance steadily for three days and nights and cover forty or fifty miles and collect, if they are good, perhaps a hundred dollars. The money pays for the elaborate costumes of the two principle dancers (which may cost, depending on the expectations of the band and the credit of its manager, between $15 or $100 dollars apiece), food and drink for the three days and nights, salaries for the drummers and dancers, and what is left goes in the pocket of the director.

After Mardi Gras is over, practice for rara season begins at once and goes on until Holy Week; dancing begins at twelve o'clock on Thursday and lasts through Monday. At this time the band may pick up two or three hundred dollars. But more of all that when I see more of it during the next month. I am positive of this much, however, that the rara and Mardi Gras bands themselves do not do all this simply and solely for pleasure and prestige, because in a little poverty town where I spent the night some time ago, there was no rara at all. The country people, slightly better off, did have Mardi Gras bands, but the costumes were entirely of home manufacture. Of course, in Port-au-Prince, where the money of Haiti is largely concentrated, the Mardi Gras season is at its best, and some of the bands net a mine of money, just how much I shall discover next week.

[First part of paragraph illegible] . . . the spectator-participants, each band with its loyal adherents and its fickle stragglers. Each of the groups singing a different song and dancing to a different rhythm, and when, occasionally, two groups would defile through each other in an attempt to attract away adherents of the other party, the conflict in the two powerful rhythms made one's soul crack. So long as I watched, however, no group of drummers lost their beat, even when it had been practically defeated in one of these mock encounters. Trailing behind each band was a little island of light and warmth and clarin and cakes floating through the air on the precise head of a woman viewer. When business was dull, she danced along behind the band from her community and consoled herself for the dullness of trade by wiggling from the navel down. Of course, all this time she paid not the slightest heed to the wooden tray with bottles, glasses, candy, etc., which slid along through the air, balanced on her head.

The group that, after all sectional loyalty had [been] thrown into the balance, was the most popular was the *chaille-o* [*chaille-au-pied*] band. Despite the fact that Revolie has repeatedly insisted that his older brother Saul furnishes the best Mardi Gras music in the world . . . [torn page, text missing] *plaine* of the Cul de Sac, last night, as he heard the *chaille-o* coming down the road, he admitted that "*li passer toute.*" I entirely agree with him. There is something about the melodies that accompany the sensual puffing and clicking of the bamboo *vaxines* [iron or bamboo trumpets]. One is an iron pipe, which carries, so to speak, the melody: "*Condi, pi pi, condi pi pi, condi pi pi dedans trou*" ("Stick the prick, stick the prick, stick the prick in the hole"); the second, a bamboo pipe of about the same length (that is, two feet, more or less), says, "*trou rouge, trou rouge, trou rouge*"; the third, which carries the base (a big fellow two and a half feet with a mouth that swallows your face when you set in to blow it), says simply, "*trou—ou, trou—ou, trou—ou.*"

The singing is male and very exciting, in fact, coffee porters all over the southern part of island use the same tunes and the same accompaniment to encourage them in their work—that and clarin. But that's another long story.

One links arms behind the major and his drummers, shuffles along with bent knees—ONE, two, ONE, two—and suddenly one is hunting one's enemy in the jungle. The major flings his arms out from his sides, crouches like a great bird about to fly, and goes racing off through the tall grass; and you race after him, hiding, running with your spear, ready to throw. The drumbeats or the pulling of the *vaxines* measure your heartbeats.

There the enemy comes, his lights and his generals announcing him, and his drums speaking against our drums. One sings louder, and suddenly the major flies away to one side; and the enemy is gone from one's eyes. One locks arms tighter and sings triumphantly and there is the enemy again. This time we march triumphantly through his whole army and pull along—with the magic of our rhythm and singing—some of his weaker-headed adherents.

Then we wheel off by ourselves in the darkness behind a hut and dance a dance of triumph. The singing stops (the tune has been carried for perhaps as long as fifteen or twenty minutes) but never the *vaxines.*

Presently some voice rises up with a new tune, continues serenely to conquer the arguments, the shouts, and the babble of our disorganized little army, until we are all singing again and off on another march.

An hour and a half of this and I was ready to go home. But when I woke again at seven the next morning I could still hear the drums going from all over the plain. This was only practice, advance notice of what is to come on Mardi Gras, a little exercise.

Well, here is my first impression of Mardi Gras and rara. It is obvious of course that I know next to nothing about it. But I have a month to learn about the details of the institution, and nowadays, when I am able to speak and understand Creole to some extent, I have a chance to gather better material. The very first thing I shall do, of course, is to buy a tape measure for measuring the dimensions of the instruments, but I really need a Leica—as this overwritten letter so well testifies—to supplement my measurements. Is there any chance that you could help me get a camera? I need a Leica with an angle viewfinder, because these people will *not* pose for pictures. I would appreciate your help in talking to Strunk, et al.

This letter is being finished . . . [torn page, missing text indicated by breaks] it began to unwind of various . . . in the south of Haiti listening . . .

eyes and making notes, but without . . . [aluminum recording discs] did not arrive, because of strike . . . a week ago. And I not only want . . . all at the age of twenty-two but . . . my fiancée is coming in on the boat from . . . be married as soon as father sends . . . hope to heaven. You see, under Haitian law I will be a minor until I achieve the magic age of twenty-five. I did not know all this until rather too late to do anything about it, and I rather expect a major mess to arise; but I am psychically, though not financially, prepared for it. There will be quite a bit of scandal manufactured here, but I have saved the good name of the Library in advance by explaining the situation to the highest officials.

When I get back home I will have more to tell you, but for the present be satisfied with this, and let me know how things have gone with my bastard bibliography, with my prospects for a job with that swell friend of [Thomas Hart] Benton's and his wife, with yourself, [your] wife and delicious children. I should also like an off-the-record opinion of Strunk's reaction to the records and report I plan to send this next week some time. I hope to have a letter from you soon, although not necessarily a brief biography like this one. In the meantime I remain.[16]

Alan and Elizabeth were married in Haiti, following Alan's plea to Estenio Vincent, the Haitian president, on February 13, 1937:

I come to you with an unusual request, the granting of which will both facilitate a scientific work, important to Haiti, and make possible the happiness of myself and my fiancée. As you are perhaps aware, I have spent two months in Haiti registering for the Archives of the Library of Congress, Washington, D.C., imperishable discs of Haiti's national music. This work, all-important from the scientific and cultural point of view, will occupy me some time more, since the richness of Haitian popular music is not to be comprehended in a day. At present, however, my investigations are more or less at a standstill. A short time ago my fiancée arrived in Haiti, where both of us believed we could be quickly married and spend a happy and profitable honeymoon. Unexpectedly we discover that the European custom of the publishing of bans has been perpetuated in Haiti and that our marriage is thus postponed for two weeks. This means lost time for me since I have already finished my work in the Cul-de-Sac and had planned to travel North to make recordings of that rich and distinctive musical culture. As matters now stand I am forced to remain in the neighborhood of Port-au-Prince where my fiancée can be properly chaperoned. My time is limited here and I need my fiancée to help me in my work. Without your good offices we will be forced to spend two embarrassing and almost fruitless weeks here. I understand that you are alone empowered to waive the publishing of the bans, and, therefore, I appeal to you to aid the Library of Congress and do me the great personal favor of employing this power in our case, a rather unique and embarrassing situation. My fiancée and I will be grateful for this act of kindness which we hope and believe will be done for us. [ALC]

In a short letter to his father on March 27 from Port-au-Prince he gave a few details about the trip:

I suppose you are all pretty sore at me because of my long and inconsiderate silence, but I have had neither the time or the energy to write. I discovered just the other day that I have had a mild case of malaria ever since a week before Elizabeth came. I am already well, but I have really felt rotten for a long time and have had no energy to do anything more than take care of Elizabeth and do my work. At this moment I should be in Leogane with the rara bands. In the states you never find out what the muchness of material means and here I have an ambulating house-hold to run, a servant to manage, an immense sea of material to swallow—all without a car on very little money and in a language that I still have troubles with. There are no places to have batteries charged outside of two or three large towns. In the village where we live there is hardly anything to eat and the water is foul and thick with germs. We have to send to town for everything. Besides that I sit all day and explain what I am doing to every kind of Haitian there is and haggle with the most money-minded people on earth about how much I will pay for the material they give me. You all will simply have to excuse me and wait for news from us until we come home. We hope to see you in Washington the 28th of April. What we will do after that is simply in the laps of the Gods. Now is too all-occupying. Please send my special regards to Johnny [his brother] and tell him that I would have been absolutely sunk without his wedding present. As for you and Deanie [Ruby Terrill Lomax, his stepmother] I know you're having a fine time somewhere and I send you my love and beg you to send a little family news. Bess [his sister] is the only one who writes me any more and she has given me up too for the moment. [ALC]

Alan reported on the complications of his filming experiences in Haiti to Herbert Putnam on March 29:

The American Minister has just advised me as follows in regard to the importation of the camera and film the Library has sent me. 1) That it was a mistake on my part not to have brought the camera with me when I came and not to have arranged the whole matter in advance through the State Department.

2) That, as the case stands a letter must go to the State Department stating: why a series of movies is an essential supplement to the scientific study of Haitian folk-music that I have already recorded, what the camera will be used for, that the Library will guarantee that none of the photographed material will be published or that any part of it will not be published (if the Haitian foreign office so desires). 3) That the State Department be requested to advise the American Minister at once to ask the Haitian Foreign Office to admit the camera and film duty-free and to make all necessary arrangements with the Haitian Department of Interior for the use of the camera in Haiti.

Everyone is very discouraging, but this is a country where people like to multiply difficulties to keep from moving from their chairs. As I said in Saturday's letter, Dr. Léon had let me understand that there would be no difficulty in regard to the camera here, but in the interval between our two conversations he seems to have changed his mind completely.

The camera will be used: 1) To photograph musical instruments and how they are played; 2) to photograph singers in the act of singing; 3) to photograph dances.

All the recent material in regard to the scientific study of music of whatever kind but most particularly of folk and primitive music, stresses the necessity of moving pictures as supplementary to phonographic recordings. In the first place, unless the collector learns to play every instrument that he records, it is impossible to understand the origin or the reason for certain rhythmic and melodic peculiarities of exotic musical instruments, unless one can watch in detail the techniques of their performers. For example, unless one has a film of how the hands are used on the drums here, it will be impossible to understand how the different tones are produced on the drums and the origin (often purely physiological) of certain rhythmic patterns. The same thing is true of the close-ups of the faces of singers in the act of singing, since a study of the use of the lips, teeth, and body in singing often throws light on the characteristics of the songs themselves. But the most important thing, of course, is to have movies of the dances. As I have written you before, dancing and singing in Haiti are simply two sides of one integrated phenomenon. The types of melodies and rhythms grow out of the dances and at the same time influence the dances in a complicated fashion that I imagine a student better trained than myself could only understand if he had both recordings and moving pictures.

I think if the matter is explained to the State Department in this fashion and the point is made that in the Library such material is strictly reserved for the use of technical experts, the whole thing can be very easily arranged. Dr. Melville Herskovits and others have arranged to use cameras here and have taken pictures of dances, and I see no reason why the same privilege should not be allowed the Library of Congress. So far as I know, these gentlemen were not required to promise to restrict the material in any fashion, and perhaps that part of the matter can be best arranged at this end. I leave that to the judgment of yourself and the State Department.

I want to apologize again for all the trouble this may cause you and for the fact that I misinformed you about the camera, but the person whose attitude I had previously had no reason to question—I mean Dr. Léon—suddenly changed his mind about the camera. I hope, too, that you will not regard this letter as an impudent instruction sheet or anything of the kind. I do not intend it as anything but a set of suggestions that will save you time and will prevent delay. I think in view of the fact that Dr. Léon has at all other times made my road easy here, that he deserves a letter of appreciation from the Library. He is the kind of man who appreciates being appreciated in a rather extravagant fashion.

P.S. Dr. Spivacke asked me to write at once if I needed any additional photographic supplies, etc. I should guess that Eastman has sent me a good apparatus equipped for use here. What I shall need, however, in case the camera is admitted, is money to pay the performers. To make decent movies requires rehearsal. Haitians are money-mad and they don't like to be photographed. I imagine that for best results at least $100 will be necessary.[17]

While in Haiti, sometime in late March, Alan reported to Spivacke in an undated letter:

The camera has turned into quite the white elephant. The American minister won't admit the damn thing without a second special authorization from the State Department, and my friends here in Port-au-Prince have for some reason changed their mind about the advisability of my taking any pictures at all. On top of that, international postal rules won't allow me to inspect the camera and accessories without paying the duty, which is a hell of a lot more than I can afford. So I will have to depend upon you to take care of the situation. It is absolutely essential to have some sort of filter, I think about equivalent to the ordinary cloud filter, to take soft, rich pictures in the sort of sun we have here. Furthermore, to prevent all chance of glare, it is essential that the camera either be fitted with or have as an attachment a sunshade for the lens.

If these things were not sent with the camera, you'd better have Eastman airmail them to me at once. As for film, I'm sure that my time will not allow me to make more than six good rolls. I do wish that you'd send all color film, because everything is cursedly beautiful here.

The whole mess is really the fault of the bastards in the foreign office here who haven't the good grace to make a broad interpretation in my case in favor of admitting the camera under the same authorization that they had from the State Department in regard to the recording machine. They simply won't listen to any reason—even when one quotes [George] Herzog and tells them that with a species of folk songs that is eminently for, by, and of the dance, one must have movies of the dance to make anything out of the songs. They just don't respond to anything but a lot of show, prestige, or money, and if you violate one of their damn rules of procedure and give them the chance, they rejoice in knifing you in the back. "Very unfortunate."

I wonder if you would call on Dr. Putnam for me and ask him to write a special letter to the Minister of Interior (M. Frederique Duvigneaud) explaining the Library's reason for wanting those pictures (I have detailed the reasons in a recent letter to the August Right Honorable), that the pictures are not destined for publication and are only intended for the use of specialists in the field of folk music. Please tell old Voorus for me that if he doesn't get my checks for special and extraordinary expenses (from February 11 to March 11) to me here in Port-au-Prince before the tenth of the month, I won't be able to leave Haiti or make a long-planned and most necessary trip to the North on my way out. But, Spivacke, darling *caiman*, the next two weeks are going to be the most exciting of my life—if I don't get arrested. P.S. All these requests have exclamation marks of urgency behind them.[18]

Alan and Elizabeth, returning in late April, had enjoyed a fruitful time in Haiti (although for a while both had signs of malaria), which he partly captured in his article "Haitian Journey—Search for Native Folklore," published in the January 1938 issue of the *Southwest Review*.[19] Alan wrote to Dr. S. H. Reiser,[20] a helpful contact in Haiti, on May 15:

I hope that Revoli explained why I didn't come out to see you before I left Haiti. It was a question of either making the boat to New York or seeing you and naturally the deal had to go against you. As Revoli may or may not have told you, our last week in Haiti went so fast and furiously that during the last four or five nights none of us scarcely slept a wink. Zandor, Martinique, Wou etc. [. . . in original]

June 25, 1937[:] I must begin another set of apologies almost a month later. I have been helping father edit the revised edition of his Cowboy Songs, working about twelve hours a day and have had no time to think about Haiti or my obligations to you. But the manuscript went away in the mails a day or so ago and I have caught up on my sleep, and this morning have made for you a couple of duplicate records of some things I thought you might like to remember. I'll send these two records under separate cover and leave the customs officials to you. It is the only sort of present I can afford to give you now, since my salary here at the Library has not begun to come in and Chavella

[Elizabeth Lomax] and I are living at the bottoms of our pocketbooks, but I hope you will feel that the records show my appreciation of the way you helped me in all my straits. Later on, when the Library installs a really good duplicating device, I'll send you some duplicates we both can feel proud of; but at present these are the best we can produce and are emphatically not for public display but for the pleasure of Cecile, Anna, Don Fred, Ciceron, Lieutenant Auguste, George, Madame Theoline, and yourself. I have tried to calculate what would give the most people the most pleasure. If there is something essential that I haven't sent, write me and I'll be glad to supply it.

Elizabeth and I had an exciting time on our departure from Haiti. After a frantic morning, we finally got all our parcels on the Haiti, just as she was lifting her moorings. At Cap Haitien, we stayed overlong at the Citadel, and on reaching the wharf, saw the propeller beating up the white at the Haiti's stern. Luckily for us, an American yacht happened to be in the harbor and her master at the moment ascending the wharf from his little runabout. He popped us in this speed boat, and we ran the Haiti down and managed to make her slow up enough so that we could leap from deck to ladder. As you can imagine, we were persona non grata to the officers for some time. At Port de Paix we showed Calixte's letter to the Port officials and were taken on a tour of the town, which was mighty pleasant, for we had been almost two days away from Creole and from Haiti and were beginning to feel a little lonely among the American passengers. The trip to New York was as stormy as our three days of parties there. And since then, as I've said before, we have had little time to think about Haiti. Certainly you seem very far away, you and Revoli and Ciceron and Dodo and Saul and Madame Degras and Cecile, but now that all the worry and press and illness that followed me though the last three months of my stay there have passed, you seem very close and delightful. Cecile and new dresses and her dancing and her [   ], Ciceron and his spare intensity and honesty, Revoli and his cosmopolitan resourcefulness and charm, Madame Degras and her transformations from simple old lady to queen, and you with your Western whole-hog hospitality and camaraderie. It is delightful to have these three hundred records to bring back all the lights and all the dancing and all the fun. The Library has put me in charge of the folk-song collection here which now amounts to about thirteen hundred records and when my regular job begins July I shall have my hands full, especially with the facilities this Library offers for research. The salary is very small but the opportunity is pretty marvelous, so for the time being E. and I will be here in Washington. I hope you'll get a chance some day to come and work on your books here in the Library where I will have a chance to play host to you for a time. Will you give Revoli all my love and tell him that we miss him every day and all the time. Tell him I shall send him a present as soon as I'm "unbroke." I should like him to write me if he can ever take time from his jardin. Ciceron's drums have been much admired as have Cecile's and Anna's singing. I have never had time to put on a real Haitian show for the people here at the Library but when I do I think that it will lay 'em in the aisles. Let me repeat again that I am and always will be grateful for what you did for me with the help of all the strange and kindly people of Pont Beudet. [ALC]

As Alan informed Reiser, he was indeed appointed director of the Archive of American Folk Song, officially titled Assistant in Charge (technically he was a "Junior Library Assistant"), on July 1, 1937, while his father remained as the unpaid Honorary Consultant and Curator.[21] In July Alan wrote to a few of his friends in Haiti, with thanks and news. Indeed, he was usually keen to keep in the good graces of those who assisted in his field work. On July 8 he contacted Mrs. Magny in Port-au-Prince:

The longer I live the less I regret the dreadful mistake you tried to save me from. Perhaps things were a little more difficult because of it, but what of that. You'll have to excuse us for not calling again in Port-au-Prince, but our lives were too full of work and food-getting and illness to allow for any calls. I do wish there was something I could do to repay you for the favor you did me and to somewhat blot out the memory of my hysteria. If you can think of anything that the Archive of American Folk Song—of which I am at present in charge—can do for you, let me know. [ALC]

Also on July 8 he communicated with M. Dartigue of the Department of Rural Education in Haiti.

I have been afraid that perhaps the record I made for you was not satisfactory. You can expect, therefore, under separate cover, a substitute with Leogane rara on one side and the singing of your Chatar drum quartet on the other. Later on, I hope to be able to send you some duplicates of better quality but at present I am not equipped to do better work. I have accepted a place here in the folk-song archive for the next year, and if this puts me in the position to do you and your rural education movement any favors, I shall be delighted. . . . Please give M. Sylvain my best regards and tell him that I am very sorry not to have seen him again before my departure from Haiti. [ALC]

The following day, July 9, he wrote to Suzanne Comhaire-Sylvain:

First, I want to thank you for the favor you did me by writing *Le Creole Haitien*. It proved a very useful book to a collector who arrived in Port-au-

Prince and was expected to record Creole folk-songs without any knowledge of Creole or of French either. Then I want to express my sorrow that I was forced to return to the United States before your return from Paris. I had met your two charming sisters and had been entertained at Kenscoff by your hospitable brother, and they had prepared me for meeting a very delightful person. My wife and I were sorely disappointed when we learned that you had stopped over in New York. Dr. Herzog told me the other day that the American Folklore Society plans to issue your volume of Haitian folk-tales in Creole and I eagerly await its publication.[22] In the meantime, however, I should like to know where the Library can purchase the thesis that you published in French, I believe, on Haitian folk-tales. I would be very grateful to you if you would send me the name of the book and the publisher. [ALC]

On July 13 Alan followed to Dr. Rulx Léon:

My wife and I have thought about you a thousand times here in Washington, about your countless kindnesses, about your endless patience with a couple of young and harassed Americans. We remember with gratitude your graciousness and your real concern with our welfare. And I hope you will forgive my not having written sooner when you learn how busy I have been since my return here. From the first of May until the first of this month, I worked as many hours a day as I had strength to in helping my father edit a revised edition of his 'Cowboy Songs' and since that time I have been adjusting myself to my new job here at the Library, as assistant in charge of the Archive of American Folk Song. And I have been trying all along to make the records I promised you, but breakdowns in the apparatus and the use of the machine for other purposes have forever interrupted me. At last, however, I snatched some hours yesterday, found a fully charged battery, and made you two duplicate records, which I hope you and your family will be pleased with. Of course they are not quite so good as can be made, but they are the best that the apparatus we have now can produce. Later on, when the Library is given a real duplicating machine, and I hope that will be soon, I will make a better set for you, but I hope that for the present these will answer your purposes. I should like to know whether you and your family and your visitors enjoy them and if there is something else you might possibly like to have recorded. If there is, you have only to let me know. The other night we saw a little of Haiti in the newsreels—the market and the palace square with its gendarmes. We felt very home-sick. The United States seemed for a long time after our return a very colorless place with a disappointing sea and a sky that was positively plain. . . . P.S. I wonder if you could find a place for Revoli at Pont Beudet. During his time with me, he proved completely devoted to his job, intelligent, resourceful, and honest. It struck me particularly about this man that his most important motivation was the need to do his job well. I hope you can employ him. [ALC]

Not quite done with Haiti, three days later, July 16, he communicated with Katherine Dunham at the Department of Anthropology at the University of Chicago. Dunham got her Ph.D. in anthropology at the university, but devoted her life to African American dance and choreography; she had arrived in Haiti in 1936 to study Vodou:

I heard so much about you in Pont Beudet and Port-au-Prince that I feel I almost know you. Cecile and Theoline and Ciceron and Dr. Reiser all seemed to think you were the only anthropologist and the only real collector who ever came to Haiti. And I have been anxious to write you for some time wondering if the Archive's records, three hundred of which I made in Haiti, would be of any use to you. Reiser told me that you were doing a Haitian ballet and if that is still the case I should like to lend a helping hand—that is, if my records would do any good. Besides, I would like to know anyone who has been to Haiti since I shall need some little advice in preparing and translating the song texts for the Haitian records. And the more I can find out about the little Pont Beudet hounfort at Le Roux, the happier I shall be. You can imagine my problems, I suppose. Having been warned away from any personal participation in cult activities, I never had my head washed as I believe you did and so was never given a great deal of "big secret." The *language* is a particularly bitter thorn in my side at present. Old Ti Cousin offered to teach me all the *language* he knew for a hundred dollars but I thought the price was a little excessive. Besides, I didn't know how far I could trust the old man himself. Have you published any material so far that has to do with Haiti? If so, I am most anxious to get my hands on it. And a letter from you would be most welcome. [ALC]

He also wrote on July 16 to the anthropologist George Simpson, Herskovits's postgraduate assistant, then himself doing research in Haiti:

After a long and ungrateful silence, many thanks for the pictures. They seem to have turned out splendidly, and it is pleasant to see Lila and her mama again. I am anxious to hear how your work is going forward and whether you have found your novelist friend of much assistance and whether you have managed to be comfortable in your little cay or not. Plaisance remains for me a brilliant and a little unpleasant dream. I did not know until I got back to Port-au-Prince just how sick I had been. It seems that I had been inhabited by several millions of benignant (what a bitter irony) malaria germs for

several weeks before I came to the mountains of the North and that they
had concealed themselves behind influenzic and dysenteric symptoms during that whole time. Even though I cleared up the malaria itself with a couple
of weeks of quinine, I was scarcely well again while I was in Haiti. As perhaps
you know, I spent my last month on the island near Leogane and there I
did some work with rara and Petro I am fairly satisfied with. I came away,
however, fully satisfied that one would have to remain in one community
for several months to be able to get an adequate picture of even the dance
activity. If you ever travel South, I suggest that you stop and call on Tanice
and Ti Cousin in Carrefour Deux Forts, the first village on the road South
of Leogane. Tanice is interested in Erzulie and Ti Cousin is one of the most
interesting men I have ever met. He would be well worth your trouble. I hope
that someday I can see you sans malaria. Perhaps you will be able to come
to the Library to see me when you return to the states. In the meantime if
there is anything I can do for you at this distance, please let me know. P.S. The
records are turning out rather splendidly. Please give my best regards to Pere
Toussaint and ask him to remember me to Pere Kodada. [ALC]

In his official report on the Haitian trip to the Library of Congress, Alan stated:

On December 10, 1936, I was sent to Haiti to make a field-recording study of
Haitian folk music. I returned to Washington the latter part of April with 58
ten-inch and 236 twelve-inch aluminum discs on which Elizabeth Lomax and
I had recorded some 1,500 Haitian songs and drum rhythms. These records,
along with 350 feet of motion picture film of Haitian dances and with the
notes pertaining to the songs and dances, have become part of the Archive
of American Folk Song.

For the Haitian peasant, singing and dancing are integral parts of every-
day existence. He calls his voodoo gods, wheedles favors from them and
dismisses them with ceremonial drumming, dancing and singing. To find a
group of men in the field with their hoes is to discover a gay festival of music
and, when a Haitian tells a folk tale the crux of the plot is likely to be a little
song learned from his grandfather.

As one might expect in a country where communication has been and is
so difficult, each little cluster of houses produces and preserves its own folk
songs. And along with the new songs that grow up with tropic luxuriance
in every hamlet and for every occasion worthy of a dance, the Haitian sings
many airs that he maintains were brought over from Africa by his ancestors.
The 1,500-odd tunes, therefore, that we recorded in four localities (Plaisance,
Pont Beudet, Port-au-Prince and Leogane) will serve to give an inkling of the
rich realism of Haitian folk music. The important types of songs represented

in the collection are Voodoo, Rada, Petro, Zandor, Congo, Rara, Mardi Gras, Romance, Combite and Conte.

For their kind efforts in our behalf and for the interest they took in the success of the Library's Haitian collection, I am especially indebted to Dr. Rulx Léon, Dr. S. H. Reiser, Miss Zora Hurston and His Excellency Estenio Vincent. But it is to Revolie Polinice, who cooked, carried, fought and talked for us during the whole four months that I shall be eternally grateful.[23]

After returning Alan plunged into the work of the Archive, for example writing to Endicott Hanson at Stanford University on July 1, 1937:

I am sorry to say that for the present the Archive's only material on Acadian and Creole folk-song is inaccessible to the public. The songs are all recorded on discs and since these discs are irreplaceable, and, besides, wear out upon repeated playings, they cannot be played by anyone, much less leave the Library. We hope to arrange for the duplication and general distribution of these records as soon as we get the equipment for making such duplicates. At present, however, the material is not available even to a serious student like yourself. I am sincerely sorry, and I shall let you know as soon as we can furnish duplicates of the records you might be interested in examining. We should be happy to receive a copy of your thesis. [ALC]

On July 30 he answered a letter from music collector Frances Densmore[24] about the situation in Haiti:

Your inquiry about the naming of Haitian drums has been referred to me for an answer. Since I have just returned from a four months recording trip to Haiti, I am able to supply a certain amount of information on the subject. The best reference I can supply—and this will probably answer your question satisfactorily—is pp. 272–7, "Life in a Haitian Valley," by Melville Herskovits, published by Alfred Knopf, 1937. Herskovits speaks for the region of Central plain about Mirebalais. I can confirm his observations in regard to the baptism of drums and other cult objects from experience in the Plain of the Cul-de-Sac near Port-au-Prince and from the plain of Leogane to the South. I was present at the baptism of a large mama drum at Pont Beudet where essentially the same ceremony that Herskovits describes was performed. Sometime later I had Ciceron, the "Mait tambou" of the same village, make a set of drums for me. After the work on the drums had been completed (and this varied only in details from the process that Herskovits describes) I was advised to finance a ceremony in which the drums were to be given souls. I was told that without this ceremony their voices would be weak and unsteady and they might burst if they were strenuously played. Ciceron, an important person in the local vudou cult and sometimes consulted in cases of illness when the priestess is not in the neighborhood, conducted the ceremony. He sent for a bottle of clarin, the native rum, two oranges, a candle and two eggs. When these had been delivered, he led my interpreter and myself into his little mud hut where the drums had been laying completed, but unbeaten for nearly a week, and closed the door. It was evident that he did not want an audience. Whether this was because the ceremony was his secret, or, because he didn't want to be bothered by the children who were hanging about, I don't know. The drums were laid side by side on the floor and designs in flour (reves) were traced on the floor around them, as shown in the accompanying sketch. Simbi is the deity who is Ciceron's "mait' tete." Damballa is the most "popular" of all the Haitian gods. The Marassa, the twins, are special intercessors with Bon Dieu. Papa Agwe is the god of the sea and he, likewise, may be an especial patron of Ciceron's.

Libations of clarin were poured on the eggs, the bodies of the drums, the heads of the drums and at the altar in the corner of the room (a miserable little pine box with a few sacred stones and a bottle for rum). We all drank. Then an orange was split open on the floor so that if any loa or any of the dead should come, they might eat. I was then told to raise the kata, stand it on its legs, figuratively. An egg was broken on its head and the white rubbed into the top surface. The yoke was poured into the butt end of the drum and sloshed about on the inner surface of the skin. Then the mama tambour was given to eat in a like manner of egg and orange. The heads of the drums were then covered with clean white cloths and they were set in a corner to dry and await baptism. I was then instructed in the care of the drums. I left sixty cents in the ropes of the drums to be distributed in bits to everyone who came to the house and at the crossroads so that when the drums spoke everyone would have to assemble. It happened that I never had time to have the drums actually baptized and given names in the regular fashion; but I was told that, although my drums would never serve as part of the paraphernalia of a "hounfort" (vaudou cult house), that they would because of the ceremony I have described, have the "heart" to make music for a dance.

In the south of Haiti I saw the batons that are used by the principal dancers of the rara bands "raised up" and 'given drink" in essentially the same way. Yet, some days later, they were baptized, received names and gifts from various god-mothers and god-fathers, and "grace et misericorde" was asked for them by the bush priest. The pots, jars, flags, canes, handkerchiefs of the vaudou cult are baptized. Even the "hounforts" are baptised. At such times these cult objects received names. At the baptism that Herskovits describes the drums were named after African deities and he seems to regard the specific names as important to the drums. On the other hand I was told at the drum baptism I attended that the name the mama drums was given was of no consequence, and indeed it seemed to me that the names I have heard given the various objects I have seen baptized were of no particular importance. The object is often given several names, particularly if there are a number of people present to serve as godmothers and godfathers who may be able to give their god-child a present of money. These names are sometimes names of the African gods sometimes of the saints and sometimes what fancy suggests. If it is worth anything as evidence, I, at various times, named a handkerchief "Francois Villon" and a baton "Rabelais" and was not corrected nor could I note any surprise or even interest in the voice of the officiant who repeated the name after me. Care in choice of a name and whether the name is remembered depend, perhaps, on the importance of the object. In the case of a hounfort [Vodou shrine or temple], I feel sure that the name is remembered, since that is the way it will be known to the gods when they visit the earth and it is so mentioned in numerous songs; but, in the case of most baptized objects the great thing seems to be to ask for "grace" from Bon Dieu, and not to give the objects a name by which they will be known in the future. I can't say, therefore, that vaudou or other drums are or are not known by the name throughout their period of use. A drummer once names his three Petro drums for me: "Porter-aller, Nouvelle, and Rose Marie," but he may have been interested in pleasing me or merely in contributing to my ignorance.

There is no doubt, however, that the vaudou drums are personified. A better way of putting it would be deified. As Herskovits says, the drums are the center of activity at all vaudou dances and if anything of importance takes place it takes place before them. When a dancer is possessed by a god, one of the first things he or she does is to pour a libation of water or rum before the drums and then later to crouch down and kiss the earth before each of the three. I do not know whether the possessed person is bowing down before the gods or saints after whom the drums may be named or before the special spirit "hounta" that is supposed to inhabit the drums. I include to the latter opinion, since, after kissing the earth before the drums, he similarly salutes the center post of the tonnelle or palm leaf shed where the dances usually take place, the "poto mitans." I rather incline to the opinion that neither "poto mitans" nor "hounta" are names of spirits or any thing of that sort, but rather the names of places or things or the "essence" of places or things which are of great ritual and psychological importance. I am afraid that this letter, despite its length, does not answer your questions. Letters to Melville Herskovits, to Katherine Dunham, University of Chicago (whom, I have been informed, knows vaudou in Haiti perhaps more intimately than

any student of anthropology in this country), to Zora Neale Hurston (who is
at present at work in Haiti), and Dr. Reiser, Pont Beudet, Haiti, (who can tell
you if he will), might clear up the problem entirely. At any rate I hope I have
been of some assistance. [ALC]

While continuing his interest in Haiti, Alan mostly turned his attention to domestic
matters. For example, he contacted Rose Warren Wilson in Martins Point, South Carolina,
in August (an undated letter):

In the course of my cataloguing work here at the Archive of American
Folk Song I have just come to and played through the records of Plantation
Echoes and I can say with all sincerity that I wish I could have been there to
have enjoyed the fun. The singing of spirituals was beautiful and the whole
performance was simple and unaffected folklore, and that from a folklorist
means that he liked it. There are various difficulties in the matter of cataloguing the records and thus giving an accurate account of the play to posterity
that you can help me clear up. I feel sure that, although the task may be a
little tedious you will be interested in helping me. Act. I[.] 1) The first musical
number after your announcement, with humming and singing, what is its
name and who played the guitar? 2) Who led He Never Said a Mumbaling
[sic] Word, and could you send me the words they sing? 3) Who led "Amen"
and what are the words? 4) Who led "I've Got an Ark on the Ocean Sailing,"
and what are the words? 5) What was the name of the woman who spoke the
long and beautiful prayer of Act I? 6) Who led "I wonder If I Ever Shall Reach
Home["] and what are the words? 7) Who preached the sermon about Jesus
and Zacharias? 8) Who led the hymn Jesus Love Us which came directly after
the above sermon? 9) Who led Jesus on the Mainline Too and What are the
words? 10) Who led THIS OLD WAR DON'T LAST ALWAYS and what are
the words? 11) Who led I HEARD THE ANGELS SINGIN' and what are the
words? 12) Who led MARCHIN' THROUGH AN' UNFRIENDLY WORLD
and what are the words? 13) Who led COME WITH ME and what are the
words? 14) Who led Drinkin' of the Wine and what are the words? 15) Who
led I'M GOIN' TO MEET YOU IN THAT LAND and what are the words?
16) Who led Till We Meet Again and what are the words?
    Act II 1) Who led WAIT FOR ME and what are the words? 2) Who
preached the short sermon that followed? 3) Who led I'M GONNA STAY
RIGHT HERE and what are the words? 4) Who preached the short sermon
that followed this song? 5) Who led "OH, BLESS GOD["] and what are the
words? 6) Who led Goin' Inter the Wilderness and what are the words? 7)
Who led LET YOUR WILL BE DONE and what are the words? 8) Who led
DANIEL IN THE LION DEN and what are the words? Act III 1) In act III

there are four dances that come before the Ring dance and the conclud-
ing dance, Snaket. Do you remember the order of the dances the night the
records were made and could you give me the titles? 2) After the dance an ex-
slave told a brief story of his experiences. What was his name? 3) And finally
what was the name of the man who made an announcement at the end of the
last record about the meeting times of the congregation and a description
of what each kind of meeting was for? I know that this letter must look like
a request for a week of your time, but I felt that you were anxious to have a
full and adequate record of Plantation Echoes made and that, therefore, you
would be willing to give a little of your time toward the furtherance of that
task. If you can't get immediately to the job of copying off the words of the
songs, would it be too much to ask of you to give me the names of the performers and correct me in case I have made any mistakes in titling the songs?
Please give my regards to the members of your delightful cast, whom I feel I
know almost as well as if I had sat and patted my foot with them, and allow
me to congratulate you on a splendid job esympathetically and imaginatively
done. [ALC]²⁵

Alan was anxious to plunge into a fresh collecting trip, this time in the South, as he
explained on August 14 to Harold Spivacke, the new head of the Music Division of the
Library of Congress, who had replaced Oliver Strunk.²⁶ While Alan was aware of the difficulty of discovering "traditional" songs because of modernization, he was not discouraged,
and certainly had few illusions:

Kentuckians divide their state into four more or less well defined regions
with north and south dividing lines. From East to West these are: The Mountain, the Blue Grass, the Knob and the Penny Royal areas. The regions I have
in mind for the projected survey is the first of the group, the mountain country, which comprises approximately thirty-seven counties in the Allegheny-
Cumberland mountain belt. It would be sanguine to expect to complete the
collecting work in this area in two months, but, on the other hand, it would
be dangerous, in any matter as chancy as the collection of folk-songs where
Acts of God, bad roads and bad tempers so often intervene, to restrict one-
self to too small an area. Indeed all I suggest is that after two months, the
Library may feel that its Kentucky mountain collection provides an adequate
notion of folk music in that region. I hope I shall be able to leave Washington
for Kentucky by the first part of September because later on the weather may
seriously impede travel and make impossible outdoor recording of dances
and baptizings.
     There is another and more important reason, however. Professor Barni-
cle, of New York University, plans to work in that region during September

and she has offered to accompany me and to introduce me to the singers she has discovered in three or four summers of collecting in Harlan, Pine and Bell Counties. As you know, Mr. Harvey H. Fuson of Harlan [a local ballad collector] asked us to send someone to make records of the singers he has located, but I should like to complete this job, if possible, before Miss Barnicle comes down from New York and be free to work with her, and have the benefit of her rare understanding of the problems and techniques of field recording of folk-songs in this particular territory. When she leaves Kentucky I shall be part of the family there and will have friends of her friends in every community I later visit. I therefore urge that, if possible, the trip began in the first week of September. The shortest and best road to Harlan enters the Shenandoah Valley at New Market, Virginia, and runs straightaway southwest through Staunton and Roanoke to Bristol. Then one heads up into the mountains through Gate City to Pennington Gap, and on country roads over the Big Black Mountains into Harlan. There one is in the heart of the mountains that have protected for generations a rich heritage of Elizabethan song, manner and speech, and at the same time have hidden the veins of coal that are leading to the disappearance of this tradition. And so one finds in Harlan and nearby communities the mountaineer—the so-called mountain eagle—and the miner—a modern workingman. Both types have produced folk-songs, and Omie Wise flows naturally into The Hard-Working Miner. Here the mountains have formed culture eddies where one can find the music of the American pioneer, in all degrees of purity, in some isolated spots little affected by nearly a hundred years of change in the "outland," in others acquiring new vitality in the mouths of the miners. From Harlan, Bell, Clay and Knox, the coal-mining counties north into Pike and Breathitt, I shall be journeying backward in time and adding to the Archive materials essential to the understanding of the development of American folk-music, material that at present it particularly needs.

It will be advisable and interesting to try out as many types of entrees into the region as possible. First of all, I have, through Mr. Fuson, Miss Barnicle, Miss Jean Thomas and their friends, a large number of personal contacts in the Southern and Northern extremities of the area. Second, I can ask the advice of Miss Mary Newcomb and Professor Josiah Combs, both Kentuckians and balladists, and letters can be sent to other collectors who have worked in the area. Third, in the counties where I do not have personal contacts through other collectors, I can establish them by letters to county school superintendents, to Miss Mary Breckenridge's mountain nurses and to the mountain schools that have been established by Northern philanthropy. Fourth, the senators and congressmen from Kentucky can be consulted and asked for assistance. They should be able to furnish valuable letters of introduction.

I have already done considerable reading about Kentucky and have looked into the collections of songs that have been made there. The notes from this reading, the field notes and the records, should add another colorful panel to the mosaic of American oral literature and music that the Archive is occupied in piecing together. At the very least we shall give certain melodies and tales, that Kentucky mountaineers have already chosen as worthy and beautiful, more rich years to live. [ALC]

In preparation for his trip south, he wrote to a number of individuals—for example, the southern collector Loraine Wyman, on August 17:[27]

Perhaps you recall that John A. Lomax and myself requested the use of your "Lassie Mohee" from your "Lonesome Tunes" in "American Ballads and Folk- Songs." Recently, in planning a recording trip to Eastern Kentucky for the Archive of American Folk Song, Library of Congress, it occurred to me that you would certainly be able to offer some valuable suggestions, perhaps supply some names and addresses of good singers or of people who know how to find the best singers. As you perhaps know the Library of Congress has been building up an Archive of American Folk Song, made up of manuscripts, cylinder and phonographic recordings of American Folk Songs. It is interested in preserving, as the transcript in some ways fails to do, the manner and voice of the singers of old and new folk-songs. The present survey of the Eastern part of Kentucky will allow me to spend two months in the mountains there, and I am sure that your suggestions will be invaluable. I note that your songs come from Knott, Harlan, Jackson, Estill, McGoffin, Letcher and Pulaski counties. Which of these sections do you suppose to be the richest? May I hope to hear from you before September first at which date I leave Washington for Kentucky. [ALC]

On the same day, August 17, he requested similar assistance from Mary Wheeler and Ann Cobb of the Hindman Settlement School in Kentucky, as well as Ethel Ferrill McLane and Mollie Wilcox at Berea College:

During the months of September and October this fall I shall be in the Eastern part of Kentucky making records of folk-songs for the Archive of American Folk Song in the Library of Congress. I am anxious to meet and work cooperatively with the collectors who have worked in the region in order that the Library may feel doubly sure that its Kentucky collection will be truly representative of the quality and variety of Kentucky folk-song. I feel sure that through your work in the Hindman Settlement School you have established contacts with interesting singers and communities that should be represented in the Archive and I feel equally certain that you are able to offer me valuable suggestions in regard to collecting in your neighborhood. I should like to know whether or not you will be in Hindman during the two months I plan to spend in the mountains and whether you would be willing to help me in the Archive's work there. I would greatly appreciate a letter from you, as detailed as you care to make it, about your work in Kentucky folk-song, about the region or regions in Eastern Kentucky you are well acquainted with and about the singers that you know. I plan to leave Washington about September the first. [ALC]

Also on August 17 he connected with the musician, collector, and composer John Jacob Niles at the John C. Campbell Folk School in Brasstown, North Carolina:

I plan to be in the Eastern part of Kentucky during September and October recording folk-songs for the Archive of American Folk Song. When the project was first suggested, I at once thought of you and the pleasant meeting we once had (where, as I remember, you played the dulcimer and sang and I presently responded with Negro work-songs) and I wondered whether you would be so kind as to point out to me some of the interesting singers and communities that you know of in Kentucky. The main purpose of the Archive is to record the living song, whether it has been published or not, and thus to preserve the voice and style of the folk-singer in some permanent form for study in the future; and then, as soon as possible, to make available its folk-song material to anyone who wants it. We are anxious to be as useful as possible to collectors of folk songs in America and we ask their help in the cooperative building of worthy Archive of American folk music. I will greatly appreciate whatever suggestions, addresses, etc. you are able to offer me. [ALC]

August 17 was a prolific day for correspondence, when he also informed Josephine McGill:

In planning a recording trip to the Eastern part of Kentucky for the Archive of American Folk Song in the Library of Congress, I found your book and felt sure that by asking your advice about singers and singing communities in that section, I would establish some valuable contacts in that area.[28] As you perhaps know the Archive of American Folk Song is devoting itself to the accumulation of American Folk Songs in the form of manuscripts, cylinder and phonographic recordings. It is interested in preserving, as the transcript in some ways fails to do, the style and the manner of American Folk Songs. It has on hand at present over a thousand double sided records made in the

field and two months in Kentucky should make a valuable regional addition to this collection. I note that you have transcribed ballads in Knott and
Letcher Counties. Which communities and singers in these counties do you
remember as being the most interesting? May I hope to hear from you sometime before September the first? [ALC]

On August 17, as well, he requested the help of Josiah Combs, a professor at Texas Christian University in Waco:

Do you remember the summer of nineteen thirty-two when John A. Lomax
and I came through Fort Worth and spent an afternoon with you while you
sang us *Ground Hog* and some other hill ballads? That version of yours, to a
Sharp tune went in the ballad book and, while this procedure may have been
unutterably unscientific, at least the song profited considerably. The project I
shall now broach to you is, on the contrary, rather unutterably scientific. The
Library, as you know, is in earnest now about building up an Archive of American Folk Song. One of its projects will send me to Eastern Kentucky for a two
months survey recording trip in that area in September and October, and I
have hoped that you would be able to supply me with some valuable letters of
introduction and direct me to some virgin territory and some inexhaustible
singers without which and whom the trip would not be half so profitable. I
shall read your volume over again carefully before I go, but I have thought that
perhaps you could send me some collectors' information that is not between
the covers of your book. At any rate I should greatly appreciate a letter from
you with whatever advice and suggestion you may give me. [ALC][29]

The following day, he wrote to Bess Owens at Pikeville College, Pikeville, Kentucky:

During September and October I shall be in the Eastern part of Kentucky
making records of folk-songs for the Archive of American Folk Songs in the
Library of Congress. I am anxious to meet and cooperate with all the collectors in the region, doing whatever I can to help them in their work at the
same time as I ask their assistance in forwarding the work of the Archive. I
was delighted to discover in reading the last issue of the "Southern Folklore
Quarterly" that there was at least one ardent collector in Pike County. I have
no contacts in that area and it seems likely to be one of the most interesting
from the point of view of ballads in the whole of Eastern Kentucky. Will you
be in Pike County during September and October? Would you have time to
talk over with me the problems of collecting in the region and perhaps help
me to find some of the best singers in the county? The Archive will appreciate whatever assistance and specific information about folk-songs in Pike

County you feel able to offer. I hope to hear from you before September the first, when I plan to leave Washington for Kentucky. P.S. Were the ballads and songs attributed to you in the "Southern Folklore Quarterly" collected from your students or from other sources? [ALC][30]

He followed up on August 19 in a letter to Mrs. Edings Whaley Wilson (Rose Warren Wilson's married name) at Martins Point:

Thank you for your kind and interesting letter and for the list of singers. We will greatly appreciate all the additional information you can send us in regard to Plantation Echoes. I regret to inform you that I shall not be in Washington during September and that the Library is taking no active part in the Sesquicentennial Celebration. It is being directed [by] Mr. Sol Bloom, Representative from New York. As concerns the re-recording of the spirituals and songs of Plantation Echoes, John A. Lomax has perhaps told you that we are not yet equipped to do the work. When we have the equipment we will then be in a better position to discuss the matter. I am indeed sorry that you cannot come to Washington to tell me about Plantation Echoes, both because of the assistance you could render the Archive and because I should like very much to meet you. Perhaps that will be at the World Fair. In the meantime, however, your letters will prove of great assistance to us. [ALC]

Alan also wrote to various school superintendents in Kentucky on August 19 about his upcoming trip (and a similar one to John Crisp in Sandy Hook, Elliott County, on August 26):

For the past several years the Library of Congress has been engaged in building an Archive of American Folk Song, to serve as a national depository for phonograph records of American folk-music, that is, the old ballads, reels, hymns, cowboy songs and the like that have been handed down from generation to generation or have been composed by and sung by people without the aid of writing or print. The Library has already accumulated thousands of songs from all over the country, particularly from the Southern States, but Eastern Kentucky, which we believe to be very rich in this type of material, is not very well represented in our collection. For that reason I am being sent to Eastern Kentucky on the first of September for a two months survey of the folk-music in this section. I shall bring with me a portable machine that makes excellent records and I will be interested in meeting and recording the singing, the fiddling or the dancing of all the individuals who know the old songs, tunes or dances. When these records shall have been made, they will be deposited in the Library of Congress for the use, instruction and pleasure of the American people. I feel sure that you, as county superintendent of schools, can be of great assistance to the Library in your section of Kentucky. It is not unlikely that you know many people who are singers or good fiddlers and perhaps you may know of some occasion, such as a Sacred Harp Singing Meet or an old fiddlers' contest or a family reunion where the Library's project could be furthered. I should greatly appreciate a letter from you giving me whatever information you can in regard to the music of your county and I should like to know at the same time whether or not you think you could help me, or would be interested in doing so, when I visit your county this fall with the Library's recording machine. [ALC]

Since he was interested in visiting Berea College in Kentucky, he wrote to its president, William J. Hutchins, on August 25 about his plans:

During the months of September and October I shall be traveling in the Eastern part of Kentucky engaged in making records of folk-songs for the Archive of American Folk Song in the Library of Congress. In planning this trip, I have all along intended to visit Berea College to renew the acquaintance I made with it several years ago when my father, John A. Lomax, came there to lecture. I have already written three members of your staff (Mollie Wilcox, Gladys V. Jameson, and Ethel McLure) asking for their help and their suggestions, but I should like to enlist your aid, as well, in this project. I feel sure that at Berea I can find the material for many delightful and valuable records and will be able to establish splendid contacts through mountain boys and girls with mountain communities rich in folk-songs. I hope that I can depend upon your personal assistance in furthering the work of the Archive. [ALC]

Unfortunately, he learned that Mollie Wilcox would not be present at Berea, and he wrote to her on August 30 about his disappointment:

I am indeed sorry that you will not be in Kentucky this fall for I am afraid my collecting work will be confined to that area. If you ever come to Washington, as I hope you shall some day, I should like to record your songs for permanent deposit in the Archive of American Folk Song. In the meantime, if you should feel ready to deposit your collection in the Library of Congress, we should be happy to accept it under any reasonable restriction you would care to impose. Your mention of a "contest" in "Bloody Breathitt" interested me greatly. Was it a folk-song contest? And, if so, who was in charge of it? I hope that your collecting trip to Eastern North Carolina is a successful one and I regret not to be able to accompany you. [ALC]

Anxious to be on his way, he wrapped things up at the Library, including this letter to
Kay Dealy in Philadelphia on September 2:[31]

John A. Lomax has sent me your letter and I should like to tell you for the
Library that we are much interested in the songs and ballads you mention. Would it be possible for you to send copies of your collection to us for
examination and possible permanent deposit in the Archive of American
Folk Song? I know the song you mention, but at this moment I am packing my equipment for an early departure tomorrow morning for Kentucky. I
shall be there for two months making records of Kentucky folk-songs. In the
meantime, however, let me refer you to two books where you can, perhaps,
find the song: English Folk-Songs from the Southern Appalachians, by Cecil
Sharp, Volume II. Folk-Songs of the South, by J.H. Cox. We look forward to
seeing your collection. [ALC]

Accompanied by Elizabeth, Alan hit the road for a fresh research trip to eastern Kentucky, which he would soon describe in his official report:

Throughout most of this region, especially in the coal-mining counties, the
tradition of ballad singing and that which is associated with it—the dulcimer, the five-string banjo, the fiddle, the country dance, the play party, the
traditional airs and the oral memory—seem to be in process of rapid degeneration or of transformation. Commercial music via the radio, the movies
and the slot phonograph is usurping the place of traditional and homemade
music, but that their case is not entirely hopeless I shall have occasion to
point out later on. The mountains have always been poor but, so long as
that poverty also meant comparative isolation, the tradition of homemade
music could survive more or less unchanged. In the last decades, however,
rural music and the mores associated with poverty have found difficulty in
resisting the competition of metropolitan intrusions backed by wealth and
prestige. This condition is most marked in coal-mining areas. The miners
only shook their heads when the titles of the old ballads were suggested,
and the ballads recorded were largely fragmentary or sung by the aged or
the infirm. In the purely agricultural counties, however, the story was somewhat different. There, where cultural competition was not so extreme and
poverty not so marked, it was easier to find banjo pickers and ballad singers. . . . The tenacity of the tradition of homemade music even in the mining
area, however, is evidenced in three ways: in the use of traditional tunes by
union-conscious mountaineers in the composition of strike songs and ballads, in the tremendous vogue of "hillbilly" and cowboy music and in the
resurgence of song-making in the Holiness and Gospel churches. . . . The

"hillbilly" musicians on the air have furnished another outlet for the home-made music of the mountains. Many of them come from rural backgrounds and their hopeful imitators in the hills of Kentucky are legion. The tempos of their square dance tunes have grown faster and their concern with the "mammy" song and the sickly sentimental love song greater, but they also sing some of the indigenous mountain ballads and "blues" and their production of new songs is large.[32]

He arrived in Harlan, Kentucky, and contacted Anna Bertram, at the Lewis County Board of Education, on September 8:

I am happy to know that you are interested in furthering the Archive's work in Lewis County, and I was glad to hear that you know of two definite informants. Are these two individuals whom you refer to, singers, mountain people? Would you be interested in planning a county folk-singing contest to stimulate interest in the preservation and use of the ballads and songs that are the South's richest literary heritage? I imagine that such a contest would not be difficult to arrange and it could culminate in my arrival with my recording machine with which I would make records [of] the best songs. If the Board of Education would be interested in sponsoring an affair of this kind, it will have ample time to arrange it. I shall not reach Northern Kentucky before the last of October. I should like to hear from you again in regard [to] this matter. [ALC]

Also on September 8, he informed Ova Haney in Ashland about a proposed contest:

It is gratifying to learn that you are so interested in collecting the folk-songs of your section. I am much interested in helping all I can in your singing contest. You realize, of course, that to really get the best singers, and by this I mean, the genuine folk-singers, to participate in such a contest great tact must be exercised. It would be adviseable, I imagine, to divide the contestants according to age, in say, three groups or four. Fiddlers should compete against fiddlers, Dulcimer players against others of their kind. Groups against groups. If it is possible to find groups of children or grown-ups who know how to dance the Kentucky Running Set or any of the other traditional forms, they would add a great deal to the fun. Perhaps you could find other groups to play the old play party games—Skip to My Lou, Go In and Out the Window, Green Gravel. And it is especially important to call for the traditional songs, secular and religious, and frown a little on popular songs of the day. I hope I have not been presumptuous in offering so much un-asked-for advice. If I have, you must forgive me on the ground that I do not yet know you. As to the matter of the participation of one or several counties, I hate to advise you. It might add greatly to the spirit of the occasion if several counties entered contestants. On the other hand it would be possible to supervise the selection of contestants more carefully if it were a one-county affair. I can be in West Liberty Saturday the 23 of October, if that date is suitable; and, if you would like me to come up on Friday and give you any assistance I might be able to offer, I should be delighted. Perhaps it would be advisable to call for an afternoon and evening, instead of trying to crowd too much into one short evening session. I should add, by the way, that I have a movie camera with me and colored film and if you find any groups that can perform the old time dances briskly, perhaps we might make pictures. [ALC]

He wrote a brief, undated letter to Spivacke soon after leaving Washington:

I'm sorry I missed you in the afternoon. This evening I drove round & round the part of town where your house was but I couldn't find it. I've appreciated all you've done in helping me to get this trip. I established new contacts in Harlan today who will help me solve the Barnicle-Fuson conflict. [ALC]

By mid-September he was deep into his Kentucky collecting, with Mary Elizabeth Barnicle's help, as he reported to Spivacke around the 19th (the letter arrived in the office on September 20):

Fuson turned out, as I suspected, quite an unprofitable contact. His people are all local and no better than other contacts I might have made on my own hook. Barnicle has just departed. Through her I was able to get in touch with what might be cautiously termed the progressives of this part of Kentucky and to learn all there was to know about the progressive songs of this country. I traveled a good deal and learned the lay of the land and made contacts. There were various troubles, however, with the machine. Several little things, unimportant, but causing delay. And the batteries turn out to be a major problem. They are likely to go down a lot too fast and it is the very devil to rent anything that is any good. I would suggest even that, subject to your best judgement you might send me a couple of real high capacity batteries. I have made so far 32 records, some of them quite marvelous, some of them mediocre, but all necessary—ballads, local and otherwise, Baptist hymns, Holiness hymns, blues, sentimental hill billy stuff, radical songs. From Smith's point of view I have made two important discoveries—one local ballad, never written down before, and something that appears to be an English broadside ballad that is not in print so far as I know. As soon as the machine is fixed up I shall be able to work much faster than before, I believe. On the other hand

I have learned things and seen people whom I should never have known existed otherwise. Would you advise that I move fast and get something out of every county or take my time and do thoroughly what places I do visit? The [Francis James Child] *English and Scottish Ballads* I have with me. It is an essential part of my field equipment. I really need the two volume [Cecil] Sharp as well. [ALC]

He next wrote to Spivacke with news of his progress, such as it was, around September 23:

The parts from Presto, which you so kindly ordered for me, arrived yesterday morning and I installed them with very little trouble. The machine now walks and talks properly again and I am off today into the hinterland of Leslie County that I spent the weekend exploring. Leslie County is perhaps the most backward and the most isolated section of Kentucky. Until two years ago there were no roads into her county seat, Hyden, and it was only two months ago that the power companies finally brought electric power into the county. Hyden has a population of at most 1500 and it is the metropolis of the county. A rickety courthouse, a sinister brownstone jail, unshaven loafers around the garage and country store. These remnants of the unhurried past of Leslie County watch the automobiles on the pike and the old ones curse while the young ones rejoice. Ten yards on either side of the road, however, thy have no need to be disturbed, these oldsters, for the ways through Leslie are foot-paths, wagon-roads, or sled-tracks at the best. Last weekend I set out to drive from Pine Mountain Settlement School, just over the border from Leslie in Harlan, Ky., to Hyden, about thirty miles distant. I was two dusty days on the road, driving through some of the loveliest country I have ever traveled. On the way I stopped and talked to almost everyone I saw. The young people were so shy that it was hard to find out what their names were, but the oldsters, as soon as they had been made to understand several times that my name was such and such and my station thus and so were very willing to help. From them I learned the name of singers up and down the road—Betsy Napper, a seventy year old banjo picker and buck dancer; Singin' John Caldwell, ballad singer; Old Jim Bolan, the oldest Baptist preacher in the region; Farmer Collett, who lives on Jacks Creek near Roark's store and whose multifarious musical activity extends through harmonica blowing to fiddling; old Granny Space, 87, from whom Sharpe collected thirty-five of his best Kentucky ballads and who in years gone by was at the same time the county's best ballad singer and its gay lady. Most of this county down the Middle Fork to Beech Creek, across the mountain in Red Bird is virgin ballad territory and I have great hopes, when I revisit it toward the end of the week with the recorder renewed and repaired, of finding some fine material.

For the first two weeks of my stay in Kentucky I have been mainly pursued with hard luck. There have been constant difficulties with the machine and then the coal camps have turned out to be quite disappointing from the point of view of ballads. Traditional material has been ousted by the influx of records and radios. The ballad singer and the fiddler have been driven out by the Holiness preacher and the "hill billy" singer who copies the broadcaster slavishly. Mr. Fuson's singers were, too, a disappointment. Blind Jim Howard wanted money. Mr. Vowel was exhausted in a morning. The gypsy family "somewhere near Middlesborough" could not be found. Miss Barnicle and I were both disappointed by the coal camps. Her contacts on Straight Creek, near Paintsville and around Middlesborough did produce the best material I have so far collected but one had the feeling about it that it was somewhat forced and artificial. Since then all the singers and fiddlers I have talked to have been sick or had a death in the family or there has been some other good and obvious reason why they couldn't sing or perform. I have before had such streaks of bad luck and for that reason I'm certain that things can't go on forever like this. I feel sure that up and down Beech Fork and Red Bird, under the aegis of Miss Breckenridge whose Frontier Nursing Service covers the same territory, that I shall at last find the people I have been looking for. My mailing address until I advise you to the contrary will be General Delivery, Hyden, Ky. I would greatly appreciate your advising the Disbursement Office of this fact so that my salary check and my vouchers may reach me without delay. I will send you another letter in a week's time ad let you know what my progress in Leslie County has been. [ALC]

He sent a short telegram to Spivacke on September 28:

Machine running. Work booming. But pocketbook empty. Speed vouchers or wire money. [ALC]

As promised, Alan followed on September 30 with more of an explanation to Spivacke from Hyden:

If you will recall the last week of my stay in Washington and our many conferences about batteries, you will recollect that I never liked the idea of taking low-capacity batteries with me, but that, due to the fact that Presto had sent the wrong specifications in their first letter and that the Superintendent of the Building could not be re-convinced of the validity of a second set of specifications sent by Presto, I preferred to make my departure rather than discuss the matter further, especially since a) you were convinced that I would not often need batteries and b) the Superintendent and his assistant were convinced that I did not need high capacity batteries. I hope by this time that my attitude toward Fuson is clear, but perhaps I better make it a littler more plain. He wrote the Library, as I recall, that he had a hundred or so songs to be recorded. When I began to work with him in Harlan I found that he had four sources of information: 1) G.D. Vowel, whom father and I had recorded before and whose stock of songs, though limited, I again recorded, 2) Jim Howard, a professional blind beggar who wanted more money than Fuson and I could pay together for singing a group of songs he did not know very well, 3) a family of gypsies in Cumberland Gap whom Fuson could not locate, 4) Pine Mountain Settlement School, to which Fuson introduced me, but where I had planned to go myself and where I could have made my own entrée more pleasantly. Fuson, himself, told me that most of the songs in his book were collected for him by a poor boy to whom he gave work one summer out of charity. I forgot one other source—a John Surgener, who knew, so far as I could discover, two songs. Please understand that I have recorded some of Fuson's material and that I have parted from him on the most amicable terms. He is a fast friend of the Archive. In the past week I have recorded about ten ballads that have been composed in the last decade, several of them from the singing of their authors.

The most flourishing genre of singing at the present in Eastern Kentucky is that associated with the Holiness, or as it's enemies term it, the Holy Roller Church. These people have swallowed the whole of the Southern tradition: Negro spirituals and blues, Baptist and Methodist hymns, the ballad form. One of their composers, a manic woman named Mrs. D.L. Shepherd sang me several ballad of her own composition last Monday night: one descriptive of the death of her own son who was run over by an automobile, the second retailing the facts of the kidnapping of Lindbergs' baby, the third voicing the Christian thoughts of a group of miners trapped in a mine, the fourth telling of the death of an old woman run over by a train, and so forth. She believes that the voice of God speaks in her soul as she sings. For the past two days I have been recording the songs of an 87 year old woman who sang for Sharpe when he visited this country. I have made movies of her singing and numerous records of her rather remarkable ballad performances and I believe she can typify one of the many colorful characters in the story of folk-song here and in England. For years she has been the gay lady and sometimes the bootlegger of Hyden and at the same time she has been the best ballad singer in the region. For all I can discover the real ballads are still to be found in the isolated parts of the country, difficult to reach by auto. I have made more records that I am proud of since I have been in Hyden than I have during the whole of my stay in Kentucky and I shall continue to work here in Leslie County, probably the most backward County in the state until I have my fill of material. Then I shall get on to as many counties in the state as I have time for. The trouble is in covering this sort of country that one has to make friends of the people everywhere one goes and that takes time. They simply won't sing for you until they feel that you are friendly or that you are friends of friends of theirs. I will need a new stock of records as fast as you can get them to me. I suppose you might as well send me a hundred in care of the Express officer in Hazard Ky. And ask them to notify the telephone operator here in Hyden as soon as they arrived. I imagine that I shall be out of records by the time they arrive. Please send me also a number of Library franks so that I will have no trouble in shipping you my material. It appears to me at this time that we will be disappointed in our aim of making three hundred records on this trip. Two hundred and fifty will be nearer the figure and this only if my present good luck holds. [ALC]

A shorter letter to Spivacke on October 6 contained details about both collecting and administrative matters:

Yesterday I recorded Ky. 101. We are both exhausted. The roads are terrible in dry weather, but in wet they are something fearsome. The people are very timid, religious and shy about performing. I would feel, however, if I had to leave Kentucky tomorrow that the 101 records give a good representative picture of folk-singing in this state. The only thing I lack is a dulcimer record and I would have had that last weekend if my gallant old Studebaker hadn't failed me on the most terrible hill I have ever encountered. Enclosed you will find a bill from the Weston meter people, signed by me. I think it can legitimately count on my hundred dollars of extras, but at present I haven't the cash to pay it. Could you arrange for Mr. Morgan to foot the bill? I have three boxes of records ready to send, but due to the fact that I have no shipping franks I can't send them. Would you send me a few along with a few more envelopes by return mail. I received the shipment of one hundred records yesterday and this afternoon in spite of a light case of flu I'm starting into Clay County to see what I can find there. Yesterday I recorded some fine ballads from a man who refused to sing for Sharpe when he was here. He says that I'm more persistent. [ALC]

An undated letter to Spivacke, from Hazard, contained more details of a generally successful trip; yet money was always on his mind:

Your wire reached me yesterday in Hyden where I was recuperating from a week of hard work and a bout with the flu in Clay County. The flu and the work being concomitant I have been hard put to it in the evenings to do anything more than crawl into bed and groan, even though writing you has been on my conscience. I made fifty records in Clay County during my week's visit there, most of them from batteries, and carried the machine up and down hills so steep that the natives had not even tried to plant corn on them through the cold and wet. These records are inscribed with several Child ballads as yet unrecorded by me, two feud ballads, some fine fiddle music, banjo picking, camp meeting hymns, local ballads and the like. Last evening I bagged two U.M.W.A. [United Mine Workers of America] ballads of which I am very proud. It seems that I am very nearly ready to lay down my life for the Library, if not to defend the capitalist constitution, for one evening I was very nearly stabbed by the most religious man in Clay County. This sixty year oldster was mortally jealous because I was helping his perfectly rotund wife up and down some steep clay banks and finally turned on me with his knife open vowing that he intended to rip the guts out of this young black s----tch [son-of-a-bitch]. My mild protestation would doubtless have been my last, if a friend of mine who can lift a seven hundred pound steel rail singlehanded had not been of the party. He held the old fellow while I beat a safe retreat. I understood later that I should have received lead in my vitals from a gun if the irate husband had had his 44 in his pocket. He had pure neglected to bring it. Again, no longer than two nights ago, I had to offer to fight ten young bullies one after another if they would not stop their racket. The racket was making recording in the hotel impossible and the proprietor would do nothing about it. For some reason, perhaps because they did not know what weapons agents of the Library of Congress carried, they wandered away before my boastful threat and left me uneasy victor in an empty hotel lobby.

Do not suppose, however, that all my adventures are like this. Most of one's encounters here in Kentucky are as pleasant as one could well imagine. Everywhere you go you are invited to spend the night and forced to eat a meal. Indeed, on account of the fact that one cannot establish any sort of impersonal relationship with these people, it is difficult to collect songs quickly. Count Oct. 16, 1937, 156. I do not quite understand the letter about the Cosmos club. What is the metaphysical organization? Do they want a lecture on the influence of the dichotomy on European philosophy or what? Are they above the mention of money? And was your letter intended to show me that the Library wanted me very much to make a talk to the Cosmos Club or were you merely enthusiastic?

Today is the first day in some time that I have felt able to write anything. I shall work on the report and get it off to you either today or tomorrow by airmail. Please send me fifty records and three dozen needles to West Liberty, Ky., General Delivery. I am sorry if I have caused you anxiety, but I have had more on my shoulders this last week than I was designed to carry. Four days ago I sent you the little Delcos, having just purchased two new batteries. One of them was cracked, and not by rough handling either. Perhaps some particularly rough bit of road did the poor little thing in. Yesterday I expressed you five boxes of discs. I wish you could do something about getting my mileage vouchers through more quickly. I have a garage bill owing in Harlan County and the Studebaker grows more expensive to run with every mile as these rough mountain roads devour its entrails and fret its extremities. Please forward my mail through Monday to Hazard and after West Liberty, Ky. [ALC]

While on the road he conducted other business, for example in writing to Rosa Warren Wilson, Martins Point, South Carolina, on October 12 about her program "Plantation Echoes":

I enclose a letter concerning your program which I trust may be helpful to you in securing a hearing of your interesting group of Negroes. I hope you won't mind a few suggestions from me: 1. The tune used in the crap shooting beginning does not seem to me Negro music. 2. Some of your spirituals are widely sung. Why not include only those peculiar to your section? 3. Your audiences will generally be far more interested in the primitive elements of the singing than in the beauty and finish of the program. 4. Omit all "white folks" music except the old long meter tunes. 5. Probably too much clapping is employed, and it begins too early in the program to be most dramatically effective. 6. Somewhere in your program you should include some of the beautiful work songs sung in the fields; also some of the "hollers." It is easy, I know, to criticize. You will know best if my suggestions are feasible. [ALC]

Spivacke was generally delighted with Lomax's progress, although he worried about his health, as he expressed to Alan in a letter on October 20:

You seem to forget that our estimate of 250 records included about 100 from Fuson. You seem to forget also that I am not a slave driver. I am satisfied that you are trying your best. . . . Father [John A. Lomax] and I have been discussing the advisability of sending you on to Akron, Ohio to record the singing of Captain [Pearl R.] Nye. The venerable captain has been sending his songs on sheets of paper over 15 feet long! Do you feel up to it and would you be willing to go if I can arrange it? Let me hear from you soon about this. [ALC]

Alan responded to Spivacke on October 26 from Salyersville, beginning with an apology:

I am sorry about the Haitian report. It simply won't come out of me fast. But I'll send it along as soon as I can force it into existence. I don't know what is the matter with me now, but I can't write what I want to. I suppose this will mean my expulsion from the Library, but I shall have to bear the disgrace as best I can. Thanks for your consolatory letter. It cheered me no end and changed my luck, it seems most decidedly. Last Saturday night I found the most delightful old time banjo player I have yet met. At 71 he thumps away at his instrument and sings about Liza Jane and all the rest with more than the enthusiasm of youth. This afternoon the best fiddler I have heard in Ky. is coming to play, plus a banjo picker and a singer and an old ballad singer and his two daughters. Tomorrow morning at seven thirty, an old fellow is coming who is said to be the best ballad singer in this county. I will need four or five extra days to run about over the rest of this section and make records in a few more counties so that the trip will seem more like a survey than it does at present. I am convinced that a real survey of this large section of the state would take six months at least, unless there were a crew of four or five people working in the territory. May I make a formal request, then, for four or five days more than my allotted time? That would bring me back to Washington sometime between the fifth and the eighth of November. Write me General Delivery, Pikeville, Ky., whether or not you approve of the idea. Please enclose two packages of cutting needles. About to put this in the mail and having as yet received no money from the vouchers that I sent in on the 8th of the month, I regret to inform you that the Kentucky Expedition address will remain General Delivery, Salyersville, Ky., until funds arrive. [ALC][33]

Alan and Elizabeth survived their trip to Kentucky, then headed to Akron, Ohio, for a brief visit, as he informed Spivacke by telegram on October 30:

Total Ky. 229 discs. Am on my way to Akron. Apprise [Pearl R.] Nye send me his address general delivery. Forward salary check. [ALC]

Spivacke wrote him there on November 2.

You must have misunderstood my letter because I had not yet obtained the Librarian's approval for your trip to Akron. However, that has been settled satisfactorily and a two weeks extension of your trip granted. . . . I suggest that your return to Washington by way of Pennsylvania and visit Bucknell College [site of George Korson's Pennsylvania Folk Festival in 1936], which I hear has long been a center of Pennsylvania folk songs. If there are any other interesting points in Pennsylvania which you should care to visit on your way back, do not hesitate to do so. The total count for Kentucky is indeed marvelous. [ALC]

Alan wrote a short letter to Spivacke on November 4 from Akron, apparently before receiving his message, so there is no reference to Pennsylvania, which they bypassed in returning to Washington:

I am sorry there has been this misunderstanding. I imagined from the number of times you mentioned Akron in your letters that you were very anxious for me to go there and already had secured the consent of the Librarian. Elizabeth has been ill for some time and I have felt criminal in keeping her in the field as long as I have, but we thought that we'd come by Akron to please you and father. Here we came and yesterday exhausted Cpt. Nye with thirteen records. But now, two weeks extension or no we are on our way home. Perhaps after I take E. to the doctor we can go out again if you consider it important, but right now I am sick of record making, tired, and E. should not be kept out of town any longer. So expect us shortly after you receive this note. [ALC][34]

Once back in Washington, he wrote to Bess Alice Owens, Pikesville College in Kentucky, on November 26:

Your letter, sadly enough, did not reach me until after my return to Washington from my two months' trip in Kentucky. I am sure I could have greatly benefited from your help in that region. The size of your collection is, indeed, amazing and I should like to learn more about its nature. How much of it has been recorded on discs? How much on cylinders? How many of the tunes are only written down? For what portion of the songs do you have the airs? I hope it will be possible for the Library, which is the natural repository for all folk-song collections I think you will agree, some day to have the words and texts of all your songs, whether you publish them or not. Would it be possible, therefore, for you to give me some information about your collection? [ALC]

1938

Alan was soon settled in at the Library of Congress, where he kept in touch with some of his contacts in Kentucky, such as Clay Walters in Hendericks, on January 14, 1938:

I am disappointed that you could not play the duplicates I sent you and I want to remedy this sad state of affairs if possible. Will you send the records back to me and at the same time write and tell me what machine or machines you have tried to play the records on? I'll try to make some duplicates for you that will work a little better when I receive this information. In the meantime I wonder if it would be too much trouble for you to write out the words to—"Twas in the town of Jacksboro/In the year of '83,"—the song about the buffalo hunters—for me. There is nothing I would enjoy more than making another visit to Salersville and to your home in the hills. Perhaps I will be able to stop by again some day or, at the worst, send some one else by to see you. I wonder if you have kept your promise to me to practice up on the old songs you know and to write down? Give my best regards to Mrs. Walters and to the other members of your family. [ALC]

On February 1 Alan had a request for Chick Ritter of the Sound Engineering Division of the American Foundation for the Blind in New York:

As you know, Barnicle has just come back from Kentucky with a hundred new records. I should like to arrange for the deposit of duplicates of these records in the Library of Congress and Barnicle has agreed to allow the duplication. Would it be possible for you to do the actual work of dubbing if we furnished the acetate and Mary Elizabeth Barnicle fed you the originals as she prepared them? If so, can you quote me a price for the job? I suppose we could get this work done through one of the regular channels, but Barnicle will be constantly using the records in her classes and your personal contact with her would make the duplication more feasible. I should like to hear from you soon in this regard and also should like to have your latest report on pick-ups. [ALC]

About this same time, in an undated letter to Spivacke, Alan continued about the Barnicle recordings:

Professor Mary Elizabeth Barnicle stopped off with me for a short visit January 31st on her way back from a recording trip to the Kentucky Mountains. She reported to me that during her stay in Kentucky she made 100 acetate discs of the religious folk-songs of the mountains. I think that these discs would be a most important addition to the Archive's collection and that they would be particularly pertinent at this time, in view of the recent acquisition by the Archive of 258 discs of secular folk-songs from the same region. I strongly urge that the Library take steps to secure for the Archive the originals or duplicates of this important collection. I feel sure that Professor Barnicle's friendliness toward the Archive will facilitate this acquisition. [ALC]

He followed on February 11 with more details to Ritter:

I suggest that you make us an estimate based on my first letter if you want the job, in a letter addressed to me, in care of the Archive of American Folk Song. I am writing Barnicle today about the same matter. Indicate in this estimate how much time you think the work would take. Thank you for your information about pick-ups and the invitation. [ALC]

He did write a lengthy letter to Mary Elizabeth Barnicle on February 11:

I have just written to Chick for an estimate on the dubbing of your 100 Holiness records and I would like to have, officially, your confirmation of this project. Perhaps, in the course of the dubbing job, Chick might discover that he could improve on the originals in his duplications for your purposes, which I presume are for demonstration mainly. In that case, if you like, you can keep the duplications and we will be only too happy to gobble up the originals.

I am beginning work the first of next week on the duplications that I promised you last winter. The machine seems to be in good condition at last! I would like to know what records you need at the moment in your class work, or whether you will trust me to pick out the most exciting things from the whole collection. Do you want complete renditions of folk songs or would you prefer to have more material in slightly abbreviated form? Please write me your notions about these matters.

I have started my class at Federal Workers' School and it seems to be a success. The first evening, the class learned eight songs that were new to them and roared them out very lustily. I wish we had a chance to talk more about your classes, because I need all the good advice that anybody can give me. The one thing that I do very much need at the moment are your Georgia and Bahama notes, and if you are not using them soon, would you lend them to me for six weeks so that I can have them typed and put where they belong—with the records. Give my best regards to your Kentucky tribe and to Margaret. [ALC]

He was soon thinking of a trip to Indiana, as he explained to the folklorist Paul Brewster in Bloomington, on February 12:

I very much appreciate your invitation to talk at the April meeting of the Hoosier Folklore Society and it is quite possible that I may be able to come. It is important, however, that such a trip should mean the addition of records to the Archive of American Folk Song. You have formerly expressed an interest in helping the Archive record the folk songs of Indiana, and I should like to know whether you might be able to give any of your time to this project in

April. Would it be possible for me to visit at that time the informants from whom you collected material? If so, can you estimate for me the number of songs I might be able to obtain from them? Does the Hoosier Folklore Society have contacts in Vincennes or other Indiana communities where French folk ways are still alive? Are there songs to be found in these communities? I hope you will be able to excuse this rather inquisitorial letter, but it is part of the procedure for me to make a forecast of field trips before I set out on them. If I've been a negligent correspondent in the past, it has been because I have had more work than I could possibly do, and I'll try not to sin in that direction again. [ALC][35]

On February 26 he clarified the copying arrangements with Chick Ritter:

I understand that it will be impossible for you to be paid for the dubbing, according to our first arrangement. It is against the law for the Library to pay wages for outside technical help. Therefore, send me one more estimate—just an estimate this time—for the price of the completed duplicate, this including the cost of the blank itself. This should, I feel, not exceed a maximum of $1.25 a record. I should appreciate your sending me this estimate as quickly as possible so that we can begin work next week. [ALC]

Alan was now arranging for a trip to Pennsylvania, as he explained to Dr. Edwin Fagel in Fogelsville, on February 28:

I am planning a recording trip into Pennsylvania for the Archive of American Folk Song. As you know, the Library of Congress has established the Archive with a view to concentrating in one comprehensive collection all the folk-song versions collected in the United States, particularly those items that are or will be recorded. Pennsylvania, so far as I know, has been sadly neglected by the recording machine and it is [a] most important forward step in building the Archive to add to it records from Pennsylvania. I am sure that you will be interested in collaborating in this effort and I should appreciate any suggestions you might be able to offer. [ALC]

Also on February 28 he repeated about the same information to Dr. L. B. Stoutt in Allentown:

I am planning a recording trip into Pennsylvania for the Archive of American Folk Song. I understand that you have invited John A. Lomax to come to your folk festivals on several occasions, but he has always been somewhere between Texas and Timbucktoo and couldn't make it. Sometime this spring or summer, however, I want to bring a fine recording instrument into Pennsylvania and make for the Archive specimen records of Pennsylvania folksongs. I am sure that both you and the German Folklore Society can be of the greatest assistance to this project. Will you be in Allentown this summer and with enough free time to give me the lay of the land, at least? May I expect to hear from you in the near future? [ALC]

Alan dedicated a much longer letter to the Pennsylvania folklorist Samuel P. Bayard on February 28:[36]

I remember with what pleasure I looked over the material you sent John A. Lomax and myself in 1933 for inclusion in "American Ballads and Folk Songs," and when I saw mention of your collection in the Southern Folklore Journal and other places, I was able to imagine just what it looked like. You must know that the Library of Congress has brought a very healthy Archive of American Folk Song into existence. We lend recording machines (in a very limited way) and do duplicating work. We have at least two field trips a year and have grown to respectable proportions—2,000 discs, 1,500 cylinders. The next field trip that we plan to make, sometime within the next three or four months, is into Pennsylvania. I should like to meet you and it will be most pleasant if we can do some field work together. I don't know whether you have ever made any recordings in the field. If not, you should find it a most interesting experience. The Archive, although it is primarily interested in collecting the best material and freeing it for public use, also understands the problems of the collector. If, by any chance, you are interested in pre-publication restrictions, we could settle that matter very simply. This letter, of course, is a cast in the dark. I shall await your reply with much interest. [ALC]

Before traveling to Pennsylvania, however, he scheduled a trip to Indiana, as he noted on March 7 to Louise Pound at the University of Nebraska:[37]

The Archive of American Folk Song is sending me to Indiana in April to make recordings of Indiana folk songs, and I wonder if you have any suggestions to offer in regard to interested individuals, interesting regions or possible informants in Indiana or the nearby Midwest. It makes relatively little difference, I think, whether the records I make are of songs that have already been published or that will be published, since, in the first case, it is important that there be exact versions, and in the second case, the Library will restrict the material so collected until its discoverer has an opportunity to publish. I have wanted for a long time to discuss some of the issues you raised in your book on the ballad. I think I have two ballads, "Po' Laz'us" and "The Grey Goose" (they appear in partial versions in American Ballads and Folk Songs, the Lomax one not the Pound one) which have emerged from a complex of miscellaneous work song verses. I should appreciate very much any suggestions you might make about the Indiana recording trip. [ALC]

He continued to plan the Midwestern trip in a letter to H. M. Belden in Columbia, Missouri:[38]

The Archive of American Folk Song is sending me to Indiana in April to make recordings of Indiana folk songs, and I wonder if you have any suggestions to offer in regard to interested individuals, interesting religious or possible informants in Indiana or the nearby Mid-West. It makes relatively little difference, I think, whether the records I make are of songs that have already been published or that will be published, since, in the first case, it is important that there be exact versions, and in the second case, the Library will restrict the material so collected until its discoverer has an opportunity to publish. I can't be positive whether or not I have met you at any Meeting of the Modern Language Association I have attended, but I have heard my father speak of you many times. Is it possible that you will attend the meeting of the Hoosier Folk-Lore Society in Bloomington in April? If not, I should greatly appreciate a letter from you with any suggestions you have to make in regard to this recording trip. [ALC]

Alan also wrote to Mabel Neale Hunter on March 7 in Atlanta, Georgia:

The Archive of American Folk Song is sending me to Indiana in April to make recordings of Indiana Folk-Songs. I have studied your Brown County [Indiana] Collection, and I should like your permission to revisit your informants and make records of the ballad and folk song versions you collected from them. If your experience has been like mine, you must have been forced to leave many possible informants unvisited and still others whose stock of songs you felt you have not exhausted. I should greatly appreciate any suggestions you would care to make in regard to work in Brown County, or in Indiana in general. As you undoubtedly know, the Library of Congress has set up the Archive for the purpose of helping students in the field, and I am sure that we will be able to cooperate to the fullest extent. [ALC]

Since his trip would take him through Ohio, he wrote to Professor H. L. Ridenhour at Baldwin Wallace College in Berea, Ohio, on March 9:

The Archive of American Folk Song is sending me to Indiana in April for a brief recording trip. This will be my first experience at collecting in the Middle West and I should particularly welcome any suggestions you might have to make in regard to regions and singers. My route to and from Indiana lies, of course, across Southern Ohio and I plan to do some recording there. If your singers are not too inaccessible, I should like to put their material in permanent form in the Archive. I don't know whether or not you published this material or plan to publish it, but, if you do intend to publish it, it can be deposited in the Archive under any reasonable restrictions you care to impose. I imagine we could arrange to furnish you a certain number of duplicates for use in your classes and so on. I hope we will be able to work together in this project and that I will be able to call on you some time in the course of this trip. [ALC]

As a most careful collector, Alan also wrote to Edith Dell Hopkins in Boonville, Indiana, on March 9:

A friend of yours, Miss Wilkin of Denver, who spent a great deal of time in the Music Division last summer, spoke to me with great enthusiasm about you and your mother and the fine stock of folk-songs that you knew. She promised to write you about the work of the Library of Congress in collecting the folk-songs of America in a central, permanent depository and this, I presume, she has already done. Naturally, I have wanted to come collecting out your way, but the opportunity for such a visit has only just presented itself. The Library is sending me to Indiana in April. Will it be possible for me to visit you and your mother and record the folk-songs that you know? If so, what time during April would suit your convenience? Do you have any suggestions about other informants, or about interesting regions in or near Indiana? [ALC]

Another letter of March 9 went to Professor Louis W. Chappell at West Virginia University:[39]

I saw Thompson some weeks ago and he told me that you had bought one of his field recorders. I should like to know what you think of its performance, and whether or not you have found it practicable for your field work. The Library is sending me to Indiana in April to attend the first meeting of Hoosier Folk Lore Society, and to do some recording in the state. My route lies across West Virginia and I should like to stop by for a visit with you. Furthermore, I should like to know whether you have any suggestions to make about recordings in West Virginia that I might be able to pick up en route. Even if this work repeated something that you have done or plan to do, I do not feel that a little duplication of effort in regard to folk songs is wasted, since it is valuable to have recordings of the same song and the same singers made at different times. [ALC]

On March 12 Alan also informed John Harrington Cox, who was also teaching at West Virginia University, about his upcoming Midwestern trip:[40]

The Library is sending me to the meeting of the Hoosier Folk Lore Society in April in Indiana, and since my route lies across West Virginia, I should like to drop by and call on you. I have found your book extremely useful in connection with my work here at the Library in cataloging folk songs, and I have many things I should like to talk over with you. Do you think there is any recording we might do in or nearby Morgantown that would prove interesting? I shall have the Library's portable recording machine with me. May I expect to hear from you soon? [ALC]

Before leaving for the Midwest, he helped organize a concert, held on March 13 in Washington, for the United Federal Workers union. Half of the concert included classical music; the other half featured Lomax performing music from his collecting in Haiti and the Bahamas, as well as white and black music from the South.

The business affairs of the Library were never far from his mind, or worries, as seen in his report to Spivacke on March 14. In planning for his trip to Indiana, and to take care of the Archive's needs, he first requested various supplies (acetate discs, cutting needles and playing needles, movie film, storage batteries), then explained:

In order to finance the forthcoming trip to Indiana, I should like to request an advance of $100.00 be made against the per diem vouchers for the trip. As surety for this advance, I have established a bond with the Fidelity Bonding and Deposit Company of Maryland. The bond's no. is 4246869 and is paid up to August 25, 1938. I would suggest that the date of my departure for Indiana be moved back to the 25th of March, so that I may be able to visit the Ohio Valley Folk Festival which is being held in Cincinnati on the 27th of March. This festival, directed by a widely known collector, Bascom Lamar Lunsford, should afford some valuable recordings for the Archive's collection.

With reference to the attached bills and memoranda: 1) Verbal authorization was secured from the Superintendent of Buildings in both cases. 2) In the case of the Capital Radio Wholesalers, it was ascertained that this dealer was the only one in Washington who carried the particular type of equipment necessary and the purchase was authorized verbally by the Superintendent of Buildings before the order was placed. The mistake I seem to have made was in ordering the material myself instead of letting the order come through the Superintendent's office. At the time, however, I did not understand that this was the wrong procedure. No one, before that time, had ever informed me that such procedure was incorrect and I had been accustomed to having the machine repaired in the field on my own initiative. 3) In the case of the bill from Mr. Fred Kohl, the Superintendent authorized me verbally to call Mr. Kohl in for repair work on the Archive's recording equipment when I had told him that Mr. Kohl had estimated his charges would be in the neighborhood of three dollars. As the repair work progressed, however, the equipment, which has seen several years of hard service in the field, developed more and more defects and it was only after several consulting technicians had volunteered their suggestions and after some ten or twelve nights of work by Mr. Kohl that the equipment was finally repaired. I submit that it was impossible for either Mr. Kohl or myself to foresee that these difficulties would arise and that Mr. Kohl has presented a very reasonable bill, since in point of fact he spent twice as much time on the equipment as he estimates in his bill. [ALC]

Once on the road with Elizabeth, they first stopped at Lunsford's Ohio Valley Folk Festival at the Cincinnati Music Hall. The brainchild of John Lair of the Renfro Valley Barn Dance and National Folk Festival organizer Sarah Gertrude Knott, Alan found the Ohio festival most disappointing.[41] He expressed his feelings to Spivacke from Bloomington, Indiana, on April 1:

After a very stiff, *501* mile, drive over the mountains to Cincinnati Mrs. Lomax and I found a very sloppily run and stupid hill-billy show masquerading under the title "Folk Festival." I recorded only two songs while the festival was in progress and they were hardly worth the acetate. [Bascom Lamar] Lunsford, as you might have expected, rather boycotted me, and, after the festival was over, dashed away with the hope that he would see me in Washington. He gave me not one scrap of information about who was [a] folk-singer out of the huge drove of yodeling, crooning, Alabama-mooning Kentuckians he had assembled. I was able, however, in the course of the most horrible exhibition of Anglo-American, blond, blue-eyed sentimentalism and musical gaucherie that I have ever endured to single out a few genuine informants. As a result I have made four visits in the past four days which have brought to the Library 28 very good records. High spots: A Very complete version of Fair Charlotte, one of McAfee's Confession, neither of which we had recorded before, both rather rare pieces of Americana; two very rare banjo pieces having to do with the Coal Mines at Coal Creek, Tenn., The Coal Creek March and the Coal Creek Pay-Day; ten fine records of the best banjo player I have met up to date

[Pete Steele], playing and singing Child, English and American ballads and blues, the Pretty Polly being a masterpiece; a group of new Ohio fiddle tunes. Two of my informants were taken quite unaware by my visits and swore that they knew many more old songs and would be able to supply them when I came back to see them.

I am, therefore, extremely well pleased with my trip so far, from the point of view of material. The prospects seem very interesting. Paul Brewster has, of course, already paved the way for me among his informants and Dr. [Stith] Thompson has arranged for me to record the traditional hymns of the Mennonites and Amish communities of Northern Indiana, communities I had intended to visit but in which I feared it could be difficult to gain friendly help. Expenses have been very heavy. A dead battery, several punctures and trouble with some as yet mysterious portion of the alimentary tract of the Plymouth have wasted my substance frightfully. Will you personally see to it that my salary comes out or has come out to me muy pronto. The express shipment of records and so on came today. I do want to warn you, however, that I may be very broke by the end of ten days and may need to call for ten or so to tide me over. If you have any suggestions, make them now. P.S. I have forgotten the reason for this letter, which is to ask you to have Dr. Putnam mail me a letter of introduction to whom it may concern in care of this address. [ALC]

In his later, official report, however, he found it expedient to give a much more positive take on his experiences in Cincinnati:

In April I was invited to speak at the first meeting of the Hoosier Folk Lore Society in Indiana and, due to the good offices of Bascom Lamar Lunsford and Dr. Stith Thompson, was able to make a group of valuable records on this two weeks' trip. Mr. Lunsford, as manager of the Ohio Valley Folk Festival, had assembled a huge crowd of fiddlers, square dancers and singers from the neighborhood of Cincinnati and, though we were unable to make records during the festival itself, we met individuals who later gave us material. In the festival we again found evidence of the vitality of rural music. Cincinnati is at once a center for "hillbilly" broadcasts and one of the gateways for migration out of eastern Kentucky and West Virginia. Many mountain families have moved across the Ohio river to work in factories in and near Cincinnati and they furnish both the talent and the audience for the almost hourly "barn dance" programs of Cincinnati radio stations. Through these programs the prestige of rural music is maintained and various individuals are encouraged to keep their heritage of traditional music fresh in mind. Typical of these mountaineers away from the mountains who have renewed their interest in traditional music are Robert L. Day, of Cincinnati, and Pete Steele, of Hamilton. The latter is an extraordinary banjo player. In Bloomington, through Dr. Stith Thompson, founder and organizer of the Hoosier Folk Lore Society, we met Indiana balladist Paul Brewster and the officials of the State Writers' Project. Mr. Brewster, who has discovered an amazing number of Child ballad variants in Indiana, kindly introduced us to his best informants and we recorded fine versions from them. We were somewhat astonished, however, to discover that many of Mr. Brewster's best ballad sources either did not know or could not sing the tunes of the ballads they remembered. The W.P.A. Recreation Project helped us locate singers in Bloomington and in Brown County and, through the Federal Writers' Project, we met Oscar Parks and his family in the backwoods of Crawford County. This delightful Kentucky family sang several fine ballads for us. Through the Writers' Project, too, we found Aunt Phoebe Elliott, of New Harmony, and Mrs. Josephine Caney of Vincennes, who, at more than eighty years, is still a witty encyclopedia of the music and manners of the French settlers of that city. Dr. Umble, of Goshen College, introduced us to Jonie Easch and Eli Bontreger, two of the singing leaders of the large and flourishing Amish community near Goshen. These two singers recorded the tunes of thirteen traditional Amish hymns and thus opened the way for valuable studies in the traditional religious music of the Amish settlers in America. ["Archive of American Folk Song: A History, 1928–1939," 58–59]

Upon returning to Washington, he spent some time catching up with his correspondence—for example, to Mrs. R. W. Fray in Spottsville, Kentucky, on April 21:

Recently, while collecting old songs in Indiana for the Congressional Library, I saw copies of some of your songs. One of them, a song about the Civil War, I found particularly interesting. I wonder if you would be kind enough to send me a copy of this song for deposit under your name in the Archive of American Folk Song. You would be making a real contribution to our knowledge of the songs of the past, thereby, especially if you could tell us where the song came from and how long you have known it. [ALC]

On the same day, he wrote to Robert L. Day in Cincinnati, Ohio:

I hope you haven't changed your plans about coming to Washington. I want to see you again and we have the pallet on the floor already made up and a bed spoken for at a friend's house. Thank you again for the fine contribution you made to the Library and the Archive; your songs will have a chance to outlive your grandchildren. Give my best regards to your family. Elizabeth and I both felt the world a more pleasant place to live in after our delightful visit with you all. [ALC]

April 21 was a heavy day for correspondence. Alan also contacted Professor John Umble at Goshen College in Goshen, Indiana:

I regret not having met you on my visit to Goshen, if you are one tenth as pleasant company as Mrs. Umble and your son. Certainly we did appreciate the friendly help they gave us. Amish hymns are a valuable and unusual addition to the Library's collection. It is a pity that both Brother Bontreger and ourselves were in such a hurry that we couldn't record all of the twenty-one "melodies" of the Amish, but on my next visit to Goshen, which I hope will be a little more leisurely, all of the tunes will be taken down. In the meantime, let me thank you for your help in the name of the Library and the Archive. The Amish music seems to be very old, indeed, and I hope you plan to make an extended historical and social study of it. If there is any way I can assist you in this enterprise, I should be delighted. [ALC][42]

He also briefly thanked Doyle Joyce of Vincennes, Mrs. Josephine Caney of Vincennes, Mrs. Dora Ward of Princeton, Mrs. Rogers of Bloomington, and Aunt Phoebe Elliott of New Harmony for their recent collecting assistance. Mrs. Thomas Bryant of Evansville received a thoughtful message:

Our visit with you was the high point of our trip to Indiana and you may be sure that the old songs you recalled for us will be kept in a place of honor in the Archive. It is rare to find one person who remembers as many as you do. I feel sure, too, that you have not half exhausted your store of material and that you will be able to recall many more fine pieces with very little trouble. We must keep up a correspondence and you must keep busy jotting down the songs so that we'll have a good excuse to come by to see you and your bevy of beautiful daughters again. Elizabeth and I want to take this occasion to thank you for your hospitality and I want to assure you of both the Archive's and the Library's appreciation of your kindness in our behalf. With very best regards to you and all the other Bryants, big and little. [ALC]

Alan's interest was not just focused on Hoosier folksongs, however. The following day, April 22, he corresponded with Mrs. Rudolph Roy in Lafayette, Louisiana. She had written that she would be representing Louisiana musicians at the forthcoming National Folk Festival in Washington, D.C., in May, and he responded:

I have been interviewed several times in the past few months in regard to my work in folk-lore, and I always mention the "Cajun" field because it is so rich in vital, new, and colorful material. I am shocked to discover that the Times Pica-yune ["Music of Cajuns Termed Untapped State Resource"] quoted me in the fashion that it did, but you must realize that newspaper reporters tend to color their stories to make them as sensational as possible. I have never worked in the community that I had a higher regard for than the Louisiana French. And when we meet at the National Folk Festival (after performance) I hope you will realize how sorry I always have been that I didn't grow up in a community where French and English were both spoken so that in my work in Louisiana I often had to ask for help in translation from friendly Cajuns. [ALC]

On April 23 he sent information to one of the House of Representatives members from Indiana, John W. Boehne:

Your letter of inquiry of April 14 has just come to my attention, as I returned to the city from Indiana only a day or so ago. The Archive of American Folk Song was established several years ago as a part of the Division of Music for the purpose of collecting and preserving American Folk Songs. In the begin-ning, when recording instruments were unsatisfactory, this work of preser-vation was carried on in largely manuscript form, but in recent years with the development of fine portable recording machines, the Library has been steadily enlarging its collection of records of folk-songs made in the homes of the people who know them. The Archive now has over 2,000 records from fourteen states and two neighboring West Indian Islands and has grown into one of the largest collections of its kind in the world. Through it the songs of the American people, which have been handed down from generation to generation have the opportunity to live alongside the more sophisticated published music that makes up the major part of the Music Division. Songs of cowboys, lumberjacks, Negro convicts, mountaineers; the fiddle tunes and banjo tunes to which our ancestors used to dance and which our rural popu-lation still enjoys; the traditional songs of the English, French, and Spanish settlers of the United States have been recorded from the people who have made or preserved them. The task of the Archive is to record this rich folk culture and prepare it for the use of scholars and other interested persons. The trip to Indiana, during which I met your constituent, brought into the Archive a large body of valuable and beautiful folk-songs, and I feel that in my three weeks visit I only sampled Indiana's rich stock of folk-music. The newly formed Indiana State Folk-Lore Society and, especially, the Indiana office of the W.P.A. Writers' Project cooperated with me and made the trip a delightful one. Most of the songs were English folk-songs from S. Indiana, with French songs from Vincennes and Amish hymns from Goshen to add an exotic flavor. I must say that I was surprised to find the state such a rich field for the folk-lorist, but I am anxious to go back and do a more thorough job of collecting there. [ALC]

On April 25 he thanked Ross Lockridge, Bloomington, Indiana:

Your contacts in Indiana proved most useful to me and your letters of introduction made my path a very smooth one. I only regret that I had to hurry back to Washington as soon and did not have time to pursue more of the many leads I had in Indiana and to inspect the folk-song material on file with the Writers' Project in Indianapolis. You are certainly well liked and much admired over the state and your letters were open sesames to the homes of the folk-singers. When I return to Indiana, I hope to be able to express my appreciation for your efforts in behalf of the Archive personally. [ALC]

That same day, Alan corresponded with James F. Broussard, a professor of Romance languages at Louisiana State University. Broussard was concerned about an article in the *Times-Picayune*, a story from the International News Service, "Music of Cajuns Termed Untapped State Resource," quoting Lomax, who did not seem to know about his university's collection:

Your note makes me regret the fact that I did not insist on seeing the interview you mention before it was published. In fact, when I discussed the Acadian material with the reporter, I emphasized the importance of Miss Whitfield's work (I have read her thesis) and I mentioned the fact that some work was being done at the University of Louisiana. I did not know, of course, that the Department of Romance Languages had purchased a recording instrument or that it planned to do systematic work in the field. The last time I visited the University, I heard of no project of this sort. Naturally, I am delighted to learn that progress is being made in this field, since my cursory contact with folk-music in Southern Louisiana convinced me that your state is an extremely rich field for students of folk literature and music in the country. I hope that the Archive of American Folk Song may be of some service to you, and that whatever material is collected may be deposited in duplicate in our files. What I did hope that this interview would do, of course, would be to arouse some widespread interest in Louisiana and folk song and to bring support to whatever projects there were for the collection of this material. [ALC][43]

While always busy with collecting for the archive, he still had time for more fanciful thoughts, as in this letter of May 19 to the music critic for the *New York Times*, Olin

Downes, who was in charge of music and dance for the 1939/40 planned World's Fair in New York City:

Nick [Nicholas] Ray[44] and I have talked over the Fourth of July pageant for the past several days. We have encountered a number of technical difficulties and have, at the same time, found some exciting ideas from which we might proceed. The difficulties arise largely from our ignorance of certain technical details. We need to know: The dimensions of the stage and auditorium. Whether they are indoors or outdoors. Whether the performances are to be by day, by night or both. The size of the cast, that is how many choruses, etc. are necessary. How much money may be spent on the production. Lacking these concrete details, we can only give you a few ideas from which a fine script might be built.

Title. *Yankee Doodle Comes to Town*. Central Idea: New York City, during her first hundred and fifty years, from 1639 to 1789 exemplifies the growth and the struggle for independence of the whole nation. This period, ending with the successful conclusion of the revolutionary war and the establishment of American institutions as we know them, presages the progress of the city for her next hundred and fifty years until 1939. America's struggle for liberty was early crystalized in New York. Founded by Flemish Huguenots who came to the wilderness in search of religious freedom, its people fought against the tyrannical colonial policy of both the Dutch and English governments and even before the revolution had won a very influential popular assembly. In 1689 Jacob Leisler led a successful revolt against the Stuarts and governed New York himself, for nearly two years thereafter. In 1770 the Sons of Liberty fought the British mercenaries in the streets of New York—the first battle of the American revolution, the Battle of Golden Hill.

Nationalities: New York City has always been a cosmopolitan town and it will be amusing to portray the arrival of the first Chinaman, the first Negro, and the first Jew. Music: For musical material we will utilize Dutch and English folk-songs, and shanteys, pirate songs (Captain Kidd was taken into custody in or near New York harbor and there is a rousing folk-song that tells in the bloodiest details his history), the popular airs of the revolutionary period (see "Popular Music of George Washington's Day," Engel, Strunk, and Sol Bloom),[45] and Indian music. Yankee Doodle will come to town dancing in Dutch wooden shoes, stick a feather or two in General Howe's behind and march out triumphantly with the revolutionaries of 1789. Contrasts and analogies: The first Nine Old Men, the first argument about the Mayflower, the first gangsters, the origins of the first great fortunes (in the Bolting milling monopoly and piracy)—such things can make some rare comedy.

Techniques of presentation: Huge backdrops: Manhattan and the bur-
roughs done in the flat dull green of the wilderness the Dutch found in 1609.
On this the growth of the city can be shown in lights as the pageant progresses, from the lighting of the first campfire to the building of the World's
Fair of 1939. Shadows: Against the gigantic masses of the land and sea on the
backdrop the early settlers and citizens will cast the long shadows that their
almost legendary character warrants; as the pageant moves on the shadows
will dwindle in size until at last the men move small and unimportant against
the glowing face of the city that they have built.

Choruses: As each episode is concluded, its characters will withdraw into
the shadows beneath the backdrop and there separate into two groups which
will participate in the action of the pageant as it progresses. One group might
be called, 'The People,' and the other, 'The Mighty.' These groups, growing as
the city grows, representing the living and the dead of the city, will comment
on the action that goes on before them, will try to win the living characters
over, will join in their songs, will at times participate in the action on the stage.
Imagine the dramatic way these groups might be used in the revolutionary
scenes: The Mighty marching behind General Howe singing 'God Save the
King' and then scattering before Washington who leads 'The People' out of
the shadows with Yankee Doodle riding high. (This may sound a bit didactic
but if the modernisms of the 17th and 18th centuries are played up it can be
made extremely effective, viz: the Madison Square Garden pageants.)

We suggest these techniques as a few supplementary ideas, already assuming that we will utilize our experience with Living newspapers, the Meyerhold technique[46] and with folk plays to the best advantage. P.S. Don't worry.
I am not going to leave Washington until you need my nearer advice and
you needn't feel too concerned at the moment about my present relationship
to the World's Fair. I am sorry I have so delayed in getting this World's Fair
material into your hands, but this week has been a bad one for me. Please let
me know when I can help you. [ALC]

Professor John Umble had responded to Alan, who answered on May 26:

I hope you can forgive me for not having replied sooner to your very kind letter. I think you are most gracious in not holding me responsible for Mr. Bontrager's reaction to his first experience with folk-lore, since I do feel now that
perhaps if I had emphasized more strongly the official nature of the recordings he might not have responded as he did. I have discussed your suggestion of a letter from President Roosevelt with the Librarian and he feels that
perhaps this should be our last resort. He suggested that later, when Congress has departed and the President is a little less busy, we might arrange

to play for him one or two Amish records and ask him for a statement of appreciation at that time. In the meantime, however, the Librarian will write Mr. Bontrager on the most official Library stationery and thank him in the most official manner possible for his songs. Would you be kind enough to let us know what effect this thank-you has on our sturdy singer? What is Mr. Bontrager's address? I hope that perhaps he will have changed his mind by the end of June because I expect to be passing through Northern Indiana and I should very much like to re-visit the Amish community in your company and make further recordings. The material I recorded last spring was most unusual. I look forward to seeing you. [ALC]

He was not yet finished winding up his Indiana affairs, as he noted to Paul Brewster, now located in Oakland City, on May 26:

The old gentleman in Brown County is named Marion Stogill and he lives in Elkinsville. You had better hurry because he is very old and feeble. You can reach Mrs. Josephine Caney through the Federal Writers Project in Vincennes. I am terribly sorry I did not send you these addresses sooner, but I had more work recently than I could get around to. It may be that next summer I will come through Indiana on the way to Wisconsin and Minnesota. In that case I look forward to seeing you and to doing further field work with you. I would like to suggest that you visit Mrs. Dora Ward and her friends in Princeton. I felt that when I saw them that I had stumbled into a very valuable group of ballad singers. P.S. Would it be possible for you to send me copies of all the material you obtain from the Parkses and the Bryants? [ALC]

On May 26, he dashed off another note to Mrs. Thomas Bryant in Evansville:

Elizabeth and I were delighted to hear from you again and to know that you and your family were well and that you were continuing to discover new songs. I will certainly insist that Mr. Brewster send me copies of all the new songs that you recall. As for the pictures, we have not seen them ourselves yet, but as soon as they are developed and printed we will send you copies of the best ones. With very best regards to you and your hospitable family. [ALC]

Lomax took a different turn when writing to Ralph S. Boggs,[47] a professor in the Department of Romance Languages at the University of North Carolina and the founder of its Curriculum in Folklore in 1939, on May 26:

John A. Lomax is in Europe and I am holding the bulk of his material for him until he returns. In the meantime let me thank you for him for the re-print of your bibliographical article. I should, on my own account, like to know how long your bibliography has been in publication. If there have been any issues previous to that of 1937, can you tell me where I can get my hands on them? Would it be possible for you to put the Archive of American Folk Song on your re-print mailing list? It would be most convenient to keep this bibliography bound in a separate volume for reference purposes. [ALC]

Since his father was now traveling in Europe, Alan kept him up to date in a long letter dated May 26:

I am now dictating all of my correspondence to my brand-new secretary, and you can blame her for all mistakes in diction, grammar, etc. My work here was piling up to such mountainous heights that I barged in and asked God for some help and in a week I had it. I feel very much relieved about the whole situation here in the Archive. Last week the Reverend [Professor George] Herzog descended from the academic heights of Columbia [University] to finally inspect the Archive for the Foundations, who at long last have heard of my little request for a duplicating machine. Dr. Spivacke and Putnam handled him masterfully and he went back to New York feeling very sympathetic toward all our problems, so sympathetic in fact that all of his criticism will be aimed at giving us more money than we asked for. Everybody, including Putnam, is now agreed that Charley is essential to the development of the Archive and he may be my boss by the time I next write you. I am completely free now to work on Ballads No. 2 and I hope that before I go on my next recording trip I will have all of the texts finally and forever done and will be well along in the job of writing the head notes, so don't bother your head about the book any more for the moment. In reply to your question—No. 1: I do not know why Stith Thompson did not answer your letter, as I told you he was as friendly as any body could be, and I would guess that he merely wanted to avoid any sort of unpleasant controversy with a person of whom he is as fond as he is of you. I have no doubt that Herzog was largely responsible for killing your projects at the Yale meeting. When he was here he confessed that although, of course, he felt no such prejudice, other folklorists have been jealous of you because of the commercial success of your books, and he, along with the others, felt that you and I were trying to hog the whole field of American folk song. Herzog objected to that on purely scholastic grounds, of course.

No. 2: Miss Knott of North Carolina gave a mildly successful folk festival in Washington the first part of this month. It was the usual uncritical hash of everything you can think of and Miss Knott played her ordinary dumb but beautiful role, sweeping across the stage in a long white lace dress and pushing folk singers around like a professional checker player. All the folklorists, from Miss [Martha] Beckwith on down, spent their time in the lobby wishing that folk festivals had never been heard of; there is a movement on foot to attempt to depose or at least demote Miss Knott. I locked horns again with Colonel [M. J.] Pickering [business manager of the festival association] and I am afraid it was only my official position and his extreme age and fragility that restrained me from letting him have it. If I get my chance in New York, I think that this wen [Wednesday?], the National Folk Festival, may be carved off the name of American folk song. No. 3: Waters tells me all the copy on *Cowboy Songs* is done and Mr. Putnam told me only ten days ago that they expected to publish the volume in August. I am a little nervous about the textual side of the book, since Waters has refused to take any responsibility for it and I have not had a minute to look it over, myself. No. 4: The Schultz matter seems to be well shelved. U.F.W.A. put its pressure on at the proper moment and that seems to have been all that was additionally necessary to kill the matter for the time being. I am delighted to receive you into the stuffed shirt bosom of Phi Beta Kappa. The stupid part of this is that you were not a member years and years ago, because if anybody deserved to be made a member, you did. You shouldn't be afraid of a little grand feeling on the subject, because the Lomaxes, in keeping with the rest of humanity, are a vain race. Please write me as much as you can about Austria, Switzerland, etc. You mention them as casually as though they were just other corn-fed counties in the Midwest. Everyone here in Washington continues to ask about you with real affection and Elizabeth and I are flourishing. [ALC]⁴⁸

On May 26, he quickly followed his earlier letter to Olin Downes at the New York World's Fair office with more advice:

While I think of it, here is another suggestion that you might find valuable and I will send it along to you, altho' perhaps some one else has thought of it first. You may not agree with me that the ragtime-jazz-blues-swing tradition is the most important American contribution to sophisticated music, but at least this tradition deserves a great deal of attention at the World's Fair. I have encountered a Negro here in Washington who might fit into the World's Fair program very nicely and who I think could represent this tradition as well or better than anyone I know. His name is Jelly Roll Morton. He is well along in his fifties and grew up with jazz as it developed in the tenderloin district of New Orleans and spread up the river to Chicago. His brother-in-law brought the first jazz band to New York; and Jelly Roll Morton, himself, is rated in *Down Beat* as the most versatile and fertile man in the field of jazz from 1910–1929. I am recording for the Library all of his compositions, all of the folk tunes that he knows along with very full biographical material. I think the musicologists of the future will find in it essential material for writing the history of American music. Jelly Roll is still a great pianist and a fine singer and he has had wide experience in the organization of orchestras, in arranging and composing. He also knows personally everyone who has ever had anything to do with jazz or swing. He might be the ideal person to put in charge of the World's Fair *Jam Session*, without which, of course, the World's Fair would be musically incomplete. What about "Yankee Doodle Goes to Town."? [ALC][49]

Two days later, May 28, he had some queries for Mary Elizabeth Barnicle, back in New York, about their previous trip:

Two questions: What was the name of the boat on which we sailed to Cat Island and back? What was the name of the lady at the Old Bite whom you fed during our stay there and who, besides, as you recall, was one of the Captain's numerous wives? These two pieces of information are going to be put on the Bahaman pictures which I have finally had mounted. I have at last got a very good stenographer at the office and have the opportunity now to accumulate the background material that should go in with our recordings. An important part of that will consist of Georgia, Florida and Bahama stuff which I can still remember and which you have in your notes. Would it be possible for you to lend the Library these notes for, say, a month or two this summer, and [in] return for this loan we could furnish you with a typed copy for your own use; and the notes, themselves, could be restricted in any fashion you care to stipulate. The same would be true for any or all of the Kentucky material you care to let out of your hands for the time being.

I feel a little bad about asking you for any more favors for the Archive, since you have done all of us many favors and we have never been able to give you the records you need so much for your classes. I think you know the conditions I have worked under. Things are beginning to move very rapidly here now and the first thing we will get is a dubbing outfit that will be practical and ready to go in the next week or so. The first thing that the dubbing outfit will do will be to make you the duplicates that you need, and then my conscience will be a little less heavy with my obligation to you. It seems rather likely now that the Archive will soon get a real duplicating set and perhaps we will be able to bring Charles Seeger[50] into the picture as director of the work here. You know what that means for me and what it will mean for folklore work in general in America. Among other things, I hope it will turn me back to freedom and the sort of life Elizabeth and I really like to lead. Of course it may be that by that time we will be so fat and settled we won't want to leave Washington.

We didn't get a chance to really talk all the time we were in Wilton, and I hope you were as sorry about that as I was. My buzzing about in New York brought some results. Olin Downes has asked for me as folklore adviser at the New York World's Fair, and it may mean something very handsome within the next year; and I will be able to see you every week or so. That is one of the most important things that motivated me from the beginning to try the World's Fair project. Will you please come to see us as soon as you can and remember that we love you more than anyone else in the world, Bess and Steve respectively excepted, perhaps. Give my best wishes to Tillman [Cadle]. [ALC][51]

On June 2 he informed Harold Spivacke about a request from Alistair Cooke,[52] then in the United States, who had a radio show on the BBC:

After having discussed the matter thoroughly with Mr. Cooke, I can find no objections to the Archive furnishing him with duplicate recordings for his projected broadcasts on American music. Mr. Cooke astonished me by his grasp of the field of American popular music and I feel that the material will be properly handled by him. The records, themselves, are unrestricted so far as I know, with the possible exception of those recorded by Mollie Jackson; and Mr. Cooke plans to call on her in New York and ask her permission to use these recordings before he has them recorded. [ALC]

Also on June 2, he followed up with Ralph Boggs in Chapel Hill:

I shall forward your letter on to my father and urge him to bring his bibliography up to date. He has published a number of articles in the past year or so which are not generally known, and I am sure he will be glad to furnish you with this material. If it would not be too much trouble, could you send me a list of the publications (with dates) in which your Folklore Bibliographies have previously appeared? Do you plan to carry a recording machine on your folklore expedition into Mexico and to use it in recording folk songs? If so, I should be most interested in hearing what the results of the trip will be. My best wishes for the success of your expedition. [ALC]

He usually kept up with his father—who had left for Europe in early February with Miss Terrill, Bess, and her college roommate, Elizabeth Watkins—as he did on June 3:

1) I have recently been raised to $1800 a year. 2) The Writers Project plans to expand its folklore activities very considerably and Buck and I are gong to

push for the establishment of a folklore archive here in the Library, in connection with the present Archive of American Folk Song. Will let you know what develops. 3) The British Broadcasting Company has asked for a large group of records to be used in a program on American folk music. As you know, BBC is not a commercial outfit; on the contrary, it is a state owned and state financed company and we have decided to loan them the records for that reason. I will let you know when the programs are gong on the air so you can listen in. The producer, with whom I had several long talks, is a very bright fellow and really knows more about American folk songs than nine-tenths of the folklorists. 4) If you can tell me where I can find the dates of your recent magazine articles, I will forward this material on to Boggs for you. 5) I hope I have not made a mistake in giving Miss Smith permission to use your material. It seems to me at the moment more important to lend assistance to composers than to try to squeeze a few dollars from them for permissions. I hope you agree with me on this. If not, let me know in general what you want me to do in regard to future requests. Elizabeth and I are both very hard at work on numerous projects and continuing very happy. [ALC]

On June 8 he informed Spivacke about his recent Midwestern trip and future possibilities in that part of the country:

The material gathered on the Archive's exploratory trip to Indiana and Ohio has afforded us a partial idea of what has happened to Anglo-American folk music in the Middle West. Both of these states, however, have been influenced more by currents of cultural migration from the south and less by the intrusion of foreign language groups and by the flow of migration from New England than other Lake States. I feel it is important, therefore, before venturing further west that the Archive turn its attention to the Lake States—Michigan, Wisconsin and Minnesota—a study of which will give us a picture of an area culturally different from the Middle and Far West and yet important in the growth of these areas. In sounding folklore resources of this region, the Archive will be able to record what remains of the once vigorous lumber-jack culture, to explore the musical potentialities of the many foreign language groups of that area (Swedish, Norwegian, Finnish, Gaelic, French-Canadian, etc.) and to observe what have been the results of the mixing of these cultures with the Anglo-American matrix. Since the northern portion of this territory is hardly accessible the remainder of the year, I suggest that this expedition be planned for July and August, when woods and rural areas will be completely accessible. Two months in the field will be the briefest period possible for a survey of the region because I plan to ask the collaboration of local folk-lorists and field workers and interest them in the work of the Archive. [ALC]

In June, Esther Petersen of the Bryn Mawr Summer School for Women Workers in Industry requested Alan to speak to the students. He first wrote to Kay Dealy in Philadelphia on June 13:

I am going to Bucknell for Saturday, Bryn Mawr on Sunday, and would like to spend Monday with you and Granny [Jenny Devlin] in recording her folk song material. Let me know at once if that date is possible for you or if Granny will sing for me solo. [ALC][53]

On June 14 he gave Robert Allen at Ohio University a hint of his summer plans:

I'm departing the slums of Washington for the summer sometime in the first two weeks of July. Couldn't you manage to get here before that time? We have a good many things to talk over, besides which I'd just plain like to see you again. Please let me know when you are going to arrive. [ALC]

He gave more details of his upcoming travels to Spivacke on June 15:

I have been asked by the Bryn Mawr Summer Labor College to lecture there Saturday, the 18th and Sunday, the 19th and to record whatever folk songs the students who have come from all over the country know. The College is willing to pay my mileage or railroad fare there and return. . . . The Pennsylvania Folk Festival will be held on Saturday, the 18th, at Beaver, Pennsylvania. Although we have been invited in the past, as yet no person on the Archive staff has attended this important folk festival; and I feel it would be advisable, in view of the Archive's connection with the World's Fair and for other reasons, for me to attend this gathering. . . . Miss Kay Dealy of Philadelphia, Pennsylvania, has discovered an old lady nearby the city who has quite a stock of traditional ballad tunes. I have seen the manuscript of this collection and I feel it would be a valuable acquisition for the Archive. I have arranged to do this recording on Monday, the 20th. . . . For this reason, I should like to request per diem for these three days. [ALC]

Alan's ideas for the World's Fair became increasingly more inventive and expansive, as he outlined to Olin Downes on June 18 (just before traveling to Bryn Mawr):

The following statement is intended as supplementary to the plan I presented to you in May. It has grown out of a great deal of thought and discussion and

is therefore, I hope, more systematic and at the same time more comprehensive than the earlier outline. It might be thought of as the maximum of
what the Fair might do, whereas the May outline presented the minimum
plan. I presume that the idea of restaurants that utilize the color of foreign
and exotic cultures is so obvious that it must have been planned within the
Fair some time ago. . . . More important for the World's Fair cultural program, however, that these concessions will be the night spots for American
folk lore. In the May plan I suggested four, the most important among them
a Negro honky-tonk and a mountain square dance hall. The number and
variety of such places could, of course, be almost endless. For example: The
French Quarter of New Orleans . . . A Pennsylvania Dutch tavern . . . A Haitian house with voodoo dances . . . A real Western saloon . . . A down-Easter
fish house . . . A Mexican patio . . . An Acadian Fais-do-do hall . . . A Negro
church social . . . A Hawaiian house. . . . [Here follows considerable detail
on the arrangement of these locations, for example] I have in mind at this
moment a number of mountain people who could fit into the break-down
house very naturally: Aunt Molly Jackson, Sarah Ogan, Pete Steele, Luther
Strong, Walter Williams, Uncle Alex Dunford, Crockett Ward, Fields Ward
and many another. . . . What I propose, therefore, is to set up a series of
strategically placed open air stages throughout the Fair Grounds and there
to present at crowd level, folk singers, banjo players, balalaika orchestras,
Indian medicine shows, spasm bands from New Orleans, Haitian voo-doo
dancers and what have you. . . . These performers at the street level would
serve not only to bring back into the Fair the ancient feeling of gaiety that
our stream-lined commercialism has smothered, but besides advertise the
further delights that await the Fair visitor in the folk lore night clubs, from
which the performers had been drawn. The fore-going sections of this plan
have discussed the manner in which folk lore might fit unobtrusively into
the ordinary entertainment scheme of any large fair. Folk lore should, however, be presented in a more serious fashion in a theater of its own. . . . An
American Folk Theater[,] however, if it were carefully edited, could present a
continuous series of programs covering all phases of American folk culture
from the buck and wing to Katherine Dunham, from the mountain ballad
singer to the orchestral suite, from the folk anecdote of the academic lecturer to folk tales. . . . Symposium on American folk music with lectures by
Dr. Charles Seeger, Dr. George Herzog, George Pullen Jackson, Lawrence
Powell, Dr. Robert Gordon, J. Rosamond Johnson, Frances Densmore, etc.;
Symposium on hot jazz with Benny Goodman, Louie Armstrong, John Ham-
mond, Charles Smith, Sidney Martin, George Bell, Hugh Panassié, Duke
Ellington, etc. . . . Conference on the ballad in America with Dr. Robert
Gordon, Dr. George Lyman Kittredge, Dr. Louise Pound, Herbert Halpert,

Robert [George] Korson, John A. Lomax, Dr. Reid Smith, Dr. Davis, Fanny Eckstrom, etc. . . . It might be further interesting to trace through a series of performances the development that led from spirituals and the buck and wing to minstrel to ragtime to cake walk to jazz. Then, perhaps, the development of popular song, both sentimental and comic, through the course of the nineteenth century and up to 1920 where it merged and was influenced by jazz could be woven into a delightful musical production. . . . In such a theater, I hope, every sizeable foreign group in America, as well as native, would have the opportunity to exhibit its traditional lore and its traditional artistic techniques and, besides, the development that has taken place within these techniques in America. [ALC]

Shortly following his trip to Bryn Mawr, he wrote to Esther Peterson on June 21:

I am sorry to trouble you with my folk songs when you are so busy, but I discovered twenty miles down the road that I had left some recordings in your office. Would you be so kind as to forward them to me here as soon as it is convenient? You will find a frank enclosed. Let me take this occasion to thank you and your whole school for a most delightful weekend. [ALC]

An article on Alan's Jelly Roll Morton recording sessions appeared in *Down Beat*, the jazz magazine, in June 1938,[54] and on June 28 Alan wrote to Melvin Oathout in Fulton, New York, a jazz bibliographer:

The recording you have heard of consists at the present time of a set of fifty records made by Jelly Roll Morton—the folk songs and blues that he knows, the old jazz and ragtime styles that he remembers, his own compositions along with discussion and explanation of all this. We hope to add extensively to this material in the future as we encounter other distinguished hot jazz musicians. The function of the Archive at present, however, is to collect and organize recorded material pertinent to the field of American Folk Song and I don't know whether an extensive bibliography on jazz, which of course would have to be expanded as time went on, would fit into our program. The Division of Music, on the other hand, of which Dr. Spivacke is chief, already has a considerable bibliography of jazz music and would be, I am told, very decidedly interested in your work; and at the very least would like to use your bibliography as a supplementary check list of materials on jazz. I shall, therefore, turn your letter over to Dr. Spivcke and you will hear from him shortly. Of course, I am personally, if not officially, very much interested in your work and shall give your material my personal attention when and if it comes to the Music Division. I have, besides, a question I should like to ask you on behalf of the Archives. Do you have in your bibliography references, besides those which recently appeared in "Down Beat" on Jelly Roll Morton? What is your own opinion about him as a figure in the history and development of hot music? I should greatly appreciate whatever answer you can give to these questions. [ALC]⁵⁵

Alan was now planning a collecting trip to the Upper Midwest, as he explained on June 29 to Professor Theodore Blegen,⁵⁶ an expert on Scandinavian music at the University of Minnesota:

The Archive of American Folk Song plans to make this summer a rapid recording survey of the folk music resources of Wisconsin, Michigan and Minnesota. I am well acquainted with your work in Norwegian immigrant folk lore and feel sure that you would be of the greatest assistance in the field of Minnesota material. The Archive is interested in building a collection of records for the use of musicologists, folklorists, composers and teachers and naturally looks forward to collaboration with the scholars in the region where its work is being prosecuted. Some day we hope to be able to supply the needs in terms of records to any student of American folk songs and to exchange our collections with the great Archives of Europe. I look forward to my work this summer in the Lake States and I will greatly appreciate whatever concrete suggestions you could send me in regard to the field of folk music in Minnesota. [ALC]

On June 30 he wrote to Kay Dealy in Philadelphia, who had assisted in recording Jennie Devlin, a font of traditional songs:

The Archive of American Folk Song is glad to accession Mrs. Jennie Devlin's records and accept the restriction that you mention in your letter of June 21st. The list of songs she recorded on June 20th runs as follows: The False Lover, The Lady of York, The House Carpenter, The Wife of Kelso, The Banks of Sweet Dundee, Johnnie Sands, Tarry Trousers, Geordie, The Frog and the Mouse, Sing Song Kitty Won'tcha Kimeo, The True Paddy's Song, Your Father and Your Mother, Love, The Brooklyn Theater Fire, Shanghai Rooster, The Orphan Child, Do You See Them, Some for the Girl of Dresses Neat, The Little Pallet of Straw, When I Was a Little Boy, Miss Riot, Martha Decker, The Old Indian, Will the Weaver, James Bird, The Irish Washerman, Oh, The Irish Ain't Much, When I Was Young and In My Prime, As We Went Bobbing Around, The Long Fol-de-Rol, There's Many a Batchelor Born to Wed, Rocking the Baby to Sleep, Rock the Baby, John, The Converted Indian Maid, The Little Valley, Young Charlotte, Poor Jim, the Newsboy.

You could do the Archive a further kindness by sending us copies of all the songs you have recorded from Mrs. Devlin's singing or recitation. As you know, there was some difference at times between the versions she dictated to you and those that she sang for me. A comparison of the two groups of versions would prove very interesting for the folklore scholar in the future. I should like to have a set of uncorrected versions if you have them, and if your supply of copies is too limited, we can have the manuscript micro-filmed for preservation here. [ALC][57]

On the same day, June 30, he wrote to William Myers of the Federal Writers Project in Indianapolis:

I have never thanked you for the very real help the Writers Project gave me in Indiana, largely because I have not had the time until recently to catalog and play over the Indiana recordings. Through you and Mr. Lockridge a short visit to Indiana proved very fruitful for the Archive. Mr. Doyle Joyce and Mrs. Caney in Vincennes, Mr. Wolfe and Mrs. Elliott in New Harmony, Mr. Dixon in Mt. Vernon and indirectly Mr. Parks of Crawford County were among the most useful informants. My very cursory view of the Writers Project folklore work in Indiana convinced me of the fruitfulness of folklore in the WPA. Some of your workers, particularly Sudie Knight and Luane Creel, have done a particularly fine job. Miss Creel is a natural collector, one of the few I have ever met and I hope the Indiana Writers Project will find a way to make her more useful. There are two bits of material that I should very much like to add to the Archive collection. The first is the material gathered in Vincennes that pertains to the customs, songs, dances, etc. of the old days. The second is a group of songs collected by Sudie Knight, District 11. The titles are: The Girl with her Dog and Gun, Pretty Maid out in the Garden, The Steamer Little Clyde, Gambling on the Sabbath Day, The Bumble Bee Joe, The Ballad of the Green Willow Tree, The Ballad of Fair Ellendar and Sweet William, An Old Fashioned Singing in Crawford County, Happy as a Birdie, The House Carpenter, On the Banks of the Sweet Dundee, The Roving Soldier, Shoo Fly Don't Bother Me, There Was an Old Man, You Bet I Was a Different Lad When I Left Arkansas. I don't know whether it is possible for you to get me copies of this material, but if so, the Archive would accept it with what restrictions you care to impose. [ALC]

Careful to maintain his Hoosier contacts, he also corresponded on July 1 with Samuel Dixon in Mt. Vernon, Indiana:

You must believe by this time that I have forgotten my promise to return the song sheets you lent me in April. As a matter of fact, I have returned to the Indiana material for the first time last week; and in going over it, decided to ask the WPA for copies of the sheets that you lent me. If, however, the WPA cannot furnish me with these songs, would it be possible for you to present the Library with your copies; or if not, to allow them to remain in our hands until we can have them copied? That, I suppose, will be sometime next Fall. I want to take this occasion to thank you for the friendly help you gave me in Indiana. [ALC]

The same day, he wrote to Paul Brewster at Indiana University:

Would it be possible for you to send me the words to the *Ballad of Stone River* and the other songs that the Parkses sent in to you? Besides these, I would appreciate the texts of Mrs. Bryant's, Mr. Kirk's, and Mr. Swallow's and Mrs. Hopkins' songs. If you are not able to have them copied yourself in the department, I could have this done here in the Library; and of course the songs will be restricted until you have published your thesis. I saw Bob Allen the other day and he told me about your new job in the University of Missouri. This summer I am to work in the Lake States, with the possibility, perhaps, of coming by Bloomington for a short visit. I hope to see you then. [ALC]

Also on July 1, he informed Marjorie Edgar in Marine-on-St. Croix, Minnesota, about his upcoming trip:

The Archive of American Folk Song in the Library of Congress is planning for this summer a rapid recording survey of folk music of Wisconsin, Michigan and Minnesota. This work is to be done by a modern field recording machine, with the idea in mind of getting down in the most accurate fashion the folk tunes and folk styles of the region, for preservation and scholarly study. We naturally look forward to collaboration with scholars in the regions in which we carry on our work and Mrs. Sidney Robertson has written me about your extensive work in the fields of Finnish and Gaelic songs. She has further indicated that you might be willing to offer me some assistance in my field work, especially in regard to suggesting reliable and fertile informants. The Library will greatly appreciate whatever you will be able to do and we can, I believe, work out without any difficulty a plan which would completely protect any material you wish to publish until such time as you are ready for it to be made public. Do you plan to do field work, yourself, this summer? Do you have any suggestions to make in regard to interesting regions and informants? I should appreciate an early reply to this inquiry, since I plan to leave Washington on the fifteenth. [ALC]

The same day he sent a similar inquiry to Art Ford in Laona, Wisconsin:

Sidney Robertson has written me at length about the songs that you and your family and Charles and Bob Walker know. I am coming to Wisconsin this summer to make records of Wisconsin folk songs for the Library of Congress and I want to come to see all of you and record the songs that you know. I would like to know when you are gong to be at home and what would be the best time for me to drop by and call on you. [ALC][58]

The following day, July 2, he informed William Schlecht in Washington, D.C.:

Thanks for your delightful letters of introduction. I very much needed contacts in both Minneapolis and Duluth, and the Dingum Shop crowd and Cal Harrison sound delightful. Where in the world is Cal Crosshaul, the lumberjack who hasn't shown up in Washington? Is he handling a peavey on the Kennebec? Please send me his address or his route and I will try to catch him. [ALC]

He also wrote to John Collier in Bloomington on July 2:

I have just been playing over the Indiana records and have greatly enjoyed you and your fiddle—your *John Roger the Miller* and your *A Little too Small*. The Library greatly appreciates the kindness you have done it in recording these songs and in helping out down Brown County way. [ALC]

On July 2 Alan thanked Doyle Joyce in Vincennes:

I have recently written to Mr. Myers , asking for a complete copy of the Vincennes material for deposit in the Archive. In the meantime, I am having copied certain of the songs that Mrs. Caney sang and I have found that I have no French text for *Mon Amour*, sung by Mrs. Caney, also by the WPA group. If it is not too late, I would like to make some suggestion about the Vincennes book; that is, use Mrs. Caney's songs just as she sings them and print in their entirety the texts that you have dug up in the Vincennes files, for the purposes of comparison. In that way you will show that Mrs. Caney's songs are genuine folk songs in a process of change, and at the same time lose nothing of the freshness of her very interesting French dialect. It is extremely important that her dialect be transcribed accurately because it is the nearest thing to Vincennes French that we have any specimen of today, and as such stands as an important historical document. I think I can interest the central office here in having that done by a really competent scholar if you have not already found one. May take this occasion to thank you for your efforts in behalf of the Archive last spring. Mrs. Caney's songs have proved a valuable contribution to American folk-lore and you are to be thanked for endeavoring to have them preserved. [ALC]

On July 2, a busy correspondence day, he updated his father, still in Europe but just about to leave the continent for England:

A couple of my letters must have missed you somewhere because I have not been so neglectful as you think. Besides, as you yourself must admit, you have not been in Europe the most prolific of correspondents. I haven't written much to anyone except on business matters for a long time. Even Bess has been sadly neglected and I suppose this has been due to the fact that I have been frightfully busy in a sort of routine way and I have had no particular news to tell anyone. It is quite definite now that I am going to Michigan, Wisconsin and Minnesota for the summer on the 15th, to return about the 15th of September. If you have any friends in that part of the country, I would certainly appreciate your writing to both them and me about the trip because it is a terra incognita and everything depends on helpful natives.

Before I go, I expect to have the textual side of the book complete, with Mrs. [Ruth Crawford] Seeger's work so well laid out for her that there will be nothing further to do in regard to the book by the end of the summer except to write notes and introduction. I hope that you will be in Washington so that we can work on the introduction together, but if not, I think we can bang one out in a couple of weeks through the mails. The notes, which should certainly go in, should amount to about a month's part time work and I am willing to engage in it. I would like, though, to do it all at once, in a piece, with the design of the book very much in mind so that the book will read easily from page to page with as much connection made between songs and sections as possible. Before I go away, I will lay the book out and take the layout with me and think about it over the summer and do as much writing as I have time for. So much for the book. The warmest news in the building at the moment is the resignation of Dr. Putnam, effective as soon as a new librarian is appointed. I hope, along with the Union, of course, that it will be John Vance and I understand that his chances are very good.

Elizabeth is on the point of getting a job with the WPA, possibly at the same salary the Library is generous enough to give me; and if that works out we will be able to live a little better and perhaps even save some money next year. And on top of that, unless something happens in the meantime, I shall next year be spending part of my time in preparing the folk-lore program for the World's Fair. This may grow into a very important scheme or not, but there will certainly be the chance for a great deal of interesting work. Plans are at last in the air for an Archive of American Folklore. Dr. [Stith] Thompson and the president of his folklore society have petitioned Senator [Sherman] Minton [of Indiana] and others to submit a bill to Congress; and although neither Spivacke nor Putnam is very enthusiastic, it may very well go through under Vance, in which case I feel I will be totally and forever submerged in this marble palace. Not that I should complain at the very soft and exciting and pleasant job, but sometimes the whole thing still seems a little bit childish and certainly it has come my way too easily. I keep thinking that perhaps the best thing for me would be to let go with both hands and try something else that hadn't been handed me on a silver platter.

I was very much surprised at how gloomy your last letter was. I certainly hadn't realized that you were worried or homesick or sad or anything of the sort. Your other two letters had seemed so cheerful, in fact, that I had told a person or two that perhaps you would stay on in Europe a while just for the fun of it. I am terribly sorry that I caused you worry by not having written. Your five dollar check was very much appreciated and any others that follow will be received with the same pleasure. As to the Seegers, Charlie has recently been appointed on the music project of the WPA at a very good salary. Ruth may get on the Writers Project, but in the meantime plans, as I already said, to finish up the ballad book—so you see, everything is rocking along very nicely. [ALC]⁵⁹

On the same day, he wrote to his sister Bess in Paris, with an elder brother's sarcasm:

Jealousy has had me in its thrall all spring—jealousy of you in Hungary and on the Danube and in your hostels in Germany, but now I'm beginning to feel a little less envious. In fact, I expect after this summer to be much more cosmopolitan than you, despite your European tour. The reason:—Dear Sir: The Archive of American Folk Song plans a rapid recording survey of Michigan, Wisconsin and Minnesota during the summer. If you know of the location of any Jugoslavian baroto blowers or any Swiss chantey singers, I would greatly appreciate your calling me by long distance before morning.

By the middle of September, I hope to be speaking an interesting dialect composed of Norwegian, Swedish, Icelandic, German, Canuck, Hungarian, Finnish, Polish, Russian and Oshkosh. You may expect to receive an autographed photo of me holding up my first muskie by at least the end of this month. The work is going to be very interesting. I'm going to Detroit armed with letters of introduction to all the fractions of the United Automobile Workers and to the Mesabi Iron Ore Range of Minnesota and the I.W.W. of Duluth for union material, that assuming a galaxy of all sorts of exotic songs and instruments plus all their Americanizations.

Besides which, Elizabeth may by that time be doing field work in an official capacity for the Writers Project of the WPA, visiting their state collections and sizing up their field workers, which will make everything much more interesting. Your letters have been consistently superb, but there are a couple of items of news that I'd like very much to have. Do you have any inkling of father's and Deanie's [Ruby Terrill Lomax] plans for next year? Have you made up your mind with great firmness to come to Washington for at least a week with us before you go to Bryn Mawr? I note that in your last letters your sympathies are becoming decidedly Fascist and I want to be notified at once as soon as you join the Bund so that I can follow suit here in Washington and we can greet each other in a true Aryan fashion when you arrive. The Nazis have, by the way, decided to make me organizer for Washington, despite the fact that my ancestry is not strictly German; but because they realize that folklorists make admirable and serviceable fighters in the great campaign against the Semitic degeneration of world society.[60]

Chavella [Elizabeth] and I are still worse than broke. My first act on getting a raise was to lose nearly half of my pay envelope, and we are still paying back the debts we accumulated. We can invite you, therefore, to bring us a lot of nice presents from Europe. But I hope you have picked up a lot of funny papers, cartoons, magazines, propaganda and stuff of that kind for me. It's the sort of thing I really enjoy more than anything else—just a lot of miscellaneous and very popular printed material—notices of meetings, handbills, advertisements, popular song books, etc. I would like some day to design a real archive of popular literature with such material as its basis. I hope that you will persist in writing us because your letters are a great deal of fun, and perhaps when I get to Detroit, we'll write you a little about Poland and Hungary, etc. In the meantime, since there is no more news and it's time for lunch on Saturday, I will bid you a sad farewell. I have one commission for you:—deliver my love to all Fascists that you encounter and tell them that I sympathize with them in their persecution of Jewish war mongers. [ALC]

On July 8 he informed Louise Caton of the Office of the Librarian of Congress:

I append copies of Music Division reports for 1933–1938 wherein the recent activities of the Archive of American Folk Song are discussed. You will find, besides, a mimeographed check-list of the recorded items brought into the

Archive before November, 1937. You will note that there is a great deal of Southern White folk song material in the body of the collection and recently this type has been greatly augmented through extensive collections from Eastern Kentucky, Western Virginia, Southern Ohio and Southern Indiana. Part of this material has been deposited with restrictions of between 2 to 5 years, but the large mass of it is open. [ALC]

Alan continued to have hopes for an expansive World's Fair, but was discouraged after receiving a copy of a letter from John Krimsky, entertainment director of the fair, to Olin Downes, dated July 11. After congratulating Alan for

an extremely well written plan,

Krimsky cautioned that

there is a deal pending with the Federal Theatre Project to utilize some of their best vaudeville acts on small platforms throughout the Fair Grounds.

Moreover,

The Negro Honky-tonk has been let as a concession to the owners of the Savoy Ballroom in Harlem. The Dutch Tavern will be built and sponsored by the Heineken Beer Company, The Hawaiian entertainment will be provided in the South Sea Island Village. I was pleased to read his description of the incidental folk and professional entertainment of the minstrel character, as I am placing great importance upon the diversified type of entertainment which will breathe life into certain sections of the Exhibit Area. [ALC]

Downes followed with more details in a letter to Spivacke on July 18, explaining

that it would be difficult for me to appoint Lomax, as I wished to do, as representative of a coordinated folk music division of the Fair. [ALC]

On July 11, Alan informed Theodore Blegen in Minnesota of a slight change of plans for his upcoming trip:

Thank you for your kind invitation. I am very sorry that I will not be in St. Paul for your lecture of the 14th. The material in your volume on Norwegian immigrant ballads is extremely interesting and I hope that I shall be able to record some of it in my work this summer. It has been necessary to postpone my trip for some days but I shall leave sometime before the first of August and should be in Minnesota at the very latest by the first of September. I hope you will be somewhere in the state at that time. I have already written Miss Edgar and I suppose I will hear from her as soon as she feels able to write. Perhaps she will be well again by the time I have worked through Michigan and Wisconsin. Please let me know what your plans are for the latter part of August and early part of September so that I can hurry on to Minnesota if you are to be away. [ALC][61]

The next day, July 12, he corresponded with Marjorie Edgar in Minneapolis:

I was terribly sorry to learn that you were ill and in the hospital and that your folklore work will not be carried on during the Summer. It is certainly very generous of you to offer to help me with the Hiberderdian [sic] songs and as soon as I know definitely when I shall be near Duluth, I will let you know. That, however, will probably not be before the first of September unless my plans change. I am already in touch with Dr. Blegen who has kindly offered his cooperation in my work this summer. Of course it will be impossible for me to make an adequate study of the Finnish folk songs but I would like to record a few good examples for the archive so that visiting musicologists will be able to find out more or less what there is available in Minnesota. Perhaps in view of that approach, you may change your mind about the advisability of my visiting any of your Finnish informants, however, I certainly do not wish to pass you in this regard since I fully appreciate your hesitancy in the matter. [ALC]

While planning his Midwest swing, he continued to serve in his administrative role, as noted in his July 12 letter to C. A. Middleton in Iowa City:

John A. Lomax is at present in Europe and so I am answering your letter before I forward it to him. He is no longer in charge of folk lore of the Writer's Project, Mr. B. A. Botkin now holds that position and I suggest that you write him for additional information. Your thesis project is quite suggestive and I should like, for my own sake, to be able to look into it more thoroughly than I can now. I am leaving in a few days for a summer field trip and will not be able to do more than make a suggestion or so before fall. Last summer I recorded a fragmentary version of "Harvey Logan in Kentucky" (enclosed) and I forward it with the stipulation that it will not appear in print before the publication of American Ballads and Folksongs no. 2 [*Our Singing Country*] to appear in 1939. As for the other ballads, I am afraid I can furnish you no information at the moment although next fall I might be able to find some material. There is a whole category of Bad Man ballads that you have neglected and that allow for historical treatment more easily than any other group of indigenous narrative songs. I refer to the feud ballads of Kentucky and Tennessee, the "Rowan County Crew," the "Vance Song" and others. You can find a number of these in [John Harrington] Cox [*Folk-Songs of the South*, 1925]. I should like to hear more of your project as it advances and will be happy to cooperate in any way I can. [ALC]

He also kept in contact with his southern informants, for example in a letter to Rosa Wilson of Martins Point, South Carolina, July 18:

It was a shock to learn that you had been so ill and that had found it necessary under these trying circumstances to send the script of your "Plantation Echoes." I want you to know how deeply I appreciate the work that you have done on this script and I want you to know that I understand the difficulties you have been faced with. Perhaps I shall be able someday to hear these negroes sing in Charleston. I feel that your work in preserving these negro folk ways is a very worthy one. [ALC]

He filled in Herbert Hollins, in Cambridge, Massachusetts, on July 18 of his travel plans:

I am leaving on another field trip to the Lake States this Friday. I will probably be in New York for 3 or 4 days, Saturday, Sunday, Monday and Tuesday and can be reached there through the Presto Recording Co., 139 West 19th Street, New York City. I wish you could come down from Cambridge for a day or two because I don't see how I can take the time from what is left of the summer to drop by Cambridge. If you cannot perhaps I will be able to go to Boston on my way home in October. Last April I called at your house in Pittsburgh at four o'clock in the morning to discover that your family had moved to Atlantic City. The funny thing was that the people there were still up when I arrived and when I looked through the window I saw a round dirty-green hat exactly like the one I remember you wearing. I was sure that you had just gotten home from Boston and could hardly believe my ears when I found out that the people had never heard of you. Please communicate to me your plans, prospects, and adventures, past, immediate, present and future. 213-B street, N.E. 'till Friday. [ALC]

Just about to head west, he wrapped things up at the Library in late July, when he wrote to G. P. Putnam on July 21:

In the absence of Dr. Spivacke, Chief of the Music Division, I am unable to give final answer to your inquiry. I will leave your letter on his desk and you may expect to hear from him by airmail early next week. Duplicates of a small portion of the Library collection have already been made. These records are not satisfactory as high fidelity recording specimens because many of them have been cut on portable apparatus both as masters and duplicates and besides they must be played with an especial type of needle (either thorn or casein) and with a light and flexible pick up. If, however, with these various disabilities understood, you still desire to audition a group of records I see no reason why the Archive should not draw upon its unrestricted list to lend you a group of twenty records. Tomorrow noon I am going away on a two months field trip for the Archive and I shall leave a group of twenty selected records in Dr. Spivacke's care to be forwarded on to you as soon as necessary arrangements can be made. Of course, I am not aware of the use to which you plan to put these records; but I think it advisable, if your interest is in any wise commercial, that you consult further with Dr. Spivacke in regard to restrictions and so on. [ALC]

Spivacke tried to salvage some role for Alan in the World's Fair, while Alan, not easily dissuaded, contacted Olin Downes on July 21:

I'll be in New York on Saturday and through Tuesday and I would very much like to see you Monday if possible so that perhaps later appointments could be arranged. I will call your office at that time. If, by any chance, you can see me over the week-end, send me a wire and I'll turn up. [ALC][62]

Alan was on his collecting trip to the Upper Midwest from August to November, following a few days in New York City still trying to have a hand in structuring the World's Fair. He first sent a telegram to Spivacke from Detroit on August 2:

Very official letter of introduction absolutely necessary for work among racial minorities. Air mail same address. Will send Michigan schedule and much news soon. [ALC]

He soon followed in an undated letter to Spivacke from Detroit:

Sorry to have bothered you by wire [of August 2], but it appeared to be necessary. I have spent a couple of days in getting the contacts the W.P.A. has and shall work out of Detroit for a few days more before departing Northward. I should appreciate your sending me some franked envelopes. My visit to New York will prove to have been very productive. I saw Krimsky, even got tight with him one night, and sold him on the idea of folk-lore in the fair and me with it. He promised to let me know definitely in the next month or so whether there would be a good job available. Actually went so far as to have me interview the personnel officer. I don't feel, however, that it is yet time for you to intervene your authority—might scare them. Downes is as much interested as ever and somewhat impressed by my progress with the Krimsky crowd. American Ballads Number 2 [*Our Singing Country*] is in a considerable mess. The contract, I find, calls for only 400 pages and we have already got together more than that amount of material. Therefore, if you have done nothing about the Mexican stuff, hold it until father gets back Sept. 5th. In case the fair people wanted me to come back in September, what would you advise me to do? If you have not yet sent the Putnam records away, would you mind holding back the record that contains "Go Down Old Hannah" and "Ain't No Mo' Cane on the Brazis" for Ruth [Crawford Seeger]. [ALC][63]

In a most sour mood, he followed up to Spivacke from Detroit on August 11:

The tale of my disasters in the past few days is almost epic, indeed, if I were a voodooist, I should certainly now be consulting a doctor and he would be bathing me in some direction or other. 1) Monday night I stayed late in Dalray, the Hungarian section recording Hungarian songs and after two o'clock, when the singers were tired and I had packed the machine in the car, they asked me in for a glass of something cool and we chatted until three. The next afternoon in another part of the city, I unpacked the equipment to record Serbian gusla music only to discover that the acetate cutting head had disappeared from the place I had left it beside the recording machine on the back seat. I went back to the house hoping that I had by some crazy chance dropped it there. (I am staying at a private home on 16th street.) Then I drove out to Delray and looked up the people who had helped me load the equipment the night before. They confirmed my opinion that the machine had been completely loaded and the car locked before I had gone back upstairs for the chat. There was one fellow on whom the finger of suspicion rested, though very lightly, but he had nothing to offer that was helpful.

2) By this time it was nearly eight o'clock, at which time I had an engagement to record Negro spirituals in a tent church across town. I rushed there and after attempting to use my aluminum cutter with little success I set out about 11:30 for a cruise through the Negro section with an intelligent Negro man I had met. This man is a Writers Project worker and completely reliable. We had scarcely driven around the corner when we heard a guitar singing the blues, stopped the car, and went back to discover one of the finest Negro informants I have ever encountered. We listened to him for a half an hour and went back to the car. There were a couple of other stops in the Negro settlement before I drove home about two o'clock. The next morning when

I went out to the car, the machine was gone along with my guitar. For some reason no records, no film had been stolen. The camera was still where I had left it.

I called a squad car at once and they took the report and later on I went down to the local FBI office and put the matter in the hands of the G-men. From that place I wired you and Presto—this last to get for the police the serial number on the equipment. Then in the afternoon I called on the Negro lieutenant who knows his district better than anyone and made a special appeal to him to locate the stolen goods if he could. He promised to work on the case. The theft of the cutting head seemed too inexplicable and the attempt to locate it so hopeless that I had decided, so far as I had decided anything in the rush of events, to buy a new one out of my own pocket. I have just received my first report from the police and from the FBI. So far they have found nothing at all and they are not very encouraging, although they feel sure that it will turn up eventually. They say it may be within a week or within one month. They suggest I hang around for 10 days, anyway. My present plans, therefore, are as follows. I will go away from the city for a couple of days—it is fearfully hot here—and rest up and write my year's report. If I have not jumped into the Detroit River by that time, I will have heard from you and perhaps will have decided what to do, myself. The Presto agent here wants $8.00 a night for the rental of a machine and I'm not going to be that extravagant without specific advice from you. It would be a shame to interrupt this trip, I think. I have a superb list of contacts throughout Michigan, more than I can visit and the same thing will be true of the other states as I work West. The material I gather here will be, as you know, a completely new field for the Archive and, besides, I will be gathering addresses that will be absolutely essential if the World's Fair Program is to be put on.

In regard to the World Fair's, by the way. I saw Krimsky's report as soon as I got to New York and felt that it was not very encouraging. Krimsky saw me more out of courtesy to Downes than out of sincere interest in my plan, but after two conversations with me, he sent me across to the employment office to put in a tentative application and the personnel manager hinted that if I wanted to stay on as a part of the publicity staff until the other job came through they would take me on. I turned down the offer because I felt that my summer's work here would be more useful all the way round, both to the Library and to folk lore for the World Fair than anything I could possibly do in New York. That evening I went to Krimsky's apartment and we talked about the Horse Opera he is putting on next season in his American theatre. He told me that he might want my advice there. Downes was greatly delighted by the progress I had made with Krimsky and felt that I might be more useful to him, Downes, in Krimsky's office, functioning as a sort of liaison man between the two, than if I were working directly under him (D.). He added, however, that he would try to arrange something for me when and if his budget was approved. Both of them urged me to keep closely in touch with them, so they could wire me at any point on my itinerary.

For these various reasons and especially in view of the fact that we have felt for some time that the purchase of a new and better recorder was in order, I suggest, that, unless there is some obstacle in the way that I know nothing about, a new recorder be purchased and shipped to me here. I would be only too happy to take a week or so of leave while I was waiting for it. I am quite tired and a little Michigan lake sun would do me good. Perhaps I should be a little more specific about my contacts. Professor I. H. Walton of the University of Michigan has made a very important collection of Lake Ballads and Lake chanteys. He has agreed to work with me in the field. I have letters of introduction to various collectors of Lumberjack material all over the state and a number of contacts in Cornish, Polish, Bohemian, Finnish and French Canadian mining and frontier communities upstate. Downes wanted me to find someone to sing the Kalevala for him at the fair, but that would only be the beginning of things. Sunday a Serbian played his shepherd's flute for me—virtuoso performance by a steel chipper who reads and writes little and still plays his pipe for his amusement in the shadow of the automobile work. Goat like, leaping. Really I could stay here in Detroit for a couple of months and never run out of material. The guitar player responsible indirectly for my disaster, commutes between here and Memphis and knows more of the Negro ballads (Brady, Stagolee, Stavin' Chain, etc.) than any other one person either father or I have ever encountered. Please write me as soon as you can of anything definite. I feel very discouraged. [ALC]

A few days later he had cooled somewhat, as he informed Spivacke from Detroit on August 17:

Your letter arrived yesterday at 10 AM but as I wasn't at the given address, I had to swear to everything but to my sex to get it out of the hands of Special Delivery people a half hour ago. I am sorry that the purchase of better equipment takes so long as to make it impractical. If it were a matter of only a couple of weeks, I might take a week of leave and then spend another week making advance recording contacts in the field—a thing which I have long wanted to do and which will probably be a regular part of Archive technique in the end. If we assume, too, that the World's Fair program is really coming through and that anytime soon, I could find a lot of important material for it in these intervening two or three weeks. Of course the Presto [recording machine] is not bad especially with sapphires on the new discs (superb I think) but we do need and require a better piece of equipment than they offer. I suggest 16" 33 rev/sec turntable as a possibility and the best cutter they have. Also it may be difficult to plug a $15 mike (dynamic) into an expensive outfit. If we buy Presto, strongly urge them to cut down on overall size. There is no sense in their machine being as large as it is. Use of metal tubes, perhaps. I hope you like my report. [ALC]

On August 27 he supplied more positive news to Spivacke from Beaver Island, Michigan:

The new machine is doing very good work & the material is quite interesting. It belongs to the private preserve of Prof. I[van] H. Walton who organized the U. folk lore society.[64] Irishmen, fishermen, sailormen, lumberjacks & their ballads. Battery difficulties, but no trouble finding songs. When I get back to Charlevoix Tuesday I'll be mailing you 2+ boxes of records + I wish you would send me 1) 3 boxes of discs express, Charlevoix—2) Purchase a dozen reels of film and I'll let you know where to forward it. This country & the people are very photogenic. I'm feeling a lot better and am able to work more hours & more effectively. The only trouble with these Irish is that they take more treating than any group I've struck. It may be that I'll need another $50 advance. At least you can help extensively by airmailing my salary to me at Charlevoix, as much in advance as you can arrange. [ALC]

Within a couple of weeks things were definitely looking up, as he detailed to Spivacke on September 1 from Charlevoix:

The past week, spent on Beaver Island in Lake Michigan, where there is a large colony of Irish fishermen, has been, as you will judge from the enclosed list most interesting. Mr. Green, in my experience, is the most prodigious ballad singer so far encountered. He sang about fifty whole ballads for me, most of them of Irish broadside vintage, and he knew at least fifty more. The only reason I left the island was the press of work ahead of me on this field trip and the fact that Mr. Green was, temporarily, tired and a little bored with recording. I left him, however, in the hands of a former WPA worker, and a competent field worker, Mrs. Woods, who promises to write the texts of the ballads that yet remain hidden in his cavernous memory. Beaver Island is, perhaps, the most isolated and the most purely Irish colony in the United States. Besides the Irish, there are, perhaps, a hundred Indians who do the dirty work and live to themselves pretty largely, one or two Poles, one or two French and a couple of Germans. These latter, however, are entirely submerged in the Irish sea and when they lift their heads it is not long before a green wave playfully slaps them down under again. The people, particularly the older generation, live in vivid memory of Ireland and they curse the English landlords with the venom of native Irishmen. This, even despite the fact that there are few of them who were actually born in Ireland. From Green and his friends I was able to obtain a great many ballads that originated on the Lakes and at least three quarters of them are about sailors and ships and were much sung by the sailors. But not one chantey! Dr. I. H. Walton of the University of Michigan, drove a hundred and fifty miles to accompany me to the island and to introduce me to the islanders. He has been working on the folk-lore of the lake region for many years and has accumulated a superb collection of Lake songs that Michigan Press will bring out soon. We must make it possible for him to obtain copies of these songs sufficient for the transcription of the tunes as cheaply as possible, because of this favor and for the additional reason that he is the leading spirit in the Michigan States Folk Lore society. I told him that it would be possible for him to reserve the records from use for a period of two years (although he is anxious to free them as soon as his obligations to his University press are satisfied) with the privilege of an extension of two additional years if he deems that wise or necessary. He has furnished me with the names of all of his informants along my route.

As you know, Elizabeth is in Mexico, due to a sudden change in our plans, and this added to the effect of the sad accident in Detroit and the unusual expenses of the past week, have completely drained my pocket. I suppose it might be possible to get along on my salary as it comes in, but I think if you can possibly arrange to have another advance of fifty dollars made me, I will be able to work more comfortably and freely. If that is not possible, perhaps I can borrow the money on my car. I will, if my salary arrives tomorrow, leave here for a week's work in this part of Michigan, planning to arrive in Mackinac City in a week's time. Have word for me there of what you have been able to arrange, please.

Under separate cover I am expressing you fifty acetate records (I have made 66 so far). And tomorrow I am sending you three sapphire needles for re-sharpening. They do not last the hundred records they are advertised to, at least not without quite a bit of surface noise. The Reeves acetate, bought from Sound Scriptions is, I am nearly convinced, better than the Presto, so, if you have occasion to buy more buy that please. Upper Michigan is full of old lumberjacks, much to my surprise, and I expect to get this next couple of weeks enough lumberjack songs so that we won't have to go begging to any of the local folklorists for material. I don't know where Dr. Putnam is, but I am forwarding to him a copy of the Indiana field notes, fully corrected. If he is not in the Library, I hope you will see to it that they are forwarded to him. I would like him to know what I can accomplish for the Archive with help.

Why wasn't the second machine insured or was it? This is a pretty important step after the Detroit debacle, it seems to me. I am writing to [Edward] Waters in hopes he can begin to forgive father for the terrific mistakes he made in regard to Cowboy songs. I only hope he doesn't believe that I had anything to do with the title page. In fact, I was terribly surprised to see what they had done. The new machine does nice work and I am gradually learning how to record at 33 without too much surface. [ALC]

Money troubles continued to plague Alan, as he expressed in this short postcard to Spivacke on September 7:

Sorry to be such trouble—I am in funds now to the extent of $12.68. This will last me about five days. If you think my reimbursements will have reached me by that time, o.k., otherwise an advance might be in order. I am not wastreling—but songs in Mich. absolutely require beer. My address for next three days will be St. Ignace, Mich. Will arrive there in a day or two. [ALC][65]

Spivacke worked on getting Alan more money, for which he thanked him from St. Ignace on September 12:

I am sorry there has been all the confusion about food for me. The trouble seems to be that the mails here in Northern Michigan are terribly slow. It takes your letters four days to get to me there and your special about finances didn't reach me until I reached Mackinac City. I'm praying that the check really arrives tomorrow, because I've been cutting down on my diet a little more than I can stand. It's too bad I'm stuck here, too, just at this moment. There are fine singers around, but one of them just had a death in the family and is off on a three weeks bender, another has an awful cold, another had a serious operation not long ago and yet others want pay and are suspicious and elusive in the way that the French Indian mixtures so often are. Please add the enclosed letter from Capt. Nye to our files on the vagaries of folk lore and heed his warning to close his collection to the public if that has not yet been done. Mr. James Green's address is simply St. James, Beaver Island, Michigan.

I think that the purchase of another hundred discs from Sound Scriptions would not be a bad move, although I don't know whether this trip will yield more than a couple of hundred records in all—unless my luck changes very much. Not that the country isn't fertile, but it is stubborn and the people

simply can't see why they should sing for me without pay. This is a question
we shall have to take up at some length on my return. The proper answer,
when you are asked, flatly,—"Well, do you get pay for this?" Nothing I have
thought of so far seems to be quite adequate. This is the region that I want
to return to for my next summer's field trip, however. I think two months
in this upper peninsula would yield remarkable finds for American folklore.
I'm leaving the Indian and the mixed blood problem until that time. Now
would be a very good time to talk about my return to Washington. I hate for
the Library to have spent the money to send me out here without some sort
of return on its investment—i.e. over two hundred records. If you think it
advisable, I should like to postpone my return to W[ashington] until the 15th,
setting that as the nether dead-line. That will give me a chance to explore
Northern Wisconsin and Minnesota very briefly, at least. [ALC][66]

Alan continued a while longer in Michigan, writing to Spivacke from Escanaba on September 19:

Since I am advised to be forehanded, I will say now that I'll need another fifty
dollars advance before the trip is over. I'm having good deal of car trouble
and entertainment of singers is coming partly out of my own pocket. So the
sooner with a $50 advance the better. You can calm Mr. Rabbitt by telling
him that vouchers already submitted by me already cover the amount so far
advanced. They will go in airmail tomorrow morning. I still think that unless
I have word from Downes or Krimsky I will prolong the trip until the 15th
of October. I am beginning to feel much better now and I'm learning a lot.
I want a chance now that I have explored lumberjacks & lake sailors a bit to
take a whack at the miners, the Finns and the French and I want to urge now
that I be sent back into this area next summer. In many ways it is the most
interesting country I have ever traveled in.

   Will you ask Mr. Waters to give me an account of how much leave I have
coming to me. Several plans are revolving in my head and according to some
of them I will take two weeks or more leave before returning to D.C. Last
week I ran into a couple of possible collectors items. 1) A set of broadsheets
of songs 1–666 (practically complete) published (1–200) by E. Nason & Co.
& (200–666) by J. Wehman, 50 Chatam Ave., N.Y.C. Late 19th C. I remember
[Robert] Gordon crowing over his complete set as a rare collector's item. Do
we have them. 2) An 1822 almanac, nicely get up—a copy of the title page of
which is inclosed.

   I have now about 50+ discs on hand and I suggest you order more. Three
sapphires will come to you under separate cover shortly for re-sharpening

and I hope you can rush them—although the steel cuts aren't so bad. I don't know where Capt. Nye's letter is now but it isn't very important—I have answered the enclosed, telling him that you will write. I will send you an idea of my itinerary as soon as I have completed my plans. [ALC]

Two days later, September 21, he added more to Spivacke on the condition of the car:

I discovered yesterday after I sent you my last letter that the brake lining was completely finished in my car and that besides new linings I shall probably need a new set of drums. That makes the matter of an advance a little more urgent than I had at first thought. Also I think you had better hurry along a shipment of discs as fast as possible. I have fifty left and I hope my luck will be good for the next few days. My schedule will be as follows so far as I can plan it: Ironwood Michigan, 26th and 27th, Oct. 1st Duluth, Minn. Let me know in Ironwood how long it will take you to ship me 75 discs and I will airmail you instructions as to where they should meet me. Would it be possible for you to arrange the advance to meet me in Ironwood? Sorry this has come up, but how could I know I would have twenty dollars in repair bills so soon. [ALC]

A telegram to Spivacke on September 28 gave a succinct account of the situation in Calumet, Michigan:

Am getting such grand stuff cant afford to leave can you wire me my salary or my advance here tomorrow by Western Union. [ALC]

He followed with this telegram from Calumet on October 1:

Check not arrived from Ironwood not received requested wire of salary have completed work here but cannot proceed please send money by return wire. [ALC]

But three days later, October 4, he sent this brief postcard:

Both checks arrived safely. I hope the records meet me in Ironwood safely tomorrow night. Will let you know future addresses in a day or two. [ALC]

Two days later, September 30 (the letter has Sep. scratched out, replaced by Oct., but obviously this was written in September), he was still in Calumet, as he informed Spivacke:

When I wired you first I was ready to leave this region & go on toward Ironwood, but I planned to take it slowly and work my numerous contacts between here and there—it is 120 miles there. I thought, of course, you would be able to send me my salary by wire or my advance (as I did not suppose it had yet reached Ironwood). A word of explanation about Ironwood—when I came here I did not plan to stay more than a day or two and thought I would then go on to Ironwood, where I have still not been. When your wire came, I presumed you could still wire me my salary and I could go ahead with my trip to points between here and Ironwood, so I wired the postmaster there to hold my mail and you to send my salary. Yesterday when I did not hear from you I countermanded the last Ironwood order and asked him to forward my mail. This he did—and this morning I received all of it—all but the advance— and I suppose he is now so confused he is afraid to let it go. So I'm in debt here and can't leave unless I get a favorable response to today's appeal to you. Of course, I'm terribly sorry this has happened, but the situation is as much a result of the nature of this job as of my bad planning. I'm still not able to predict in advance how a community will turn out—it is only by chance, for example, that I met the person who gave me my entrée to the Finnish people here and further South. I have been profitably at work here meantime and have recorded a lot of good Finnish stuff. So these days of waiting have not been wasted at all, but to go any deeper I need to know the language (it is not very difficult). The records—75 of them you can express to me at Ironwood. Enclosed are two sapphires that need resharpening. I think that, barring accidents, the two received of Rapidscriptions will do until I get home, but it still would be safer to have these two sharpened and mailed back to me. I await your reply to this morning's wire anxiously. I made last night the 165th record for this trip. [ALC]

On October 8 he was in Ironwood, as he explained to Spivacke:

I suppose you are disgusted with me as well as too busy to write, and I do feel sorry to have raised so much cain again about money. However, I had extras on the car and then trouble with the slowness of mails here—much worse than in Kentucky, for example. Neither was I aware that government money could not be wired. I shall never again change my schedule when a check is in the offing. My plans at the moment are as follows: 1) Today and Sunday in Marinesco, lumberjack center. 2) Monday and Tuesday in Champion and Baraga, where I found French singers last week—the patriarch of the family died the night I rolled in and of course I couldn't do anything—I am beginning to think I am Death's special herald. 3) Wednesday morning, an old lumberjack in Green; and 4) Three or four days to visit folk-lorists, etc., in Wisconsin and Minnesota in preparation for next year's work. 5) Chicago—where I may stay for a week or a month—on leave. 6) Back up to Mr. Pleasant to see Dr. [Earl] Beck, who has collected lumberjack songs for ten years and should have a machine—a very touchy individual on whose territory I poached a bit this summer and who should be mollified and won over to our point of view. 7) One or possibly two days in Flint and Detroit where I found material I could not record on the way up. Altogether I may need a week or ten days extension of my time, not all in a lump, but groups of days. Please signify your approval or disapproval by an aye or a nay addressed airmail general delivery Ironwood. I hope you enjoyed yourself in New England last week as much, at least, as the Czechs enjoyed the Munich parleys [this is a reference to the Munich Accords, signed on September 29, in which Great Britain and France did not object to Germany moving into Czechoslovakia]. What do you think of the middle of the road anyway [this seems to be a reference to neutrality]. [ALC][67]

On the same day he thanked Edward Waters at the Music Division of the Library of Congress for shipping the discs, although some arrived damaged. He also added a bit about his advance:

Thank you for your promptness in getting the records to me, as well as the money. I had no idea that in emergency a government salary could not be wired, but I think you are being a little over-solemn about "no more money." What does this mean? Am I to be cut off without a penny or am I already discharged? [ALC]

He further updated Spivacke on October 15 from Ironwood, Michigan:

Thanks for your cheerful letter. I wish I didn't have you pictured as some kind of ogre or right now I would be square dancing with a French Canadian girl in Baraga. But here I am, feeling very easy and pleased with myself. Since I wrote you I've made 45 swell records—and tired as hell & ready to come home. I'll let you know my plans as they develop, but right now you can help if you'll airmail my salary to Madison General Delivery & along with my other mail. I'll send you a list of the records tomorrow or the next day. Why not the same group the BBC people used—or some of them. Of course try them out first. Try Willy Reilly by Capt. Nye—East Virginia—Rosie (the latest acetate)—Moise-o (Haiti)—The Lady of Carlisle—Go Down Old Hannah (sung by the group on the Central State Farm). . . . [ALC]

Alan remained in the Midwest a bit longer, as he explained to Spivacke on October 23 from Chicago:

I arrived in Chicago this afternoon after my swing through Minnesota and Wisconsin. I think the trip was worth the trouble; for I arranged for a very fruitful summer of collaboration with practically all the local collectors and I think made them interested friends of the Archive. I have Archer Taylor, Tom Pete Cross, Katherine Dunham and some friends to see here and then I think I'll head for Washington by way of Detroit and Dr. Beck, as explained. I won't, however, go to New York unless I hear from Olin Downes and Krimsky. That should bring me back to the loving arms of the Library along in the first week of November. If you think there is sufficient reason for me to make a quicker trip I'll accommodate, but I'd like to know the reason. I should like to spend a couple of weeks at the Archive sort of cleaning house and settling whatever business there is to be settled and then go away for a real vacation. I am not exactly tired, but I am developing a very bad temper and my relationship to my work is certainly not what it should be emotionally, although I am still quite hard at it. I find it quite hard at this distance to recall the names of the best records, but I should suggest these tentatively: Pretty Polly, Pete Steele, East Virginia, Sayersville, Ky., Ain't No Mo' Cane of de Brazis, Go Down, Old Hannah, Earnest Williams, Sugarland, Texas, Any of Elita or Julien Hoffpauir's Cajun French ballads, Go Down, Red Rising sun. Ask Mrs. Seeger, who has the copies of the best ones in her hands. I've heard so much Polish, Finnish, French, Lumberjack, etc., that the Library set of names completely escapes me. [ALC]

By early November Alan was back in D.C., where he rushed to catch up with his correspondence, as he did on November 7 to William Myers at the Federal Writer's Project in Indianapolis:

I wrote you on August 18 and the letter never got into the mails. Perhaps it was just as well since I did not have time to stop by Indianapolis on my way back to Washington. The foreign groups you speak of there interest me very much and I hope that in the course of your work you will be able to develop a series of contacts for a future visit of a recording machine. Perhaps this will be next spring or early summer. I would suggest that if there are any large and interesting segments in the population that your field workers be of that group or at least able to speak the language in question. I want to take this opportunity to thank you and the Indiana Writer's Project for the very real assistance you rendered the archive on its Indiana field trip. [ALC]

On the same day, November 7, he gave his father a vivid account of his return:

Thursday morning at 11 o[']clock the Plymouth wobbled up to the library stop light and came to a drunken stop. There on a corner waiting for a car was Dr. Putnam, dapper and incisive in the sunlight. In telling the latter to the round table luncheon he said that he had already noticed this car and thought it belonged to some poor farmer that had come to town with his vegetables and squalling family. When I leaned through the window and flagged him I could see the color rise to his cheeks. The same color came Saturday morning when, in the midst of a chat about Michigan, he suddenly said "You will never make another trip in that car, Mr. Lomax." It cost me about $200 this summer and now it is literally falling to pieces like the old one horse shay. But I console myself that whether or not I will have a car at least the Library will, in the future, send out a sound truck when it goes after folk songs in the field. This morning I felt rested for the first time in months and even glad to be back. One of the things that made coming back pleasant was your long letter, which I appreciate more than I can tell you as much for what it did not say as what was written there. And I am more relieved than I can tell you to know that you are all at work and facing things with so much courage. I think it would be an extremely good idea if we let the book rock along for six or nine months. It is quite out of balance now and that is something that can be helped only with time and consideration and there is no question that we have done books faster than any other team in existence. My plans are as follows. Next week-end with Bess then another week of clearing desks at the library, then two or three weeks vacation "with Nick [Ray] on Cape Cod" where we are going to do a play on the growth of jazz, a play already well mapped out and exciting in its possibilities.

This reminds me that I think the B.B.C. certainly gypped you when they paid you what they did. They are a very wealthy corporation and you gave the best fruits of your labor and experience of the last 4 or 5 years which they could have got from no other person. If they come back for more for heaven's sake work through an agent. To matters of business. Mr. Blossom, assistant reference librarian here, wants to propose you for membership in the Cosmos Club in Washington. Good food, reasonable hotel rates and the most distinguished authorities on anything you like in and out of Washington as members. I will tack on notes about costs of membership on end of this letter when I sign it. Frank had not sent your books because you had not given him very definite addresses. They went into the mail Saturday, however. I will work on the Cole publishing matter when I come back from seeing Bess and let you know, and will also let you know what Colonel Beauvais of the

Copyright Office thinks about your chances. His advice is naturally the best you can get. Your generous offer of a year in the woods or in college are naturally tempting and I will hold them in reserve. I think, however, I can get 6 perhaps 9 months of college on my own and I will write you about this soon a little more definitely. . . . P.S. So many people have asked about you and sent their regards on the trip it would take another letter merely listing them all. The Crosses (Ellen is happily engaged) and Archer Taylor are merely typical of the group. [Carl] Sandburg was away. [ALC]

On November 7, moreover, he wrote to Mason Palmer in Newberry, Michigan, one of his usual post-recording acknowledgments:

I remember with pleasure the evening I spent in your home and as soon as I can get to it I will mail you a copy of one of your records. As I recall you recorded 12 songs on the 3 or 4 records and a number of them were quite good. I would have sent you a duplicate long ago except that I only returned to Washington four days ago. [ALC]

The next day, November 8, he wrote to John Green in St. James, Michigan:

Perhaps you think I have forgotten you, but that is certainly not the case. Instead, I have been over my ears in work in Michigan until a day or so ago. You should know that you have the largest stock of ballads of anyone I met in the whole state and that the archive is many times richer for the addition of material you were kind enough to give us. I am sorry now, of course, that I did not stay longer on the island. If you remember your young days of traveling you will know how I felt. But I certainly look forward to coming back and spending more time on the island. You may expect from now on through the years a regular procession of my friends because they have all heard or will hear about the place and you and Dominick. In Escanaba I called on some of your friends. The former Mayor Gallagher was very pleasant but neither he nor Mrs. Gallagher could think of any people who still knew the old songs. Scaley Willy, as you must know by this time, had just lost his wife and did not feel in the mood for singing, but promised to sing the next time I came back. All the other people you directed me to had either moved away or were dead so I wished again I had stayed on the island longer.—Mrs. Kovis and I had a chat.—"Help yourself to the mustard." You remember when I left, you and Mrs. Woods had promised to get together and finish up the job you and I had begun. I hope you have stuck to your promise as much for your own sake as for the Library of Congress's sake. A complete collection of all the songs you know would stand as a monument to you and to the Beaver Island

Irish long after the houses have tumbled down and the gravestones turned to dust. I feel sure that you know at least 200 songs, and, perhaps, if we can get them all together it will be worthwhile publishing them as a united collection. Anyway it is worth working on and if you write me I hope you can send me, along with the Beaver Island news, a report that this job is being done. [ALC]

On a different note, he responded to Ruth Roark in Mozelle, Kentucky, also on November 8:

I am grieved to hear of your father's death. I remember him as a fine gentleman and a delightful musician. As I recall I sent Mr. Collett a copy of one or two of his records, shortly after my return from Kentucky in 1937. Perhaps you do not know of these records and they might suffice for the time being. We do not have here at the Library at the moment the best facilities for duplication and your father's original records should not be played unnecessarily as they might show wear. If you feel it is possible for you to wait perhaps a year for additional duplicates, at that time I believe you may be able to obtain duplicates of much better quality for by then we hope to have regular facilities for duplication in this division. I am deeply touched by your request and if you feel that you need a record at once I will do my best to make one for you. [ALC][68]

Alan was continually involved with small official matters, as in this letter to Anne Scott West in Washington, November 10:

It is difficult to send you the "correct words" of your "ghost story" since this song is, like so many folk songs, current in a number of different versions. However, I can give you a reference to published versions of the songs and you can chose the one you like the best. Page 483, *Folk Songs of the South* John Harrington Cox, Harvard University Press, 1925. In this source you will find references to other versions, both English and American. [ALC]

Alan tried to keep in touch with his informants, as he did with the Forster family in Lauriun, Michigan, on November 11:

You have not heard from me because I only got back to town last Thursday and I can tell you that I have been as lonely for you as you have been for me. Everyone I saw in the rest of my trip I told about you and how if they were to have a good time they should come and see you. How long it will be before I can come, I do not know just now. I have an awfully busy winter before me and that means an equally busy spring. There is a chance that I might dash

out to Upper Peninsula for New Years but that is very unlikely. I am awfully
sorry to learn that the Yalmer has been ill and I hope he is better by this time.
Don't forget me and as soon as I can I will send you a record with everybody
on it. Tell Abo [Johyani] that his peppermints were really very effective and
give him my greeting in this sentence that I learned in Minnesota "Ken kansa
halveksu sortuvi niinkuin jureton puu." ["When anyone scorns the people /
he topples like a rootless tree," from Arvid Genetz, "Heraa Suomi."] [ALC]

In his official report on the trip, Alan detailed his collecting successes:

A two and a half month reconnaissance survey of folk-music in Michigan brought into the Archive a group of about a thousand songs, lumberjack, lake sailor, Irish, Southern Negro, Finnish, Serbian, Polish, Canadian
French, German, Hungarian, and Croatian. Dr. Ivan Walton of the University of Michigan, Dr. E. C. Beck of the Michigan State Teachers College, and
Mr. Howard Newsome, Director of the Federal Writers' Project of Michigan, were of assistance in locating singers. After ten days spent in Detroit
recording a few of the many types of foreign minority music still orally
current there, notably records of Serbian diple and douduc players, I visited
briefly a few of the fine lumberjack singers Dr. Beck had located near Mt.
Pleasant. It was then arranged for me to join Dr. Walton, the authority on
lake sailor songs, at Beaver Island, Michigan. There he introduced me to
two remarkable Irish singers, Dominick Gallagher and Johnny Green. The
latter one of the most amazing ballad singers who has turned up in America,
recorded over a hundred come-all-ye ballads—forecastle, lumberjack, lake
sailor, Irish, popular, etc. Since that time he has written that he has recalled
a hundred and fifty more. The Beaver Island singers were all Irish and ended
their songs in the fashion described by Barrie as "parlando rubato." Indeed,
wherever a lake sailor or lumberjack of fifty years or over was recorded this
type of ending was noted. A visit to Posen, Michigan, brought the Library
an interesting collection of Polish ballads and fiddle tunes. Many of the
latter had been learned from local fiddlers when the Polish settlers arrived
and now among young people are passed under Polish names as Polish
tunes. Here, as all over Michigan, even including Detroit, a great revival
of interest in old dance forms was in evidence. Local bands were expected
to be able to play national music, jazz, and American square-dance music.
The Upper Peninsula of Michigan proved to be the most fertile source of
material. After six weeks of recording a mass of lumberjack, Finnish and
French folk-songs, I felt that there was material enough in the region for
years of work. Near Newberry, Munising, Greenland, and Ontonogan, it
was comparatively easy to find lumberjack singers. Everywhere through

the Copper country and south of it, Finnish singers generously furnished me with more material than I had time to record. And in Champion and Baraga I found French ballad singers who still enjoyed ballad fests that lasted all night long.[69]

There were always odds and ends of matters to deal with, as he explained to Esther Bell Beachy in San Antonio, Texas, on November 18:

I have just retuned to the city from an extensive field trip in the Lake States and find your distressing letter on my desk. The clipping[70] you mention came into my hands only shortly before my departure this summer and it is now somewhere among my papers here in the Library. I shall commence an intensive search and send you a letter on Monday with the clipping enclosed, or else send an airmail request to the Kansas City Star to supply you with another. I regret very much that this whole instance occurred and I hope you will be patient for a few more days. It would be of material assistance if you will send me the date and the page number of the clipping. [ALC]

A few days later, on November 21, he contacted Thomas Outram in Sheffield, England:

The exact texts for the two songs you request can, unfortunately, only be obtained from the records which you heard. Neither of these records happens to have come from the Archive's collection. In fact, I believe them to be dubbings from commercial recordings which you may be able to buy. This information would have to come from Alastair Cooke, since he chose the recordings originally. The text to the "Night Herding Song," by J. A. Lomax, New York The Macmillan Company, 1938. I believe the text of the other song is in the "Hobo's Hornbook," by George Milburn, New York, I. Washburn, 1930. I would have answered your letter before, but I have been away on a long field recording trip. [ALC][71]

Then next day, November 22, he kept in touch with Earl Beck in Mt. Pleasant, Michigan:

As you doubtless know, I came to Mt. Pleasant last August shortly after you had left on your Nebraska vacation and not having found you at home to my very great disappointment, I made inquiries, found a couple of your best singers and recorded several of their best songs for the Archive. I did the recording with this reservation clearly in mind—that after I returned to Washington, I would write you and place these records at your disposal and deposit them in the Archive with whatever restrictions you cared to impose. I can prepare and send to you, if you like, a list of the songs and fragments of songs that Bill McBride and the others gave me and if you would like to have copies of the same, that can be arranged too.

My trip in Michigan was full of a great many fruitful surprises. Among these was my discovery that there are still a great number of lumberjack singers in the state with good voices and healthy memories. It is extremely important that these singers and their songs be recorded before it is too late and since you have already done such extensive work in the study of lumberjack ballads in Michigan, I feel that you are the person who ought, if you are interested, to do the job. The Archive of American Folk Song desires to give as much help to competent collectors as possible and therefore it may be possible to arrange for you to use one of our portable electric recording machines for a period or to send a machine and an operator to Michigan to work under your supervision. [ALC]

On November 22 he wrote another of his mostly joking, personal letters to his sister Bess, now back at Bryn Mawr College:

I broke several hearts with your letter from Czechoslovakia but assure you that this has not proven very successful. One positive suggestion that has been made is that you advertise for the lady in the various foreign newspapers (Czechoslovak and liberal German-American) that are printed in the United States. Some Czech paper might even be willing to run the letter entire and some honest widower's heart might be broken with practical results for Miss Lowinger.

Nick [Ray] and I are going out into Maryland for a week of work on the play I told you about beginning this afternoon and you can expect to hear from me only after we come up for air next Monday. Have you forgotten that Jean ought to be writing a story about your Austrian boy in McGee, Arkansas?

When you have read this paragraph, seal your lips forever and burn the letter. In other words, this is confidential. Spivacke and I this week have spent in imagination $38,000 on a new Archive. (P.S. I don't think we'll get it!). That is all the news I can think of now except that you're generally regarded here as the white hope of the generation and everyone, including myself, is very fond of you. Please convey my greetings to Eddy and if you have anything to be looked up in the catalogue, write the Librarian. [ALC]

On December 3, he sent off a pleasant letter to Mildred Stocker in Detroit:

As it happens, neither of your pictures of me are accurate. The Library sent in another recording machine and I left Detroit about a week after I saw you for three and a half months in the field. I am delighted that you find your present job so unsatisfactory because I have half an idea that there may be an opening here in the Archive within the next month or two. If there is, and your application is at hand, I feel sure you will be, as the personnel office says, "seriously considered." Please let me know if you are interested and consider seriously how many seasons of American folk-lore you can stand before you answer. [ALC]

A few days later, December 8, he informed D. G. Rowse of the British Broadcasting Corporation (BBC):

In response to your letter to Mr. Elam, who had charge of shipping the records in the absence of both Mr. John A. Lomax and myself,—I see no reason that you shouldn't keep the whole group of Archive recordings until after Christmas. I feel sure that, in your hands, they will receive the very best care. One of the disappointments of my summer in Michigan was that I failed to hear Mr. [Alistair] Cooke's programs on American folk songs and, in order that this will not happen again, I would appreciate your sending me the notices of future programs. I presume that these programs are broadcast by short wave or is that the case? Through some oversight, we have not received the recordings of the broadcasts of last summer and I take this opportunity to remind you of the promise that Mr. Cooke made the Library last summer in this regard. [ALC]

On December 8 he kept up his exchange with John Umble at Goshen College in Indiana:

Unless my plans change, I will not be able to attend the American Folk Lore meeting in New York this Christmas. I believe, however, that it will be possible to send you a duplicate record of two of the Amish hymns for demonstration purposes. This request of yours will have to be approved by the Librarian and for that reason I cannot make a definite promise at the moment. In the meantime, however, you can choose from the enclosed list which of the hymns you prefer to have duplicated in case this recommendation is approved. [ALC]

He also responded on December 8 to a letter from Earl Beck in Michigan:

I think perhaps you have exaggerated the difficulties attendant upon the operation of a portable electric recording machine and I feel sure that with a few days practice in the field, you would be able to take very successful records. It may be possible to send a portable recording machine and an operator into Mt. Pleasant next spring and I certainly agree with you that it is important that this particular piece of recording be done as soon as possible. At the moment, however, the Archive cannot commit itself that far in advance, especially since by that time we may be able to arrange the recording work locally.

It would help considerably if you could estimate just the number of songs and singers that would be available next April. And there are various questions which it would be most helpful for you to answer. First, do all the singers whom you have located live near Mt. Pleasant or are they scattered throughout Michigan? How much time do you estimate it would take to make records of the ballads you have in your collection? How large a collection of important folk songs have you accumulated? If the recording will take more than a week, will you be able to leave your University duties for that long a time? With this additional information at hand, we should be able to let you know by next February or March whether this trip will be feasible or not. If you care to have a list of the recordings which Bill McBride and your other performers made for the Archive, we should be happy to furnish it along with duplicate records of three or four of the songs. I hesitate to choose these records myself since my preferences might not match your needs. [ALC]

Alan communicated with Harold (i.e. John) Krimsky on December 9 concerning his reluctance to give up on his World's Fair plans:

On the second anniversary of your promised letter, I feel like the third year bride whose husband is calmly eating his baked beans and talking about the boss and has forgotten orange blossoms and sweet romance. What has happened, if anything, in regard to the program we discussed for the World's Fair? Since the matter is semiofficial at least, and rather affects all my plans for this next year, I should like as definite an answer as you can give me. I realize, of course, that at the moment perhaps things are very much up in the air, but let me hear from you. [ALC]

That same day he wrote to Mrs. Whitelaw Reid Stryker in New Orleans:

I must apologize for not having replied to your letter earlier, but it came to me in Michigan where I was doing folklore work for the Library and I postponed an answer until my return to Washington. Your daughter's program sounds most interesting, and yet I am afraid I can suggest nothing further at the moment than that she put herself under the direction of a competent agent. As I understand it, this is the practice of most singers and lecturers nowadays. Perhaps you would like to send me your daughter's New York address so that I can call on her the next time I am in the city. I should be delighted to meet her. [ALC]

He again connected with John Umble on December 20:

Under separate cover, you will receive the duplicate recording of Amish hymn-singing which you requested. I included on the "B" side, parts of two hymns in the hope that one of them would meet your requirements. Mr. Bontrager did not sing any one hymn entirely through, since he felt that the first, or in some cases the first two stanzas, would be enough to give me the melody. This record should be played with a good quality medium tone needle and the hook-up used should be light and flexible, preferably a crystal pickup. The record plays from inside out, and should be good for forty or fifty excellent playings if it is carefully handled. It will reproduce only on an electric phonograph. [ALC]

On December 20 there was a short letter to John Shawbitz, one of Alan's contacts in Bessemer, Michigan:

The Archive does not have the facilities at this time to supply duplicates to the general public, but in view of your cooperation in our work in Michigan, I shall try to prepare a record for you within the next six weeks. [ALC]

The next day, December 21, he followed up to Earl Beck:

Thank you for your informative letter. As soon as the Archive plans for the spring have been made, I shall let you know, and you may be sure that we shall do our best to have a recording machine in Michigan as soon as possible. The list of songs recorded by Bill McBride will be prepared for you after the holidays. With my best regards for the holiday season to you and to my friend, MacBride. [ALC]

He made a quick trip to New York in late December, where he recorded part of John Hammond's expansive Spirituals to Swing Concert at Carnegie Hall on December 23, 1938. As he reported to the Library of Congress:

With the help of John Hammond, organizer and mainspring of the New Masses swing concert at Carnegie Hall, and the Allied Recording Company, who lent their machine for two days, I was able to make for the Library recordings of five of the most remarkable Negroes in American music:

Albert Ammons, Meade Lux Lewis, and Jimmie Johnson, the "boogie woo-gie" pianists; Pete Johnson, the blues pianist and composer; and Saunders Terry, the blind harmonica player from North Carolina. These recordings were documented in the fashion described above and represent the finest performances of these Negro folk-artists.[72]

On December 27 he wrote to Joe Arnstein at the Adult Education Program of the Chi-cago Board of Education, who was collecting labor songs for a proposed book:

Forgive me for not having replied to your letter before, but my correspon-dence has been unusually heavy recently. The songs collected by the Archive of American Folk Song are still almost entirely on the original master record-ings and as yet we have no facilities for duplication of these records. Perhaps within the year the records will be generally available and of course whatever request you care to make at that time will be given due consideration. A great many of the songs you are interested in can be found in published collections such as *American Ballads and Folksongs*, by Lomax; *The American Songbag*, by Sandburg; *Negro Work-a-day Songs*, by Odum & Johnson; *Songs and Bal-lads of the Anthracite Miner*, by Korson; *Negro Songs of Protest*, by Gellert. If further information is desired, I would suggest that you be much more specific because your request covers the entire field of American folksong. I suggest further that you communicate with the Co-ordinating Commit-tee for Folk-lore in the Works Progress Administration, of which [Benjamin] Botkin, of the Central Office of the Federal Writer's Project, is chairman. I feel sure they can give you material aid. [ALC][73]

LETTERS, 1939–1940

1939

In late December 1938, Alan requested permission from Harold Spivacke to move temporarily to New York City, mostly to further his studies, as he explained in a draft of this undated letter:

I should like to suggest a project to you which I believe will be of interest and value to the Archive of American Folk Song in the Library of Congress. This project is one that I have thought over at considerable length and that I hold personally very dear. It is important to the adequate performance of my duties as assistant in the Archive of Folk Song that I have more systematic academic training in anthropology and in the anthropological approach to primitive and folk music. To this end I should like to spend the spring studying anthropology and musicology at New York University and Columbia University in New York City. At the same time I look forward to continuing my work for the Library on a part time arrangement, recording the great store of folk music of New York City and investigating the extent of American folk song items already recorded by commercial concerns. The courses I plan to take are the following: In New York University, Primitive and Oriental Music, Dr. Curt Sachs. In Columbia University, Folk Music, Dr. George Herzog. Problems and Methods in Field Work in Ethnology, Dr. [Ruth Leah] Bunzel. Psychology and Ethnology, Dr. [Otto] Klineberg. This program might, of course, be changed somewhat when I should come to know the individual professors more intimately, but the intent of the year's work would remain the same. I might add that I plan to study music with private instructors. The expenses connected with this semester of academic work will be: Registration and tuition $250.00, Living expenses $600, Total $850. I would expect to add to the Archive in this period at least two hundred

FISK UNIVERSITY
SEVENTY-FIFTH ANNIVERSARY
CELEBRATION
APRIL 29-MAY 4, 1941
Nashville, Tennessee

A Program of Negro Folk Song

I. REELS AND WORK SONGS

    Alan Lomax, *commentator*
      Assistant in Charge, Archive of American Folk Song,
      Library of Congress

II. BLUES AND BALLADS

    Sterling Brown, *commentator*
      Associate Professor of English, Howard University

III. SPIRITUALS

THE GOLDEN GATE QUARTET

Willie Johnson, *tenor*   Henry Owens, *baritone*
Clyde Reddick, *tenor*   Orlandus Wilson, *bass*

JOSHUA WHITE and his guitar

TUESDAY, APRIL 29   8:15 P.M.

FISK MEMORIAL CHAPEL

Program to the Fisk University Seventy-fifth Anniversary Celebration, 1941. Alan Lomax's lecture, "Reels and Work Songs" was part of our program. (John A. Lomax and Alan Lomax Papers, AFC 1933/001, fol. 302, American Folklife Center, Library of Congress) records important in the study of American folk-music, and at the same time to acquire training which would make my future work for the Archive more valuable. [LP, folder 4]

While waiting for permission to relocate to New York, he wrote a postcard to Spivacke on January 4, 1939, when briefly in that city:

I've been asleep since I got to N.Y. —from 12 to 14 hours a night. I've done not a jot of work. Tomorrow I'll stir about a little bit + in the meantime you can reach me at 158 E. 26th St. (*not 258*). Hold my mail. [ALC]

On January 11, back in Washington, he updated his father about work on their new book, *Our Singing Country*, which would not be published until 1941:

I returned from New York a day or so ago and found a stack of letters from you which had not been forwarded. I hope that you are not worried or angry about my neglect of you, but it was simply a matter of not having received the letters. The Cowboy Song and American Ballad matter I will take care of before the end of the week, in regard to the replacement of copyright material. Last night Ruth [Seeger] and I talked over the work to be done on the ballad book and we are going to have a long session either tomorrow or the next day, after which I will write you at length about what should be done. Two things, however, seem necessary before we can do anything. 1. That we know how many pages Macmillan is going to allow us, whether it will cover more or less than necessary for the amount of material already accumulated. 2. We must either have the manuscript of the book itself, or at least the table of contents so that we can make the necessary deletions and round the rest of the material out with the new songs that are coming to the Archive. Perhaps it would be a good idea for you to send the table of contents on to us at once and we will go straight to work on it. I think that probably we can do the whole job by correspondence if you don't feel like coming to Washington; at least we can get along very well for a month or so. My plans at present are to spend the next few months at Columbia University taking anthropology and other things, and I think I can arrange the finances for this period myself. As soon as I have any definite news on any of these scores, I will write you again. P.S. I think you should sue the Oxford Book of Light Verse. [ALC]

Two days later, January 13, Alan updated Spivacke:

In the course of my recent authorized trip to New York City, December 22–25, 1939 [1938], I had the unexpected opportunity of making a group of very valuable records of the artists who performed in John Hammond's concert in Carnegie Hall, "From Spirituals to Swing." The Allied Recording Company was kind enough to lend me a very fine portable recording machine for the work and from them I purchased recording needles and blanks. The expenses for the recordings are itemized below: Blanks and needles . . . $23.00. Rent of recording studio with pianos and sound-proofing for 6 1/2 hours at $1.50 per hour . . . 9.75. Fee to negro harmonica player, Saunders [Sonny] Terry . . . 5.00. Refreshments for informants . . . 5.00. Total $42.75. These expenses were taken care of out of my personal funds and I shall appreciate an early reimbursement. From the point of view of recording, these records are the best that have so far been made for the Archive and their historical interest is great. From the point of view of content, they interest Mr. Hammond so much that he wants a full set of duplicates. [ALC]

On January 14 he corresponded with Stephen W. Smith at the Hot Record Society in New York:

The Music Division is delighted to accept the set of records issued by the Hot Record Society for permanent deposit in its phonogram collection. It is hoped that we shall be on your permanent mailing list, so that this set can be kept complete and up-to-date, and that besides that we receive the bulletin which parallels the recordings. . . . May I take this opportunity to thank you and the Hot Record Society in behalf of the Library and the Music Division for this significant addition to our phonogram collection. [ALC]

While still in Washington, he contacted Ruth R. Roark, Mozelle, Kentucky, on January 17:

I regret that my reply to your letter has been delayed so long, but I have been in Washington very little in the last month. I am sorry to hear of Farmer Collett's death, and, of course, I want to help you get copies of his records if I can. At the time he sang for me, he also accompanied the singing of a number of other people, but the list of songs quoted below were sung and played entirely by Mr. Collett: Jackson Jail Blues . . . The Butcher's Boy . . . I'm Gonna Cross That White Oak Mountain . . . I Would Pawn You My Watch . . . Buck Creek Girls Won't Go to Somerset . . . John Henry. The type of record I suggest you have made is of aluminum. While these are not entirely satisfactory, they are at least fairly durable if they are played with the proper needles. Twelve-inch duplicate aluminum disks of Farmer Collett's songs will cost seventy-five cents each, and it will take five twelve-inch records to include all of his songs. This would make the entire cost $3.75, to be paid in advance since the work is done outside the building by a private concern. [ALC]

The same day, January 17, he responded to John Umble at Goshen College:

I should like to know why Mr. Bontrager and his friend refuse to make more recordings. If this is due to any mistake made by my wife and myself in dealing with these elegant old Amish gentlemen, I should like to know in detail what mistake or mistakes were made, so that I shall not repeat them in the future. I am delighted to hear that you found the duplicate record useful and if there is any way in the future that the Archive can assist you in your studies of Amish music, please let me know. It might be possible that we could lend you a simple recording device with blanks if you ever had occasion to make a series of recordings of the music of this interesting Protestant sect. If you are interested in knowing the policy of the Archive regarding the loan of recording machine and materials, I suggest that you read Doctor Harold Spivacke's article on the Archive in the March 1938 issue of the Southern Folklore Quarterly. [ALC][1]

Spivacke did agree to allow Alan to temporarily relocate to New York, as he acknowledged on January 19:

I recommend that Mr. Alan Lomax be authorized to transfer his activities to New York City from February 1, 1939 to June 1, 1939, on a half-time basis during which period he is to receive half of his present salary. I recommend further that, while in New York City, Mr. Lomax be authorized to negotiate for the rental of a recording studio to be used in making records for the Archive, to encourage gifts to the Archive from commercial recording companies and others, and to carry on research for the Archive as directed by the Chief of the Music Division. I recommend also that Mr. Lomax make periodic visits to Washington (possibly once a month) to report on his progress and that he receive railway fare and per diem for there [sic] trips as well as railway fare for his initial trip to New York and his return to Washington in June, to be charged to Increase. [ALC]

While preparing for his move, Alan was involved in the new book with his father, *Our Singing Country*, as well as other matters, as he wrote to John on January 21:

The "Fiddler-crab Song" was delightful according to Bess, Elizabeth, myself, Doctor Spivacke, Mr. Waters, Miss Rogers, Miss Andrews and all and sundry who have seen it. That you have not received acknowledgment is due, first, to the coldness of heart induced by the climate and the tempo of life in these parts, and second, to straight ingratitude. Try to forgive us all correctively [sic]. I bought Bess for Christmas a large camel's hair coat costing about $39.00, and had to spend the rest of the money on Library business. When I get paid back I shall buy myself a $21.00 Christmas present in kind memory. I was as astonished as you were to find *American Ballads and Folk Songs* in the "Oxford Book of Light Verse." Also, to hear that two of our songs were in Marc Connelly's recent flop "Everywhere I roam" without acknowledgment. Also to learn that our version, word for word, of Jessie James was used in "Missouri Territory," another Broadway production. One more word about Bess. She is already something of a leader on the Bryn Mawr campus, because of her charm, earnestness and intelligence. She is very happy there and is growing in every sort of way, probably too fast to be able to write about it well.[2]

I can't find the copy of *American Ballads and Folk Songs* you mentioned in your letter of the 15th, but I have talked the matter of revision of the music over with Spivacke, Waters and Mr. Seeger. They all feel that extensive correction of Mary Gresham's work has to be done, and do not feel that Mr. Strunk's correction would be sufficient. A number of the songs will have to be corrected directly from records, and it seems best to have one person do most of the job. A little more about the machine—Doctor Spivacke is anxious to find out how long a trip you want to take, so that he may make out the necessary request for mileage and per diem. The machine will be ready a month from now, probably, depending on what condition the Detroit thieves left it in. We need some good acetate recordings of work-songs for possible inclusion in the suggested album for Pan-American republics, etc., and I suggest that you go by Huntsville, Darington, and the other prison farms in Texas and Arkansas, and stay as long as you can and get bang-up recordings of group work-songs, also as many blues with guitar accompaniment as possible. We have made one fairly serious mistake all along, and that is not repeating songs until really good recordings were made in all cases. The disks and needles you will be using this time are going to make a lot of difference in the quality of the records you can make.

I have one town in Kentucky which I suggest you visit—Salyersville, about a hundred miles south of Ashland. The best banjo player I ever heard and one of the best mountain singers lives there. His name is Walter Williams. Another singer there of great interest is Clay Walters. I can give you other names if you decide to go. It seems a great shame not to keep closely in touch with such a remarkable person as Roscoe MacLean, and not to make some additional recordings of his voice. On your way through Louisiana, if you come that way, why not try to run down the story of the Batson affair. It is one of the most interesting of American ballads and abut which even Gordon has practically no information. I can give you some good names in New Orleans, too, of early jazz musicians who know folksongs and jazz tunes which were not written down. Elizabeth's uncle lives in a little town in the no-man's-land on the Texas edge of Louisiana. Elizabeth says that he has a natural amateur's interest in folksongs and knows all the fiddlers and singers of that section, and he could probably lead you to very good material. All of which, in addition to contacts you have, sounds like a good month and a half of work. I hope you can arrange this trip to stay in prison camps longer than you have hitherto been able, and don't forget Bowlegs, for Heaven's sake, he is one of the great and when he gets out of Parchman will be lost to us forever. About the Great Lake songs, I know Mr. Walton quite well and last summer recorded a number of his songs in Michigan. I think I can get permission for us to use four or five of them and I shall pick these out in the process of looking at the records. Mrs. Seeger and I are going to spend all this afternoon and as much time as we get to in the next few days on the ballad book. Please let me know as soon as you can about the loan. P.S. I shall get copyright on the two cowboy songs looked up this afternoon. [ALC]

An undated letter to Spivacke went out sometime in early February:

My address for the present is 46 W. 96th St., Apt. 3-W. Elizabeth and I are very comfortable there but we will undoubtedly move once more before we finally settle down. Under separate cover I'm mailing Miss Rogers some letters for typing. You might take a look at some of them so they won't have to be done over twice. We had a Hell of a trip up here in the fog with plenty of car trouble. I am a little groggy from the experience, especially after such a crush of work the last two weeks I spent in Washington. I need to hear at once about the Strong Loan. Please write me. [ALC]

Also about this time, in another undated letter from 46 W. 96th Street, he gave Spivacke some details of his current situation, while enrolled in three anthropology courses at Columbia University from February to June:

I met a very much surprised Dr. Herzog at Columbia this morning, a Dr. Herzog who told me that I had made a great mistake in coming to school to take his course this term, that I should have come next term, should have come next year and for a whole year. Such a neurotic little academic man you never saw before. It seems that the catalogue was wrong, that he doesn't give his course in folk music this term, but primitive music, and that primitive music follows folk music as he has his course arranged. He and I are going to have a conference tomorrow morning, however, and he is going to try to arrange some way out of this terrible dilemma for me.

Wednesday I spent with the gentleman from the French Broadcasting Company and discovered that he wants more variety than he led me to believe in Washington. His needs can be satisfied if you will send me the exhibition acetate records which are all together in a group on the shelf above the recording machine along with the records made by Fred Carriere in Michigan. Mr. Carriere filled about fifteen blanks between numbers 190 and 220 in the recent Michigan series. Mr. Henderson can find these records easily enough or, if he is not there, they can be found in the last of the tin boxes (beyond 1700) in the Archive. I will give him only one of these and insist that NBC give us a master duplicate of the record he chooses so that we can consider that one playing as having lost us nothing. The other masters I will return without any playing at all. Mr. Berger, the gentleman in question, will be our very good friend in Paris and I think it will do us no harm to render him every service we can. He is talking about possible recording trip to Africa. Why not ship all my stuff to me via American Express at one time. Should get there by Wednesday or Thursday.

I am enclosing a letter I received this morning from BBC and which I will have long distanced you about I hope before you receive this. Other letters for your approval and Miss Rogers' typewriter. My friend Pollock in Detroit, whom I had asked to look at the machine, reports it in good condition and can be shipped when we make provision for its packing. I shall so inform Mr. Dumaine and shall follow his instructions. Will write you tomorrow or Monday. [ALC]

He penned a short message to Spivacke on February 16 from their new address at 124 West 12th Street:

Elizabeth is still in bed. Columbia is lot's of fun. Thanks for the loan. [ALC]

From 124 West 12th Street he also wrote to Spivacke in another undated letter:

I just came across your old letter about the Lead Belly album. A Harrison Special is a small, highly portable revolver, deadly at short range, but mainly carried by amateurs and young boys. Pulling a doey is having a hell of a party, raising cane, etc. [ALC]

One of Alan's projects was to obtain copies of commercial folk records for the Library of Congress, starting with Columbia Records. He was quite aware of their importance, and was certainly not only interested in field recordings. As he wrote to Spivacke in this undated letter:

I saw John Hammond on Tuesday and he told me about the outcome of your visit to Columbia. He said that besides the classical records affair, he believed that in the next two weeks Columbia would have agreed to send you their race list—in all about five or six hundred records. Naturally they have many more than this out of print. Upon hearing this I suggested my old plan of making a bibliography of commercial folk recordings, including those of which the masters have not been destroyed. He said that he could get me into the factory with a carte blanche to hear everything that the Library wanted. He was very enthusiastic about the bibliography and felt that this is an excellent way to introduce the other recording companies to our desire to have folk and popular issues and I shall, therefore, study their catalogues carefully (he says they have a fairly complete file) and visit their factory. With the information thus obtained I shall then be able to approach other companies in town and by the end of the spring I think I should have 1) found out what they've done in the way of folk recording 2) completed a fair bibliography and 3) perhaps obtained from them certain promises regarding special Library of Congress issues. Naturally I want your suggestions about this. For one thing, if I discover a lot of old and valuable catalogues in their files, do you want me to arrange for microfilming and deposit in the Library? For another, would there be an objection to my editing an album of folk records for Columbia in case I find enough good stuff or do you feel that that might hurt our chances at the moment? As you know it has been extremely difficult for me to get around to all my work with Elizabeth in bed, but I feel that from now on things won't be so hard. Columbia is a great deal of fun and my connection with the Library of Congress is, as you have suggested, most helpful in getting me in to see all kinds of people. I shall call on your friends, Clarke, Smith etc., next week at the latest. [ALC]

The following to Spivacke, also undated, apparently was attached to the above:

I left one tangle behind me when I left Washington—the duplication of the Farmer Collett records. By mistake she sent me a money order to cover the duplication and I returned it to her with instructions to send it to Radio-scriptions. I believed that she would return the order to them before I left Washington. It has just reached my hands. I suggest that the simplest way to settle the problem is to send the records down to him along with enough acetate (six or seven 12" blanks) and allow him to mail her the dubbings. That will rid us of any responsibility to her. The list of records can be found in the files in my last letter to Ruth Roark or Nonie Collett. Mr. Henderson can find the originals for you, the truck can deliver the material and I will write Coar a special letter of instructions today about handling the discs. Enclosed you will find a letter from Presto Recording Company which mentions a letter I never received. Perhaps you opened it and kept it on your desk. I shall not call on them until I hear from you. You may recall that the cutting head was sent to them for examination only and no repair was authorized by anyone. . . . Elizabeth is much better but is still confined to the house and a long way from being completely well. [ALC]

On February 24 Spivacke warned Alan to be cautious about his commercial records project:

I approve heartily of your plans for the bibliography of phonograph records. You may remember our discussion on this point almost two years ago. Go right ahead on this at once. Please follow my instructions *to the letter* in your dealings with the Columbia Phonograph people. Do nothing independently lest you spoil our entire plans. . . . Do *not* ask for any records yourself. Send your recommendations *to me*. Your remarks about Mr. John Hammond show me that you have already misunderstood my letter on the subject. The President of A.R.C. (which owns Columbia and others) had already offered me *anything* I wanted! The Vice-President, Mr. Wise, suggested the race records and *others* but agreed that we should postpone discussion of this until *after you* make a survey. Furthermore, my suggestions to Mr. Wise regarding the possible utilization of your services (personal) went much *further* then merely re-editing old records. I suggested *commercial* recording trips under your supervision etc. But do not press this matter! Let *him* bring it up. I must insist for your own sake that you leave certain things to me. I have absolute confidence in your persuasive powers but wait until I indicate when and where you are to apply them. You will be called upon plenty *later*. So visit Messrs. Wise and Taylor as soon as possible! You will find them both delightful. Report to me as soon as you see them. [ALC]

On another matter, Alan sent a telegram to Spivacke on February 24:

Secretary of Labor wires asking my presence conference Washington Friday March third. Can you arrange travel order for that weekend as my regular monthly visit library. [ALC]

Alan provided more details to Spivacke on February 26 concerning his collection of commercial records for the Library:

Certainly my last letter to you did not convey my feeling about the Columbia phonograph matter. What I tried to do was to ask your advice about that step

I should take next. This is what happened. Not having been told that Columbia was of a mind to present the Library with hill-billy and race records, I went to [John] Hammond who was the only person in the concern I knew to be directly interested in the matter and made to him the same proposition I have made to several officials of Columbia before—i.e., that I return for free access to their factory files. I would tell them what good folksong records they had. Hammond then practically offered me the company and I was so surprised that I wrote you to ask what to do about it. I shall certainly call on Mr. Wise [Columbia Vice President] and Mr. [Davidson] Taylor next week to try to straighten the matter out.

I have sent off an airmail request for my Texas [university] record and it will be in your hands shortly. The Presto letter turned up among my papers yesterday and I am sorry you cannot take a small bit of kidding. Of course I had no idea that it was on your desk. I shall call on Presto next week and see if I can't fix the matter up. I thought you might be interested to see the Department of Labor letter. Do you think you can use NYA [National Youth Administration] help in the Archive. The last person I saw in Washington was Aubrey Williams [director of NYA] and he practically swore at me for not having asked the NYA in on the folk song business. Would you like me to arrange to see him when I come down this weekend. I would not have wired you about the travel order if I had not received a wire from Mary LaDame [Special Assistant to the Secretary of Labor]. This led me to believe that she wanted action on this appointment. I presume the Department of Labor is dearly concerned, and certainly it is pleasant to have them come to us for material. Please forward me a travel order for the train trip down. I will come Thursday night or Friday morning early and go back Saturday night or Sunday depending on how much there is to do in Washington. At that time I can have Nonie Collett's record duplicated and sent on to her. Elizabeth is much better, but for a while she was quite sick and had to have steady nursing. [ALC][3]

He quickly followed up to Spivacke, in another undated letter, with more information on the negotiations with Columbia, and other labels, as well as his prospects for a radio program:

This past week I have had several conferences with Mr. Wise and Hammond. They are both greatly interested in the bibliography, but there remains one difficulty in beginning serious work—space and facilities for auditioning records. It has been agreed by everyone that this must be done at the factory in Bridgeport, but the O.K. of Mr. [Edward] Wallerstein [President of Columbia], himself, must be obtained before this can be done. In the meantime I have called on the Decca people, who claim they sell more records than any other company in the world, and have found a very swell guy called

Capps [Dave Kapp] in charge of their hillbilly department. He thinks he can arrange for me to go through their material and besides he is going to introduce me properly to Ink Williams, the Negro who grandfathered the so-called race-business. The Musicraft people are interested in our having their material but for the moment they plead poverty. They strike me as a little ignorant, but otherwise good guys, very earnest and sincere, and I think I will do them a couple of favors that the Columbia Company doesn't want anyhow—A Lead Belly album with texts and some Aunt Molly Jackson and bring them around. There is one person in the Victor business who can be a lot of help to me. His name is Frank Walker and it seems that he started the early Gennett hillbilly lists. I want to come down to Washington and go over our Victor material before I see him, however.

Eric Clark seems to be not quite sure of me or else not ready to offer me a traveling lectureship. I urged him to urge you to take one, however, and whether you like it or not, I think it's a good idea. Davidson Taylor has got a big program on American music up his sleeve, in which he wants a couple of spots of folk music a week. He says if the plan goes through he wants me to scout the material up and bring it into local stations once a week. That's a hundred a week and expenses and if it starts at all—he's not sure—it means right away. I'm four hundred dollars in debt waiting for my scholarship and I do like Columbia and as much studying as I have time to do. What do you think? Would the Library give me leave? Poor father seems to be fading away with impatience in Texas. Can't the machine be rushed on to him? Please let me know when you do send it so I can forward a letter of instructions. [ALC]

While involved with other matters in New York, he also wrote to Professor Umble at Goshen College on March 16 about Library business:

I am pleased to hear that the Library duplicate of the Amish record has served you so well. More such records must certainly be made, before any really adequate notion of Amish music can be arrived at. Amish singing technique must, it seems to me, make the task of notating their tunes particularly difficult. Plans for my next summer's field trip are as yet indeterminate but it appears that I shall be somewhere in the Middle West. Perhaps at that time I could do the recording in Iowa you mention. Otherwise I hope arrangements can be made for you to borrow a machine. If that arrangement is made, I should like to see records which are a little more representative than those I made near Goshen:—regular congregational singing with women in the group, women singing some of the tunes, the same tunes sung by persons of different age groups and on different occasions (in order to discover the degree of melodic fixity), the same tunes sung in different types of congregations, in addition to some of the Mennonite tunes themselves in order to point the similarity or difference of the music of the two denominations. Thank you for your kind assurances about my role at Goshen a year ago. [ALC][4]

The following day, March 17, he responded to Paul Hanna at the School of Education, Stanford University:

The Library of Congress has accumulated in its Archive of American Folk Song a large amount of material which would be, I should think, very helpful in preparing the study to which you refer. Unfortunately, however, most of this material is contained on master phonograph records which we have no means of duplicating at present. In lieu of this material, however, I can suggest several references from which you may obtain valuable suggestions. 1) The American Journal of Folk Lore, Volume Iff. 2) The Southern Folklore Quarterly, which has many valuable bibliographic suggestions. 3) The Publications of the Texas Folk Lore Society. 4) The Journal of the Folk Lore Society of the North East. 4 [sic]) The American Songbag, Carl Sandburg. 5) American Ballads and Folk Songs by John A. and Alan Lomax, in which as an appendix you will find a fairly comprehensive bibliography with many references to books and articles on the folk music of different parts of America. 6) Bibliography of American Folk Songs, by Mellinger Henry. 7) Folk Songs of America, Robert W. Gordon, obtainable from the National Service Bureau of the Federal Theatre Project, New York City. I hope that among these references you will find the type of information you need. [ALC][5]

He updated Spivacke on March 21 concerning the recordings he made from the Spirituals to Swing concert at Carnegie Hall a few months earlier:

Enclosed you will find two of the lowest estimates I have been able to get on the dubbing of the Boogie-Woogie Carnegie Hall recordings. I asked for an estimate on the basis of five sets: One for John Hammond, one for the Library, one for the New Masses (if they will pay for it), one for you, and one to be distributed among the singers (as promised). If the New Masses is not interested or not financially able, Eric Clark has expressed a desire for some of the material and we could undoubtedly place others of the records strategically and well. . . . Isn't there any news or have you decided not to write me? [ALC]

Alan had more to report to Spivacke on March 26:

I received your distressful note this morning and feel sorry that I have been so busy. Your notes about the Lead Belly records certainly delighted me, and, since there is so little to my credit these days, I might at least take what's rightfully mine—I did send you the records. Father has written me several encouraging notes about his work lately. I enclose the last one. I am writing him this afternoon to persuade him to investigate one Robert Johnson of Robinsville, Mississippi, on whom Hammond and I are going to do an album soon. Hammond was much delighted by the plans I submitted to him for reediting their old commercials and I think a contract for me will emerge out of this in the next couple of weeks. In the meantime, however, I want to come to Washington and begin work on the Ballad Book, Number II, which I am anxious to get done before the Halpert, Botkin, Seeger, etc. group even begin theirs. I am, however, so broke that I wonder whether I can even get out of town. What has been heard from the revered and highly learned committee on the subject of my grant? I am already, by the by, working full time for the Library again and I thus expect to be able to adjust my leave during June equably. The Writer's Congress has asked me to speak on the subject of folk-lore on June the Fourth. Shall I stay on here until then and finish up a couple of recording jobs and try to complete arrangements with American Record Company or do you wish me to appear on June the First. I suggest the former course.

What have you heard from Mister Frank Walker of Victor? Will it be possible for you to send me franks to cover shipment of Library records back to Washington or do you want me to send them express collect? Shall I get a bargain price on a new recording machine or shall I arrange to have a new cutter and a new microphone installed on our presto? I think, if you can afford it, it might be a good idea to invest in a sixteen inch recorder which would serve all sorts of purposes for us later on and would cut masters for us from the beginning. I shall consult you, of course, before I enter into any contracts with Columbia Phonograph Company. I hope you can get something done about that grant. I still have one course to pay for at New York University. I have one new Ford contracted for on which the success of my summer's trip depends. Thanks for your continual encouragement. [ALC]

Five days later he briefly informed Spivacke,

I'm off to Bridgeport this morning with [John] Hammond. Much news later. [ALC]

On April 8 Spivacke learned of Alan's progress in New York regarding his commercial records research:

There are a number of things of some importance I want to tell you in this letter and I must ask your tolerance for not having written you about them before. First of all, in regard to record albums. Musicraft, a small but very flourishing company that does specialty recording, has just finished an album by Lead Belly—the first genuine album of American folk songs that has yet been done. Hammond assures me that this in no way hurts my relations with American Records [ARC/Columbia]. Second, as you probably have learned from Mr. [Daniel] Wolfert Gamut records wants father to collect an album of material from them on this trip. Gamut is even smaller than Musicraft, but they have done very nice things and they are the subsidiary of one of the best recording studios in town—Reeves, where our acetate is made. Their offer to father is 15% of royalty with no advance. Since none of the big companies, so far as I can learn from Hammond and others, are quite ready to try this, I see no reason why as a sort of trial balloon for everyone concerned this Gamut experiment should not be tried. From the enclosed letter from father, you can see his feeling about the matter and, if he hasn't written you already, I think you might write him directly and personally what you feel should be done.[6]

Third, in regard to the record bibliography. Last week, after days and weeks of stalling around and waiting, I finally got to go out to Bridgeport in Hammond's company. I spent about three hours in the factory and learned the following: a) They have between twenty-four and twenty-five thousand masters there. b) If you pick a record out of a old catalogue that you would like to hear, they have no copy of it for you to play and c) In order to discover whether or not they still have the master from which a pressing could be made they would have to spend five to fifteen minutes running through their complicated, incomplete and disorderly files. d) They do not have anywhere near as complete a set of catalogues as has New York Public. e) They feel that most of the records I would be interested in have already been junked, although as you know that scrapping process has been completely discontinued. f) They are in the process of revising their filing system and think they will be through next year. g) In the meantime they clearly indicate to me and to Hammond they are too busy to bother. I am inclined to agree with them.

The reason I have not sent you any catalogues with marked numbers has been that the more catalogues I have looked at the more I have felt that we should get everything that we can lay our hands on. The output of the commercial companies in the field of folk and semi-folk music has been for the past fifteen years simply amazing. Further I thought at the time I wrote you last that, by going through the records completely could at the one time a) estimate accurately what the companies had already done, b) order our material on the basis of some selective categories (rather than purely by title), c) tell both Hammond, Taylor and Wallerstein what they could further do both on the air and in recording trips. I had established the first couple of hundred cards of a catalogue system, by artist, and expected with NYA help to collate with a title index and all the biographical and geographical material I could dig out of the files. I had also planned to get as much material on sales figures, by year, by type, by content and by singer along the way so that the basis would be laid for a really intelligent study of American taste. My visit to Bridgeport naturally discouraged me a good deal and when I learned that there were as many as 76 active companies producing records in America in the twenties and that at one time their annual output was something like three hundred millions platters a year, I decided that my plan was a little ambitious.

What I plan to do, therefore, is to play through the current catalogues of Decca, Vocalion and Bluebird (if you can arrange a trip to Camden for me later) and supplement this with visits to Hammond's collection and those of other people in the city. Then I'll see what should next be done. If, however, you want to write Wallerstein at once, my opinion is that the commercial recording companies have done a broader and more interesting job of recording American folk music than the folklorists and that every single item of recorded American rural, race, and popular material that they have in their current lists and plan to release in the future should be in our files. Next week I will call on Jack Capps [Kapp] of Decca and try to get an answer from him in regard to placing the Music Division on his mailing list. In addition I shall be ready to ask Musicraft to give me their material—and they have some very fine stuff. I should also like to go to Bloomfield's and see what they have of their former large stock of Paramount releases. As you may know, Paramount was the first big "race" company in the country and since its demise there has never been such another group of "race" recordings. Decca has what's left of their masters—about forty—and I should like, with your permission to consider buying everything Bloomfield's has—if they turn out to have a large stock—for the Library. I should also like to visit Port Washington, Wisconsin, where the records were pressed, next summer and see what they have left.

I learned this afternoon that Downes has definitely bought the Labor Stage show "Evening of Negro Music" for the world's fair. Lead Belly was featured in this show—at my suggestion—and the rest of it stunk—although it did get good reviews. I feel a little sore at Downes for not having at least let me know about this or mentioned me in connection with it and I wonder whether a letter from you might not help. One more thing before I close this long—and what must seem to you—exhausting letter. Miss [Sarah Gertrude] Knott has scheduled her show significantly for the end of April. I wish there was something that we could do about keeping it out of the fair. I am sure there isn't, but I wondered what you thought. . . . P.S. I can now notate simple tunes, sing all intervals at sight and write fair phonetics. [ALC]

About the same time, in an undated letter, he gave Spivacke additional information on his commercial records project:

Enclosed you will find the list of the Vocalion releases which we should acquire for the Archive. Vocalion is the label under which the American Record Company now releases all hill-billy and "race" records, whereas formerly it printed such records under Melotone, Perfect, Oriole, etc. etc., labels. The recordings that we particularly want at this moment are marked with a star. The name of the person in the Victor RCA Corporation who could be particularly helpful is Mr. Frank Walker. He was one of the first people to interest himself in hillbilly recording and can, besides giving me access to the Bluebird and other Victor folk material, tell me many important things about the history of folk song and semi-folk-song on commercial records. I should greatly appreciate it if you could arrange an interview with him for me. In this connection, I have just written Miss Flanders and should hear from her within a few days. At that time I will be able to tell you when it will be possible for me to go to Camden to complete my bibliography. If it is possible for me to audition their records there I will need at least a week and one person to assist me in writing the cards. I have just received a letter from Mr. [Harold] Schmidt of Fisk University and am writing him to invite him to the Library of Congress sometime in June when I shall be there. [And on the back of the letter he added] On second thought, it might be a good idea for you to wait a bit before making your request to Columbia for records. I shall have finished my inspection of their material in a few days. [ALC]

While Spivacke encouraged Alan to continue his collecting and discography, he cautioned him on April 14:

I did not expect that the acquisition of the commercial recordings of folk-music would be a simple matter. But even if certain records are not immediately available, your bibliographies will not be wasted at all. They will serve as necessary want lists at the proper time. Whatever you do, refrain from dumping quantities of records on the Library at the present time. Our present staff cannot cope with it at all—cannot even check the shipments for acknowledgment! We are just now finishing the count of the initial shipment from Columbia. We shall of course welcome gifts from Musicraft, Gamut, etc., and a systematic acquisition of folk-material. But no dumping—please! [ALC]

Alan responded three days later, April 17:

I spent Friday going over the two thousand Paramount records that are still
left in the loft at Bloomfields. As I understand it, it is the only large group of
Paramount pressings left in the country. Out of this group I chose two hundred and twenty five records—some of them, probably not especially significant—but, as the few samples I was able to play indicate, most of them are
fairly important to the understanding of Negro secular music in the United
States. Quite a number are collector's items. Bloomfield's price is .15¢ (fifteen
cents) a record and I, at least, can make them go no lower. They are holding
this group of records for me for a time, but naturally they would like to hear
from you in this regard fairly soon. My talk with Mr. Wolfert the other day
makes it quite clear that he wants to present the Library with the Gamut
recordings and, besides, put us on their review list. He expects to hear from
you in this regard before he actually mails the records. I think their list of
recordings is decidedly worth having in the music division since it includes
only such items as have never before been recorded in the United States. His
final terms for father's work for him were—20% without any advance.

This week I shall run over the Vocalion material and try to look at the
Decca stuff. This, however, will be merely a formality on my part, so far as
the acquisition of material by the Library is concerned. I think it is important
that we have everything they will give us and it is toward this end I shall work
unless I hear from you to the contrary. Hammond, by the way, plans to do an
historical album with Jelly Roll.

I have been thinking lately about summer plans. The three items on my
program that are fairly definite are: 1) The completion of American Ballads
and Folk Songs [the book with his father]—three weeks of straight work. 2)
Visit to Miss [Helen Hartness] Flanders in the early part of the summer [on
a collecting trip]. 3) Visit to the Mt. Pleasant, Michigan, lumberjack-song
authority sometime before the end of July. The deadline on the book has
been set for the end of June—will mean publication by next Christmas. I
should, perhaps, be able to visit Miss Flanders for two weeks beginning the
last week in May, and then return to Washington for two weeks of uninter-
rupted work on the book. That would mean that I could leave Washington
for the West at the end of June. I should like this trip to be more leisurely than
my other trips have been so that I could get somewhat better acquainted
with the communities in which I record songs and besides so that I can make
potential master recordings in every case. What do you think of recording
from this time forward on one side of the record only so that in the case of
master pressings the other side will neither have to be dubbed off or lost?
One thing more—I should like to see a little of the Southwest before I come

back to Washington—first, to poke my nose into the field of cowboy singers and to see what there is to be done in the Mexican field in New Mexico.
Do you think it would be possible for me to spend, say, September in New
Mexico or perhaps return there during the winter, provided we do not decide
that another year of college work might not be amiss. These are some of the
matters I should like to discuss with you soon. Perhaps it would be a good
thing for me to come down to Washington for the folk festival for three days
and see you at that that time. [ALC]

Spivacke liked Alan's plans, but wondered how he could do so much in such a short
period of time, as he wrote on April 22:

Your plans for this summer are wonderful but for the life of me I don't see
how you can possibly do all that in less than a year. You seem to forget, if you
see Miss Flanders, you must do so before July and still you suggest going to
Michigan at almost the same time. [ALC]

Alan had arranged a recording session for Lead Belly with Musicraft on April 1. The subsequent album, *Negro Sinful Tunes,* included "The Bourgeois Blues," which Spivacke particularly enjoyed. As he assured Alan on May 13:

I am always so ready to criticize that I feel that I cannot—must not delay in
complimenting you on your excellent piece of work. We sat up last night until
well past midnight listening to the Lead Belly records. To say that we enjoyed
them would be putting it mildly indeed. The Bourgeois Blues is the finest
song that I have heard in years. Your fears regarding this song are unfounded.
We Americans have a good sense of humor and can take it. Carolyn said that
she always wanted a good description of this town and has at last found it in
Lead Belly's song. . . . All in all though, it is the most successful piece of work
you have yet done. I feel sure that we shall be responsible for the sale of many
albums. [ALC]

While Alan surely enjoyed the praise, he was busy with many other projects, as he
detailed to Spivacke on May 28:

Things are coming down a little too fast for me these days. 1) [John] Hammond definitely assures me that Columbia wants to sign a contract to do
some albums and that, if the revivals of old records prove to be successful, he
wants to do other material actually recorded in the South. He adds, however,
that he does not completely trust me in the matter of Negro material, but
that he'll leave the hill-billy things entirely up to me—he's a very impudent

young lad, indeed. 2) Conversation with Davidson Taylor [of CBS] yesterday, when I was very tired, broke and dirty. He asked me to prepare them an outline for a twenty-five week program for their American School of the Air on American Folk Music and to submit this outline by the end of the week. I am somewhat non-plussed and would like your encouragement and your suggestions. If they like my outline, as I feel sure they will, that will mean they will want me to work for them steadily, more or less until the program is complete—which will mean the end of next year. What do you think? What do you think of my suggesting Charley [Seeger] for the job? Naturally they will eventually acquire a lot more musicologizing than I can offer them, at least for some time to come. Agreeing to do this will also mean that I won't have time to complete the ballad book in June as I had planned. Don't write Dave [Davidson] Taylor or tell anyone but Carolyn about this, please, but give me some advice. I don't want it talked about until its settled one way or the other.

3) The American Writers Congress has asked me to sing at their reception when [Eduard] Benes [former President of Czechoslovakia] is to speak, etc., also at the Folk Lore panel on Sunday. I have until Monday to get Dave Taylor his outline so I think I'll stay over, if that's O.K. with you. In addition I want to complete arrangements for the Columbia album right away. 4) As you probably know by the papers I am to play a banjo for the king and queen next week in a very august assembly of performers. Will Dr. Putnam permit it or not? 5) I have just this afternoon completed my eightieth [eighty] second record for the Library. Aunt Molly [Jackson] 61, Captain Dick Maitland 21. Two very fine and very complete bodies of material, thoroughly documented. Aunt Molly turned out to be a regular gold-mine. You know she has composed some Union songs, using old tunes, but her best stuff turns out to be ancient Baptist hymns. I enclose two recommendations for payment of these two people. They both have certainly earned. Aunt Molly gave me nearly a solid week of her time.

6) Enclosed you will find the bills I have contracted lately for recording materials. If you have received a bill from Reeves, pay it no attention for the moment, because the two sapphires did not prove to be very satisfactory. I am naturally distressed to hear about the decision of the Carnegie Foundation. Wouldn't it be possible for us to get an Allied or a Fairchild with a double turntable. We could probably set up a pretty fair duplicating outfit for $1,500 if we were satisfied to cut all the corners. Couldn't you persuade Mr. Bond to go that far for us and, if we could get somebody to run the machine, just any bright college boy, we could begin to turn out a certain number of duplicates. We could make some sort of arrangement to borrow the Archive's technician to train this person in the fundamentals and he could probably do some quite

nice jobs for us. You know, of course, that the Department of the Interior is doing the duplication for the Fine Arts Committee's trio? Perhaps we could turn our material over to them. The various enclosures speak for themselves. When you write next, will you tell me when you think the Committee will be able to send me my grant? I will forward the Mississippi letter on to father this morning in South Carolina. In the meantime I can see no objection we could possibly make to the WPA making use of the Parchman records, provided that father is consulted and given due credit. [ALC][7]

In his subsequent official report, Alan described his recording sessions in New York City in May:

Captain Dick Maitland, aged 82, of Sailor's Snug Harbor, in two days of singing filled nineteen records with his version of the clipper ship shanties. Not only were his melodies what Joanna Colcord calls "a generation older than most of those in print," but Captain Dick explained in his terse and seaman-like fashion just how each shantey was used aboard ship. Aunt Molly Jackson, formerly of Clay County, Kentucky, and a sort of walking encyclopedia of the oral tradition of her people, recorded her singing biography for the Archive on some sixty-one records. Story led to song and song to story. There are representatives of every type of tune sung in the mountains—English ballads, feud ballads, banjo tunes, fiddle tunes, sacred tunes, love songs, etc., with an exhaustive discussion of each type by Aunt Molly, who can tell stories as well as she can sing.[8]

A pleased Alan wrote a short letter to Mortimer Graves at the American Council of Learned Societies, on June 9, regarding their financial assistance:

I am delighted to accept the grant which you so kindly made me and I shall submit a report on my activities when they have been completed. [ALC][9]

In an undated letter, Alan updated Spivacke about the proposed CBS radio show:

The Columbia Broadcasting Company [CBS] has asked me to supervise their musical program on the American School of the Air during its next season of twenty-four weeks, beginning October 10th and ending the second or third week in May. According to the present plan I am to act as advisor on script, commentator and in some cases singer on this program. The series is designed to reach school children during school hours and I am told it goes to more than 120,000 classrooms across the whole country on their coast-to-coast hook-up. It provides, I feel, at once a rare opportunity for stimulating a general interest in American Folk Song, but also will create a situation in which the Archive of American Folk Song can begin at once to play a vital role in American culture. I might add that it is planned to commission twenty-two of America's leading composers to write brief works especially for presentation over this program. I am naturally delighted at this opportunity to do a creative and at the same time authentic piece of work, and, since I feel that my participation in the program would not injure the future of the Archive but on the contrary enrich it, I feel justified in asking for a certain amount of leave without pay during the season of the broadcast. This leave should not extend over more than two days a week during the actual broadcast and in all likelihood, after a certain routine has been established, the day of the broadcasts, themselves, will prove to be sufficient leave. [ALC]

Working on the radio show, Alan wrote to Davidson Taylor at CBS from Washington on June 16:

It has occurred to me that the outlines I have sent might have seemed a little vague on the score of suggested titles of songs, etc. The reason for this omission was that I wanted to make the outlines as brief as possible, and I saw no particular point in making final or semi-final decisions about the songs until the material for the broadcast was finally decided upon. Naturally, too, the programs were only a selection out of a large group of possible programs, and if there is material in which you are interested which is not included, please let me know. In outlining the two series that I did, I avoided a great deal of contemporary social documentation which someday I hope the songs will be given over the air. As I told you, my experience in collecting has been with poor farmers, workers, etc., in the main. It would perhaps, be interesting to emphasize this contemporary background on the programs and use more social documentation than I first suggested. I should have discussed this problem with you before I left New York, but it had not occurred to me then. I hope to hear from you within the next two or three days. [ALC][10]

He had not given up on a new collecting trip, however, as he wrote on July 17 to Helen Hartness Flanders in Vermont:

I finally received your letter of June 2nd, and in the same mail the issue of the Proceedings of the Vermont Historical Society which contains the article and check list on Vermont folksongs. The publication is of great interest and its scholarly finesse will no doubt be fruitful for other such publications in the future. At the moment, I can see no obstacles in the way of my visiting Vermont in September. The trip, if your check list is any indication of the available material, will not only result in important additions to the Archive collection but a most interesting field experience for myself. I look forward to the prospect of collaboration with you with great pleasure. [N-JB][11]

Also on July 17 he updated Earl Beck on another possible trip to Michigan:

I have delayed this long in writing you again because I hoped up to the last minute that I would be able to come to Michigan as I had planned. Work at the Library will probably keep me in Washington until the end of August, and by then I presume you will be away from Michigan on your vacation. The material which you can make available to the Archive will certainly be among the most important collections in the country and I still look forward with great eagerness to collaborating with you in putting the voices of your old lumber jacks on permanent recordings. In this regard, if you can tell me when you plan to return to Mount Pleasant, I feel sure that John A. Lomax or myself will be able to visit you at some time in the coming fall. I did not know before a few days ago that you and my father are old friends and if I am not able to come myself, perhaps his coming would mean a very pleasant get-together. He has asked me to send you his very best regards and to ask you whether you would give him permission to use the version of "Little Brown Bulls," which I recorded last summer, in his forthcoming book *American Ballads and Folksongs, No. 2*. I look forward to hearing from you again. Please accept my apologies for such a long delay in replying to your last letter. [ALC]

Alan mailed off a brief response to David Spaziani in Hartford, Connecticut, on July 18:

Thank you for your postal. It is a great pleasure to know that there are people interested in cowboy songs at Hartford, and I certainly think that someday there will be such a society as you suggest. In fact, it sounds like a very good idea. [ALC][12]

On August 16 he finally informed Spivacke of his current activities:

Enclosed is my year's report. I finally wrote it out yesterday after two or three days of preparation and of trying to get it done. If I have not done it before, it has been because it literally wasn't in me to do. I have attempted it several times, but it was not until yesterday after a few days relaxation in the sun, that I could manage it. As this goes in the mail, I shall return to Detroit and see what has been done about finding the machine. I'll write you again before I sleep. P.S. There is space for one name I couldn't recall on the top of page 14. It can be found in the Archive file under Galax. [ALC]

While in Washington for the summer, Alan contacted Davidson Taylor at CBS on August 17:

In writing a request this morning for a regular schedule of leave without pay, so that I can work on the folk music series, it occurred to me that I have as yet no contract with Columbia. Knowing nothing whatsoever about such matters, I must present the problem to you as a friend. In engaging myself to work on the program, I have to allow the Library to allocate my pay for the time I take official leave without pay elsewhere. In this way I involve myself in the risk of a lowered salary in case the program for some reason does not turn out to everyone's satisfaction. What about a guarantee of some sort. Please don't feel that I am dissatisfied or any thing of the sort. It is merely a desire on my part to have everything perfectly clear between us before I go ahead with my work. Perhaps you will cast your eye over the progress of the syllabus, keeping in mind the fact that we want as many songs squeezed in as we can possibly manage. [ALC]

Alan was eager to prepare for his CBS radio series, *Folk Music of America*, part of Columbia's American School of the Air, designed for children, to be aired each Tuesday morning. As he informed Leon Levine, the series assistant director, on August 17:

There is one matter I failed to attend to while I was at work on the syllabus. At the bottom of each page where a song is reproduced, there should be mention of the source from which the song was taken. Just to make sure that you will have this material and so that it can be easily inserted, I will list the songs and their accompanying sources. [Here follows a list of sixteen songs and their printed sources.] This indication of source is our obligation to Joanna Colcord and John A. Lomax who own the title to these songs. Please let me know at once if I can be of further assistance. Your Mr. Wiebe was a pleasure to work with. [CBS]

He kept up with Library business, for example to Beal Taylor in Medina, Texas, August 21:

Both Doctor Spivacke and John A. Lomax are out of town and I am therefore replying to your letter of the 11th. The records which you made for the Archive collection are among the most interesting renditions of cowboy songs that we have acquired. We should be delighted to send you copies of everything you sang for us at once, but at the moment, we have no facilities for duplication of these records in the Library of Congress. In the next three or four weeks, however, I shall endeavor to have some duplications made for you and they will be sent to you free of charge because of the valuable service you have rendered the Division. [ALC]

On August 24 he contacted Richard Allen at Indiana University:

It has been impossible for me to reply to your letter sooner. I have been busy for the last six weeks with a new Lomax ballad book and all official business has been let slip. Doctor Spivacke and I have both been at work on plans for a folklore archive. We feel that in a month or so there will be definite news for you. In the meantime, I deeply appreciate your consideration of me and your concern about the Archive. Doctor [Stith] Thompson's interest will certainly be invaluable in bringing this project to its realization. Perhaps you will be interested to learn that The Columbia Broadcasting System has put me in charge of their music program of the American School of the Air for next year. The program is, as you know, aimed at stimulating interest of children in basic subjects of the school curriculum and my part of the series will consist of very simple and straightforward presentations of American folk music and folklore. I hope you will be able to listen in and give me the benefit of your expert criticism and experience. Please give my very best regards to Doctor and Mrs. Thompson. [ALC]

Probably in late August, he wrote an undated letter to Marjorie Sanborn at the CBS Educational Department, about songs for his upcoming radio programs:

My best address for now will be Library of Congress, Washington, D.C. I can give you a weekend address later on. The reason that my reply to your letter has been delayed is that it had to [be] forwarded to me.

The Chisholm Trail—P[age]. Cowboy Songs
Santa Anna—This Singing Country (to be published this winter)
Ox Driving Song—This Singing Country—
Springfield Mountain—P. Cowboy Songs
Shoot the Buffalo—p. 296, American Ballads and Folk Songs
I Married Me a Wife—This Singing Country
Samson—This Singing Country
The Cowboy's Lament—p. Cowboy Songs
Tamp 'em Up Solid—p. 17, American Ballads and Folk Songs
The Boll Weevil—112, American Ballads and Folk Songs

You will notice a couple of changes of title here. Please let them stand. Pagination for *This Singing Country* is impossible.

Before I left New York Mr. Levine assured me that there would be no songs cut out of the manual copy unless I was consulted. I note that four songs have been omitted from the list—*Lolly-too-dum* from the program entitled Courting Songs; *Joe Clark* from the program entitled *Square Dances*; *The Lowdown Lonesome Low* from Sailor's Songs; The Grey Goose from *Negro Gang Songs*. I am absolutely opposed to the elimination of these songs from the booklet and I hope that it has been simply a piece of carelessness on someone's part that they were not included. Please bring this matter to Mr. Levine's attention at once and ask him to write me in regard to it. *Lolly too dum* comes from *This Singing Country* as does *The Lowdown Lonesome Low, Joe Clark*, page 277, American Ballads and Folk Songs; *The Grey Goose*, page 242, American Ballads and Folk Songs. The fourth song was "The Boston Come-all Ye" from Joanna Colcord's "Songs of American Sailormen" page 188. Miss Colcord can be reached at The Russell Sage Foundation New York City. She, however, does not own the copyright on the songs in this book. It belongs to W. W. Norton, whom she suggested I contact myself. Mr. Levine felt that your office should handle the matter. In writing Norton you can tell them that Miss Colcord was delighted at the prospect of her material on The American School of the Air. Please let me know your final decision about the four songs I discussed above. [ALC][13]

He continued with his correspondence to Paul Brewster at the University of Missouri on September 2:

I believe that the texts of the "Two Sisters" which we have in the Archive will not show important differences from those you have already assembled. There are, however, one or two folk tale versions of the story from the West Indies that may be of interest to you. The difficulty here is that the texts of these stories have not yet been transcribed from the records, but if you believe that this material will be useful to you, let me know and I shall attempt within the next few months to have it transcribed. I can make no promises about this. With very best wishes for the success of your project. [ALC][14]

Alan continually mixed his fascination with collecting in the field and the commercial recordings of hillbilly, cowboy, and African American songs. In continuing to compile lists of commercially recorded folk songs, Alan wrote to R. P. Wetherald at RCA Victor on September 8, as he began to develop plans for a new book of political/labor/protest songs:

Enclosed you will find the lists which I promised to send you some time ago. This addition to the records that you have sent the Archive of American Folk Song will largely complete the collection of folk and semi-folk recordings from Victor. I presume that a more careful study of the records during the next two or three years will reveal a few minor gaps in this collection, but for the moment, will you accept my very deep appreciation for this valuable contribution to American folk song? I have not written you further about the matters we discussed last a few days ago, because I have been waiting to hear from you in respect to my father's offer. I have, however, gone through the

Bluebird and Victor records which we have here and am more than delighted with the material I have at hand. Despite what anyone may say the Golden Leaf Jubilee Quartette is one of the most remarkable singing organizations in America. I should like to know what have been the results of your correspondence with my father.

I am in the process of preparation of a collection of songs which have come out of the past five or ten years of depression. I have wished to include four or five numbers in the Bluebird catalog. They are as follows: *Weaver's Life* sung by the Dickson [Dixon] Brothers, (Bluebird B7802A); *Project Highway* sung by Sonnyboy [Sonny Boy] Williamson (Bluebird B7302); *Insurance Man Blues* sung by Sonnyboy Williamson (Bluebird B8034); *Down and Out Blues* sung by Uncle Dave Makin [Macon] (Bluebird B7350B); *Welfare Blues* sung by Speckled Red, (Bluebird B8069A); *C.C.C. Blues* sung by Washboard Sam and his Washboard Band, (Bluebird B7993B). Would it be possible for you to obtain for me the addresses of these singers so that I can ask each one his story of the origin of the song along with a brief biography? I am sure you realize that the use of these songs in book form will help the sale of the records. [ALC]

Also on September 8 he wrote a message to his father:

A small note of inquiry only—a cousin of Ben Robinson's called me yesterday to ask whether you had received the book of old songs by Elija Owens which Ben has already sent you. Ben has not received notification that this book has come, and would like to know about it. If you have not received it write him and let me know, too, so that I can run it down here either at Hyatsville or at the Library address. Not much news from me except that I am very busy. I will be in New York Monday, Tuesday and Wednesday for the International Congress of Musicologists. These appearances are on the cuff; the Library pays my way. [ALC]

In a letter to Stanton H. King on September 14, Alan continued to pursue the Library's song collecting:

Evidently I did not make clear in my first letter to you exactly what the Music Division wants. We are making a collection of authentic renditions of American folk songs on records, and in process of this work we send portable recording equipment into the field, visit authentic singers and record the old songs they know first hand. I felt, perhaps, that you were a chantey singer, yourself, or that you might know some individuals who were. In that case, a trip to Charlestown might be arranged and in that way the old songs might be set down accurately in a way that is impossible to achieve in print. What is important here, of course, is not the voice of the singer, but the way he renders his material. I should like to know your reaction to this proposal. [ALC][15]

Alan's busy schedule at first seemed to postpone his visit to Vermont to meet with Helen Hartness Flanders, as he informed her on September 14:

Your telegram reached me after some delay, since I was in New York when it came to Washington. I then had to return to Washington to consult with Dr. Spivacke before I could make any reply. I certainly hope that the dates I suggested will be possible for you, since I have been much concerned by having to break my promise to you and have devoted considerable time to making this room for the trip on my busy fall schedule. I shall not be able to leave my desk before the tenth of October and from that time until the 1st of November I shall be scuttling back and forth to New York. Perhaps if it is impossible for you to be free to go with me in November, I can make an attempt on my own for a few days to visit persons whose addresses you can leave for me. At any rate, please let me know how your plans fit in with mine and if the above dates are impossible for you, perhaps I can think of another way out. In regard to duplication of your cylinders, you already know how much the Library appreciates your generous offer. At present there is no equipment in Washington adequate to the job. We do, however, expect to arrange for such a setup within a few months, two months or three at the most, I hope. As soon as we have made the necessary arrangements for equipment, I will notify you at once. In the meantime, I shall hold off any final decisions in regard to my schedule for the next six weeks until I hear from you. [N-JB]

He followed up to Wetherald on September 15, discussing future projects as well as his upcoming CBS radio show:

Too many people seem to have been on their vacations the last two weeks. I understood that Father had written you and received an answer in Niagara Falls where he last was. He wrote me that in reply to your original offer he had made a counter-reply and was prepared to stand firm on that ground. Did you ever receive a letter from him asking two cents a record for editing the albums? If not, I suggest that you write him again at 1618 Avenue Y, Lubbock, Texas. I did not know where he was myself for nearly ten days and he did not stop in Washington on his way to Texas.

It has occurred to me that one possible effect of the albums of reissued records that we discussed might be to legitimize further recording of this sort in the eyes of the Union. By the time you have come to some understanding with Mr. Walker and the company I shall have made further progress in my study of material already in the Archive. The Columbia Broadcasting System has no objection to my recording and working with Victor, and as soon as it is convenient I will be happy to consider whatever offers you may care to make. It will be six weeks, however, before I will have any time outside of the work I have already on my schedule. [ALC][16]

Always involved with the details of his upcoming radio show, Alan complained to Leon Levine, the Assistant Director of the CBS Department of Education, on September 14:

Having read the manual over at more leisure, I am somewhat annoyed at a lot of changes that have been made, seemingly without any particular rhyme or reason throughout the material. The most important changes were made in the arrangement of the program—its sequence, and I want now to register my objections to them.

The series, logically—and there is logic in the ordering of this material as well as any other—should develop as follows: 1) Preview, 2) Cowboy Songs, 3) C[ountry] S[ongs], 4) Gold Rush Songs, 5) Sea Shanties, 6) Forecastle Ballads, 7) Lumberjack songs, 8) Nonsense and Animal Songs, 9) Courting Songs, 10) Square Dances, 11) Play Parties and Negro Reels, 12) Love Songs, 13) British Ballads in America I, 14) British Ballads in America II, 15) Negro Spirituals, 16) Negro Work Songs, 17) Railroad Work Songs, Negro, 18) Railroad Ballads, 19) Hobo and Jailhouse Songs, 20) Outlaw Ballads, 21) Poor Farmer Songs, 22) Blues (Not, for sweet Mary's sake—"Blues" songs). It is regrettable, to say the least, that you failed to send me proof of the booklet. I write this letter in hopes that something may have delayed the appearance of the booklet and there may still be opportunity to make these important revisions. Let me hear from you and send this letter on to Mr. [Sterling] Fisher [Director of the CBS Department of Education] for his information. [CBS][17]

On September 18, he sent a short, positive message to Helen Hartnett Flanders:

Let us pray that the rural roads will still be passable and set our time together from the 3rd to the 13th of November. I can be in Springfield the night of the second and we can make a respectably early start on the morning of the 3rd. If everything does not work out as fast as we hope, I can come back again later on. I am sure there is much more than can ever be done in ten days. When the time draws nigh, it might be of advantage for you to send me a rough itinerary. I have two or three local contacts of my own buried in my files which I should like to work in if possible. I am sorry that the contests did not yield expected results. In some ways the balladist fights a losing battle against changing cultural attitudes. In the end, though, what we want will win. [N-JB]

Also on September 18, he informed Nelson Sprackling in New York regarding song permissions:

My father is in Texas. I am forwarding your letter to him, but in the meantime I am sending you the answer that I am sure he will agree with me on. "Whiskey Johnny" in our book is quoted from Carl Sandburg's "American Songbag" and we cannot, therefore, give you permission to reproduce it. This permission will have to be obtained from Mr. Sandburg, himself. I quite understand your situation and wish that I could help. Captain Dick [Maitland] mentioned you to me when I saw him in New York in May. He was amazed at your ability to get the old tunes down correctly. I look forward to seeing your book. In the meantime, if you locate other authentic shantey singers, I would appreciate your letting me know about them. The Archive of American Folk Song which we are building here in the Library of Congress is attempting to accumulate recordings of all Americana folk-songs, authentically sung. [ALC][18]

He continued to assist Paul Brewster in Missouri, in a short note on September 25:

I will try to arrange for transcription of the folktale version of the *Two Sisters* sometime this fall. I will also make a search in recent library acquisitions for possible variants of the ballad which I had not before found. [ALC]

On September 26 Alan corresponded with Cornel Lengyel, a poet and music critic, who was connected with the WPA (Work Projects Administration) Music Project in San Francisco:

I want to express to you my admiration for the excellent work that your project has done in the preparation of the first two volumes of History of Music in San Francisco Series. Not only will these books prove to be valuable in reference work but they will besides, make good reading for a long time to come. I should be very grateful if the Archive of American Folk Songs were put on your mailing list, and if it were possible for you to supply it with the two volumes already published.

     I hope that the series will be continued and that at some point an entire volume might be devoted to personalities of the persons who composed the miners ballads. There certainly must be more background material available than you were able to include in these two volumes. Sidney Robertson, who is recording songs for the WPA under our sponsorship, tells me that she has already accumulated a good deal of this kind of material: a joint publication might be most profitable. On November 14 I am presenting a program on Songs of the Gold Rush Period on the American School of the Air for CBS. The songs to be used are mostly those found in Put's Songsters. Is there anything known about the person who compiled songsters under his pseudonym? Was he author himself or merely compiler? Was he a singer or merely some employee of Appleton Company? Any information you can supply me on this mysterious individual I should deeply appreciate. [ALC]

He was naturally nervous following his inaugural radio program, as he informed Spivacke on October 2 (there was a preview broadcast on October 1, while the first show, "Preview of Song," was officially aired on October 10):

I'd like to hear your verdict on the first performance. Personally I feel much relieved that it's over and much surer about going ahead with subsequent performances. On my arrival I was given a thorough raking over the coals by Levine and Fineschriber who evidently felt it was time to take me down a notch. I bore this with calm and good humor, although they were not entirely honest or just in what they said. My relationship with them is completely smooth now and I'm working on the first scripts with Fineschriber. Unless you need me urgently, I think I'd better stay here and rehearse and write steadily until after the tenth. I really need a week to get my soul set for the first show. After that it'll be easy. Please forward my mail at once to Hotel Albert, 64 University Place, NYC and special delivery my pay-check—which the disbursing office failed to do after having promised me to. If you need the report before the tenth, let me know. Otherwise I'd rather ruminate in peace on radio. I've discussed publicity with the proper department and I'd like to make the Times, etc. Possibly you could write [Olin] Downes? Suggest other names to me of writers who might be interested. May I express my gratitude for this opportunity you have helped me to. I'm going to have a marvelous time at it. [ALC]

Alan shot another letter to Earl Beck on October 4, regarding his radio show and demonstrating his concern about details:

I am preparing a series of non-commercial broadcasts on American folk music for the Columbia Broadcasting System's American School of the Air. One of the programs will be devoted to songs and ballads of lumbermen. [Franz] Rickaby, in his book, "Ballads and Songs of the Shanty-Boy," writes of

Billy Allen. Can you tell me if there has been anything further written about him, and if the origin of *The Little Brown Bulls* is definitely known? Are there any biographies, diaries, or stories about lumberjacks that would contain more than straight informational material about the process of lumbering and would give more about the men and their recreations? [ALC][19]

Despite his busy schedule, he had not given up on a trip to Vermont, as he informed Flanders on October 12:

It is difficult for me to tell you how much I appreciate your continued gener-ous anxiety to share the folk music of Vermont with the Archive of American Folk Song and the rest of the country. Your letters are fine examples of what the attitude of most workers in this field should become. I assume that it would be wise to follow your suggestion and postpone my trip until the mid-dle of next May when the roads will be more open and your list of contacts a bit more certain. In case the itinerary is already set I can, of course, still plan to come. Keep me informed about this, please. Your survey is, at the same time, ambitiously and simply planned. It should eventually be very fruitful. We, at the Library, will be glad to help in any way we can. By the time we will be ready to make duplicates of Vermont recordings, say within nine months or a year, and we may have equipment of our own. It would, therefore, be fruitless now to try to make any estimate on the cost of the set of records. Your interest in the traveling libraries is a sample of your unusually generous spirit. [N-JB]

He followed on October 13 to E. C. Beck in Michigan:

I am very grateful for your generosity and interest in my work. I shall write Mr. George Lutman at once and try to get a look at his reminiscences. [Stew-art H.] Holbrook's book [*Holy Old Mackinaw*] I find rather repetitious and somewhat lacking in regional understanding, although, of course, it is the best piece of work in the field. I would like a lot more Lumber Jack and less Hol-brook per page. A book of life histories and stories transcribed from the old lumber jacks that you know, would not only be a valuable contribution, but a commercial success. Time was too short for me to record any of Perry Allan's, although, of course, I realized that he had a great deal of material. I am still concerned with getting a machine out to Michigan to visit you within the next nine months, in the meantime, many thanks, and very best regards. [ALC]

The same day, October 13, he did indeed write to George Lutman in Traverse City, Michigan:

Dr. E. C. Beck of Central State Teachers College, has written me enthusiastically about your manuscript of reminiscences. I have collected a large number of Lumber Jack songs and I have been reading everything I could find about the "Good old days." One of the things I looked for but have not found, is the book of just the sort Dr. Beck has told me you have written.

Would you consider lending me your manuscript for two or three weeks for my own pleasure and information? I could at least give you some fairly good advice at the end of that time, as to how it might be prepared for publication since I have some experience in that field. Perusal of a book of this sort would make me feel much more sure of my ground in speaking to the school children of America about Lumber Jack life and songs, as I shall in the month of November. I am talking about old-time songs over the air for the Columbia Broadcasting System every Tuesday morning on a program called the American School of the Air and one of my subjects is The Songs and Ballads of the Lumberjack. You can feel perfectly sure that the manuscript will not only be handled with the greatest of care, if you send it to me, but will also not be used in any other way unless you yourself desired it. I should simply like to read the biography of a real old-time lumber man to sort of get the feel of the thing. As you know, most of the books on this subject are written by outsiders. At any rate, I should like to hear from you and if possible, when I come to Michigan next to visit you with my recording machine. In the expectation of an early reply. [ALC]

With his radio show on his mind, Alan sent a request to Julius Mattfeld at CBS on October 13:

I am under the impression that you still have a number of my music manuscripts, if so, please mail them to Ruth Crawford [Seeger], 9609 Fairway Avenue, Silver Spring, Maryland, as soon as possible. If not, drop her a note saying so. I think I am going to be in New York, or near New York, most of next week, so I can straighten out with you the rest of our problems at that time. Charles Seeger is going to have his scores microfilmed and sent to you soon. Ruth Crawford and I are going to decide about her place on the program today and I am on the track of some possible scores for the symphonic end of the program. [ALC][20]

On October 15, he wrote briefly to Philip King at the Maritime Commission in Washington, D.C.:

I wrote your father some time ago asking whether he could still sing shanty. He apologetically disclaimed any ability to sing, but suggested that I write you. I am looking for a single man or group who sing shanty in the old time "not glee club" way. Have you any suggestions? [ALC]

On October 18, following Beck's suggestion, he sent letters to Lewis Torrent, Baddy Miles, and Bill Duchaine in Michigan:

Some time ago, I wrote my good friend, Dr. Beck, of Mount Pleasant, Michigan, asking him for material on old-time lumberjacks in Michigan—character sketches, biographies, autobiographies, descriptive material, anecdotes. He gave me your name and said that you might have such material and would be willing to lend it to me for the purposes of my study. Another [thing] I would like to know, is the story of the origin of the Little Brown Bull chantey or lumberjack ballad. I am also particularly interested in knowing what songs were popular among the lumberjacks in Michigan. How, where, and when they were sung. The Library of Congress is making a collection of lumberjack songs and I would appreciate your cooperation. [ALC]

Still planning a trip to Vermont, Alan wrote a memo, apparently to Spivacke, on October 23:

As you know, Miss Helen Hartness Flanders has been planning for sometime to sponsor a Library recording trip in Vermont. She has gone to a great deal of trouble to arrange an itinerary for me between the 3rd and 5th of November (see correspondence file for this trip). I suggest that a new recording machine be purchased and since the time is too short to look into another model, perhaps a Presto portable with a one B cutter and a lever mechanism for lowering the needle would be advisable. I shall be in New York until it is time for me to leave for Vermont and will be glad to assist in the purchase of the machine at the Presto factory. I recommend further the purchase of 400 green seal Presto recording blanks and 6 sapphire cutting needles. The blanks will be necessary for the field trip and should also suffice for our duplication work for the next two or three months. [ALC]

Three days later, October 26, he informed Spivacke of his travel plans:

The enclosed letter from Mrs. Flanders indicates that she is at last ready for the Archive to send its recording machine to Vermont. Since we have discussed the desirability of this trip at length I will at this point merely discuss the details of the trip. (One) I can be in Springfield, as requested, on the morning of November 3, and be free to work with Mrs. Flanders until the 13th, at which time I must be back in New York City. (11 days) (Two) I shall use my own car for travel and for carrying the recording equipment, and should not imagine that the mileage for the trip should total more than fifteen-hundred miles, including the distance between New York and Washington. (Three) I am sorry to inform you that both the machines which I might have expected to be able to borrow are not free for this period. Miss Barnacle's machine is in use, and Mr. [Herbert] Halpert informs me that the only way to get the loan of his recording machine is for you to make a request direct to Colonel Summerville. Rental of a machine for nine days is out of the question because of the expense involved and I should therefore recommend that a new machine be purchased for the Archive, preferably equipped with a two speed turn-table motor and a one-b cutting head.

Jean Evans[21] will hand to you, next week, Miss Corse's latest letter about the Florida folk-song work. Her only additional request was for the loan of our BC-AC Genemotor for use in recording the songs of the fishing fleet en scene. The Rickard records are to be found in boxes numbered 2589 and 2728. They were made in Kingsville, Texas, and I think they will be found at the beginning of the series. It might be a wise idea to stall a little bit and find out from father what records were promised Mr. Rickard, although there may be so few as to make this not of great importance. (Father will write airmail.) I have had great trouble in locating a person to sing shanties for my next CBS program. I think, however, that I shall be able to put together an annual report tomorrow and have it on your desk by Saturday morning. I can be reached here until next Wednesday morning, after which time my mail should be addressed c/o Helen Hartness Flanders, Smiley Manse, Springfield, Vermont. P.S. Sidney Robertson has made a set of copies of her Gold-Rush records which were expressed to me some days ago, care of the library. Please rush them along, express-collect, care of the Hotel Albert as soon as they arrive, because they will contribute greatly to the success of my next performance. [ALC]

In an undated letter, probably in late October, he updated Spivacke from New York:

Here's the annual report, to be cut if you like. You might ask Charley [Seeger] to look over the Arts Committee portions of it, if you feel at all uncertain about details. Two things only: *Please* that Miss Rogers should special my salary on to me c/o Feinschrieber, CBS, along with mail. Keep me in touch per Mrs. H. H. Flanders, Smiley Manse, Springfield, Vt. My address Tuesday afternoon, night, Wednesday morning is c/o William Appleby-Robinson, Cornwall, N.Y. He has a phone. [ALC]

He tried to keep Spivacke up to date, as in this memo on November 16, partly about his trip to Vermont:

As you know, Dr. Ivan Walton of the University of Michigan assisted me materially during my Michigan trip in 1938. At that time I promised him duplicates of records which he assisted me in collecting and you approved the recommendation. On his recent visit to the Archive he picked out the records which he wished to have, to the number of forty. I should like to recommend that these records be duplicated and sent to him as soon as may be. My ten day trip to Vermont resulted in 76 twelve inch acetate records of excellent quality. I should like to recommend that we make a duplicate set of these records for Mrs. Flanders. She plans, by the way, to have certain of these records sent out in the Vermont State Traveling Library which goes to country schools. [ALC]

Alan briefly connected with his father on November 17:

I've got to get proof that the Darby Ram with the "Didn't he ramble" refrain is a folk song and not written. Of course I know that the verse is part of an old English song but I do not know about the refrain. Will you look through your files to see what you can find on this? If you find a version with the given refrain please mail me the ms air mail, special delivery. Let me know as soon as you possibly can. [ALC]

He again contacted R. P. Wetherald at RCA Victor on November 20:

Father has written me that you two have at last reached an agreement. I shall make the suggested selections of records within the next month and send you the list so that you can ship them to him. But I would first like to have a look at the other records that I picked out of the catalogue. If you can get them to me sometime soon we can start the ball rolling for father. Besides, I would certainly find a few items in the group to include in my bibliography which I must complete very shortly. [ALC]

Also on November 20 he briefly replied to Sheldon Dick's recent letter:

Your letter reached me just as I was going out of town for a few weeks. I will be able to give it my full attention when I return on the 22nd. In the mean time, thank you for letter and the enclosures. [ALC][22]

The following day he wrote to Edward Jennings in Pawlet, Vermont:

Your letter comes most opportunely in one way and in another not. I have just returned from a two week recording trip in Vermont and the letter which was to bring your address to me reached me after I returned. I made one attempt to find you in Bennington but failed so gave up hope. I still remember after two years your remarkable records of spirituals and I welcome your generous offer to the archive from the bottom of my heart. We now have facilities for duplicating records so can bring your spirituals into the archive at no cost to yourself with the benefit of the best possible acetate recording. Please let me know when you can come. My days here at the library are from Wednesday through Saturday of each week. Another matter which I am anxious to discuss with you is the possibility of your cooperating with Professor Harold Thompson of the New York State Teachers College, Helen Harkness Flanders of the Vermont Archive of Folk Song, and the Library of Congress in extending the collecting of New England folk songs on records. The library will be able to furnish discs and needles, Miss Flanders mileage for the car, and I think we can get a machine from someplace. We all thought of you as the best worker in that region and when you come down I hope I can play you enough material to interest you, if you are not already interested, in this significant and important undertaking. [ALC][23]

Alan thanked Flanders on November 22 for her recent cordial assistance:

I deeply appreciate your interest in my radio programs and I'm glad you enjoyed the last one. CBS has informed me that they will not be able to use any piano scores on the programs but I still plan to sing The Frenchman's Ball at some point before the series is over. Mr. [Elmer] George is going to sing on the next program. I hope you will be able to listen in. I want to thank you again for your hospitality. I enjoyed staying in your home and I shall remember that period in Vermont as a high spot. [N-JB]

He was continually catching up with his office work, as in this correspondence with David P. Bennett in Chapel Hill, North Carolina, on November 25:

Mr. [Bascom Lamar] Lunsford's[24] records cannot be used without his permission, so a preliminary step in making the material available to you would be a letter from Mr. Lunsford giving you permission to use his material. At present we have no duplication facilities in the Library of Congress. This means that we cannot make records available to you unless they are duplicated by a commercial recording company outside the Library. The average price for a twelve-inch record is between $1.25 and $1.50.

I regret that I am unable to send you a check list of the North Carolina material that we have, but a lack of secretarial assistance in my division makes it impossible. I shall try to prepare a provisional list within the net two weeks, meanwhile I shall await the results of your negotiations with Mr. Lunsford. His songs form the largest single unit of North Carolina material in the Archives. Other material has been recorded by Herbert Halpert, Federal Writers' Project of the W.P.A., New York City, by John A. Lomax, through the courtesy of Doctor Frank C. Brown, and by Mrs. Sidney Robertson, Federal Music Project of the W.P.A., San Francisco, California. I suggest that you write Mr. Halpert, Doctor Brown and Mrs. Robertson for their permission to use the material in the Archives. We have a total of 145 records made in the mountains of North Carolina. This will amount to about 400 titles of separate items. I shall be glad to hear from you after you have got in touch with these various collectors. [ALC]

On November 29 he again reported on the Vermont trip to Spivacke:

Last summer Mrs. Helen Hartness Flanders of the Vermont Folk Song Archive was in Washington. At that time she offered (1) to allow the Archive of American Folk Song to duplicate her cylinder recordings of Vermont folk songs and (2) to assist the library in recording on discs material available to her in Vermont. In return for this Dr. Spivacke and myself both promised that the Vermont Folk Song Archive would be presented with duplicates of all material so recorded. In a field trip authorized by the library from November 3 to November 14 I made, with Miss Flanders' assistance seventy-six recordings of Vermont folk songs. I recommend that she be furnished with a set of duplicates of these recordings in return for her great services to the Archive of American Folk Song and in expectation of further collaborative work. [ALC]

He followed with a message to Spivacke that same day:

I wish to recommend that the Department of Interior Radio Broadcasting Division duplicate for current work in the Archive of American Folk Song [blank] archive discs. Two of these are from the recent Vermont recording trip and since Miss Flanders expects (see accompanying memo) duplicates of this material, I recommend that double duplicates be made for these two records. The total number of blanks requested will be [blank] and this number is available from the stock left over from the Vermont recording trip. [ALC]

Also on November 29, Alan contacted Roy Mitchell at the International House in New York:

You and the Consort must both forgive me for having neglected your letter for so long. This has been a case of unwillful neglect on my part because I am delighted at the prospect of working with you. I shall today send a recommendation down to Dr. Spivacke suggesting that the duplicates you have asked for be sent you when proper arrangements have been made and that we work out some cooperative recording project soon. Something should come of this very soon, I think. I heard you on the Pursuit of Happiness program last Sunday and was doubly delighted. First, because the stuff was so good, and second, because I had a hand in recommending you to CBS. I hereby take my bow and pass it on to you. [ALC]

About a week later, December 7, he connected with Sheldon Dick in New York:

I have sent the recording "There Are Mean Things Happening in this Land" under separate cover. It should reach you in a day or two. "Silicosis is Killing Me" as sung by Pinewood Tom [Josh White] is on a Perfect recording, number 6-05-51 (18733). I am very much interested in this film which you are making. Is it on silicosis or on industrial disease in general? I would appreciate anything you wish to tell me about it. [ALC]

Always concerned about his sister Bess, he wrote on her behalf to Dean Manning of Bryn Mawr College on December 9:

This letter will serve to add my voice in behalf of my sister Bess Lomax's vacation plans. (1) My father is quite old and really needs to see Bess over the vacation. It would be a terrible deprivation to him if she could not go to him. (2) On the other hand, there is no one else available who can sing with me on my American School of the Air program on January 2. The songs to be sung are duets and in order to give the children an idea of how these were sung early in the history of this country it will be necessary to have a girl's voice. My sister and I are accustomed to singing these songs together. Without her the program will be only half as valuable as otherwise.

Since this program is agreed on as being of no little educational importance, and since you undoubtedly realize my sister is an earnest, extremely sincere person, I hope you can cooperate by making as light as possible whatever regular penalties her cuts would entail. She is willing to return to Bryn Mawr after the 2nd and make up for the hours she will have lost before

Christmas. The whole family will appreciate your help in this situation. [ALC]

Also on December 9, Alan responded to Edward Jennings in Vermont:

I know your spiritual recordings are valuable material. We are faced with this problem at the moment: We cannot make pressings. We can, however, make you duplicates of your records on aluminum which would stand up under a great deal of playing. When the records are finally pressed, if ever, we would certainly furnish you with a set of pressings. I don't know what you mean by *hard* records. I hope you mean aluminum. Miss Flanders has offered to pay mileage for a month's recording in Vermont and I have taken up with Dr. Charles Seeger, Assistant Director of the Music Project and Chairman of the Folk Arts Committee of WPA, the matter of compensating you for such time as you might spend in the field recording. This might possibly be on the WPA music project. You will hear from him in this regard. In the mean time I will inform Miss Flanders and Mr. [Harold] Thompson of what has been done so far. [ALC]

In a short letter to Frank Frazier of the J.B. Lippincott Company, December 15, he thanked him for sending a new book:

Mr. Harold Thompson is one of the most scholarly and at the same time most fertile figure in American folk lore. His rich and salty compendium of New York lore is a testament to a rich man in a rich state. I shall try to place a review of the book in some periodical. Thank you for a delightful addition to my library. [ALC][25]

Preparing for the holiday season, on December 15 Alan requested a number of records from the Columbia Recording Company. (He sent a shorter request to RCA Victor the same day, with a few records to the same people, as well as to Roy Harris.) The list seemingly indicates his taste in recent commercial records:

I would like to order the following records: For Mr. Nick Reynolds, 1811 N. Oak St., Arlington, Va.: Melotone 20120, "New Stranger Blues," sung by Tampa Red; Vocalion-7-04-60 (SA2631), "Hell Hound On My Trail," sung by Robert Johnson; Vocalion 1454, "The Dirty Dozen," sung by Leroy Carr and Scrapper Blackwell; Melotone-5-11-59 (18023), "You Got To Give Me Some Of It," by Pinewood Tom and Buddy Moss.

For Miss Jean Evans, 1811 N. Oak St., Arlington, Va.: Melotone 13193 (15493), "Collector Man Blues," by Walter Roland; Perfect-6-05-51, "Silicosis

Is Killin' Me," by Pinewood Tom; Vocalion 03416 (SA2580), "Kind Hearted Woman Blues," by Robert Johnson; Perfect 7-12-63, "Sinking In The Lonesome Sea," by the Carter Family; Vocalion 03075 (01921), "Louise, Louise," by Big Bill Broonzy.

For Miss Bess Brown Lomax, 7426 San Benito Way, Dallas, Texas: Melotone 13193 (15493), "Collector Man Blues," by Walter Roland; Melotone 20120, "The New Stranger Blues," by Tampa Red; Vocalion 03416 (SA2580), "Kind Hearted Woman Blues," by Robert Johnson; Vocalion 7-04-60 (SA2631), "Last Fair Deal Gone Down," by Robert Johnson.

For Miss Elizabeth Harold [Alan's mother-in-law], 118 S. Rosemont, Dallas, Texas: Vocalion 1637, "Things About Comin' My Way," by Tampa Red; Melotone 13193 (15493), "Collector Man Blues," Walter Roland; Perfect 6-05-51 (18733), "Silicosis Is Killing Me," by Pinewood Tom; Melotone 20120, "New Stranger Blues," by Tampa Red; Vocalion 7-04-60 (SA2631), "Last Fair Deal Gone Down," by Robert Johnson; Perfect 7-09-56, "Hell Hound On My Trail," by Robert Johnson; Columbia 15349-D (147330), "Cuba," by The Sacred Harp Singers; Perfect 7-12-63, "Sinking In the Lonesome Sea," by The Carter Family; Melotone 5-11-59 (18023), "You Got To Give Me Some Of It," by Pinewood Tom and Buddy Moss; Perfect 7-01-67 (20141), "Georgia Hound Blues," by Tampa Red; Brunswick 212, "The Lady Gay," by Buell Kazee.

As it is necessary that these records arrive in time for Christmas would you please give this matter your immediate attention? [ALC]

The next day, December 16, he mailed a short request to Mrs. Glen Noyes in Turnbridge, Vermont:

I should like to see copies of four ballads that you mention: "One Stormy Night, Who's That Knocking?, How Paddy Stole the Rope, The Apples are Ripe." A letter will go to Mrs. Hough this afternoon. In the mean time thank you for your kind interest in helping me. [ALC]

He quickly followed with a letter to Mrs. John Hough in Brandon, Vermont, also on December 16:

A friend of yours, Mrs. Noyes, has told that you know a number of old ballads sung in Vermont when you were a girl. The Library of Congress, in collaboration with Mrs. Flanders of Springfield, Vermont, is making a collection of New England ballads for the Archive of American Folk Song. Mrs. Noyes mentioned particularly *Fair Ellen* or *The Black Bride*. I would deeply appreciate it if you would write out the words of all the songs you know and send them to me. [ALC]

Concerning his financial obligations in working for CBS, he contacted Sterling Fisher at the company on December 16:

Attached you will find a memorandum of various expenses incurred by me in preparation of material for the School of the Air programs. I feel that these are definitely extra expenses which are not taken care of in my weekly stipend. I believe my contract reads prepare script material and this has amounted to my writing the scripts. These have been used entire except for minor corrections and cuts by Mr. Fineschriber. The preparation of this material has entailed my missing many days from my regular job at the library. Salary for these days has been deducted from my pay there. I feel I should be reimbursed at least for my expenses. I'd appreciate your giving this your immediate attention. I've been interested to hear of developments for your Latin American program idea. The bill amounted to $57.00. [ALC]

That same day, December 16, Alan sent a short message to John Hammond at the Columbia Recording Company, who was organizing the second From Spirituals to Swing concert at Carnegie Hall on December 24:

I am delighted to hear that Charles Smith is working with you on the Christmas concert. I am going to call on the Golden Gate Quartet day after tomorrow and I'll try to hand them some work songs for you. You certainly should get together a group of New Orleans musicians with Jelly Roll for the concert. I think his recent Bluebird recordings completely vindicated him as a musician. Sorry I cant be there but best of luck. [ALC]²⁶

Also on December 16 he contacted Alec Saron of Cabaret TAC (Theater Arts Committee) in New York, the sponsor of the upcoming From Spirituals to Swing concert:

After you called I spoke to Peter Seeger and Lawrence Gellert in regard to the folk music program we discussed. Gellert knows Negro singers in Harlem and that should round out our program completely. I suggest that you give Mr. Seeger and Mr. Gellert full leeway in planning the program until I return on the second of January. Then we can all get together. [ALC]²⁷

He was continually involved with library business, as in this letter of December 18 to Dorothy Dunn Morrison in Falls Church, Virginia:

Thank you for your interesting song. I believe that it is what might be called a barroom or college student folk-song. It will be filed in the Library of

Congress, and if you know of more I would like to see copies of them. In appreciation of your intelligent response to the program, I am. [ALC]

Alan was approached by R. P. Wetherald of RCA about putting together a new record album, and he responded on December 22:

I have two suggestions to make about your square dance album. First, the price you offered Mr. [Pete?] Seeger and myself is fairly small for two such busy people as we are. Second, the records which you left with me are mostly pretty bad, not worthy of Victor or of American folk music. There are three possible solutions for your difficulty. A: Get in touch with Ruth Crawford, 9609 Fairway Ave., Silver Springs, Md. She is co-editor of my father's and my new book which is to appear in the spring and a Guggenheim fellow in composition. B: Make a good set of records with calls, using one of your current hillbilly orchestras under expert supervision. C: Bring out an album of square dance tunes of different kinds with directions for different dances included and using fiddle records that you already have. The experience of folk dance leaders has been that records with calls are extremely difficult to follow in most cases unless you know the particular regional figures demanded by those calls. There is great variation here. If you do a new album I certainly feel that John A. Lomax should be consulted about it. I am still waiting for the records before proceeding with my recommendations to father. I must be acquainted with the whole range of your material before I can make intelligent choices for him. [ALC][28]

Alan continued to work with his father on their forthcoming songbook, and on December 22 wrote to Annabel Morris (Mrs. John P.) Buchanan, founder of the White Top Folk Festival in 1931 in southwest Virginia, to obtain song permissions:

A number of years ago my father recorded several songs of J. M. ["Sailor Dad"] Hunt in Marion, Virginia. Recently in compiling our new book of American folk songs we decided to use two of these: *Santy Anno* and *Haul Away, My Rosie.* We wrote Mr. Hunt for permission. He replied by giving us permission but said that you had published the first and suggested that we write you for permission to use the song. Both my father and myself would very much appreciate your giving us permission to reprint this song with proper acknowledgment. [ALC][29]

December 22 was a busy correspondence day. He also notified Dora Bryant in Evansville, Indiana, concerning his CBS radio show:

The programs beginning January 2 again will continue until April 29. I am sending you, under separate cover, a manual. I would love to use some of your beautiful ballads on the air for the program but they are already over-crowded with material. I will never forget your kindness and hospitality to myself and Elizabeth and whenever we are near Evansville we will drop in to see you again. In the mean time give my best regards and good wishes to yourself and your charming family. [ALC]

Alan was flooded with letters regarding the radio program, some of which he answered, including to Miss A. G. O'Brien, in New Britain, Connecticut, on December 22:

You can find the material that you want in the American School of the Air Manual and in the bibliography given at the end of the section on music. The history and origin of American folk song is a subject for many volumes. I suggest that you look in various encyclopedias under such headings as Cowboy Songs, American Ballads, English Ballads, etc. [CBS][30]

As the year ended he informed I. S. Becker, a business manager at Columbia Artists, on December 22, of his future lecture plans:

I hope you can allow me time until after the Christmas holidays to send you the management contract. I have been much too busy lately to even think about it. I will call on you when I return to New York on January 2. [ALC]

And on the day before Christmas, December 24, Alan dropped a short note to Moses Smith at Columbia Records:

I am still so far behind that I haven't had time to prepare the list I promised you two months ago. However, in January I think I'll have some help. Remember, I do a job very similar to yours without equipment or technical assistance. Be as charitable as you can. With best wishes for the holidays. [ALC]

1940

Alan wrote a short note to Spivacke, undated but perhaps in early 1940:

Dr. Robert Gordon has asked me for a duplicate of one of [Herbert] Halpert's Virginia play party recordings in connection with his research on Dixie. The duplication could be done by Shannon Allen on the small sample acetate accompanying this original. It might be wise first to consult Charley Seeger

on the matter of permission. [P.S.] Dr. Gordon adds that he does not intend
to publish this tune but only compare it with a no. of others. [ALC][31]

Annabel Morris Buchanan answered Alan's earlier letter on January 3, giving her
permission to use Sailor Dad Hunt's songs, and Alan followed the next day with his
acknowledgment:

Thank you for your cordial Christmas present of a letter. Of course, I shall
give acknowledgment for both of the shanties. I shall write J. Fischer in G.
Schirmer for their permission to reprint the two shanties. I shall ask Schirmer
if they wish an acknowledgment of their publication of *Haul away my Rosie*. I
think your attitude about material is the only one that is possible for a really
genuine folklorist, and I certainly am glad to know how you feel about the
free exchange of songs. Naturally, I hope that the favor can be reciprocated at
some time. I will forward your letter on to my father in Texas. [ALC]

On January 3, he continued with another note to Moses Smith at Columbia about a
record order:

Please don't worry about the discount business, but pass the order on to the
department to be filled in the usual way. Last year, I asked for the same thing
and was surprised and delighted to get the discount. You seem to be doing a
grand job. [ALC]

More library business followed on January 4, with Alan's note to Marshall Bartholomew
in New Haven, Connecticut:

Your letter recalls to me a piece of recording which I have long wanted to do.
Miss Newcomb and I have visited together over her manuscript and both
mutually agreed that her songs should be recorded on disks for the Archive
collection, but something has always come up, however, to prevent this. I
will try to see to it by spring that this will no longer be true. I would greatly
appreciate your bringing to my attention any collectors or collection in any
part of the country that you think we may not be aware of. [ALC]

Also on January 4 he filled in his father on his recent activities, beginning with their
forthcoming book:

My telegram should have read, "The dummy has been in for a month and the
manuscript for two weeks" which was substantially the case, I believe. They
must have the manuscript since I received an acknowledgment for the same

recently. I have worked on the book to the neglect of a number of other really more pressing projects and I shall be able to finish the whole job including the difficult record appendix within a month. Please don't worry about it. I should have kept you more closely informed about the progress, however.

I am glad you all had such a nice Christmas and would like very much to have been there myself. I knew, however, I would not get any rest if I came. Elizabeth and I had a completely beautiful and restful week in Nassau, and without it I don't know how my spring would have been possible. I must say again, however, that one of my reasons for not coming is your invitation was not sufficiently general. Bess is staying with [the Nicholas] Rays and myself for the rest of the week and working on her school papers. She was not very well when she arrived but her cold is much better now. Don't feel concerned about her. A couple of enclosures will speak for themselves. [ALC]

The next day, January 5, he contacted E. Milby Burton, director of the Charleston Museum in South Carolina:

The Archive of American Folk Song has quite a large collection of Haitian drumming records which I made on the Island in 1937. We are much interested in making this material available to the people who are interested but we have no means of duplicating the records even for our own study. Your request will be placed on file and when we have the equipment it will be considered. [ALC]

Alan continued to juggle his various interests and obligations, for example in this letter on February 1 to Helen Whitaker in St. Louis, Missouri, about her collecting:

Many thanks for the song that you sent me a couple of weeks ago. I have not written to thank you before because I've been too busy, not because I did not enjoy the song. I feel sure you know other songs besides the children's games and play parties. If you would send me those words too, I should like to put them in the collection of the Library of Congress at Washington, D.C., in your name. One thing I'd like to know is where you played the games, how they were played and how long ago this happened. [ALC]

A few days later, February 7, a similar letter went out to Mrs. H. G. Landon in Pittsburgh, Pennsylvania:

It is a great pleasure to receive letters like yours in which games and songs are so clearly discussed. I am certain that you must know a great deal of material and I hope you will jot it down and send it to me at the Library of

Congress to be incorporated in our National Archive of American Folk Song. You cannot imagine how valuable and interesting such material can be until you see it. [ALC]

Alan tried to respond to some of his fan mail, as in this message to Ola Margaret James, in Los Angeles, on February 7:

Your letter about play party songs is one of the most interesting that I have received as a result of my request over the air. You must know a great many more songs and I should like to ask, if it isn't too much trouble, for you to send them in to me particularly "Rosa Bess' and "Doctor Montcalm." Would it be at all possible for you to send the music along with the words? The songs are twice as useful for others if they have their own tunes. My reason for asking for songs in the first place is to help the growth of the Folk Song collection in the Library of Congress of which I am in charge. Any assistance you can give me will be greatly appreciated and acknowledged. [CBS]

A similar note went to J. Teller, in Middletown, Connecticut, on February 7:

Thank you for your kind, encouraging, letter and for the text of Frog Went A'Courting. Where did you learn the song? Do you know others of the same kind? If so, if you will send them to me I shall incorporate them in the Folk Song collection at the Library of Congress. [CBS]

He also thanked Ruth E. Day of Lucas, Iowa, on February 7:

The version of Springfield Mountain which you sent is of very great interest and value to the Library of Congress collection of which I am in charge. You seem to know a ballad when you see one and, believe me, that is not a very common talent. I feel certain that you could find a great deal more interesting material from Mr. Rouse and others in your community. Would it be asking too much that you see what else he knows and send it to me? Your efforts will be gratefully received. [CBS]

That same day, he also explained using his radio program in order to solicit information in a letter to H. F. Wright in Spencerport, New York:

I greatly enjoyed your interesting letter regarding square dancing in the North and South and have put it on file in the Library of Congress Archive of American Folk Song as a useful document. My reason for asking for information over the air was to establish contact with people all over the country

interested in folk songs and to assist in our project of building up a National
collection in Washington. I should like very much to record the tunes you
learned in northern New York and to find through you other fiddlers and
singers in that region. Once these records are in the collection of the Library
they have all sorts of uses for artistic, educational and historical purposes.
Would you be interested in helping out? [ALC][32]

Charles Todd, on January 23, informed Alan:

I was doing some writing for the New York Times on the migratory Labor
Camps in Imperial Valley [California], and in the course of my wanderings,
I picked up a number of old "Okie" ballads—along with others not so old.
I managed to make recordings of some of these, and I think you might be
interested in hearing a few of them.[33]

Alan wrote back on February 7:

Did you work with Margaret Valliant of the F[arm] S[ecurity] A[dministration]
last summer? She made records of the camps about the same time. I should
like to hear your recordings and talk with you about Okies and folk lore. You
can expect me some evening at 6 Bank Street. [VFDB]

Alan thanked Corinne Brown in Waco, Texas, on March 19:

I enjoyed your letter and the songs that you sent in more than I can tell you. It
was very pleasant for me to hear from Waco, for it's only a few miles from the
town in which I was born. I want to use both of your songs on my program
of April 16th, and in order to do this I would have to have the tunes written
down, and besides, have your signature on the enclosed letter of permission.
I'm sure that if you went to some local music teacher or friend of yours who
knows music, they will be glad to write these tunes down. Do you know other
old songs besides the two that you sent me? Send me a list of them and perhaps I can ask my father to come by to see you some day and make records of
them. I would like to hear from you within a week. [ALC]

Alan, then in New York, gave details about his health issues and other matters to his
father on March 20:

As you probably noticed on Tuesday, at 3:35 [broadcast time for his American School of the Air program], I have been quite ill for two or three weeks.

A couple of days I spent flat on my back with Streptococcus throat. This is the reason why I haven't written you. I will try to reply to your letters in full as soon as possible. I have a vacation of two weeks, and in that time I will finish up the unfinished business on the book and also my unfinished correspondence with you.

In the meantime, here are two matters in which you can help me, and I think they will amuse you besides. These two old ladies have sent me the best songs of anybody from Texas, and they sound like people who know a great deal of material. I'd like to get the tunes to "Little Colen Annie" and "I Sold my Clock and Wheel." I thought perhaps Deanie [Mrs. John Lomax] might be interested in calling on Mrs. Smith and remembering her for the first contact of your forthcoming recording trip; and I feel sure you or Deanie would know someone in Waco who would do me the favor of visiting Mrs. Brown and sending me her two tunes. I want to use these songs on my April 16th program, so if anything is to be done it has to be done at once. Please return the letters within the next couple of weeks, for I will use them for speech material. The St. Louis business has been shelved for practical reasons. Elizabeth has just come back from Mexico and I am very well contented. [ALC]

Alan met Woody Guthrie at the "Grapes of Wrath" concert at the Forrest Theater in New York on March 3 to benefit the Committee to Aid Farm Workers, organized by actor Will Geer, Woody's friend. In addition to Guthrie, performers included Aunt Molly Jackson, Burl Ives, the Golden Gate Quartet, Pete Seeger, along with Alan and his sister Bess. Lomax quickly brought Woody to the Library of Congress, where he recorded him for three days in late March, and then arranged for a recording session for RCA. R. P. Wetherald confirmed certain details to Alan on April 4:

I am very sorry that you have been ill. Shortly after I saw you in New York, I went down to hear the Golden Gate Jubilee Quartet at Cafe Society. I mentioned the chain gang song idea to the leader whose comment was that he really didn't know anything about those songs. If I could meet you some time in New York, we might work out recording plans and I could relieve you entirely of the financial end of the thing if you would introduce me to Leadbelly. The list of folk song records which you sent in seems a very large batch to send to Texas to have your father go over to select a half dozen records for the album. Don't you think it would be possible to boil this down to about 100 records for this purpose. [ALC]

Wetherald followed up to Alan on April 29 with details of a recording session with Woody:[34]

I am sorry that I missed your phone call last Tuesday afternoon. Woody came down Friday morning, and we recorded twelve sides. . . . I am planning to put these out in two albums of six sides each. If you have any thought on the possible groupings, I would appreciate your indicating them to me. I am sure that I have you to thank for swinging Woody our way, in view of the high offer which Columbia made to him. I think I have things about worked out with Leadbelly if I can only convince the powers that be that it is all right to list him on Victor with the Golden Gate Jubilee Quartet and on Bluebird for his solos. I hope that you can relax now and get a good rest. I will let you know when I have the Leadbelly agreement worked out and then we can arrange for the recordings with the Golden Gate boys. [ALC][35]

Alan's radio show continued to elicit positive responses from his audience's parents, teachers, and children, for which he was thankful, as in this May 6 letter to E. E. Tucker in Great Falls, Montana:

Allow me to thank you for the most friendly and interesting letter sent in by anybody during the year. When my program reaches people like yourself, who've had troubles and fought against them and know something about life in this country, that makes me feel pretty good. But all these darn school teachers—You couldn't do anything that would please me more than to send me that "Eleven Cent Cotton" record, if you wouldn't mind.[36] I'd like to make a copy of it for preservation in the folk song collection in the Library. Besides it's a song I'm particularly interested in myself. Also I'd like to know what other old songs you know, either good or bad, pure or impure, rough or smooth, sweet or bitter—that you have heard about, picked up, sung, hummed or heard hummed anywhere between South Carolina and Montana. I'd like to hear about the songs you've heard and liked and why and I'd like to hear about them all at one time or in installments as you happen to think about one or remember it. If you lived in town, I'd drop in to see you, but Montana as the feller says is a hell of a way off for a visit unless you're going to stay for supper anyhow. So let's do it by mail and on the installment plan. And send me that record. Airmail express collect. [ALC]

He continued his messages to Annabel Buchanan, usually brief, as on May 22:

I have recently found your letter of permission. Thank you again. I shall include references to folk-hymns of America in the page proof of the appendix. [ALC]

On May 24 he informed H. C. Darnell of the RCA Manufacturing Company in Camden, New Jersey, about the song "Didn't He Ramble":

This morning I talked with Mr. Robert Gordon, one of the leading authorities on Folk Songs in the United States of America, and he told me that Rosamond Johnson told him that he (R.J.) had picked up the refrain of "Didn't He Ramble" in Jacksonville, Florida. This tallies with W. C. Handy's statement, with my father's testimony that he has known the refrain "Didn't He Ramble" all of his life and I now can present you with a printed version of the Ram of Darby with the "Didn't He Ramble" refrain dated 1888. The reference is p. 157, no. 5 of the Publication of the Texas Folk-lore Society. To recapitulate. 1. Rosamond Johnson picked up the Didn't He Ramble refrain and wrote new lyrics and a new melody for the stanzas. 2. The Didn't He Ramble refrain had been for a long time been current as the chorus of the obscene ballad about the Ram. I can furnish you versions of this from Texas, Kentucky, and Michigan, all dated before 1900. [ALC]

On June 4 he sent a request to Mr. O'Connel at RCA Victor:

Carleton Smith [of the New York Public Library] has asked me to order for him a group of selected records of American Folk Songs issued by Victor. He is leaving Friday on a plane and will appreciate your sending him collect the records on the inclosed list. Some of them may be out of print. [ALC]

In juggling his hectic schedule, there were occasional problems, as Alan telegrammed Spivacke on June 14:

Developments in School of Air make return to Washington impossible until Wednesday morning. [ALC]

Library matters were never far from his mind, as noted in this letter to Mr. Jacobs, an acoustical engineer at CBS, also on June 14:

Enclosed you will find the floor plans of the section of the Library which we plan to use for a new studio. The space is 22' wide, 11' high to the beam, 12' to ceiling. We can use as much of this space as is necessary. The lighting fixtures are the hanging type, but I hope to replace these with the fluorescent lamps. I think you have all of the necessary information regarding our plans but, if anything else occurs to me, I will send it along to you. I told Dr. Spivacke of your offer to help us and he was very appreciative. I too am glad to have some one with your experience and authority working on the studio. [ALC]

Alan also kept up a correspondence with Pete Seeger, for example on June 20, partly referring to the book of protest songs they were working on with Woody:

I know you'll be delighted to get the enclosed letter. It just came this morning. Also, a telephone call from the publicity man at Sam Goldwyn's who wants you and Woody for a party this weekend. By this time you should have obtained the material [Ben] Botkin sent from Washington. Please rush the record list back to me and enclose the list of the Aunt Molly records that you have. This is very pressing. I'll get on the trail of your introduction today. For the moment, address me tactfully at the Library of Congress because we're moving out to the country this week-end. [ALC][37]

Alan looked forward to a return trip to New England, as he informed Milton Ellis, chair of the English Department at the University of Maine, on June 21:

Father sent on to me your nice letter and I think your offer and expenses will be alright. I'd like very much to get acquainted with Maine. Sometime in May should be a good idea. I'll look forward to hearing from you. [ALC]

About this time he connected with Irene Whitfield in an undated letter:

It is sometime since we have corresponded. In the interim I understand you have arranged for the publication of your study of Acadian songs. I hope this rumor turns out to be true and I should like to know more about the venture. Since I wrote you last, I have been on an extensive field trip to Michigan (where, by the way, I recorded a lot of fine Canadian-French material), have spent a half-year of graduate study in Columbia University and am now helping father finish another ballad book. In it we plan to print ten to fifteen Cajun ballads and among these "J'ai m'ai fait une maitresse trois jours, mais c'est pas longtemps." I suppose you recall that this ballad was not complete on the record, the last words being—Je me mettrai mari, mari—.

I have not been able to find this ending in any of the books I have seen and wondered whether you had ever found the conclusion for it. If so, would it be too much to ask that you send me the references or the quotation, itself? Have you ever seen Elida or her father, Julien Hofpauir? I should add that if you can give me the date, publisher, title of your thesis, I should like to plug it in the book. I have mentioned it already in my note but without title. My best regards to your family and yourself.

And, as I end this letter, a swarm of other questions overwhelms me. Do you know my good friend, Mackie Langham Bennett, former Instructor in English at the U. of T., now married to an oilman who makes his headquarters in Lafayette? If not, you might look her up, she's an engaging person. Have you ever figured out what "Les Clefs de la Prison" has to say. There seems to be a number of ways of looking at the song. My interpretation runs as follows: a) The boy says to his [mamma] "they've given me the keys to the prison.["] b) She replies, what do you mean, the keys to the prison when the officers have them hung around their necks? c) I mean they're coming after me at nine to hang me at ten. And what grieves me most is that I've got to know my death such a long time in advance. d) His father is tearing out his hair on his knees. e) How could I have left you, have gone away from you except to prison. f) (c) again. g) yes you take my body to the grave with my beautiful (?) horse, and my black carriage and the four red wheels. Or is it a conversation between a boy and his parents. Or what? What does *shausse* mean? I have been over your transcriptions a number of times and have made what I think are some corrections. Would you like to see the results? especially in "J'ai passé au long du bois." [ALC][38]

He updated his father on June 21 about their new book, finally in production:

Our Singing Country is being set up and page proofed. There were a lot of corrections to be made on the galleys about one half of which were Mac-Millan's. Ruth's [Ruth Crawford Seeger] appendix will be done this week and my introduction this month. You will get a copy of both before they are sent in. Mrs. Prink is in no hurry for either one. The matter of splitting fees on the C.B.S. programs is as yet not beyond the lecture stage. I've already thought about that problem and you can be sure that if my income ever gets out of control, you'll be notified on green paper. The enclosures you sent me made me awful mad and I think I'm going to sue about it. Very little has been changed about the book. I've spent endless amounts of time on the two appendices and the galleys. I'll write you a more gossipy letter soon. We should hear about the summer trip about the first week in July. The reason I have not answered some of your letters is that they did not catch up with me. [ALC]

He followed on June 25 with a heated letter to R. P. Wetherald at RCA Victor:

My opinion of your friend Mr. Darnell is not very high. I suppose that matters of copyrighting sections have to be like that. It's regrettable. I particularly object to his rather tight-fisted policy to John A. Lomax. All of the songs recorded by the Golden Gate Boys and Leadbelly were first collected and published by him and almost all of them I taught to these singers. Let it be understood that until a satisfactory agreement is reached between John A. Lomax, my signature on these contracts does not apply. I have advised Mr. Lomax to accept the offer made him by Mr. Darnell provided that all twelve songs are covered by the offer. It seems to me that the same terms should apply to the library when the songs have already been published in one of John A. Lomax's books. I look forward to hear from you at a very early date. [ALC][39]

Alan worked hard on compiling a list of recordings in the Archive, as he explained to Spivacke on July 8:
In the process of completing the check list of the Archive of American Folk Song, I have found that we shall need the advice of various specialists in foreign languages, as Greek, Rumanian, Slovenian and etc. I should like to request that from time to time, Mr. Halkin of the Cataloging Division make available one of his skilled cataloguers to assist me in these foreign language problems. This, naturally, should be on official library time because the material requiring attention is part of the Library Folk Song Collection. [ALC][40]

The next day, July 9, he answered W. W. Babb, Publicity Manager of the Rock Island Railway in Chicago:

I'm sorry I couldn't answer your letter about the "Rock Island Lines" song sooner, but radio and archives work have kept me extremely busy. The song you mention has never been published, and will appear in print for the first time when *Our Singing Country* by John and Alan Lomax, is published by Macmillan Co., 60 Fifth Avenue, New York City, this autumn. The words were recorded on a phonograph record in Arkansas by John A. Lomax, who had a group of Negro workers sing it for him. The record itself is now in the Archive of American Folk Songs at the Library of Congress. [ALC]

The same day, July 9, he sent an informative letter to Archibald MacLeish, the Librarian of Congress, which appears to be his response to an inquiry by Pearl H. Staut:

The Archive of American Folk Song in which the songs you helped collect in Arkansas are deposited, has long been engaged in a program of recording the folk music of the United States. We have sent recording machines into many regions of the country to take down folk songs from the lips of people who know them and we are most anxious to continue to enlarge our collection. The cooperation of the National Congress of Parents and Teachers is naturally extremely welcome to us. It would seem to me possible for the Archive to arrange to record a sizable collection of songs which you had located in any region or state in the United States. In states where there are active collectors, we can enlist their help. In other situations, we send a sound truck to do the job. By next fall we expect to be in the position to duplicate for public use four thousand records which we already have and this practice will naturally make this material available to you and your organization, along with the material in which you actually participate. A checklist of these songs will be completed in the summer and a copy mailed to you on publication. Enclosed you will find the press release announcing the establishment of the phono-duplicating division in the Library of Congress and describing its services.

We have already assisted in the establishment of state archives in Michigan and Florida at their respective state universities, and we are anxious to encourage collections of this sort. In such cases, we have assisted a local collector in the early stages of his work by furnishing discs, needles, and etc. in return for the deposit of the original recordings in the Archive of American Folk Song. Duplicates of his records were returned to him and these made the basis of a state archive. We feel that this process can grow and continue. It would be of great interest for the Archive to learn of the work of the Association in the field of folk song and its plans for collecting. We shall be happy to cooperate in any way possible. [ALC]⁴¹

Alan kept in touch with Mary Elizabeth Barnicle at New York University, as in this letter on July 10:

Along with a flock of W.P.A. workers, I am in the middle of making a complete catalogue of the Archive. We have now got the money for duplicating and will be producing records within a few months. We have come to your Kentucky records and there's one question which needs answering. Who did the singing at Dorton Branch, Ky.? It sounds like a congregation of Holy Rollers but I'd like to have more particulars. Elizabeth and I now have a house in the woods on the Potomac and we'd love to have you and Tilman [Tillman Cadle] down any time you can come. Please don't attribute my not having called on you to any diminution of affection or loyalty. For Elizabeth and myself both you are still one of the few suns warming the cold soil of this world. [CBS]

While Alan attempted to keep up with Library business, he was also pursuing his radio and lecturing career, as he noted to Helen Scott of the Columbia Lecture Bureau on July 10:

Enclosed you will find my suggestions for the leaflet. I imagine you'll have to rewrite it somewhat, but, please send me the proofs before it is published. When you make engagements in the future, consult the schedule of the School of the Air Program and assume that I'll be in New York from the Friday preceding each broadcast through the following Tuesday night. You'd better check with Bill Fineschriber about that. I have contracted for a lecture at the Wooster Women's Club on April 9, 1941. These people wrote me independently before I signed up with you all. Would you please file the enclosed letter to Mr. Farnell. I should like for you to arrange for an advance on submission of complete script. [ALC]

Alan sent a short letter to Woody Guthrie in New York on July 15:

I lent your piece called "No Title" to Ed. Rosskam of Alliance Press and he was extremely enthusiastic. He wants you to do your autobiography for him and he will pay you cash for same. Let me recommend him as a nice gentleman and I sure hope the book comes through. Where's Pete [Seeger], where are you, hello. [WGC]

He again contacted Annabel Morris Buchanan on July 17:

The proper acknowledgments have been made and are now in our new book. I've never been to one of the White Top Festivals and I should like to come for my own edification and for the purpose of recording the whole festival for the Library of Congress. As you doubtless know, material recorded at such a time under your sponsorship can be restricted. I should like to know how you and your committee would feel about this before I apply to the library for permission to come. [ALC]

He also sent one of his lengthy letters to his father on July 17:

For the last time, your letters are not annoying, unwelcome, unpleasant, nor any other "un," except for one thing. They continually put me in a position of apologizing for faults of omission which I really can't help. I wish I could write you as often as you do me, since I can't physically, consider that I do the best that I can. 1. The sermons and other miscellaneous prose material are being gathered together for you. Elmo Newcomer's tunes are being searched. This material you will find enclosed. Tomorrow, I will go into my files and pull out the unused material from Our Singing Country and send it to you. Mrs. [Ruth Crawford] Seeger has been written about the music since she has all of it. 2. I should like very much to come to talk before the Texas Folklore Society next spring, after my programs are over and I shall try to make it coincident with a two or three month field trip into Texas, Arkansas and Louisiana which I have long wanted to explore in my own way. You might have [J. Frank] Dobie write to MacLeish in about ten days inviting me to lecture in May. 3. I think your idea about the books is a grand one, but I should also like to know what the total of my obligations are to you at present and I should like to consider including Cowboy Songs in the group since this will be a major problem in connection with the radio rights. If you feel that this deal will be of some cash advantage to yourself, I wonder whether a small cash to boot could be thrown in as I'm awfully broke this summer.

4. I've just been notified by the Library of Congress that your recording trip and your stay in Washington have been finally approved. $500.00 from the Library of Congress increase for per diem and mileage, and $250.00 for records, needles and other incidentals. A new recording machine will be bought for the trip which will be much more portable than others you have used. Besides, Mr. Macleish has got from the Carnegie Foundation, $500.00 to pay expenses for you and Deanie to stay in Washington for six weeks to annotate your own field recordings. In this regard, I wonder whether it would not be wise for you to postpone completion of adventures[42] until you can get close to your material. Let me know about your wishes and ideas about the trip. I'm already pulling out of my files all of the contacts I have along through the mountain country. This time I hope to see you explore some new territory. If I get a free minute, I'll sit down and write you a chapter on the Bahamas before August 1.

5. The enclosure from Lloyd Lewis was extremely interesting and I'm sure you will want to keep it in your files. I'm herewith returning it. Under separate cover, you will receive a summary of the History of the Archive, compiled and edited by B. A. Botkin who forwards it with his very best regards. I think I'm going to sue my slanderers. [ALC]

On July 18 Alan contacted Leland Coon at the University of Wisconsin regarding uncovering vernacular music informants in Wisconsin in order to obtain Archive support:

Dr. Spivacke turned over to me your letter of July 2 for my answer. Due to the pressure of work in the Archive I have only just been able to attend to it. My suggestion is that you obtain from Dr. Brown, Frances Densmore, Dr. E.C. Beck of Mt. Pleasant, Michigan, Dr. Ivan Walton of the University of Michigan and others, a highly selective list of folk music informers in Wisconsin. Map out an itinerary of two thousand miles (5 cents a mile) of twenty days duration at $5.00 a day and send your technician over this carefully planned route. Informants should be notified and prepared in advance so that the recorder may record already rehearsed performances in the briefest time possible. The material should be selected, 1. from the point of authenticity of performers, and 2. upon the point of view of the greatest possible variety. At the end of twenty days, if you have a good field worker, you should have at least fifty or perhaps a hundred fine records of Wisconsin Folk Music,—a sampling of the rich variety to be found in your state. This body of records can, more than anything else, make a case for the necessity of Folk Song work in the states. Lectures, demonstrations and radio transcriptions can be based on this group of records and I should think that such a program of demonstration propaganda should guarantee the continuance of the work under more favorable circumstances next year. Enclosed you will find a list of a few informants whom I know of in Wisconsin. Let us know as soon as possible when you plan to start your technician on his road, so that we can send the recording machine and the discs. We should have at least two weeks notice.

I have very few contacts in the state of Wisconsin, but I will give you herewith, those that are still in my files. 1. Art Ford, in Laona, can put you in touch with Warde Ford, Chas. Spencer, Clyde Spencer, Jack Bailey, Bob Walker, and Bud Faulkner. These singers and musicians know lumberjack and other Anglo-American ballads and tunes. They were contacted and partially recorded by Sidney Robertson, Box 354, Berkeley, Calif. She has done work in the state and perhaps can give you other leads. 2. Levine Brussoe [Leizime Brusoe] of Rhinelander, Wisc., a fiddler and Frank Uchytll of the same place [sic, Rice Lake], a lumberjack. 3. Henry Parmelee, Waukeegon is said to know lake sailor songs. 4. Captain Delos Smith of Port Washington, M. J. Barnett, 437-50th St., Kenosha, both supposed to know lake sailor songs. 5. Mellen, Wis. was represented as a good community for lumberjack songs. 6. Moquash as a pioneer Czech, a group of fifty records from Wisconsin should include, (a) Lumberjack songs, (b) Lake sailor songs, (c) Anglo-American songs and ballads, (d) Fiddle tunes and game songs, (e) Vulgar ballads and songs, (f) Finnish songs, (g) French-Canadian songs, (h) Norwegian songs, (i) Swedish songs, (j) Icelandic songs from Washington Island. I feel sure that Dr. Brown can supply you with the proper contacts, at least. For the rest, it is important to try to record the songs that Franz Rickaby collected, and to investigate such groups as the Kaintucks and the Shantyboys people in your state. [ALC and the more complete version in HS-T]

As Charles Todd and Robert Sonkin prepared for their recording trip to the Farm Security Administration camps in California, Alan communicated his detailed instructions to Todd on July 20:

Enclosed you will find a letter of introduction and authorization from the Librarian and a set of operating instructions for the recording equipment from Jerome Wiesner. In addition, I should like to make a few suggestions which will make your material more useful to the Archive. Most of these suggestions, I'm sure will be more repetition, but if they're followed exactly, the records can be much more easily catalogued. 1. Give your trip a name, viz.

"John Doe's Expedition to Kalmazoo," or something of the sort. 2. Number the records in the order they are recorded, writing or stamping the titles of your trip and the number of your particular recording on the top of each record envelope. 3. Scratch or write in the center of each side the letter *A* or *B*, thus identifying the record side.

4. The strips on each side should be Nos. 1, 2, 3, and etc. in the order of their cutting and each of these strips should be identified by giving the title of song as the singer gives it (followed by the recordist's title or other title), the name of singer(s) with instrumentation, the place of the recording and the date. The slip cover, where such notations are generally made, should then look like this: A1—Barbara Allen, sung by John Doe with guitar and with fiddle by Jim Henry, Pasadena, N.Y. Dec. 6, 1844. A2, A3, A4, etc. B1, B2, B3, B4, etc.

5. Naturally, we hope that you will be able to furnish us with a great deal of additional material surrounding the recordings, both, in terms of careful field notes and interesting interviews, recorded with the songs. You'll find a questionnaire enclosed which has been used in the field to some extent. It contains a great many pertinent suggestions for questions. My personal opinion is that it is valuable to get the informant talking eloquently for himself, rather than interrupt him or push him with questions. The recording interview can be as significant as the song itself and is valuable as a fresh field document, especially if the informant does not know that the interview is being recorded, and if he ever learns it.

6. It is very important to record the tunings of all instruments which play a part in the music, to photograph the instruments and get the informant to explain how he plays it. In the case of unusual instruments, it would be worthwhile to make accurate drawings or send the instruments where they could be drawn to scale. If part singing is recorded, it would be a real contribution to record the parts in the harmony separately. This can be done by shifting the singers in front of the microphone. 7. As you know, valuable material is to be had from comparison of different versions of the same song from different regions. So also, are different performances of the same songs in the same community by different singers, or the same song by different members of the family, or the same song by the same performers at different times. Therefore, it is not so important to us that material be always rehearsed without a mistake or hesitation. The great beauty of field recordings is that performers take their own time and do things their own way, feeling that if they make a mistake, they can try again. The results are such that no commercial recording company can ever hope to achieve. [VFDB][43]

Alan's July 22 message to Richard Erstein, at the Columbia Lecture Bureau, captured his ongoing concerns about publicity:

It seems to me that costs for advertising are mounting so high, that my lecture fees will never reach my pocket, but, I'll try this for a while. The Leaflet
copy seems alright. I've made only a few changes. Please tell Miss Scott that I
can't be in New York on the 26th for her little get-together and I'm sorry. I'd
very much like to hear what response you got from Sam Goldwyn in regards
to that matter I referred to you some time ago. Please let me hear from you.
I received a letter from "Program." I thought I had already discussed what I
wanted to do about that with Miss Scott. [ALC]

Unfortunately he had to change his travel plans to the White Top Festival, as he informed
Buchanan on July 24:

I regret to say that it will not be possible for me to come to the White Top
Festival on the 15th of Aug. A sudden business emergency calls me to New
York for that entire week. I'm deeply disappointed, but I wanted to let you
know in case my proposal had presented any problems to your committee.
[ALC]

He maintained his exchange with Helen Hartness Flanders, writing to her on July 25:

Do you know a song supposed to have been sung in the [illegible] called,
"Madame You Know My Trade is War." How are things going with your song
collecting work? I don't know if I answered your inquiry about collecting in
Vermont. Since it came, we have been rushing through a complete check list
of songs in the Archive and my memory of anything by this time is rather
hazy. My Carnegie grant does not provide for any field expenses. I think by
next year, we'll have some means of taking care of certain field trips, but right
now, we can only offer equipment and discs. If Miss Olney could arrange
to use a machine for two or three weeks, I think that might be arranged,
although, I know this must sound rather vague to you. The American School
of the Air continues next year, thanks to you and others such as you kept
writing me. [N-JB]

Alan shot off a brief message to Pete Seeger on July 25:

I'll be back in New York on Saturday and on through Tuesday and we can settle our differences there. I'm delighted about the book. Have you made it clear
about our advances? See if you can get [John] Steinbeck's agent to arrange for
a final conference the first of next week while I'm in town. [ALC]

The following day, July 26, he connected with Woody Guthrie:

All of your letters are being filed for posterity in the high dives. If you want to swap, I'll do so, carbons for first copies, which were all a mist anyhow, and I'll explain when I see you. I've heard your records which are really fine. My only regret there is that they didn't have sense enough to use Pretty Boy Floyd. See you Sunday. With the best regards that the high dives can afford. [WGC]

He saved many of the details of his life for a letter to his father on July 26:

1. The first week in May is the earliest I can come. I hope you're not pushing [J. Frank] Dobie into something for your own sake rather than bringing them something they will really like. It might seem to a lot of people like the old fantastic father to son maneuver that certain folklorists might be unusually jealous of by this. 2. I also feel inclined to let your proposition jell a bit more but I had no idea my obligation to you was so large. 3. I've come up somewhat out of the hole since I last wrote you and I feel I'll make it somehow through October. I'm awfully tired spiritually right now because of the pressure that has been on me continually for the last fourteen months. I look forward with unholy delight to taking a couple of weeks vacation at the end of August (maybe).

4. Nick's [Nicholas Ray] and my program, called "I'm a Stranger Here Myself" with Clifton Fadiman, M.C. will be given a dress try out on C.B.S. on August 19. I'm going to be tearing around pretty rapidly between now and then. If the program sells, my end will be writing the scripts here in Washington which ought to be fun. 5. I think you might be interested in a memo of mine which is going around. Please read to Deanie [Mrs. John Lomax] and return in the next mail. It's extremely confidential in character since the Library has not embarked as yet on any kind of program such as the one that I have laid out in the paper. I thought you might be interested in knowing the possible direction things may take and the direction my thinking has taken in the last two or three months. It goes without saying that it is not very well written. I did it in one evening at home.

6. The Library has just recently acquired a new passel of red tape and your trip is being untangled from the midst of it. No question but that you'll be ready to go on the first of September as you desire, and, in the meantime, we can get everything beautifully laid out for you. I'm enclosing in this letter a list of persons out of my correspondence files and past trips whom you may be interested to see, perhaps. Spivacke and I have no particular desires in the matter, except; 1. To get records extremely tuneful and interesting for release by the Library, and, 2. To get some good cowboy songs. In the latter regard, I still think that Folk-Lore Society of which you're president should furnish many contacts. I also think that the trip ought to be hemi-demi

sponsored by the University of Texas and Folk-Lore Society with the view of depositing duplicates of the Texas records as the basis of the Texas Folk Song Archive. Alex Moore[44] should be rerecorded on acetate. So should the Gants. Bill Kittrell can give you the names of two or three cowboy singers of great interest in Texas who should be recorded. I'm very enthusiastic about railroad songs recorded enscene. Vance Randolph in the Ozarks is supposed to have traced a good bit of Mountain material and should be located. However, the idea of going to a plantation in Mississippi is one that makes my mouth water. Mrs. [Ruby Pickens] Tartt[45] is always good. I'm sure you could find good material in Dallas if you try and I would as it will come in handy for broadcasting and lecture programs right at your front door.

7. The last time I saw Dr. Davis and the Wards, they promised to take me back in the mountains to see all kinds of musical fanfares. (By the way), what was Dr. Davis's answer about the material for the book? The sheriff of Derry Co., Ky., Justing C. Begley, is one of the finest banjo players and ballad singers in America. It would be worth while going by and record his complete repertoire on acetate and if I write him, I imagine he'll open up avenues to you all through that mountain country.

8. About the machine, we can send you either a small portable Presto or the larger (but still lighter than Lincoln Thompson) and handier to use than Presto, Model Y. Model Y will make practically professional records with care, but it may take some practice to get the best results out of it. It's a little more complicated. Pictures of both are enclosed. 9. I always greatly enjoy your enclosures and friendly casual notes. Please realize I always come to your defense in the Lead Belly matter and it is never mentioned by Lead Belly except with regret for his foolishness.[46] I'll visit Mr. Houston and write Mrs. Winterbotham and also send you the material of This Singing Country this week end. Spivacke will send you formal notice as soon as the form has been reformed and remade. Meantime, go ahead and plan your trip for Sept. 1. 10. Enclosed you'll find a number of address cards. Pick out those that you think you'll use and send them to me. I'll write these people from here which will save you a lot of trouble. [ALC][47]

About the same time he sent an undated, lengthy memo to Spivacke, which is perhaps the one he mentioned to his father (on July 26), as the country prepared for war:

In re, contribution of the Archive of American Folk Song in event of conscription. May I suggest that the total plan which I suggested in a memo submitted to you some time ago be considered. The burden of this memo was "to make it possible for the American people to explain for themselves what America means and has meant to them." The words and the music have already been made by the people and presumably they like it. It remains for this program to put this material together and make it speak for the whole people rather than for any special region or group. If, however, it is not possible for us to embark on a total program, I submit the following suggestions for an immediate and emergency conscription program.

1) The AAFS can draw upon its large stock of tunes and songs for material for song books for camps. These song books may be designed according to the needs of the regions in which the camps are located, according to the racial and occupational make-up of the camps. I feel, for example that where any large group of second-generation Polish conscripts are located, Polish songs should be sung. The same for Negro, Mexican, Greek, Finnish, etc. conscript groups.

2) I need not overstress my opinion that "God Bless America" and Kate Smith are both extremely dull and mediocre. They have both been elevated to an artificially astronomical position by the power of mass advertising and the star system. One of our contributions to the integration of the people and, specifically, of the conscripts would be to find and help encourage all sorts of poetry, songs, and talent of all sorts among the conscripts and to give it publication or a place to be heard. We can work through the NYA [National Youth Administration], the WPA [Works Progress Administration] Arts Program or whatever other agency will be concerned with the recreational activities of the men to encourage and foster the poets and singers of the camps.

3) I am not too narrow a specialist to realize that much of the material with which I have to do, I mean folk song and ballad material, possesses only an historical or scientific interest. Many of the songs and tunes, however, possess remarkable potentialities for adaptation into other more familiar or sophisticated or contemporary idioms. There are a great number of romantic and delicate mountain love songs and war ballads which, if adapted for such a singer as Maxine Sullivan or Francis Langford, could have an extraordinary success. This would mean a departure from the traditional singing style and so on, but I believe, nevertheless, that the resulting songs would be more useful than they now are in Cecil Sharp's ten dollar treatise "English" folk songs of the Southern Appalachians. There are besides a great number of tunes which only need orchestration for brass band and for strings to make them good marches or fine material for movie or radio music or for such small orchestras as will undoubtedly be organized among the conscripts. Dr. [Charles] Seeger and his wife, Ruth Crawford, are, I believe, shortly to be brought into the Library WPA Music program. They are both composers of great experience and are well acquainted with American folk music. They should devote (along with a staff of arrangers, if

possible) at least half their time to the problem of adapting American folk music to larger forms.

4) I refer you to my suggestions for radio programs contained in my earlier memorandum. A great many of these program ideas could be adapted for transcription and the transcriptions loaned by the Library to camps all across the country. The Library with its sound truck could go into all the camps and make up transcriptions of the life, songs, talent, etc. to be found in each camp and these transcriptions made into a series of programs to be swapped among the camps by the Library. I believe such a program could have extraordinary general appeal as well as the interest they would naturally have for the men in the camps. [ALC]

Another memo from Alan to Spivacke was written about the same time, as war loomed for the United States:

We feel that a pamphlet, containing a succinct account of the origin of the *Star Spangled Banner*, should be issued at this time. Aside from scattered short accounts, there are two books devoted entirely to this subject—the [Oscar] Sonneck *Report* of 1914 and Joseph Muller's Bibliography, issued in 1935.[48] Both books are still useful, but much has been turned up since the Report was issued, and it could easily stand a revision. In any case, both works are too long and technical for ready reference or popular use. The proposed pamphlet, although based on the best information available and designed on strictly scholarly lines, should primarily strive for readability and clear simplicity. A strictly factual account of this sort would make the pamphlet of permanent value and help to avoid the stigma of "propaganda." The text should cover the origins of the tune, the composition of the words (with sufficient historical background to fit the defense of Fort McHenry into the War of 1812), and a very brief account of the subsequent history of the song—noting particularly significant changes in the tune and the Act of Congress which made it our national song. Sufficient illustrations should be employed to make the account vivid—a portrait of Key, our copy of the first broadside, the manuscript, the first printed music, a map of the region, etc. At the end should come a straight-forward piano arrangement of the music with a good version of the words. As a special supplement, special arrangements of this version should be made available for full orchestra, theater orchestra, dance band, military band, and concert band. Spivacke approved the plan and sent it on to higher authorities. [ALC][49]

His lecture tour continued to develop, as he wrote to Isabel Scott at Columbia Lecture Bureau on August 1:

Mr. Farnell is connected with Sam Goldwyn, Inc.—publicity director I think. I understand he's now out of town but I wish you'd look into the matter anyway. The number of lectures that I have now scarcely take care of the commission and publicity costs up to this point, but if you feel that I will actually be in somebody's debt by also advertising in the special issue of Program, I'll go ahead with it. I'll see you in New York in the next couple of weeks. [ALC]

In a short letter to Davidson Taylor in New York on August 6, concerning his upcoming radio program *Back Where I Come From*, Alan wrote:

I'm glad to know the program is going on on the 19th. "Old Joe Clark" might be a good theme tune. If not, I still vote for Buffalo Gals. My home address is Route 1, Maclean, Virginia, but during the week, it is best to write to me at the Library. P.S. I like most of what [Clifton] Fadiman has added to the script very much. P.S.S. I shall need the other half of my money for my second trip to New York. I realize this is an imposition, but the summer time always finds me much embarrassed for funds. [ALC][50]

On August 8 he corresponded with William Fineschriber at CBS:

I hope you have not seen the horrible picture in the leaflet that Columbia Artists Bureau have got out. I have asked them to withdraw the monstrosity from circulation, but in the meantime, have mailed them a number of not too unpleasant photographs of my map [i.e. face]. I wish you'd have the publicity department substitute one of these for the sweetness and light pictures they used last year. I'd like to begin thinking about scripts and could think much better if I had a copy of the Manual. [ALC]

He followed up that same day, August 8, with a request to Isabel Scott at the Columbia Lecture Bureau:

Please withdraw the picture on the flyer, and use one of the other good pictures I sent you. In fact, I'll be in a position to split the expense of a new edition with you provided this one is withdrawn from circulation. It seems to me that you might have sent me galleys on the flyer before you sent them out and that you may have remembered that I protested myself about the photograph in the Program. I'm quite certain that I do not like this photograph and I insist that no publicity go out from your bureau using this photo. [ALC]

Alan kept juggling his projects and Library work, as in this letter to Archibald MacLeish on August 8:

I have shown the enclosed to Spivacke and Jamison and they think it's very fine, and etc., but I think it's very important. I wrote it for you to read in the first place and have pried the usual channels choked with red tape. Now, I'm doing a wrong wicked thing in saying here's a thing you ought to read. I'm not applying for the Radio Fellowship as everybody seems to feel. I don't think I'm qualified and I'd rather stick to my folklore for the moment, but I do feel that creative research unit with the folklore bias can do the best propaganda job for the Defense Council and can of course, furnish loads of materials for your writers. I've discussed the whole thing with Evans at some length and he has asked me for some practical estimates for presentation to the Defense Council people—all very tentative. I've also prepared outlines for four song books for conscription camps. Copies of these are enclosed. The reason for this letter is that I'm concerned about the urgency of the present situation and lie awake nights with it. I imagine you are too, even in Conway [Massachusetts], and I feel therefore justified in going over heads and if necessary crawling over hedges to get this notion to you. The section of the Radio Project was included as one series of examples, and that only, to the generalizations contained in the introductory pages. [ALC]

In an undated letter, probably in the first week or two of August, Alan updated his father on some of his current ventures, including the new radio program:

One of our new portable recording machines which has been in New Mexico for a few weeks will be shipped to you from there in a few days. It will arrive along with records from the Library early enough for you to record around Dallas and Fort Worth before your trip begins officially on September first. He assures me that the authorization will have come through by next week so that you can leave on that date. I presume that you copied out the addresses sent you in an earlier letter on cards. I misread your letter and will write these people on my return from New York. I will have a few more to add to these when I come back from New York on the 20th of the month. May I suggest that you sit down and draw a map of your trip before you begin with approximate stopovers roughly calculated. The allotment procedure of the Library is extremely strict and if you spend any more money in miles, days or records than is allotted for the trip Dr. Spivacke will be in an extremely embarrassing position. On the other hand mileage not used up on the way up can be used on your return. I don't know how your Chicago plans fit into the picture, but if they will coincide with your return to Texas, we have some extremely interesting work lined up with Dr. Beck in Michigan which has not yet been done.

I'm going to New York tomorrow night to stay up a week with Nick's and my radio program called "Back Where I Come From." My estimate at this point is "only fair," but it may work out in rehearsals. A lot of compromises have had to be made, such as having Clifton Fadiman be the MC. The only reason for this was the hope that his presence will make the program a commercial possibility. Listen to CBS, 8-9 EST, Monday the 19th. Your friend the FBI ranger[51] called and I invited him to attend the broadcast, which will be billed as "Forecast." Please call some of our mutual friends. I'll write Shirley and Bess from NY.

I'm simply awfully tired and I hope my vacation the end of this month will be possible. If so, I'm going to go to Carolina mountains and hike for two weeks and sleep in the rumble of the car. [Archibald] MacLeish is out of town, which is why you haven't heard from the Texas project. As I read the Lead Belly contract they are under no further obligation to you except to furnish you with a statement. They never made their $250 I am pretty sure. The records were badly recorded and badly marketed.[52] I've just searched through the big file of your letters in my office and I'm again impressed by your thoughtfulness and deep and completely fine regard for me—I ain't wuthy [sic]. I'll have two or three days free in New York and I'm going to wind up the affairs of our joint book and turn the final copy over to Macmillan. I'll write you again from there. [ALC]

He mailed a short message to James (sic, Joseph) Mitchell at the New Yorker on August 12:

I greatly enjoyed your article on Madame Olga and would like to get the text of the Circus Version of Root Hog or Die. If you don't have it, could you furnish me with a lead where it may be secured? [ALC][53]

Late in the month, on August 29, he was wondering about his new program to William Fineschriber at CBS:

I'm sure you'll be interested in the enclosures from J. A. L.'s [John A. Lomax] comments on CBS publicity methods in Texas. I would like to have your opinion about whether the program is going to sell. Am rather vaguely on vacation at the moment. [ALC]

The next day, August 30, he mentioned the proposed White Top Festival to Annabel Morris Buchanan:

Thanks for the kind letter about the festival. As it turned out, I wasn't able to go, but I certainly hope to see the festival next year at least. I look forward to the publication of your new book with especial pleasure that one always reserves for your work. [ALC][54]

He wrote more on his radio program to Davidson Taylor on August 30:

I think you might be interested in the enclosure. It's not possible for us to include this interesting subject on the School of the Air programs this year, but I thought you could use it elsewhere. Nick encouraged me by what he said about the success of our program. Do you think there's a serious possibility of it's being sold? If I never before have expressed my appreciation of your extreme kindness to me and Nick, I want you to know how deeply [grateful we] both are to you. Neither the program nor the present growing interest in American Folk Songs could have existed without your always tactful and fertile stimulus. [ALC]

Another acknowledgment went out to Hal Davis at Columbia Records on August 30:

Thank you for sending the Album of Chain Gang Songs to the Archive. [Josh] White did a very fine job in this album and the acoustic characteristics of the records are really quite remarkable. [ALC][55]

Alan sent off a somewhat different letter to Frederick Stokes in New York on August 30:

I greatly appreciate the copy of the delightful "American Mother Goose" that you sent me. It's a real addition to my library and I know I shall enjoy reading it. [ALC][56]

Also on August 30 he sent an additional inquiry to Joseph Mitchell at the *New Yorker*:

Would it be possible for you to give me the address of Madame Olga, the bearded lady and I'll call on her sometime when I'm in New York and see if I can get the ballad from her. [ALC]

As usual, he updated his father on September 10:

My vacation has been somewhat interrupted to say the least. I've put in seven working days out of the first two weeks, but this one I'm going to stay out of town. The enclosed letters of permissions all call for your attention. I suggest that you go hard with Mr. [Elie] Siegmeister, keeping Mr. [Earl] Beck, who gave you the song "O Meeshegan" in mind and that you go easy on [Reuel] Lahmer. He's a nice young and important musician who works with Roy Harris—Harris is a No. 1 American composer and a completely loyal Lomax fan. The Program hasn't sold as yet, but will be definitely sold before the first of October. We made a great hit. The job which neither you nor Bess nor Deanie could make anything of is a job in the Library of Congress Radio Project as folklore and folksong consultant at a considerable advance in salary. This will come through the end of October, but it's not completely certain yet. Buy Bess a tuning fork and strike it in front of the microphone before every record is begun. This is very important and is a suggestion of Harold's. Also remember in recording Negro singing, to try to get a picture of the various parts of the harmony by changing the position of the microphone so that each singer's part is recorded over and against the other. Elizabeth is calling and I'm going home. [ALC]

Alan was eager to promote his speaking engagements, as noted in this message to Edward Ward in Saginaw, Michigan, on September 11:

Your letter of the 26th has been referred to me for answering and I'm [sending] it on to the Columbia Artist's Bureau who manage my lecture engagements. I appreciate your interest in having me and I certainly hope that I will be able to come this year. [ALC]

As a follow up to the note to Ward, on September 11 he drafted a short message to Isabel Scott at the lecture bureau:

The enclosed note explains itself. I hope it may mean a date. I would suggest that you not go too steep on the price and dovetail the date with my Minnesota jaunt. I like the new leaflet much better. [ALC]

Regarding the request for song permissions from Reuel Lahmer, Alan wrote to him on September 11:[57]

I have referred your letter to my father who handles all Lomax permissions with recommendations for leniency. You realize, however, that the publishers will have to pay something to use these tunes. This has always been the case since father's books were first published. I would suggest that you ask John A. Lomax for permission to use a group of five or ten songs for publication, to be paid for when the manuscript is accepted. For performance, except over the air, I don't see why not go ahead just as you please. My best regards to you and the rest of the Harris family. [ALC]

On September 11 he also corresponded with Mrs. Abbot regarding the publishing status of the proposed *Hard-Hitting Songs for Hard Hit People*:

I would very much like a report on the present status of the Woody Guthrie song book, since I have invested a good deal of time and energy on the project. I'm sure you agree with me that the book has got great significance and I believe a large potential market. If I can be of any help in giving the book a slightly different form, assuming that its present form does not seem salable, I should be glad to cooperate. Some further work must be done in getting permissions on all the songs included and in arranging payment for some, either from an advance or from royalties. I should like to hear from you. [WGC]

> While he continued to promote Guthrie, Lead Belly, and the Golden Gate Quartet, Alan also suggested another budding performer to Wetherald at RCA on September 16:

The most charming singer of old world ballads that I know of—not in any particular authentic American style, but in a characteristic Irish style of his own which is extremely captivating is Burl Ives. I think his albums of songs will far outshine those of [John Jacob] Niles and the other dulcimer players on Columbia, whose names I can't recall, at the moment. I suggest that you see him on your next visit to New York. His address is 550 Riverside Drive, Tel. No. Monument 2-8244. I'll get you the copy of the Leadbelly Jail House Songs as soon as possible. I've not hurried because I felt one might let the scent of the chain gang album depart from the public nostril. [ALC]

> Alan sent a short request to his father on September 18:

Would you please send me a copy of the sentence that the Arizona judge addressed to his Mexican prisoner about to be hung. Nick and I would like to use it on the C.B.S. sustaining series which begins next Monday, 10:30–10:45, E.S.T. and will continue three nights a week, Mon. Wed. Fri. indefinitely thereafter. C.B.S. did not sell the program commercially and have decided to sponsor it themselves. I will use a good deal of material from your books and I think if you're still willing to make the deal about my debt, I'd consider it very seriously. I'm not going to make enough money this year to pay you back and I'd like to get it, of course, in a way that is familiar to you. Please include the rights to Cowboy Songs at least on programs with which I have something to do myself. I hope your trip is going extremely well. [ALC]

> More news to John followed on September 27:

Mr. Siegmeister wired me that his book was coming out tomorrow and asked for the permissions.[58] I said $15.00 per song and hope that it was alright. I have taken care of the notarization matter. My program is on W.A.B.C. (860 Kil.) 9:30, E.S.T. It's really worth hearing. I will be on the American School of the Air preview, Oct. 1, 10:30 P.M. and regularly after that beginning Oct. 8, at 9:15–9:45 and in the afternoon [3:35–4:00]. Bess is here in Washington and will stay on until Sunday since her friend Counts decided on the last minute not to come down to Bryn Mawr until Sunday. She looks in the pink and we're keeping her in bed and feeding her up for her year's work. She speaks with great enthusiasm about the trip and your handling of the singers. The results, so far, sound fine, folkloristically, but shy, acoustically, because of the machine. It would improve your work a great deal to record at 78 instead of 33 and I suggest that you make that change at once. If you have any more troubles of a serious nature, set back on your heels and wire us. I might even be able to wrangle a better machine for you. We have no objection to recording the entire interview between you and the informer, including the songs you sing them, the leading conversation that you use and the fullness of their replies.

It will be marvelous to see you again. I'll look the judge's story up at once in the Southwest Review and let you know what I think. Here's a quote from your letter of Aug. 8. "I now propose to transfer to you all my claims to the three books in question, ABFS [*America Ballads and Folk Song*], Leadbelly [*Negro Folk Songs as Sung by Lead Belly*] & OSC [*Our Singing Country*], by legal document, giving to me the entire proceeds other than for radio use, for a period of ten years. You thereafter to own entirely, all proceeds in any form whatever, the income, from whatever source from these books." My added suggestion was to allow me radio rights for Cowboy Songs, revised edition, where material from the same is used in a program in which I'm connected myself. As for the other books, radio rights should include any and all radio programs. It is a very generous offer and I hope suits your convenience as much as mine. May I assume that it is in operation from this date, pending a formal agreement. [ALC]

That same day, September 27, Alan mailed a short message to Davidson Taylor regarding his CBS contracts:

There are a number of problems which the contracts bring up which I'll discuss with you when I come to New York next week. I hope to see you on Tuesday morning. [ALC]

About this time, in an undated letter, Alan wrote to Clifton Fadiman regarding his CBS show and the application to the Rockefeller Foundation for funding the proposed Radio Research Project:[59]

This letter will be a strange mixture of things, and I am not counting the two-fingered typo-errors. Your letter turned the tide. Two days after it was written, [Archibald] MacLeish had included me in the Rockefeller application, not as a radio fellow, but as the folk-lore, folk-music expert. He thinks, I understand, that I am no writer and I sometimes agree with him. Anyhow he has given me the nod and I will have a chance to prove him wrong. Someday to show my appreciation, when you want to go on vacation, I'll volunteer to ghostwrite your book-reviews [for the *New Yorker*].

You know we locked horns the first time we met and, being young and childish, I took the battle very seriously. Working with you for two weeks in the back country completely revised this edition. The whole cast came around and expressed the same opinion about you. I'm no good at this, but it was good to know you.

I'm sorry that Lucky Strike and you feel tentative about the show. It ought to go on the air, while the traffic is light. The reactions I have had from the hinterlands have been extremely favorable. I am inclined to agree with your first reaction when you saw the script that a great deal of mcing is not essential and this I think will be even more the case when we have the cast that we want, including Sidney Bechet, the Coon Creek Girls, Wade Mainer and others. At the behest of various friends of mine I have been thinking of myself in the mc's shoes and I want to know what you think of it. The material and the performers might sell the show. [ALC][60]

Continuing to move between New York and Washington, he updated his father on October 12:

I am going to cast this letter on the rough waters of life of this United States and hope that it finds you. I suggest that if the recordings are not completely up to standard that you let us know and we can send you a machine that you know better how to handle and are familiar with. It's already to go whenever you are. I've just got back from New York where I did my first School of the Air broadcast and several others also. Spent the night with Mrs. Eleanor Roosevelt in Hyde Park. She's a very nice lady. I'm working my head off and I'm delighted to know that you're having such good luck. Your letter to Mr. Wiesner has just come and we all think that you should change to 78 and that you should send for the other machine if you feel that you need it. [ALC]

Back to Library business, Alan wrote to Beatrice Sawyer Rossell at the American Library Association on October 12 (with a brief follow-up on October 16):

You must by this time consider me completely undependable, but the fact is that your letters chase me to and fro from Washington to New York and back, and I've been constantly on the go until the last day or so. Your idea for records for Book Week is, I am afraid, somewhat beyond me this year. I should like to work on such a project myself for four or five days and there just isn't the time this year, and that's what I think this job would mean, nor do I have an assistant to whom I could assign this fascinating project. The Library does not at the present, lend records. We are able to furnish duplicates at a fixed price of $1.50 for a twelve inch acetate record at 78 R.P.M. For the best results with such records, you will need a good play back machine with the light and flexible pick-up rather than the victrola type.

There are, besides this, the problem of choice of material for children which we know little about. Perhaps by next year if you think it of sufficient importance, we can have prepared an album especially with the needs of children in mind. Another possible solution is for you to use copies of certain School of the Air broadcasts of last year as demonstration pieces. If this seems practical, you'll have to communicate with Sterling Fisher, C.B.S., New York City. He will have to ok the use of these records for public demonstration. I suggest using Railroad Work Songs, Poor Farmer Songs, Square Dance Songs, Gold Rush Songs and Sea Shanties for your programs. [ALC]

Still pursuing his speaking career, he wrote to Burton Paulu of the General Extension Division of the University of Minnesota on October 14:

I'd be delighted to speak on your informal interview program on Thursday November 7. I suggest that you contact me immediately after the lecture in the morning so that we can arrange the details. [ALC]

The next day, October 15, he responded to Charles Thomson of the Department of State:

Thank you for the return of my manuscript. I was delighted that your commission felt able to use it. Would it be possible to send me fifty reprints of the bibliography itself. I should like to send them to a large group of folksong specialists throughout the United States. Also, I would like to send them to some friends who have been asking about them for some time. [ALC][61]

He also corresponded with Mary Elizabeth Barnicle on October 15:

I would still like to know what the name of the group that sang hymns at Dorton's Branch, Ky. is. We're about to bring out a check list for our 4,000 records so that people can order copies made by our phono-duplicating service. Have you made any records lately which we should copy for our files before they're worn? I met Mrs. Roosevelt the other day and was amazed to see how much she looked and acted like you—with a big laugh like yours and lots of calmness and strength. Elizabeth and I would like very much to have you come to see us anytime you can. We have a place out on the Potomac that's very wild and you and Tillman might find some squirrels to shoot. If you can't come down, I'd like to see you on my next trip to New York about a month from now. How can one reach you. Varney was a little uncertain about it when I called him. What do you think of "Back Where I Come From?" My very best regards to Tillman and much love from Elizabeth and myself to you. [CBS]

The following day, October 16, he conferred with William Fineschriber at CBS:

It is now three o'clock Wednesday evening and I am just starting out to find the people for the program. I may come dragging back about Monday or sooner, but in any event, I suggest that you schedule a dress rehearsal and etc. with Miss Gillis, W.J.S.V. She doesn't sound any too happy about it. I'll write you or wire you when I have definite news about everything. [ALC]

Alan again wrote a note to Helen Flanders on October 25:

The Vermont folksongs have now been copied and when the titles have been copied on each cover, they will be ready to come to you. I want to know, first, whether you want us to send all of the vulgar songs and stories, many of which were recorded for anthropological interest only and might not be suitable for the Vermont Archive. I make here a distinction between the broad traditional ballad as opposed to the vulgar folk and contemporary vulgar song. [N-JB]

Also on October 25 he pursued getting a speaking fee from Howard Phillips in Washington, D.C.:

Thank you for your kind invitation to appear at the Wilson [Teachers] College on the program you mentioned. My fee is fifty dollars ($50.00). [ALC]

On the last day of the month, October 31, he asked his father a short question:

Will you kindly send by *airmail* your permission to reprint "Home On the Range" to be used in the Army Song Book. All of the people who have been asked have given permissions. The book is not to be sold, but, is to be used in conscription camps. [ALC]

The first of November brought a spate of correspondence, including a long letter to Woody Guthrie, somewhat concerning his radio program:

I am indeed sorry that you're no longer on Back Where I Come From. I wish there was some way that you and Nick [Ray] could get together again. The first program that you failed to appear on just about broke my heart and I don't know yet how I'm going to plan the script without imagining you taking lines. I'd like to hear your side of the story and I'd like to try to do something about the situation.[62] A friend of mine is helping to put on National Art Week. He heard about your ballad on Tom Joad and thought it would be a good idea for you to write a song or ballad about National Art Week. This project which you will find out more about in the pamphlet, gives opportunity to artists in the country to exhibit and sell their work and is aimed at making it easy for more artists to make a living in the United States. I thought this idea of finding the hidden talent in America might be right for you. The song doesn't have to be about artists, specifically, but just about the hidden, unknown, and undiscovered fine people that there are in this country. I wrote MacMillan Publishers the other day and suggested that they look at your autobiography. How is it coming along? How are you coming along? If you'd like to get away from New York for a couple of weeks, why not drop down to see us. We'd be delighted to see you and to have you. [WGC]

To I. S. Becker at Columbia Artists, on November 1, he expressed his feelings about his public appearances:

Wilson Teachers College called me shortly before your letter came and I arranged to talk for them for $50.00 on November 18th. I did not think to inquire if you had contacted them previously. This was my mistake and I'll not make it again. I'll also be glad to forward you your commission if you so desire. It seems to me that Wilson Teachers College behaved rather badly. [ALC]

Alan thanked Lexie Dean Robertson, Rising Star, Texas, on November 1:

Thank you for your charming letter and for the enclosure "Beggars Minstrel" which I enjoyed very much. I regret to say that I did not know before who was the Poet Laureate of Texas. My most cordial greetings to you. [ALC]

Concerning a different matter, he also wrote on November 1 to Gertrude Zwenig in New York:

In reply to your recent letter, I wish to state that no job is open in the Archive of American Folk Song at present. I'm sure your interest and experience would be useful and I suggest that if you wish to apply for such a position as suggested in your letter in the future, you write to Mr. Rogers, Personnel Director, in charge of applications. I'm glad to know that someone enjoyed the classes at New York University as much as I did. [ALC]

In response to an inquiry from someone in Brazil, Alan gave an overview of the collection to Spivacke on November 4:

The Archive of American Folk Song now contains over 4,000 discs, both aluminum and acetate, of folk songs, folk tales and folk melodies collected in the United States and in the West Indies. In addition, there is an interesting series of recordings copied from cylinders made by Percy Granger in the South Seas, Denmark, and the British Isles in the early part of the century. The recordings in this series of seventy additional discs, naturally, are not acoustically good in quality, but the material is of great scientific interest. Geographically, the Archive of American Folk Song represents the following states in the United States: Vermont, New York, Penna., District of Columbia, Virginia, North Carolina, South Carolina, Georgia, Florida, Mississippi, Tennessee, Kentucky, Indiana, Ohio, Louisiana, Texas, California, Colorado, New Mexico, Oklahoma, Michigan and Wisconsin. There are also sizable collections from Haiti and the Bahamas in the West Indies.

Linguistically, the songs are in English and dialects of English, with a very large section of the songs in the Negro dialect of the southern part of the United States. Other languages represented are: French . . . Spanish . . . Finnish . . . A large number of very fine examples of Slavic, Russian, Polish, Yugo-Slav, Czecho-Slav, Rumanian, Slovenian are represented in small groups of songs largely from urban centers such as San Francisco and Detroit. Others. Portuguese from San Francisco, Norwegian from Wisconsin, German from Pennsylvania and Indiana and particularly interesting and rare are some hymns of the Amish sect. Types of Songs: [Here follows a long list.] I look forward with great anticipation to a long continued and fruitful period of exchange between the two folk song collections, yours in Brazil and ours in the United States. [ALC]

He answered Helen Hartness Flanders's next letter on November 5. She had inquired about the selling of recordings of Elmer George, who had appeared on Alan's American School of the Air show of November 28, 1939, and some other matters:

I know nothing about the George recording matter. It is possible that some person who handles such business got the information from a newspaper story or from C.B.S. when he was in New York last year. I rather resent your having thought that I'd be responsible for an attempt to exploit a singer and a friend of mine and especially that I would do anything in Vermont without consulting you. The Library of Congress is planning to issue a series of folk-song albums to be distributed at cost to the general public. I've been thinking of including from the Vermont collection certain items, but I wish to be assured by you that they meet your approval. These records will be non-commercial and will make available the literature of the American Folk Songs to students all across the country. It might, perhaps, be interesting to think of the Vermont Album edited with your collaboration. [N-JB]

Since Flanders continued to be concerned about the possible issuing of commercial records by Elmer George, without his or her approval, Alan reassured her on November 15 that there was no problem:

I inquired at Columbia Broadcasting System as to whether they had recorded Elmer George or written him. They have done neither. There are firms in New York City who make a practice of recording singers who appear on the air in the hope that they can sell the records to these singers. Such records cannot be sold for commercial purposes without the permission of the singers. I do not know what firm has written to Mr. George but I imagine that he can tell you. In the meantime, Miss Linscott has written the enclosed letter to C.B.S. I'm dreadfully sorry to hear of Mrs. Sullivan's death. She was a fine and noble woman able to find this complex life interesting up to the very last. I hope you will express for me my deepest sympathy with her children. [N-JB]

In a short memorandum to Spivacke on November 15, Alan gave some of his usual supportive advice:

Dr. Mitchell of New York University has expressed his desire to begin recording in New York City and I recommended that a portable Presto machine be forwarded to him along with 50 acetate records and four sapphire cutting needles, as soon as possible. The duplicate which he requested some time ago has now been made for him and is ready to be shipped to him immediately. [ALC][63]

Continually juggling his public and private responsibilities, Alan sent a brief note to Roger Starr at CBS on November 16:

I feel rather sure that Miss Dannenberg did not return to me all of the negatives left in her hands last year and that you have in your department what you're looking for. I've just looked through my files and I can't find them. I'd like to know if you do. [ALC]

Alan next wrote to his boss, Spivacke, on November 19:

It is very important for the Archive of American Folk Song that the W.P.A. continue its present helpful practice of cataloguing new records as they come into the Archive. I understand that Sidney Robertson is shortly to deposit a group of two hundred additional records made in California with W.P.A. help, but before these records can be accessioned and catalogued, two other groups of records must be so treated: 1. Recordings made by Todd-Sonkin in California under Library sponsorship and in cooperation with the Farm Security Administration. 2. Recordings made by John A. Lomax in the south, partly with the help of the W.P.A. Music Project in Alabama. This work preliminary to the Sidney Robertson records include approximately two hundred-fifty 12 in. discs. If we would make an estimate of the number of records to be so treated within the next year, a conservative guess would be about a thousand. I would greatly appreciate your giving this your immediate attention since work in the Archive is being seriously hampered by this delay. [ALC]

Spivacke received a short memo from Alan also dated November 19:

There are in the Archive of American Folk Song forty-nine (49) records made in Indiana with the help, in part, of the Indiana Folk Lore Society and the W.P.A. Writers Project. The records contain ballads in English and French and a group of German-Amish hymns. The serial numbers are 1719-1767. [ALC]

On December 2 he briefly corresponded with Lee Hays in New York, who had recently moved from Arkansas:

I certainly thank you for the interesting ballad you sent and it will go into the special starred collection in the Library. Maybe we can record the tune someday when I'm in New York. If you have any more like this, please send them along. Your copy is herewith returned. I'll speak about the other matter when I see you. [ALC]

Hays had recently met Millard Lampell and Pete Seeger, and with Pete Hawes they had formed the Almanac Singers.[64]

On December 2 he responded to a fan, Dr. Winifred W. Curtis, in Stony Brook, New York:

Your letters are always a pleasure to receive. Perhaps, if you like the School of the Air so much, you'll enjoy a program which I write called, "Back Where I Come From," which is broadcast over C.B.S., Monday, Wednesday and Friday at 10:30. On this program I am able to take a more adult approach to the material. If you're interested in the history of "Frog Went a-Courting," look in "Publications of the Texas Folk Lore Society" Vol. 5, pg. 5 for a lengthy discussion and many versions of the "Frog's Courtin," published versions of which we have going back to 1549. We have about twenty thousand songs in the Archive. [CBS]

That same day, Alan sent a short note to Archibald MacLeish:

For the past seven years the Library of Congress has sponsored field recordings of American Folk Songs under the Archive of American Folk Song. Recently, a grant was secured from the Carnegie Foundation to install equipment in the Library of Congress for duplicating the four thousand or more field phonograph folk songs so secured. Through this equipment, copies of these records will be available to the general public at cost of duplication. A check-list of the songs in the Archive is in preparation and will be published within the next two or three months for general distribution. [ALC]

He followed up the next day, December 3, to "Archie" (MacLeish):

I think the classic essay enclosed on spitting on public library grounds deserves your personal attention. At least, it should be preserved in brass as a stimulating if not elevating human document. [ALC]

Also on December 3 he encouraged Miss Valborg Kjosness at Stanford University in California:

I am very much interested in your project to record Basque music in Boise [Idaho] and hope to be of service in getting a good job done there. The Archive of American Folk Song has a machine at its disposal to loan to competent field workers but expects them to purchase their own copies of the records they make and is not now in a position to assist them in field work. I suggest that Dr. Allen communicate with Dr. Spivacke, Chief of the Music Division, Library of Congress in this latter connection.

It will not be possible for us to get a machine to you for work this Christmas but I see no reason why you cannot make preliminary arrangements for recording during the holidays so that work can be done next summer. For background in field work, I suggest that you examine: "Folk Lore In America" by Martha Beckwith, "Research in Primitive and Folk Music" by Dr. George Herzog (a bulletin of the American Council of Learned Societies), "The Introduction to British Ballads from Maine" by Phillip Barry and F. H. Eckstorm, "Minstrelsy of Maine" by Fannie H. Eckstorm and Mary W. Smythe, "Folk Lore from the Schoharie Hills" by E. E. Gardner, "The Quest of the Ballad" and "Ballads and Sea Songs of Nova Scotia" by W. Roy Mackenzie, "The Ozarks" by Vance Randolph, "A Song Catcher in the So. Mountains" by Dorothy Scarborough, "Folk Song Variants from Jamaica" by H. H. Roberts, Vol. 38 (JAFL). I think that after you look over these volumes, some of which can be looked at cursively and some of which deserve a close reading, you'll have a pretty good picture of some of the problems that come up in field work and that your field work might touch upon. Under separate cover, I am also mailing you a questionnaire prepared by Herbert Halpert for use in the field by collectors. It also brings out a number of questions that one would like to have the answers to. I think it is up to the field worker after a certain point to decide what problem he's gong to tackle and how. However, if I can be of any further help in future correspondence, please let me know. [ALC]

Over a week later, December 13, he responded to Charles Thomson at the Division of Cultural Relations of the Department of State:

Thank you for the fifty reprints of my bibliography of American Folk Songs. They are now in my hands and will go to the persons who have requested them. I greatly appreciate your promptness and generosity in complying with this request. [ALC]

The next day, December 14, he sent a short request to Spivacke:

An order from Dr. Stith Thompson, Indiana University, has been received for 49 records. I suggest that we take care of it within the next four weeks since Dr. Thompson, through whom it really comes is a person of so much importance to us in the Archive of American Folk Song. HURRAH! [ALC]

Also on December 14, he drafted another request to Spivacke:

Due to extremely heavy correspondence during the past year, my Archive mail now amounts to at least two trays full, not counting miscellaneous papers which I can't file at all. I very urgently need a section of filing cabinet, three or four trays deep, to take care of this problem. [ALC]

Alan sent a bit longer letter to Amelia C. Andrews in Black Mountain, North Carolina, on December 14:

I appreciate your letter and the cards about Widducan Vare. I wonder if you in your course of eighty generous years, you have not learned some old fashioned songs which may be of interest to a collector of such material. If you have, I'd very much like to hear about them and have you send them in to me. P.S. Since you have enjoyed the folk song program, you may be interested in knowing about another which I write called Back Where I Come From, over CBS on Monday, Wednesday and Friday at 10:30. In this broadcast, I am allowed to take a slightly more adult view of folk material. I hope you will listen and write and tell me what you like about it. [ALC]

Mr. Allan-Allen in Bernardsville, New Jersey also received a letter from Alan dated December 14:

I am sorry that I'll not be in Washington between the 25 of December and January 1, but I hope it will be possible to arrange to meet somewhere at some time. I think, perhaps, you'll enjoy hearing the folksongs in the Archive of American Folk Song in the Library of Congress and I'd like to make whatever suggestions I could, if I may be so helpful, for program material. Meantime, if you have any material for singing groups, I'd like to hear about it. [ALC]

Apparently planning a trip to Cleveland, Alan sent a short note to Spivacke on December 16:

Do you expect me to play records in Cleveland? If so, how? I understand that Miss Bush will need a machine too. What about transportation? [ALC]

In addition to the rest of his busy schedule, Alan managed to write a couple of popular articles; the first, "Music in Your Own Back Yard," was published in the Girl Scouts publication *The American Girl* in October 1940. It briefly covered some of his recording experiences, including Lead Belly and Aunt Molly Jackson. He followed with the very brief "Songs of the American Folk" in *Modern Music* early the next year, aimed at professionals. At the same time he was involved in moving his office at the Library of Congress, as he informed Spivacke on December 17:

As you know, the project of moving the Archive into its new quarters has been in the prospect for some time, and I think that it should be pushed forward before the first of the year. I am constantly needed to assist Mr. Wiesner in business affecting the Archive; the W.P.A. project also could save a great amount of time if I were near at hand for consultation. Besides, by January 1, if I am not already working on the radio project, I shall be working in collaboration with Mr. [Philip H.] Cohen. They, too, are anxious to be established in quarters near to the phono-duplication laboratory. This will mean: 1. moving records into stack space provided for them. 2. setting up the office of the Archive to temporarily service the Radio Project and the Music Project.

Herewith, I submit the attached floor plan for the division of the office into three parts for the section above mentioned. The cases now used to shelve the Archive records can be used for this purpose. Those remaining, Mr. Wiesner needs for his use in the phono-duplicating section. The tables now in the Archive can all be used in the Archive office, and-or by Mr. Wiesner in the phono-duplicating division. I wish to have my telephone transferred for my own use in the Archive and wish to suggest, specifically, that this *not* also service the radio project. [ALC][65]

As the year ended, on December 30, he wrote briefly to Denise Chotas at the Mexican Embassy in Washington:

I think you must be quite the most pleasant person in the diplomatic service to continue to sing so anxiously about my poor records. They will be safely waiting for you when you and I are a little less busy. I haven't had the time to think about them for a moment lately and I haven't been fighting any war either. [ALC]

A longer letter to William Fineschriber at CBS went out on December 30:

In case you're worried, I am worried too! Here it is Monday morning and no script for next week's program, and I don't have an idea in at least three hundred miles. I'm completely empty of ideas. However, I'll go home and commune with nature and try to think of something. What I think of now is to have Burl Ives again.

The French-Canadian program again concerns me. [Marius] Barbeau recommends: 1. Phileas Bedard, 73 years old, from country near Montreal for a fee and expenses, speaks no English, a very great folk singer. 2. Emil Dushea, folk-like tenor, 40 years old, as escort. 3. Madame Bolduc, Montreal, who is too fat to travel. I've heard her records and she's very fine. I still think you'd better send me to Montreal if you want a good program and send me to arrive, Thursday 19th. The problem of importing singers from Canada, according to Barbeau, are extensive, involved, the problem of American money in advance, passports, and the possibility of all kinds of misunderstandings. There are very good folk singers in the neighborhood of Montreal and Ottawa and even though I am foot sore and somewhat weary of soul, I think we'd better go there and do the broadcast. Will write you again Tuesday or Wednesday, and, in the meantime, I'd like to see whatever mail there be. [ALC][66]

Even on New Year's Eve he wrote a few letters, one to Thomas Larkin in Boston:

Your Haitian project sounds interesting. I'll be glad to discuss it with you and play records for you. Do you know of the work of Katheryn Dunham, Zora Neale Hurston and Melville Herskovitz? I suggest that you give me a week or two notice as I'm often out of town. [ALC]

Another on December 31 went to George Lee Kramer in Winter Haven, Florida:

You can obtain a copy of Peter Grey which is the name of the song your dad used to sing by writing to _____ [in original] collection at Brown University Library. They have brought out a series of reprints of early American songs and this is in that series. Do you happen to remember other songs your father sang of the same type, songs of Reconstruction Days or Railroad building? If you do recall any and even if they're fragmentary, I'd greatly appreciate your sending them to me to be added to the collection here in the Library. [ALC]

In a message to Davidson Taylor, on December 31, Alan expressed his thoughts about his radio show:

I am sorry I did not see you in New York, both, for holiday reasons and because from what Nick [Ray] tells me, your opinion of "BACK WHERE I COME FROM" is not what it should be. Our mail, of which the two enclosures are typical, seems to me clearly indicative that our audience is so far a rather articulate and highly critical one, who feel that the program has something very important to say. I think it has too, and I can't understand why your attitude towards it has changed. I believe in it enough to want to continue working on it in spite of the difficulties that my new job as radio fellow will entail, and I'm going to hire an assistant to take care of some of the details of my several small concerns, and incidentally, stop this eternal problem of clearance of BACK WHERE I COME FROM. That's a mechanical matter which I can hire the disposition of. Before taking this step, I'd like some (friendly, *unofficial*, not in the slightest contractual) assurance from you that BACK WHERE I COME FROM has a clear road ahead for some time. Morally and artistically, I feel it should have, although, I know its many problems for all of us. I also know of its many strong points. I've had a grand Christmas, flat on my back, lolling about and gossiping with old tried and true friends. My best wishes for the New Year from Elizabeth and me to you both. P.S. Please post on all bulletin boards the review of the Golden Gates' magnificent performance. [ALC]

There was also a concerned letter to L. Merrick on December 31, regarding his contract with Columbia Artists:

I do not know what the statement of my account with you refers to, either, on the debit or the credit side. Please explain. [ALC]

LETTERS, 1941–1945

1941

Alan began 1941 with a short letter on January 10 to R. P. Wetherald at RCA Victor, indicating his continuing interest in commercially recorded country music:

Would you have the hillbilly department try and locate for me Wade Mainer and his Mountaineers and send me their present address as soon as possible. [ALC][1]

He also followed up with a note to Amelia Andrews in Black Mountain, North Carolina, on January 10:

I should be delighted to have copies of the songs you mentioned and it's pleasant to know that you are following the program. Under separate cover I'm sending you a copy of the American School of the Air Manual.[ALC]

The next day, January 11, Alan responded to a query from Arthur Moore in Albany, Georgia:

When I was in Florida and southern Georgia in the summer 1935, the word "jouk" was current as applied to a dance hall and drinking place of "low resort." I heard this term used mostly by Negroes and used in exactly the same sense as barrel-house was used in Texas, Louisiana and Mississippi. The word was also used as a verb, applied to a certain style of guitar playing in which the player, using a pattern of bass runs, played the melody on the tenor strings with a bottle neck on his little finger, Hawaiian fashion. They would say "jouk it boy," or "I'm jouking it now," and the style of playing itself was called "jouking." Zora Neale Hurston uses the word constantly in

ALAN LOMAX

**Authority on American Folk-Lore . . . Archivist to the
Library of Congress . . . Commentator and Artist on
"Columbia's School of the Air"**

Flyer created to promote the Alan Lomax lecture series.

"Mules and Men" and she can undoubtedly give you a great deal more information. She can be reached through her publishers, Lippincott Co., Phil. Penn. "Jouk" box I've heard only recently and I feel as though it has been derived from generic "jouk." I suggest, also, that you contact Sterling Brown, Howard University, English Department about this. I've been in contact with _____ [in original] University of Georgia in regard to starting a Folklore Archive there. Are you interested in this enterprise? [ALC]

The minutiae of his office always intruded, as in this letter to Harold Spivacke, also on January 11:

I feel it highly advisable that the cases in which the Archive records are kept be made locked cases, since the materials are more easily subject to damage and also more valuable in certain respects than materials in ordinary shelves. To this end, may I suggest that wire grating be placed back of the case in which the Archive records are now placed and that a door be installed for that case and another one for the next case adjoining. [ALC]

Two days later, January 13, he updated Luther Evans, Assistant Chief Librarian, on his father's current work:

John A. Lomax, Honorary Curator of Folk Song of the Library of Congress is working at the Library at the moment, writing up his experiences and field notes over his years of collecting. This material will form one of the most valuable parts of the Archive collection and will be an indispensable supplement to the records themselves, and I believe, one of the most important human documents in the Library itself. Enclosed, are two samples of the work now pouring out from his pen. Mrs. Lomax is devoting her full time to writing up field notes, transcribing texts and coordinating the whole with the records. The volume of work to be completed is, however, so large that stenographic help is vitally necessary. Mr. Lomax is, at the moment, employing two part-time secretaries out of his own pocket for the job. It seems to me that, in view of the contribution which Mr. Lomax has made to the Library of Congress collections during the past seven years, the Library should provide stenographic facilities for him during his stay here. [ALC]

On January 14 he was back in touch with William Fineschriber at CBS regarding the program on French Canada:

I telephoned Dr. [Marius] Barbeau and the station manager at CKAC (Biondi) to send me the list of songs which their singers know and which can be cleared and they were to have written me by today. Perhaps, the letter will come tomorrow morning, if not, I'll call them and get the information over the telephone tomorrow. You will hear from me again Thursday morning. [ALC]

On another matter, he queried Willard Z. Park at the University of Oklahoma on January 27:

Would you be willing to undertake the co-sponsorship of Miss Barry's project with us. It's the sort of job that should have constant supervision by a technically qualified person. If you should feel able to do this, I think we could furnish Mrs. Barry with the equipment she wishes. [ALC][2]

On January 30 he warned Spivacke about a rather strange individual:

Life moves so swiftly these days that one must depend on first impressions as the basis for action, perhaps, too often. I feel sure, however, that Mr. Ishtiope Robertson is not a charlatan, but a harmless and egotistical careerist who ascends by jumping from acquaintance to acquaintance, never staying too long with any one, never concerned with solving any problem. I sincerely hope that I will not have to assist or in any other way work with Mr. Ishtiope Robertson. For example: he spent the entire time that he was in my office in attacking, superficially and ignorantly, all the studies that have ever been made of Indians in the United States and all the scholars concerned with them. [ALC]

Alan mailed off a more detailed letter to William Fineschriber at CBS on January 30, regarding his upcoming radio show, *Wellsprings of Music*,[3] no. 15, "Latin America," to be broadcast February 4:

Here is what I can do in the way of clearances for Tuesday's show: I. For the Ecuadorean Trio. A. Ecuadorean Songs. 1. A San Juanito. 2. A Jaravi. 3. A Pasille. These are tunes usually played on the Indian pan-pipes or "Ronada-dor" and are the commonest of dance forms in the Andean region of Ecuador. There are numbers of such tunes in print in collections, but it is impossible to tell, which is which. All are called folk tunes. . . . [Here follows a very detailed list of tunes from Ecuador, Chile, Mexico, and Cuba, and where they can be found.]" As for the Mexican songs, "All the above can be found in the same publications as No. 1. That is, they appear in a government publication and are identified as P[ublic] D[omain]. These may be used if the other parts of the program do not work out. I believe that the singers know these because they are the commonest of Mexican songs." Concerning the Cuban songs,

"None of these can be found in any published sources that I have analyzed, although there are a few here on Cuban music. A guajira appears to be the dance of the natives of Cuba and these are probably folk or semi-folk songs based on the fundamental rhythm. E. I could find nothing on the Argentine Songs. F. Nor the Puerto Rican Songs. [ALC]

On the last day of the month, January 31, Alan dashed off a short message to Spivacke:

You'll be interested in the two attached letters. Perhaps if Victor or Columbia do not wish to do the recording, it will be a good Defense Program material for us to keep in mind later on. [ALC]

Responding to an inquiry from Ivalee Hobden, Music Consultant of the National Youth Administration in Dallas, he wrote on February 3:

Dr. Spivacke has handed me your letter for comment. Your project seems to me an extremely intelligent and creative one and I shall be glad to help in any way that I can. It seems to me basic that you buy for your project a group of the best books of material available and see to it that the boys absorb as many of the old tunes and old songs as possible. Trust them to supply their own improvisatory decoration. I might suggest the following books for their use:

"American Ballads and Folk Songs" by John A. Lomax and Alan Lomax

"Cowboy Songs" by John A. Lomax and Alan Lomax

"English Folk Songs from the Southern Appalachians" by Cecil Sharpe, Oxford University Press (This is in two volumes and is the best single source for old and authentic songs.)

"The American Songbag" by Carl Sandburg

"Thirty and One Mountain Tunes" by Bascom Lamar Lunsford

"Lonesome Tunes" by Loraine Wyman

"Singing Cowboy" by Margaret Larkin

I should like to add to this preliminary and fairly basic list of books two or three books of fiddle tunes, but I am away from my office and their titles slip my memory. I will send them to you when I return to Washington.

About records, under separate cover I will forward you a bibliography of cheap American records of folk songs most of the white stuff being done by contemporary singers with whom your musicians are probably acquainted. I feel that this list of records will be of great use to you and I would like to recommend that you allow me to pick out for you about ten Library of Congress original recordings, have them copied and sent to you. Copies of these records can be purchased at $1.50 each. This is for a 12-inch, two-sided acetate. I have discussed your project with my father who will be back in

Dallas in March and he has indicated his interest in helping you out with consultation and advice if you care to call him at his home. [ALC]

Also on February 3 he wrote to E. Z. Massicotte, Archivist of the Palais de Justice in Montreal, Canada, following a quick trip:

It was a great pleasure to meet you and to lunch with you in French with cabbage soup. I hope that if you ever come to the United States you will allow me to do the honors for you in Washington. In the meantime, thank you for helping to make my visit in Canada an extremely pleasant one. [ALC]

He followed on February 3 with a sharply critical note to R. P. Wetherald at RCA Victor:

Practically everyone in the Library of Congress feels that you have made a serious mistake by not including "Whoa Back Buck" in the Lead Belly album. [ALC][4]

There was a brief acknowledgment on February 3 to George Morgan at the Library of Congress:

Attached are two travel vouchers which I did not use on my Canadian trip. Thanks for your courtesy in getting these vouchers out for me so hurriedly that Friday morning. [ALC]

He continued his correspondence to Woody Guthrie on February 4:

I haven't had much time to take it easy since your letter came or to do any letter-writing either. Besides "School of the Air" and "Back Where I Come From," I am working every day on a really good folk song program [*The Ballad Hunter*] with my father, who should have been hired by Columbia years ago instead of me to talk about folk songs. We are putting him and his recordings on a series of transcribed records for distribution to the stations all over the country and he really takes it slow and makes it juicy. Would you mind us using your record of "Whoopee Ti Yi Yo" and "Get Along Little Dogie," which Father thinks is pretty fine?

I really miss you a lot on "Back Where I Come From." The program has become very "merry" and "jolly" since you left us. We don't have anybody who can come out and speak his mind with sincerity and honesty the way you can. Pete is on very regularly and his banjo playing adds a lot. Direction has improved a great deal and everyone likes the show except maybe Burl who is beginning to feel his oats these last days. The two finally got too high for us when the winter wind really began to blow and we've retreated into town in an apartment that's so snug it's practically underground, the address being 912 19th Street N.W. if you and your family are ever along that way or should care to drop me a line.

I don't know what to do about the Tom Joad song myself since I am also in the business but I am going to call up Steinbeck's agents and see whether they won't take action for you. It seems to me they are the proper people to handle it. If I did anything myself it would appear that I had a personal grudge against [Elie] Siegmeister, which I don't. I'll tell them to write you direct about it. I hope you are going to work more on your writing and get those short stories written. When they are ready I'll show them to everybody I know and try to help get them sold if you would like me to. I believe your job in the world is as a writer as well as a talker and singer, and I hope you keep digging at it. Give my regards to your family and to California and to those miners who know how to take it easy. [WGC]

Another letter on February 4 went to Libbie Maney in Elcho, Wisconsin:

I should be delighted to see the copies of the four songs you mentioned, along with any others that you remember hearing your parents sing. The Frog song, "Brennan on the Moor," and "Gypsy Davy" are all songs I should like to have and "McAllister, McAllister" is completely new to me. Please let me hear from you soon. [ALC]

Spivacke heard from Alan on February 4:

In regard to the letter from Mr. Getchell, I would like to point out that the next to the last phrase in the eighth paragraph of Mr. Getchell's letter is pretty far off the track as far as I am concerned. Miss Smith sings music hall ballads in a ferociously successful manner but this style would, it seems to me, rip to tatters, violate, maim, cripple and otherwise destroy the subtle and usually undersung ballads of the people. The Archive records are, of course, available to those as wants them, but I don't see why we should go after Kate Smith very vigorously. "Barbara Allen," "Pretty Polly" and "The Streets of Laredo" will be here long after she has finished writing her memoirs. The letter is a classic and if you don't mind I should like to have a copy of it for my files. [ALC]

February 4 was a busy correspondence day, with two short messages to William Fineschriber at CBS:

I think that Marius Barbeau in return for his labors on the French Canadian broadcast, deserves a set of recordings of the program at 78-rpm on 12-inch discs. Don't you?

The second was a bit longer:

Mr. Levine and I did not discuss the possibility of paying my living expenses for the French Canadian broadcast. As a matter of fact, when I came home I found that I had spent a lot more money than is usual on these weekend excursions. A number of times I entertained the cast, and then prices in Canada are high for living. I feel that this expense account, therefore, is justified. [ALC][5]

In the midst of all of this activity, Alan continued to consider further recording in the South. For example, he responded to Horace Mann Bond on February 4:[6]

I have just had the opportunity to read over your letter carefully—this month of January has been so busy that I have neglected all of my correspondence—and I find that I should like to come to your festival very much indeed and bring with me a recording machine to take down the music of all the participants. Let me hear from you as soon as you can about whether it will be possible to record continuously throughout the festival and I will recommend that the Library of Congress send me down for the occasion. It may be possible, too, for my father, John Lomax, to come too. I suggest that you also invite Sterling Brown of Howard University, whom you certainly know; Charles Seeger, Pan-American Union, Washington, D.C.; Dr. [Hugh] Hodgson of the University of Georgia, who has recently expressed an interest in collecting folk songs in Georgia on a statewide basis; Dr. Howard Odom and Dr. Guy Johnson of the University of North Carolina; and Zora Neale Hurston, who can be reached through her publisher, Lippincott, in Philadelphia. I am not completely certain that I can come because my present schedule at the Library is so full but this corroborating letter of yours would make it more certain, I believe. Thanks very much for the invitation. [FVMF]

He wrote a more personal letter to Mrs. Harold (his mother-in-law), February 5:

Elizabeth [Lomax], after quite a violent but short siege of strepto is now very much improved and up and around again. She's taking thyroid, iron and liver extract and probably by Spring will have her long delayed operation. I think by then the medicine she's taking will have her feeling a lot better. We have moved in town in an apartment. The address is 912-19th Street, N.W., and we'll both get a lot more sleep. I never met Margaret Johnson but I understand from Nick [Ray] that she looks better than she sings folksongs. Thanks for all the encouragement about Back Where I Come From. I will forward the clipping on to Nick. He needs the encouragement. [ALC]

The following day, February 6, he kept in touch with Joan Rayner in New York City:

I shall put a ten year restriction on your record, especially stating that it shall not be used without your permission. Be sure to call by the next time you're in town. It was a pleasure to see you both. [ALC]

As usual, Alan updated Spivacke on February 6:

The re-shelving of original records is becoming a very serious problem and I wish that you would make some arrangements about this soon to insure the originals against injury. [ALC]

With his radio programs always on his mind, he communicated with William Fineschriber on February 10:

Enclosed is a list of songs for clearance for the Spiritual Program. I have this day received confirmation of the invitation extended to me by the White House for the folksong party on the 17th. I have written Willie Johnson [leader of the Golden Gate Quartet], Burl Ives and Joshua White and they will also get invitations from the White House. But just to be sure that they receive the word, I'd appreciate your speaking to each one of them for me.

I don't have much money to spend so I have to arrange for the [Golden] Gate [Quartet] to take the pullman down after their show and the other two to take the day coach down early Sunday morning. They will have their expenses paid, all of them, for Sunday and Monday, but C.B.S. will have to take care of the Gate's expenses for Tuesday when they give the show with me. Do you wish me to have the scripts done down here or up at your place? And who's going to direct the Tuesday's show? I imagine our rehearsal will have to come sometime Monday morning early. I hope that you've found out that Burl has been pretty hard to handle on Back Where I Come From. He's a nice fellow but convinced of the fact that he's the best singer in the world. He can make Back Where I Come From impossible by refusing to take direction and you can make it possible by making him feel that he does not have to. [ALC][7]

Alan followed up to Fineschriber on February 19:

I hope you heard the afternoon show which was one of the best out of the forty we have produced so far. I am afraid that the morning show suffered from my not having ever rehearsed it with the cast before we went on the air. Clint did not get much of a performance out of his work with the boys and we were all very sleepy. The White House show came off well. Just to clear out slates:—The Golden Gate and Josh White were on CBS expense accounts on Tuesday and I have told them that was our understanding. Joshua White has all along been scheduled for an appearance on this spiritual show and he did a very nice job. Reimbursement expected. I think that Pete Seeger of the [Almanac Singers], Burl Ives, the Golden Gate, and myself could, with one fiddler, put on a very respectable show for the Latin Americans on March 1. I should also very much like to have Pete Johnson and a thirty piece combination to include Sidney Bechet, to be located through RCA Victor, perhaps. I am in process of composing a long letter to you and Dave [Davidson Taylor] about BWICF [Back Where I Come From], somewhat of a diatribe and jeremiad. [ALC][8]

The White House concert had been designed to boost military morale, as Alan noted to Colonel Dunkle at Fort Myer in Virginia on February 20:

Everyone who heard the program Monday night was very enthusiastic about it. I've just received a charming letter from Mrs. Roosevelt, herself, expressing her appreciation for it. I hope that it will mean, in the end, more music recreation for enlisted men in the military services. Thank you for your personal kindness to me and for your help in making this evening a successful one. [ALC][9]

Alan continued with his interest in southern black music in a letter to Davidson Taylor at CBS on February 20:

If it is not too late, this will introduce Harold Schmidt, Fisk University, who has the opportunity to make real progress in bringing a genuine program of Negro music to the Negroes in the South, through Fisk University. He is at work now on a festival for the Seventy-fifth Anniversary for the founding of Fisk and wants to have the Golden Gate and Joshua for an evening's concert. It occurs to me that it might be possible for CBS to send these fellows down as its contribution to the festival. I think the Gate would be honored to go. [ALC][10]

Concerning the Library of Congress's role as planning for the war developed, he composed a long letter to MacLeish on February 22:

After experience in the post near Washington in recording the folksongs the men know, in teaching others to them and in preparing the folk song program for The White House I wish to make the following recommendations for an Army Music Program. In general, the program would follow the desires of the men. Their tastes can be taken as the main criterion for the program. There is an enormous and basic interest among the white soldiers, the youngsters, in "hillbilly music," that is in contemporary American folk song. Basic to this interest is their enthusiasm for stringed instruments: guitar, harmonica, mandolin, banjo and fiddle, in that order of importance. A great many of the boys know how to play these instruments extremely well in the folk style, others can play a few chords, others wish to learn. Very few have instruments of their own and those that do are afraid to bring their instruments to camp.

A great many of the boys know cowboy songs and other white folksongs and like to sing them individually and in small groups. Few know as many verses and tunes as they would like to know. (These suggestions may be applied with appropriate changes to the Negro camps.) Therefore, I should like to propose the following: 1. To furnish the words for songs (cowboy songs, hillbilly songs, sentimental songs, popular songs, folk songs) in leaflet, pamphlet, and song sheet form. More leaflets, full of references to the historical & regional backgrounds of the songs should besides contain directions & calls for square dances & play party games. 2. To furnish similar types of songs on records. a. Select commercial records. b. Select Library of Congress records. c. Other records to be specifically recorded in the field for the Library for this purpose.

3. To furnish all types of stringed instruments, making them available in the barracks and in suitable recreation centers. 4. To furnish instruction books for playing these instruments, along with tunes and card diagrams to fit the types of songs about [to be] discussed. 5. To furnish recordings by folksong virtuosos who play on these instruments to be used as instruction records by the men. 6. A sound recording machine should visit these camps once a month to record the best programs by the men and the songs they have themselves made up. These records could be reproduced and used, beneficially, to circulate from one camp to another. To carry out this program, the Archive of American Folk Song needs clerical and editorial assistance. [ALC][11]

The letter of February 22 seems to have been attached to another two days later, February 24, to MacLeish:

You ask me to make recommendations for the activities of the District Music Unit of W.P.A. in the Library of Congress. This Unit can, given a little freedom and proper direction, render invaluable services to the Archive of American Folk Song. I should like to make the following recommendations. 1. That Mrs. Sidney Robertson who is an experienced and able field collector of folksongs and who has already directed a similar project in California under the W.P.A., be appointed supervisor. She is a person whom we should not like to lose in the Library of Congress and she would be invaluable to any Defense Program.

2. The Project must complete its work on the Check List, including geographical supplements, the foreign language supplements. Much remains to be done to bring to completion all the indices, by singer, place, classification, etc. for the Archive catalogue. 3. We have the opportunity to bring into the Library and to complete an index of American Folk Songs, in published form, initiated and carried two thirds to completion by Archer Taylor of the University of California. Mrs. Robertson has worked on the index in California, and under her, the project could shortly round it out. This index, along with the index of Library recordings, would give the Archive its basic working tools for any cultural project whatever. 4. It is possible for the Library to acquire for the asking all the folksongs that have been recorded on commercial records. These records will have to be indexed as they come in to be useful to us and again they are basic to us for National Defense. 5. I understand, besides, that the project is keeping current an index of American Composers and ordering and indexing the duplicate files of the W.P.A. between the years of 1935–1940. [ALC]

In a brief note to Mr. Crim at the White House on February 24, Alan recalled the recent concert:

It turns out that I gave you the complete list of the persons who participated on the program at The White House last Monday night. Will you be so kind as to send me a copy so that I can write letters to these performers. May I take this opportunity to tell you how much I appreciate your personal kindness and consideration of a very nervous performer, one who must have appeared to you as occupied in a strange musical business. [ALC]

In regard to an upcoming *Wellsprings of Music* show, he gave Fineschriber the list of performers and songs on February 24:

Here is a tentative program for the "shebang" on March 1. [Alan Lomax, Pete Seeger, Burl Ives, the Golden Gate Quartet, Joshua White, Pete Johnson,

Sidney Bechet and Group are listed along with their respective songs.] Of course, we can change the numbers a little but the last one ["Careless Love"] I'm particularly enthusiastic about because we can give the tune to Pete, then let Joshua try it out on the guitar, then the Gate, then Sidney, and in the end with a group rendition with the audience. Item Jim Crack Corn is a minstrel number with definite white influence and it is therefore appropriate for the Golden Gate to sing it with Burl as leader. Musically, it's simply delightful. [ALC][12]

Regarding Library business, he informed Archibald MacLeish on February 24:

Vance Randolph, author of the best books on the Ozark's region and one of our most important regional writers would put at our disposal his knowledge of the country and his entire collection, one of the most important in the United States. If we only had a little money to help him along with. There are a number of other cases of this sort throughout the country. If we ever get any money, it is through such people, in part, that I want to work. In the meantime, do you think we'd have a prayer to one of these here "funds"? [ALC][13]

He again wrote to MacLeish on February 26:

I do not know how much Mr. [Waring] Cuney knows about Negro folk music, it appears to be very little at this moment. On the other hand it is a fine project that he has in mind and I think that if he is sincere he ought to be encouraged. Few other Negro singers have decided to interest themselves in Negro folksong. His project proposal and bibliography indicate to me that he could learn a great deal by spending two or three weeks in the Archive before he goes South. I would suggest, also, that he buy a really good recording machine and use 12" records. There is no point in recording rare singing such as he wants to study on poor records. I think you might suggest beside that these records come to the Archive for duplication before they are worn by playing back in the field. He has asked me to write a letter to the Rosenwald [Foundation] for him and I intend to do that. [ALC][14]

Swamped with work, Alan had to beg off attending the Fort Valley Folk Festival in this letter to Horace Mann Bond on February 27:

I'm awfully sorry to have missed you and to have to tell you that I can't possibly come to the Festival as I had planned. I am, however, still trying to arrange to send a Library of Congress recordist down and will see that you have word the first of next week about this. Mr. Schmidt has invited me to the Fisk festival the end of April and I look forward to meeting you there. [FVMF][15]

No matter seemed too trivial, as he expressed in a few additional letters on February 27. For example, he wrote to Lois Pollard in Denver:

Please thank your grandmother for me for giving you the words to "Nobody's Darling But Mine" to send to me. I very much appreciate the trouble you both went to on this account. [ALC]

To Colonel A. L. P. Sands in Fort Sill, Oklahoma, on February 27:

Good friend Colonel Ike Spalding has forwarded to me the four songs you sent him. I am very glad to have them, and hope you will keep in mind my interest in having copies of any songs which may crop up from time to time. Even the very familiar spirituals sometimes acquire new words, or a new verse slipped in to express the issues of the moment, as you know. [ALC]

Margaret Kennard at the Pratt Institute in Brooklyn also received a note from Alan dated February 27:

There is a very fine example of Cajun singing on a commercial record, listed as Bl2042-B: Ta Oblis Do Vernier, performed by Happy Fats and Rayne-Bo Ramblers, singing with string band. There is also a Victor album of Creole music which has just appeared. I have not yet had time to play it through and so can't guarantee its authenticity, but you might try that. There should be something in it suitable for a Mardi Gras scene. [ALC]

He also sent a short memo to Spivacke on February 27:

Mr. Heindel informs me that Mr. Vail mentioned in his memorandum has contact with one of the last-surviving Shaker groups. I think it might be a very good idea to send Jerry [Wiesner] up this spring with a good recording machine or with the sound film apparatus which he has said he might be able to borrow, to record this music. If you think that this project is worth carrying further, let me know. [ALC]

As far as updating information for the Columbia Lecture Bureau, he informed Richard Erstein on February 27:

Nothing new this year, thanks; just repeat what you used before. [ALC]

Library business was never far from his mind, as in this message to Elsie Kennedy in Birmingham, Alabama, on March 15:

Our folk song and dance collections show no volumes for the [illegible] Fijians. The following two volumes may be of some use to you. [ALC]

Alan wrote a short letter to Charles Todd, March 17, in response to his of February 20:

[Woody] Guthrie is in California and, I hope, corresponding with his agent. Some day he will make a great book or a great man, and I wish I had time to sit down with him and stir the book in process. Your book ["Okie Anthology"] sounds very interesting and I hope it goes. A book that I suggested last year [Hard Hitting Songs for Hard Hit People], edited by Woody and very well edited, did not go. Maybe it wasn't sufficiently down the nose to suit the NYC publisher. Thanks for the new contacts. I think that Todd and Sonkin might get a machine, but our position about such matters is vague until after the appropriation hearings are over. Is it true that you're to be congratulated? [VFDB]

On March 19 he mailed off a short complaint to Leon Levine at CBS:

I herewith return to you a check which purports to cover my expenses in connection with the International Conference of the American School of the Air but does not tally even approximately with the expense account I submitted. I feel this should be brought to your attention. [ALC]

Two days later, March 21, a different sort of letter went off to Moses Smith at Columbia Records:

A friend of mine, Malcolm Rose, publicity director of the National Labor Relations Board, has written a very nice song about sharecroppers and stuff in the South, which one of your people has been interested in recording for Columbia commercially. I would like to suggest that Burl Ives do the song because it suits his style very well. I wish you'd route this letter around until it reaches the right person. Burl Ives has recently made an album of songs for you, I believe, and in that album has included a number of songs from the new Lomax book. I've told him that before he recorded those songs for you he should get permission from my father and find out what kind of acknowledgment John A. Lomax thought was necessary. My father can be addressed: San Benito Way, Dallas, Texas. I am going to do something about those albums for you before June. [ALC][16]

Margaret Reed of Philadelphia received this from Alan dated March 22:

I am very much obliged to you for taking the trouble to send me the songs you enclose. That is a beautiful version of *Perri merri dictum dominee.* [ALC]

Alan's growing concerns as war loomed were expressed to Spivacke on March 25:

Recommendations for the collections of the Archive of American Folk Song in case of National Emergency. 1. Duplication of 4,500 recordings for deposit in some secure place. Estimated cost $8,000.00. 2. Microfilming of Gordon Folksong Manuscripts. Estimated pages 50,000. 3. Deposit along with these, a duplicate catalogue of the records in the Archive of American Folk Song, now in the process of being made by W.P.A. 4. Deposit of copies of the Annual Report which contain the History of the Archive of American Folk Song with the aforementioned collections. [ALC]

On April 2, he assisted John Thompson in Des Moines, Iowa, who was interested in music from Haiti.

Forgive me for not having answered your letter until now. I have been out of town and not been able to get to it. You can find the material you are interested in these three books: [Laura Bowman, *The Voice of Haiti*, Harold Courlander, *Haiti*, and *Meringues Populaire Haitiennes*]. We have excellent records from Haiti, about 300 of them made there in 1937. Practically all of these show a mixture of French and Negro influences. A copy of one of these for your program might be just the thing, because I doubt if you can get good performance of this difficult music within a week, or if at all. These records can be purchased from us from the Photo duplication division at $2.00 each. There is also an album called Voodoo, which consists of Haitian songs recorded from natives living in New York City. These records are quite acceptable, and the album can be obtained by you for your assembly, with all convenience. [ALC]

On April 3 he fired off a pithy one-liner to Moses Smith at Columbia Records:

I really mean business this time. [ALC]

Alan wrote to H. H. Ward, director of the Educational Department apparently at Macmillan, on April 5, as *Our Singing Country* was in the final stages of production:

One of my problems with the book was the gap between the all inclusive title and the rather narrow and poor choice of material. As you point out the fiddle tunes and the play party song material is quite good, but there the book pretty much ends. Very few of the ballads are traditional folk songs. I do not like to appear captious, because I think the more attention paid to traditional music the better, but I felt embarrassed about not reviewing the book and want to explain it somehow. I think your editors made a very bad choice for the title. I trust you will not let this letter go further than your desk. [ALC][17]

About this time, in an undated letter to Spivacke, he explained his recent activities and need to get to his office at all hours:

In response to your request for explanation of my presence in my office on April 3 and April 8:—I was engaged in work on "Wellsprings of Music," Columbia's program for schools, sponsored by the Library of Congress. I try to do most of my work on this program outside regular office hours. I do feel, however, that I can legitimately request an all-hour pass. My work at the Archive requires more time than the amount required by law. I also have work to do as Fellow of the Radio Project.[18] Then there are constant calls upon me for special jobs, which require late work in my office near my files and my reference books. May I therefore urge you strongly to issue me an all-hour pass. [ALC]

A matter of a copyright issue was the concern of Alan's letter to William H. Darrow on April 10:

Attached is a copy of a statement which I made in reply to a copy of a notice sent to my publisher by one Arthur E. Garmaize, attorney-at-law. Please do not therefore quote me as saying that Alla en el Rancho Grande might be in the public domain.

The attachment reads:

TO WHOM IT MAY CONCERN: My father and I published Alla en el Rancho Grande, from the Texas Folk Lore Society Publications, in good faith, in *American Ballads and Folk Songs*, under the impression that the song was a folk song. When asked recently I said that I believed it might be a folk song. Since that time I have not found any publication of the song earlier than 1927. If I do find any evidence that the song is a folk song I will make the information public. Until that time, I shall be happy to cease and desist from saying that "I believe that this song might be a folk song." [ALC]

The following day, April 11, he wrote to Elise [no last name]:

Thanks for the list of fiddle tunes, the clippings and the good wishes. I want to know about your plunge into the deep you say that you are going to take soon, so that I can throw some rice in after you. [ALC]

Concerning his radio program, he sent some details to William Fineschriber on April 11, referring to the last of his "Wellsprings of Music" shows on April 15, which featured railroad songs by himself, the Golden Gate Quartet, Burl Ives, Lead Belly, Pete Seeger, and Josh White:

We don't need *Casey Jones* particularly. I have written the boys about the tunes for Tuesday and I wish you'd arrange a brief rehearsal for me with them Sunday afternoon, as well as the 4-hour stretch you promised me on Monday. Since it is possible this time, it wouldn't hurt to send them all scripts in advance. I am going to drive up Saturday afternoon. Tell McGill to study hard and don't forget your Sunday School lesson. [ALC]

On April 15 Alan explained to John Reynolds about his recordings in Haiti:

In 1937 my wife and I made 300 disc recordings of about a thousand musical items in Haiti—vaudou, mardi gras, etc. Harold Courlander (to be reached through Columbia University), Melville Herskovits (of Northwestern Univ.) have also taken records there. I was helped materially by Dr. Roulx-Leon of the Department of Hygiene and by Dr. Reiser of the same department. I suggest that you look at Haitian Valley by Mellville Herskovits, Haiti Singing by Harold Courlander, and that you consult the writings of Madame Suzanne Sylvain, eminent Haitian folklorist. It occurs to me that if you plan an extensive recording trip to the West Indies that you go where other people have not made records: SANTO DOMINGO, CUBA, Martinique, St. Kitts, Trinidad, etc. etc. I should like to hear further about your plans and help wherever I can. [ALC]

Sometime in mid-month, in an undated letter, Alan wrote to Carleton Sprague Smith, Chief of the Music Division of the New York Public Library, concerning recording in New York City:

I gave your rather rabbitty Mr. [Tom] Glazer enough records to listen to. He was quite secretive about his paper and about his conclusions. Even about his conclusions about the records. I was busy and so saw little of him. Last

week I suggested to Chas. Todd and Robert Sonkin of CCNY, good recordists and speech men, that they try their hand at a survey of minority music
in NYC, since no one else seemed to be working on it but Mitchell and he
mighty slowly. The people were there to advise—[Henry] Cowell, who knows
the music and the problems and the NYC field for it and transcribes like a
whiz—[Curt] Sachs who knows the instruments—yourself looking for singers and anxious to push folk-song. New York is a rare field and I think it
should think money was to be had if you really went to town to get it. We
could furnish blanks and equipment and backing would be easy to find. Like
to hear what you [think]. Let me know when I can be of help about the program. To tell you the truth I was a little miffed at the rush way you suggested
that we work it out last week. [ALC][19]

He was always encouraging budding collectors, as in this April 22 letter to Harold Nes-
tler, Poughkeepsie, New York:

Thank you for your interesting letter. I am sure the region you are working in is
alive with songs. I am astonished to hear that your informants do not sing the
songs, but recite them. Haven't tunes stuck to *any* of them? Do you know of
the work of Herbert Halpert in your state? I should like to invite you to deposit
a copy of your manuscript in the Archive where it will be subject to suitable
restriction but available to students of folklore, and folksongs. [ALC]

Also on April 22 he connected with Miles Hanley at the University of Wisconsin:

It was a pleasure to hear from you and I have passed the change of address
on to Dr. [Charles] Seeger. If anything should come up, I'll keep Dr. Hayek in
mind, and as for yourself, don't fail to come to see me when you are in Washington. By the way, did you know that we have sponsored some recordings in
your state, with the able assistance of Dr. Leland Coon. You might take a look
at the records and keep your eye on the project (from the folklore end). I think
they could stand some help. That's entirely off the record, of course. [ALC]

Alan fired off a request to Fineschriber on April 24:

Please send me copies of the following A.S.A. [American School of the
Air] scripts to complete my files: Oct. 8 . . . 2, Nov. 12 . . 1, Dec. 10 . . . 1,
Feb. 4 . . . 1, Feb. 18 . . . 2, Mar. 18 . . . 1. Please forward the enclosed letter
on with an urgent notice to Miss Hinze. I need the dough for my vacation
very badly. [ALC]

Having received Carleton Smith's response the day before, Alan wrote back on April 26 about his forthcoming travel plans:

On Tuesday, April 29, I will be in Nashville, Tenn. for the Fisk Jubilee; on May 2, San Antonio, Texas for the Texas Folklore Meeting; on May 10, at the wide place in the road, Clarksville, for my brother's first wedding; and after that, until June 10, I will be in parts unknown. If June 10 isn't too late, I'll be glad to do what I can to help your show along. If the Archive of American Folk Song gets the proposed funds for next year, I'm practically certain the Library will back a study of National Minority Music in New York City, headed up by you, [Henry] Cowell and [Curt] Sachs. We would expect to pay for material costs, at least and expect you to find financial support for it after it got underway from the city or from another place. I'll suggest that Henry Cowell come to see you about it. [ALC]

That same day, April 26, he reinforced his plea to Fineschriber:

It's easy to be polite (except with Lomax), when you are an executive of a big corporation. PERIOD, PARAGRAPH. Anyhow, suppose I was hasty, I'm sorry. Anyhow, suppose CBS was slow sending me my checks (you ought to be sorry). I asked the lady at the dispersing office to please send me a record of the checks paid me, covering my last four programs. I feel sure I was not paid for one of them and I never received my check for the banquet. I'd appreciate, dear, kind Bill, if you'd get me this information and *them checks*. Next address, until May 10, 7456 San Benito Way, Dallas, Texas. After that, I think I'm going to Mexico. I hope you have a nice time on your vacation. [ALC]

One more letter went out on April 26 to his father, whom he would soon visit:

The book came, was autographed and mailed to Mr. Hill. I have been working 15 hours a day lately. I think that we had better go directly to San Antonio and meet you there. I hadn't realized I am on the first day's program. Mr. Armstrong wrote me a letter the other day reneging the engagement. Said he couldn't promise the crowd. I was frankly delighted. I don't want the date, May 16. In fact, I don't want to do any more work after the 10 until I get back to Washington. The letter about the old lady in Comanche is very exciting, but it came too late for me to make any plans about a recording machine. We'll talk about that when I get there. It's too early to make any plans for recording this fiscal year since we haven't heard from the appropriations. The McClousky lady sounds interesting. Sounds like you should send her stuff on your Ballad Hunter program for use in her school. I guess I won't get to see her since the Waco lecture is off. I expect to see you in San Antonio, and to stop in Dallas between the lecture and the wedding. I don't know yet what the plans are, but we're going to hit the road for the mountains somewhere after that. [ALC][20]

While on his trip he apparently had little correspondence, although there is this letter of May 1 to Leland Coon at the University of Wisconsin:

I've just finished listening to the Wisconsin records for the first time. Some I like very much and others seem to be wasted acetate. The lumberjack material is uniformly interesting and certainly folky, even if the people are old. Mrs. Borousky [Borusky] is very fine. Mr. Rosseau is one of the best country fiddlers I've ever heard. A repeat visit should result in more records. Why don't you try to get at this sometime. French-Canadian ballad tradition at the north of the state is pretty sure to be oral in character. Out of all of the foreign records, I felt that only Icelandic and possibly the Swiss-zither records were worth making, from the folklorists' point of view. Singing to the accompaniment of the piano and from a book and written source by cultured voices is not the subject of study for which the Archive was started or set up. It's almost always possible to find persons in any sizable community no matter how prosperous who have received their songs by word of mouth and without interference from learned sources, from traditional folk singer informants. These people almost universally sing in the folk fashion and therefore have interesting and important musical ideas to contribute to the record. I suggest that you get in touch with Dr. Hanley of the Speech Dept. who has done a lot of field work and get him to advise on your summer plans. There's one item in the collection I'd particularly like to have and that is the full version of line "Red Light Saloon" which I'd only heard in part. Please do not feel that this letter is in any wise cantankerous or captious. Your trip may be regarded as very fruitful and you have a rich future of collecting before you. [HS-T][21]

There is also an undated official document, signed by Alan, that describes a robbery from his car in Mexico City:

Siendo las trece horas del dia dieciocho de mayo de mil novecientos cuarenta y uno, se presento en esta oficina el senor ALAN LOMAX, domiciliado en el Hotel Biltmore, cuarto numero 222, y expuso: Que viene a denunciar el robo que sufrio ayer por la noche del interior de su cocha que dejo estacionado en las calles de Filomeno Mata y 5 Mayo, aproximadamente entre las

21 y 23 horas, consistiendo lo robado en una camara fotografica con lentes especiales marca "Exakta" numero 431809, con tres lentes marca Tessar 1. 3. 5. #1573619, marca Gorlitz #712341 Ihague, asi como 4 filtros, todo esto con valor $500.00; que para cometer este robo fue forzado el cristal dei ventilador de la—puerta derecha delantera; que tambien le fue robado un abrigo para mujer, y una guitarra Sevillana. Que lo anterior se hace del conocimiento de esta Jefatura a fin de que se proceda como haya lugar. Previa lecturea, lo ratifica y firma para constancia. [ALC]

[Translation: At 1:00 p.m. on the 18 of May of 1941, a gentleman came to this office by the name of Alan Lomax, living at the Hotel Biltmore, Room 222, and declared: That he comes to report the robbery he suffered the previous night in the interior of his car that he left parked on Filomeno Mata and 5 de Mayo streets at approximately between the hours of 9:00 and 11:00 p.m., the robbery consisting of a special photographic camera of the brand Exacta and number 431809, as well as three Tessar 1. 3. 5. lenses #1573619, brand Gorlitz #712341 Ihague, and 4 filters, all with a value of $500.00; the robbery was committed by breaking the ventilator window of the right front door; also that he was robbed of a woman's coat, and a Seville guitar. That the previous has been reported to this precinct with the end of proceeding to recover. Previous report is ratified and signed for the record.]

While in Mexico City he wrote to Spivacke a long, undated letter, sometime in mid-May, from the Hotel Biltmore:

I hope you're through the toils and joys of moving. I hope your pores are open for the summer and that your summer suit is the proper weight. I hope that you've house-broken your child and work-broken your wife. I hope that every note that is played in the United States during the next two decades, in war or in peace, in whore-houses or for Henry Ford rolls across the threshold of the music division, is catalogued, filed away in special self-liquidating cans which disappear until called for and demand constant attention from a staff of three-thousand in a building that old John's Blue Ox Babe could turn around in without scratching her tender arse a single scratch. I hope and wish for you all the good fortune, the encomiums, the laurel wreaths, the good drinks of whiskey, the beautiful women that money can buy or patronage can bring. In other words, hail! It's summer.

Fisk was mighty hard work. They didn't have no turntable. They didn't have no amplifying system. They didn't have no space for Negroes on the Pullmans South of Washington the bushwah town so J[osh] White and the five man Golden Gate Quartet had to stand up in the mens' room all the way to Chattanooga and were too tired to perform. They didn't have no audience as good as the Coolidge Auditorium afforded. Worst of all they didn't have no Jerry Wiesner. But—but—we did all right—not as well as we should have, but we impressed 'em.

1) Pres. [Thomas Elsa] Jones offered me a job the next morning to come for a year or two and get Fisk started down the straight and narrow and make her the center of folk song collecting for the Negro in the South. He says Rockefeller simply can't wait to give them the money to do that job. Pres. Jones is a nice man whom Harold Schmidt and others of the faculty don't like. Maybe he saw an ally in me. Anyhow here's a swell chance for us to set up a big—with money—collecting agency for Negro songs in the South. I am to stop on my way back to Washington and have a conference with the heads of all the pertinent Fisk departments about what they should and could do.

As a first step I proposed that we should duplicate John Work's—approximately fifty—recordings of Negro folk music, some of it very unusual and that his originals, which he was wearing out, should stay with us, while he got duplicates for transcription and for Fisk. Work is a good man, suffering from obesity and a desire to write rather than collect music. I do not blame him, but the Pres. and H. Schmidt (whose praises I cannot sing high or loud enough) want a fast mover and a go-getter and an organizer.

Step two—sending Work blanks in small doses, beginning as soon as possible, for recording work in Nashville. He has a couple of old-time Negro fiddlers and banjo pickers who are worth doing entire. I have told Work, Jones, and Schmidt that *you will get in touch with Work at once about these two matters* or else turn them over to Jerry to handle. They want to get started at once. Left Nashville May [*sic*, April] 30, arrived San Antonio May 1, lecture May 2nd, attended Texas Folk Lore Meeting and heard more good papers in two days than you'll hear in two centuries at other meetings, found:

1) John [Henry] Faulk has been given a year's grant and a recording machine by the Rosenwald for a study of the Negro sermon in the Southwest. He is a very bright boy who needs blanks and help and will work with us. 2) William Owens had been made Director of Folk Lore Collecting for the University of Texas with a Presto Y and a bias against the LC. I don't know why he has a bias,—he suspects us of leanings toward monopoly. Father was reelected President and he liked my talks.

May 4 talked SMU [Southern Methodist University], Dallas, May 6, visited a wonderful ballad singer in Comanche County—eighty-four—whom father has found and was convinced again of the fact that he can use a machine. I suggest that you send him one and that he pass this on to the man in Denver [Duncan Emrich] later in the summer when he goes there to lecture. Item no. three for poor Jerry. Then, by God, I became Hymen, the genius of marriage, in rut, and Johnny took off through the moonlight after it was over with a spanking young damsel, broad and firmly made, soft-eyed and tender and trembling. It was beautiful and I took pictures of the whole thing with my flash-bulb camera.

The sad end of the letter is that Elizabeth and I have decided against coming back to the States at all. The fleas are so much quicker on their feet than ours are. The thieves are so much thicker—my new camera has gone already to the thieves market—. The roses bloom so much sweeter. Harold you should come here. This is not God's country; only the virgin Mary could have conceived it. Dave T[aylor]. wrote me he wanted me to help them get their Latin American work started and so here I am to take a look at the lie of the land, talk to Chavez, Mendoza, Campos and hear some music while drinking wine in the sun. So can you tell me the news by airmail of the Latin American Folk Song appropriation and of our own? Father is in wonderful form. Elizabeth and I both have the bellyache. This is a long letter to a man who gets too many of them. Remember, it is from a friend. Please let me have the news. P.S. Life has been so strenuous so far that I'd like to consider taking a longer vacation—possibly not returning to Washington on the 10th. Father will be in the East at that time and I believe I could induce him to introduce Fenton.[22] What's your reaction? Bloodpressure? [F-LC]

Waiting for a response from Spivacke, he wrote to him again from Mexico City on May 28:

Please reply my letter return airmail or send copy anxious. [ALC]

Back in Texas, he wrote to Spivacke from the Gunter Hotel in San Antonio on June 10:

Some long lonesome day I'm gonna scalp that [Helen Hartnett] Flanders gal. I can understand now why the Mohawks & other savages always ravaged the pioneer women. Please write to Archive of Vermont Folk Song, Middlebury College, Middlebury, Vt. and ask what sort of acknowledgment they would like for the song "Foreman Monroe" by Elmer George to be included in the Friends of Music Album. You might add that in the hurry of getting away for a long-deserved vacation Mr. Lomax possibly forgot to write for this permission. A copy of this letter with a brief acknowledgment is all Mrs. F. deserves. I have wired [Arthur Palmer] Hudson in Chapel Hill to give Morris his degree & have written Morris that I've sent his letter on to you. Item. Van der Wall has just written a cordial and urgent invitation that I come to La. and discuss the beginning of their work with him & his colleagues. Item. I think I ought to go by Galena, Mo. & personally speak to Vance [Randolph] before we give him all that money. Item. Please write me what you think of the *Nashville business.*

I have to know what to say to them. What have you & Jerry [Wiesner] done about [John W.] Work's records. I promised them action.

Item. I have promised to drop in on the Chapel Hill bunch for a chat & on Fletcher Collins who is the head of a committee on Folk Song & Ballads for English Teaching in the public schools. He would be an excellent man for one of the machines. Can you approve per diem for this four or five days of work on the way up? If you can't do it easily forget it. While you're answering this, I'll think the Brazil matter over. Naturally it sounds most attractive. There are two considerations. 1) My obligation to the radio project—a considerable one & one I'll enjoy liquidating. 2) The fact that Fisk Univ. per Rosenwald has had an excellent linguist & sociologist in Brazil with a recording machine for nearly a year—Turner of the Sociology Dept. Perhaps with the little that has already been done in S.A. it might be better to go where no work has recently been done. Arrange for father to take a machine home with him if possible. [ALC]

Returning to Washington from his western trip, he immediately dropped a brief note to Lucie Breeden in Pulaski, Virginia, on June 26:

So far as I know the two very interesting folk songs you sent have no financial value. They do, however, have interest for the collector of folk songs and for the Archive of American Folk Song. I would greatly appreciate you sending them along with others that you may happen to have at your disposal, to the Archive collection. [ALC]

He somewhat caught up with his father on June 27:

I just got back day before yesterday, after visits at the University of Louisiana, Fisk University, N.C., and with your delightful Ruby Pickins Tartt. She is all you have limned her and has a wonderful tempestuous temperament . We seem to have some recording money to spend next year, and when I am sure just what, and a little more straight about it, I will send you an outline of the whole thing. Enclosed are a number of letters which concern you, and a few more of the dictaphone texts which I found in my papers. Elizabeth and I both enjoyed very much seeing all of you in Beaumont and Galveston. I wouldn't have missed it for the world. [ALC][23]

He also wrote to William Fineschriber on June 27:

I just got in from Texas and Mexico City, part business and part pleasure. I find that no reply to my two letters to you about the two checks which I have never received. To remind you—1—for the M. C. appearance for that hideous banquet and—2—the American School of the Air checks, which your accounts over looked in the process of making out your stupendous income tax report. About this later item I am not completely sure, but if you would check with Miss Hinze about this, it was one of the last 3 or 4 checks. Mexico is a most beautiful place that I have yet seen, and the easiest place to acquire a healthy bellyache. Elizabeth and I spent our time with the bellyache, zooming all over the place from desert mesa to tropical canyon. I would like to see you. Why don't you come to the place where things are happening for a visit. We have a couch always made up in your behalf. [ALC]

Anxious to initiate something in New York, he again wrote to Carleton Sprague Smith on June 27:

I still would like to know what you think about a project to record foreign folk songs in New York? How is the School of the Air? [ALC]²⁴

Alan encouraged the work of Duncan Emrich, at the University of Denver, in a letter on June 30:

If you can move fast, perhaps I can arrange a recording trip for this summer. In this fashion, John A. Lomax can bring the recording machine to Colorado, show you how to use it, and how to carry on field work. We can, I believe, help you with some of the expenses. Perhaps you and father might travel together for a time, depending on how the funds hold out. We can not finance a trip from Colorado to Alaska, but I do want songs from that area. If you could plan a fertile recording trip for the end of the summer or early fall, which would include the recording of mining songs, good and especially bad, I should like to hear about it. Be very specific, give me the areas you would like to take a recording machine to, and the types of material available to be recorded from live folk informants. Perhaps if nothing more comes of this, your working with father in Colorado, for a week or two, that would be fine for this year. Then, in case the Guggenheim should come to you, you could do recording for the Library in this connection. Please answer my letter at once, so that I can make arrangements for father to bring the machine with him when he comes. [ALC]²⁵

In the midst of his hectic schedule, he became involved in a complex field project with John Work, which would become very productive. Lomax had attended the April 29 concert at Fisk University with Josh White and the Golden Gate Quartet, where he also met with composer and educator John Work, Charles S. Johnson, who directed Fisk's department of social sciences, John Ross of the drama department, and Fisk President Thomas E. Jones. At this meeting a field trip to the Delta was broached.[26] He began a busy month by writing to President Jones at Fisk on July 1:

My report of the project discussed by us at our last conference in Dr. [Charles S.] Johnson's office, has been warmly received in the Library. I think how that it would be best to carry out a survey of the type discussed in the Mississippi Delta Counties and to help Dr. Work in his recording in Nashville and vicinity. In this latter work, you could be of great assistance. I feel fairly sure that the recording machine needs an overhauling, and perhaps new parts. We shall check this when Dr. Work sends us his earlier records, and if it appears necessary, perhaps he could bring the machine here for the overhauling. I hope you can provide funds for this. Again Dr. Work tells me that he has no way to get about in Nashville with the machine, and I thought that possibly there was a university car that could be made available for him especially in the evenings. I look forward to hearing from you soon, for Dr. Work's recording should begin as soon as possible. [F-LC]

The following day, July 2, he contacted Louis (Lomax had erroneously written Lawrence) W. Chappell at the University of West Virginia:

The Archive of American Folk Song, has this year received funds to enable it to duplicate some of the best collections of records in private hands. I recall that a number of years ago you bought a recording machine, and I presume that you have made a good many fine records. Would you be willing for us to duplicate these records for our collection and on what basis? Of course, our object eventually is to make them available to the scholarly public. We have acquired an excellent duplicating laboratory, and are now in a position to help preserve recordings of all kinds. I should like, at any rate, to know about your work because it may be that we could be of some practical assistance. [ALC]

On July 3 he reconnected with Kay Dealy in Philadelphia:

I was delighted to hear from you, and many thanks for your contacts. They will be put into our files to be used sometime perhaps. We are so busy now, in so many different directions it is beginning to seem fantastic to record just one person. I would like to hear what you are doing with your Irish, English and Scotch background songs in Philadelphia. Are there any that need recording, this time by a good recording machine. [ALC]

Also on July 3 he continued to relay his ideas to Carleton Smith at the New York Public Library:

I have suggested a project for you to put in project form. If you have any notion that the City of New York would be interested in financing such a project and do you know about getting the money? I think it would be safe, next week to start one on the work the consort has already done for us in New York City, and we have many willing experts to do the work analysis and publish the material. May your folk song project go through your summer cady [*sic*], and fly into Mayor LaGuardia's office. I understand that we will be in Mexico together. I will tell you more then. [ALC]

Getting more involved with the Fisk/Coahoma study, he connected with Charles S. Johnson on July 7:

I feel fairly confident that the Library will see its way to finance the discussed field trip to the Delta counties of the Mississippi. I should think that 6 weeks would about take care of the problem. I suggest that we began work sometime in September. Of course there is a great deal of preparation to be done before that time. But before we go any further, may I have further assurance from you that your department can carry out its part. Our understanding as I recall, is that the Library furnish sound equipment, materials and engineer, while Fisk University furnish the field workers and carried out to the publication and study. May I expect to hear from you soon. [F-LC]

Alan mailed a rather long letter to his father on July 7:

Under separate cover, I am sending you 2 speeches of Spivacke's about the Archive; 2 press releases about the Phonoduplication Division, which speaks of me and the radio use of folk lore and folk songs, and the master sheets of the geological check list (please return to me as soon as possible); the reports on the Archive of American Folk Song from 1928–1939; and your Wild West clippings. I have never written down any of my speeches on the Archive, so that's that. The top numbers in the Archive as of today are; discs 4627, cylinders 373. We have money this year for extensive duplication of other collections and for a number of field trips. Machines are now in the field in Alabama, Alaska, Dutch Guiana, Wisconsin, South America. There are available through the Archive about 2000 songs on records from all over the country. The geological check list does not include the approximately 5000 folk songs in Spanish, French, Portuguese, Creole, Siberian, Finish, German,

Czechs, Hungarian, Italian, Greek, Russian, Lithuanian, Armenian, Turkish, and various Indian, Polynesian languages.

We are planning this year a number of trips to South America and have been awarded $6000 by Congress, for sending our records to South America for their Universities and radio stations etc. We have a fully equipped sound truck, which will travel all over American [*sic*] during the next two or three years etc. I hope this is what you need. If you want anything more write me air mail. Since the appropriation bill is now signed we can talk business about the machine. Would you like to do some recording in Texas? The Old Lady in Canancha [*sic*] county for instance, then work with Emrich in Colorado, Peter Hurd in New Mexico and so forth.[27] How do you feel about this? Your reply should arrive about the time Emrich's does, and we can make a budget then. Elizabeth and I just spent last weekend on the Kitty Hawk sands. We are both very well and hearty. Much love until later. [ALC]

Alan followed up to Carleton Smith on July 8:

It seems to me that before we put the matter into a project form that you should sound out the city fathers or whatever other sources of funds are available to take interest. I should think that Mayor LaGuardia and his cohorts would be much interested in this sort of a project now-a-days. We have already begun in collaboration with Dr. Mitchell and his Consort group. Probably the Library would furnish equipment and discs. Todd and Sonkin would be available as recordist. [Charles] Seeger, [Curt] Sachs, [Henry] Cowell, Sidney Robertson, [George] Herzog might all collaborate as advisors, editors, etc. I suggest that someone (Seeger, Sachs, etc.) be employed full time to carry out the project. A fine outlet and study group in the Mitchell singers and in the folk dance group. So let's get going. If you do not want to bother with the problem let me know, and I will take it up from this point. [ALC]

He wrote two memos on July 14, apparently to Spivacke:

I have learned from Samuel Bayard[28] that the [Phillips] Barry Collection at Harvard amounts to about 180 cylinders, 76 of which are the early Edison type, according to Bayard unplayable on modern machines. These records are, so far as he knows, unrestricted and in charge of the Librarian of Harvard University. I suggest that you write and ask for a temporary loan of the records, so that we can duplicate them for our collection. The cost of duplication would amount to $153.00 for the duplication of Dictaphone records themselves. If Harvard College asks for a set of duplicates, the cost would be approximately $200.00. I recommend immediate action on this matter. [ALC]

The second memo to Spivacke on July 14 concerned another matter:

In order to discuss constructively plans for a Brazilian field trip with Doctor [Melville] Herskovits, I suggest that it would be wise for me to go to Northwestern where I can hear some of his recordings and see him in his own surroundings. The documentary field trip is scheduled to begin the 25th of this month, so that this weekend will be the most convenient time for me to go. Exact date can wait for a reply to my letter to Herskovitz mailed on Saturday, but I suggest that you put in a travel order for a round trip plane fare to Northwestern as soon as possible. [ALC]

With financial matters constantly on his mind, Alan wrote to Fineschriber on July 14:

Enclosed is a telephone bill which was incurred doubtless in relation to the School of the Air for last year. For some reason it has come back to the Library and I wish you would take care of this. The Accounting Office has not yet written me about the other matter that is still pending. I need the money very badly and wish you would please call them up. Things, particularly documentary things, are blooming this way. [ALC]

On the busy day of July 14 he contacted Fletcher Collins at Elon College in North Carolina:

I am terribly sorry that I missed seeing you in Chapel Hill. You had just left the office for Elon College when I called and I had driven so many miles in the previous weeks that I could resolve to drive no more. Frankly, I am looking for somebody with a good recording project in hand and wondered if you had one which the Library could help motivate. If you have, let me hear about it at once so that we can do something about it this summer. [ALC]29

On the same day, July 14, he gave his father a detailed outline of his plans and ideas:

I am awfully sorry that you are feeling under the weather, and hope that you continue to get perter [sic]. All the more so, because I cannot go to Denver. I have arranged to go on a field trip with the Radio Project boys, leaving here the 24th to last until the 10th of August. We are going to document completely words, music and sound of a mountain community in Tennessee and put it together in the form of some radio programs. On the 10th of August, CBS and the Defense Council fly me to Mexico City for a performance with the Golden Gate Quartet and Joshua White. Back to Galax on the 15th, for some recording with Charlie Seeger and a Portuguese from Brazil. Then into the field again until September with the sound-truck. Don't know exactly where at the moment. I think you are silly when you say that I should go to the Denver Conference. You make the best damn speech this side of the Rio Grande and all you have to do is to put up a front like some of the other boys do to impress them academically. You should have enough material with what we have sent you and for recordings there is the story of the Archive.

Your questions three can be answered thus: No. 1. Approximately 16-thousand songs on disks in the Archive. That does not include the Gordon collection, which by rights belongs to us and would bring the total up to 20 or 25-thousand, you know best which. No. 2. Catalog will be ready within the next six months. [Luther] Evans and Spivacke will not be more definite than that. A commercial printer told me it could be finished in a week if we could give him $1700.00, but I have not been allowed yet to apply for the money, although I think it will be forthcoming. No. 3. The Archive this year has $12,000 to spend on duplicating the records in other collections, and for field trips. Plans so far:

To duplicate part of the immense [Marius] Barbeau Canadian collection in Canada; to duplicate the Barry collection in Harvard (mostly New England songs); to duplicate the Herskovits collection of songs from Africa, Trinidad and Dutch Guiana and Haiti which will give us a pretty complete picture of the development of West African music in the Western Hemisphere, the whole background of our Negro songs. Your personal Negro collection will top the heap. To duplicate the Virginia ballad collection, [Louis W.] Chappell's West Virginia ballad collection, [Edwin C.] Kirkland's East Tennessee collection and such others as there remain funds for.

Recording trips to the Tennessee Valley for the documentation of a Tennessee Valley community; two Mississippi Delta communities, a study to be made in collaboration with Fisk University of the singing habits of the Negro as related to community living. To finance Vance Randolph to record his large and widespread ballad collection in the Ozark region; to send records and other help to John [Henry] Faulk for his project; to record the songs in the migratory camps in the Rio Grande Valley; and to help Brownie McNeil record his large collection of Mexican Corridos; to help the Wisconsin Music Department continue its study of folk songs in all the languages in the United States; to help Eloise Linscott in her New England recording trip. To send a recording trip to South America for six months or a year with an additional $3500 voted by Congress to the State Department for Latin-American cooperation.

In this regard, Congress has also appropriated $6000 for sending records for radio programs from the Library of Congress to Latin-America. $3000 of this will be spent in making up a set of 25 pressings of the best Archive records for Latin-American distribution in sets, two or three to each country. We shall also make up a series of programs on American folksongs for radio transcriptions, with a commentary in Spanish and Portuguese. We intend, besides, to press within the year about 50 additional records for general distribution for those who write in for folk song recordings. These will be available in albums and singly for about 50 cents or $1.00 apiece. I have a lot of other notions stewing in my head, but the foregoing seems more than any one person can do in a year. I am told I am to get a stenographer within ten days, but I doubt it. [ALC]

On July 17 Alan wrote to John Work about furthering their plans to collect in the Delta:

I am greatly disappointed not to have heard from you in regard to the recording project which we discussed a short time ago. I have written to President Jones about the use of the car and I should like to help you initiate further recording in Nashville. However, I still think our sound-engineer should have the opportunity to audition the records here in the Library and make recommendations for repair of the equipment. If repairing the equipment seems completely impractical, send the records along anyway, because the sound-truck will be coming through Nashville about the 25th or 26th of this month on the way to the Tennessee Valley. We can stop then and give the machine a whirl and start you off on your field trip. I cannot act officially until I have some expression of interest and some sketch of your plans here in writing. May I hope to hear from you at the earliest possible date. [FVMF][30]

He was also somewhat confused about the trip to Mexico City, which he noted in a letter to Sterling Fisher at CBS on July 18:

I should like to know by return Air Mail Special Delivery exactly what the Golden Gate and myself are supposed to do in Mexico City. I want to get my part translated into Spanish and read it in that language, so give me one or two days to prepare, please. Also let me know as soon as possible about Lead Belly—if he is in condition to go or whether it will be necessary to get Joshua White as a substitute guitarist. This had better be settled at once as I told you. Before I leave Washington, I shall send you a forwarding address, but I shall be here until Wednesday. [ALC]

A letter of a different sort went out to his father the next day, July 19:

I suggest that you write to Mr. Jason and tell him that you have ideas for folksong films, but that you wish to know in advance what he would expect to spend on a one, two or three-reel film and ask him what evidence he can give you of his financial standing. Movies cost an enormous amount of money and $10,000.00 is not too much for a two-reel picture lasting five minutes, especially if it is made in the field. I think I can get competent and objective advice for you on any proposition he will make you. I am today writing Mrs. [Ruby Pickens] Tartt a long-due letter and I am drawing up a budget for a field trip for you and Mrs. Tartt. Let me hear how things go in Colorado. [ALC]

Alan was anxious to proceed with the New York City project, as he wrote to folk song collector Joanna Colcord on July 19:

For sometime I have been interested in initiating a project in New York City to record the folk songs of the foreign minorities there. There are fine singers there in every language and dialect in the world probably and there are also a number of people competent to give counsel, direction and advice to such a project. At this time, especially it seems to me, that America should make clear her concern for the cultural riches of the peoples whom she has welcomed into her borders, and no better evidence of this interest could be given than a project launched in New York City to record and make available in all sorts of ways the songs of the national minorities there.

The Library of Congress, I believe could send the equipment and discs necessary for such a project. Doctor Curt Sachs, of New York University, Doctor Mitchell, of New York University, and Doctor Carleton Sprague Smith of New York Public Library, and others in New York City could guide the project and offer their technical advice and serve as channels through which the material could be utilized. There are a number of young men in New York equipped to serve as recordists and field-workers who have already worked with us. The project could operate through the various foreign language associations, social organizations, etc., and should be expected to furnish all sorts of material for cultural programs. At the same time basic and important folksong data would be in the process of accumulation.

I should think this project could be carried forward for as little as two or three thousand dollars a year, although, of course, a great deal of money could be spent. Our experience has been that one ardent recordist given a little financial backing and good equipment can do a good deal. I wonder if you could find time in your busy life to think about how such a project might be financed. Colcord answered on September 10, expressing her interest and some ideas for financing the project. [ALC][31]

On July 23 he again wrote to Sterling Fisher at CBS:

Enclosed you will find an outline of my program for Mexico City, and the full text of my remarks. I wish you would have this last translated into Spanish and mailed to me as soon as it is finished so that I may rehearse it in that language. I notice that your letter did not mention Joshua White. Please assure me in your next that he will be included in the party flying to Mexico. I must insist that you arrange for an advance on my fee to help me take care of my expenses on the trip. I presume that I shall see you and I hope so. [ALC][32]

At month's end, on July 30, he again contacted Fletcher Collins in North Carolina:

I would like to know how many records and how much time you calculate will be consumed in recording your project described in your letter, which sounds very interesting to me. I imagine we can free a machine for your use in October. We are willing to agree on the publication restrictions if the collector is willing to allow us to press or duplicate the recordings for additional distribution, and if the restriction does not run on for longer than two weeks. I think you should think pretty seriously about an intensive recording schedule because it will make it much easier for us to help you.

The Archive is much interested in cooperating with the Folklore Committee [of the National Council of Teachers of English] and we can already furnish in recorded form the words and tune of nearly any American folk song you may want to mention. In some cases, scores of tunes or songs. We are, besides, initiating a publishing program, that is we are beginning to make pressings, as distinguished from the acetate duplicates mentioned above, of the records. If your committee can sponsor the release of a series of such pressings, which would be adapted to your purposes, the Archive would be delighted to cooperate. We are going to make up such a series for distribution in the Latin American Republics this winter, the money being already available. I am very excited about the project of publishing the words, music, and headnote in broadside sheet form so that they will be available cheaply to schools, libraries, and hoboes. Such single sheet publication would make it possible to put together regional collections, variant collections, type collections with no labor. However, this project which I think can pay for itself and which would protect the songs and ballads from the copyright raids now going on will cost a good deal of money to initiate.

The Archive would very much like to have the Delaney songbook collection. I believe we have one fairly complete copy in the Music Division but another one would be extremely useful. A gift to the Library would bring him a very nice and highly decorative acknowledgment from us. My address for the next ten days will be General Delivery Blairsville, Georgia. [ALC]

Also on July 30 a brief note went to Sterling Fisher at CBS:

For the next ten days, my address will be General Delivery, Blairsville, Georgia. I suggest you send a copy of whatever letters you may write to me in care of the Information Office, TVA [Tennessee Valley Authority], Knoxville, Tennessee. I am delighted that Lead Belly will be well enough to go to Mexico City, and the departure from Atlanta on August 11 fits in with my plans very well. You will, of course, forward to me the plane ticket well in advance of my departure. I will notify you of any change in address. P.S. It is very important that I be back in Nashville on the 16th, and would like you to route my return by Nashville with a stopover of a day and make the termination of the trip Roanoke, Virginia, by American Airlines. [ALC]

Concerning his work with Fisk University, John Work had responded to Alan on July 24, and Alan answered him on July 30:

I think you have gotten things rather mixed. When I was in Nashville, I discussed two separate projects; one, a survey project to be worked out with Dr. Johnson, and two, a small recording project to be limited in Nashville by yourself with your fiddlers and local singers at once. I am still very anxious that you begin work on this. In this second project we agreed that you were to use the Fisk machine and perhaps the Fisk campus car in the evening while the Library furnished you with our discs, needles, and copies of your records. Much depended, however, on the condition of the University recording machine which we were both in doubt about, and which you were to have checked in Nashville. Your collection of records was to come to us immediately so that we could determine by playing them in the Recording Laboratory what was wrong with your work technically as far as it had gone. I suggest that if you want to do this work at all this summer, you had better move fast because we have a number of projects under consideration which we are anxious to set up and the initiation of your project depends on you. In regard to the records you have already made, I can assure you that every one who makes a record which comes into our collection is given complete credit for having done so. The basic material contained on the catalogue card gives the title of the selection, the singer, and the place and date of recording. This in some sense protects the collection. Let me repeat that we will send you a set of copies of your records as soon as we receive them —and are able to duplicate them. I am in correspondence with Dr. [Charles] Johnson about the survey recording project which we plan to initiate sometime in October. I hope to work with you in this connection also. Correspondence for the next ten days should be sent

General Delivery, Blairsville, Georgia, and send the records to the Recording Laboratory, express collect. [FVMF]

Alan encouraged Work to focus immediately on his local recordings, while he worked
with Charles Johnson on a larger plan for the Delta, about which he wrote to the latter on
July 30:

Our plans about coming to Nashville have changed somewhat, but I would
like very much to see you about the middle of the month in Nashville and
discuss plans with you for the survey project. However, I think we can settle
some of the problems by correspondence. It had occurred to me that a visit
to the area to be surveyed during the latter part of August would be valuable.
First of all, I would like to see for myself what the problems are and, second,
much of the material to be found in such a community I imagine will take
place during the revival season which is shortly to begin. Perhaps a recording
trip of two weeks would make it possible for the truck to be in the field less
time in the fall.

I am sorry that we did not have time to go more fully into the nature of the
various communities we have in view. It might be more convenient to pick
one near at hand in the Mississippi Delta, but since the material is in your
hands, you can be able to make preliminary judgement about it better than
I. A number of people have suggested that southwestern Tennessee, which
is slightly more stable than the Delta area, would be a better region for work
than the one we have thought of already. I would like to have your suggestions on this subject so that I can be thinking about them before I see you in
Nashville. I shall come there by plane from Mexico City on the 16, 17, or 18 of
August; just which day I will let you know a little later. In the meantime, my
address will be General Delivery, Blairsville, Georgia. [ALC]

Alan was back in his office by August 21 and wrote a memo, apparently to Spivacke:

Mr. Fletcher Collins, Chairman of Folklore Committee of the National Council of Teachers of English, has requested the use of a Library machine for ten
days of recording in North Carolina. Mr. Collins has an excellent reputation as a collector of folk-songs and I feel that this project would bring good
records into the Archive. He wishes to have the use of the machine in the
month of October, so that approval of the project should be expedited. [The
budget totaled $147.50.] [ALC][34]

Concerning the looming Fisk study, Alan wrote to Charles Johnson on August 21 about
his plans:

This will inform you that I shall be in Nashville sometime in the morning of the 25th. I hope by that time that Doctors Jones and Work will have consulted about revivals in Tennessee and Mississippi and will have a recording schedule laid out so that we can leave Fisk the same day. Since our sound engineer will be in the army camps, I am bringing along Mrs. Lomax as my assistant. The equipment will take up the rear part of our sedan and therefore, it will be necessary for another car to go along on the trip. I have consulted with Mr. Wiesner, our sound engineer, and he agrees to overhaul your recording machine and install whatever new parts seem necessary. This will probably mean a new microphone and cutting head at an estimated cost of thirty-five dollars ($35.00). I suggest that you ship the machine at once so that we can get to work on it. [ALC]

That same day, Lomax sketched out his current plans to Spivacke:

I wish to urge that you approve a brief recording trip to Mississippi and Virginia which will begin Saturday, the 23rd of August and end on September 15th. 1) To record Negro revivals in the region of Northwestern Mississippi in company with various members of the faculty of Fisk University. This survey recording trip is preliminary to an intensive field study of Negro folk-song in a Mississippi Delta County, to be carried out during the fall and winter by the Fisk University Sociology Department in collaboration with the Archive of American Folksong. I believe that this survey and resultant study will represent the first scientific study in the field of American Folk Song. It will be carried out by Doctor Charles S. Johnson and his graduate students in Sociology in collaboration with the Library of Congress.

2) To record a few of the best ballad singers of Western Virginia who have been discovered by the Virginia Folklore Society. These records will be used for the compilation of an album of Virginia ballads to be released by us and edited by Mr. Arthur Kyle Davis, of the University of Virginia. An estimate of this trip is appended. [He calculated an approximate budget of $580.00.] [ALC]

On August 23, a day before he and Elizabeth arrived in Nashville, Alan updated John Work:

The 50 blank disks will be shipped to you within the next day or two. I hope by this time that Doctor Johnson will have sent the Fisk recording machine to us for repair. It should be given a thorough over-hauling before you use up more acetate in recording with it. I enjoyed the article very much and I feel that the Negro Sacred Harp songs should be further documented. Perhaps we can visit that section of Alabama while I am south. I shall see you the morning of the 25th, ready, I hope, for our trip to Ripley.[35] [ALC][36]

Alan also wrote to William McDaniel, State Supervisor of the Tennessee Writers Project, on August 23:

I have never written you to thank you for your kind letter of July 21st. The expedition left shortly thereafter and went first only as far as Knoxville. There we chose the community of Blairsville, Georgia, as one being actively affected by TVA and here we recorded enough material for two or three documentary radio programs. I am very sorry I missed talking with you and looking through the Writers Project files. I shall, however, be in Nashville within the next two or three weeks and shall come and call on you. In the meantime, I hope you will accept my apologies for not having written you sooner. [ALC]

He repeated much of the same information to Harvey Broome in Knoxville, Tennessee, on August 23:

I should like to report for the project that we finally decided on Blairsville, Georgia. We left the day after we saw you and stayed there for nearly two weeks recording a great deal of material, including the accounts of disaffected tenants who were being moved off their land. I think we shall be able to make about three programs out of it with good material and plenty of material for each one. I shall let you know how they come out. Perhaps sometime you will be in Washington and can come in and listen to some of the records we made and I think you would be greatly pleased. In the meantime, let me express the appreciation of myself and all the members of our party for your cordial reception of us in Knoxville, and for the fine party you gave for us. [ALC]

He had time to write one more letter to his father on August 23:

Your trip with Mrs. Tartt has been approved and the only reason we could not make it include the Amarillo jaunt is that there is no machine available in the Division except the one I am about to take with me today to Mississippi where I shall be for about ten days recording revivals. Doctor Spivacke is scheduled to write you as soon as your trip with Mrs. Tartt has passed the last hurdle. Your machine should be on its way to you in a week or ten days. If you can arrange through Owens or the Dean of Extension to use the Owens machine for the trip, I think we can handle the expenses. I am terribly sorry that it was too late to do anything else, but there was simply no other machine available. [ALC][37]

Lomax spent almost a week, August 29 to September 3, with John Work and his team, Lewis Jones and John Ross, recording throughout the Delta, including Son House and McKinley Morganfield (Muddy Water[s]).[38] On September 4 he reported to Spivacke from Nashville, with much on his mind:

We decided to come on back to Fisk University and work on the development of our field method a couple of days, rather than to spend any more time in the actual recording at this moment. We have made some extremely good records and the Model Y recording machine performs nobly. We'll probably leave here on Saturday and after four or five days of recording in Western Virginia, we'll be in Washington—I hope about the tenth. I will return here on the twentieth for two days of work with the students [Samuel C. Adams and Ulysses S. Young] who are going to carry out the survey; and then we'll leave the Fisk people to carry out the project until the last week of October when I'll take the machine into Coahoma County for a final two or three weeks of work.

I was delighted to hear of Mrs. Shwartz's appointment, but sorry to learn that you had forgotten my request that she be set to work straightening my files, and putting my papers in order. I believe she has enough to do to keep her busy until my return, and I think that she won't get very far with cataloging the records without my assistance. I hope you will find it possible to let her drop the cataloging project until I get there so that the work will not have to be done over again. I hope by this time the trip for John A. Lomax and Ruby Jackson [Pickens] Tartt has been initiated. They are anxious to go to work and the longer we delay, the harder their problems will be, as the weather grows worse.

Enclosure 1—The enclosed letter from Doty at the University of Texas refers to the field trip which I have suggested for Brownie McNeil. It seems now that they will not need to borrow our equipment but only want records from us. Perhaps we could send them 150 records for their field use in recording the Mexican songs along the border of South Texas. He has plenty of material to keep him busy all winter long. I know you'll be amused to see our delicate friend from recreation going down to Texas. He'll have a hard time I fear. *Enclosure 2*—Would you be so kind as to turn Enclosure No. 2 over to Ed to take care of. It is not in my line. *Enclosure 3*—Please note the first paragraph of Mr. [Vance] Randolph's letter. I think certainly that we want the pictures Mr. Randolph says he can obtain and I recommend that Mr. Wiesner purchase ten (10) film packs for his 5X7 Graflex Camera, with the material cost of the Randolph trip. I shall write Mr. Randolph that I have made this recommendation and that the rest of the letter is taken care of.

Enclosure 4—If you care to, you might ask Mr. Rabbit what happened to poor Pete Steele's check. Remember his wife is in the hospital and he is a sweeper in the factory. *Enclosure 5*—You can quote me on Mildred S. Stocker as follows: She is an excellent stenographer, typist, and a file clerk and general secretary. In her six weeks work for me, she proved herself to be a person of a great deal of talent, individual initiative and resourcefulness. I think anybody who hired her would be lucky to get her. *Enclosure 6*—Professor [Emelyn Elizabeth] Gardner has edited two of the best books in the field of American folk song Folklore from the Schoharie Hills, and Ballads and Songs from Southern Michigan. She has been carrying on an intensive survey of the folk music of Detroit, working through the students in her ballad classes there. She now wishes to borrow, during the remainder of the school term, one of our portable recording machines, along with sufficient records for her work. I suggest that two hundred (200) would be enough for the purpose. Such a project should cost us not much more than shipping cost of the two hundred disks and 200 duplicates. I have written her that I have recommended the project to you and that she can expect to hear from you before our return to Washington. *Enclosure 7*—From Willem van der Wall.

Enclosure 8—I thought you would be interested in the inclosed letter from [Norman Holmes] Pearson of Yale. I have already written him and when I get home I'll make up his records at once. But there's a possibility there I think that they will want to use a great deal of our material. This fits in with Fletcher Collins' interest I think.[39] On my way home through the Virginia mountains, I'm going to try to take as many records of the classical English and Scottish Ballads as possible. We have too few of these songs recorded satisfactorily. This is a dull letter, but Elizabeth and I were driving last night until four o'clock and I've been hard at it all day long. For the first time since I have been working for the Library, I'm beginning to feel that we're doing a job which interests me intellectually. My very best regards to you and your live wire department.[40] [ALC]

Alan was, as usual, involved with family matters, as in this letter to his sister Bess on September 4, then visiting in Chicago and job hunting:

Elizabeth and I will be back in Washington by the 10th or 11th. Perhaps that next week-end we can go to New York and try out the boys at CBS. I have written them all about you. I think that it might be a very good chance, although I haven't heard from them yet. You can reach me in the meantime in care of General Delivery, Salem, Virginia. I don't know [where] we'll all live since Elizabeth and I have given up our apartment, but come on, we'll manage it some way. I think the possibilities are here in the intervention section rather than out in that isolation belt you've been living in. I wish I could write all the news but there's too much to tell. Cora is out being trained to kill poor innocent birds in Maryland. Elizabeth and I have just finished the first laps of the Fisk field trip. [ALC]

Alan followed to his father on September 5:

I'm so far behind in my correspondence that I hesitate to write at all. But my mail has not kept up with me during the last couple of weeks. I left Harold [Spivacke] promising to get you and Miss Tartt started right away, and I have just written him again to urge him all speed. I'll be back in Washington on the 10th, and see that it is done then, at the very latest. Elizabeth and I just spent a very exciting week in Coahoma County, Mississippi, which has the highest ratio of Negro population of any county in America. I'm extremely pleased so far with the collaboration with the Fisk people. It seems to me that we establish very close contact with the Negro community on very short notice, working with these people. Whenever we ask about work songs, they say, Why don't you go to parchment [Parchman Penitentiary]? I'll send the clipping to my new secretary in Washington to have it photostated, and have her return it to you. Sorry to hear about your thumb, but keep writing me. [ALC]

Alan also reported to Jerome Wiesner on September 5:

The fifty new records arrived just as we were leaving Clarksdale, but I'll have use for some of them here in Nashville, and later in the mountains as we come home. The machine worked beautifully, although some over-cutting resulted from the effect of the intense heat on the cutting gear. It was so much fun to run that I could hardly keep my hands off it. I regret to inform you, however, that the glass records are pretty fragile. Three or four have been cracked by being bumped around in the car and one of the best records, I found today, was broken right through the middle. Perhaps we can repair it or help it in such a fashion that we can cover up the crack.

We got to Mississippi just as the revival season was being wound up so we had to work largely with other things. However, we have a study planned, which I believe is going to revolutionize the study of folk songs and folk lore in this country and we are very excited about it. There is no time at all for documentary records [for the radio research project], in fact, the community situation was so hot, as well as complicated, that I would hesitate to document it, until I knew the place better. Everywhere we went we were asked point blank, were we or were we not union organizers. Sorry I did not get to go with you to your army camps. Elizabeth and I will be home about the 10th, and if you have a spare room or so, we'll be only too happy to stay with you. [ALC]

And on September 5 there was a short note from Alan to Estil C. and Orna Ball[41] in Rugby, Virginia:

My wife and I are coming to Rugby in the next two or three days with the hope of recording some of the songs known to you and other of your friends in the community. I hope you will be able to spend an evening recording these songs for preservation in the Library of Congress. We look forward to seeing you. [ALC]

He kept his father somewhat informed of his activities on September 16:

I have just come back from New York where Bess was installed as secretary and assistant to Carleton Smith, chief of the Music Division of the New York Public Library and this year's commentator on the School of the Air music programs. Bess, in return for her twenty-five dollars a week, will probably write the scripts for the School of the Air and do most of the research and contact work. I also called on [Clifton] Fadiman and he promises to do his best for the book, which will be released on the 28th of *October*. [Henry] Luce I couldn't get to see, but I arranged for Bess to call on him. She is in a position to do well in a number of directions, I think, and I think you can put your worries at rest for a while. Don't get mad at Burl Ives, who plugs your songs over CBS five times a week, but reproach Columbia Recording Company in regard to the Cowboy's Lament, Peter Gray, Cotton Eye Joe, and Darling Corey, which are right out of our books. Sweet Betsy from Pike is his own. I didn't give him permission to use the songs, but told him that he should get C.S.C. in touch with you. [ALC][42]

Alan was soon planning a return trip to the Delta, as he wrote to Charles Johnson on September 17:[43]

November 15 to December 1 will suit me very well. In fact, I think that six weeks of field work before I come to the county will make the situation that much clearer. If it would be possible now for you to set the Fisk schedule so that I may include it in my memo to the Librarians I would appreciate it. I should also like confirmation from you about the seminar over this weekend in which I was to give the field workers an introduction to the field before they went to Mississippi. First, is this definitely projected? Second, would it suit your convenience as well to make it the weekend after next, that is the 27th through the 29th? I can come this week end and plan to come, but await word from you since I would now much prefer the later dates. Send my kindest regards to Louis Jones. [ALC]

The following day, September 18, he summarized his recent trip for his superiors at the Division of Music:

1. *Background*: The result of a number of conversations between Dr. Spivacke, Dr. [Harold] Schmidt of Fisk University and myself was that on their centennial I presented a program-demonstration of Negro folk-song much similar to that given in the Coolidge Auditorium upon the anniversary of the Emancipation Proclamation. This concert was received by the faculty, and particularly by Dr. Jones, President of Fisk University, with a good deal of enthusiasm. Dr. Jones asked me to come to Fisk for a year or two to assist them to initiate a broad program for the collection and study of Negro folklore in the South. I demurred, but arranged to confer officially with a group of department heads later in the summer. The upshot of this subsequent conference with Dr. Johnson, head of the Sociology Department and Director of the Institute of Social Research, Dr. Work of the Music Department, Dr. Ross of the Dramatic Department, Dr. Jones and myself, was the proposal that we initiate conjointly the folk culture study described in the following pages.

Briefly, the agreed upon study was to explore objectively and exhaustively the musical habits of a single Negro community in the Delta, to find out and describe the function of music in the community, to ascertain the history of music in the community, and to document adequately the cultural and social backgrounds for music in the community. It was felt that this type of study, carried on in a number of types of southern communities would afford: (1) an oral history of Negro music in the South over the past hundred years; (2) describe music in the community objectively, giving all criteria for taste and the relationship of music to the dynamics of social change; and (3) result in a widely varied and completely documented set of basic recorded musical materials. Dr. Johnson agreed to furnish the field workers to supervise the editing of the material at Fisk. I proposed that the Library furnish the recording equipment, the records, and a set of duplicates for the Fisk Library, and my own services as field worker and co-editor of the study.

This project received the general approval of Dr. Spivacke and Mr. Clapp, and in the month of August I made a first exploratory trip to the region in question, namely Coahoma and Bolivar Counties, one hundred miles south of Memphis, where the Negro population is higher than anywhere else in the United States. This week of field work was highly successful. It resulted in twenty-five sixteen-inch records, approximately twelve hours of recordings of all types of music in Coahoma County. The party returned to Fisk with a completely clearcut notion of the field problem involved. Two days were spent at Fisk in collaboration with Dr. Louis Jones, field supervisor for Dr. Johnson, in preparing the outline of the study attached.

2. *Work still to be done*: The Fisk faculty strongly urged that I return to Fisk at the end of this week, that is for the twentieth, twenty-first, and twenty-second of September, in order to train the graduate students, who are to carry on the field work, in the field of Negro folk-song and its problems. The plan will further entail a period of field work at the end of October or the beginning of November of from two to three weeks. At that time it is projected that I take the Model Y machine and document the socio-musical survey that the Fisk workers will have carried out between September 25 and the last of October. The records will then be brought to the Library, and copies sent to Fisk University for transcription and study by various members of the faculty. By the middle of December Dr. Johnson and I look forward to having the material well in hand for final editing. This final editing will probably entail at least one more trip for conference to Fisk.

3. *Objective*: So far as I know this study marks the first occasion on which a great Negro university has officially dedicated itself to the study and publication of Negro folk-songs. I believe that the result will be the establishment of active South-wide folk lore work at Fisk University, and this again will have long-term, deep rooted cultural and scientific results. The type of musical study which is herein projected and laid out will lay the basis, it is believed, for contemporary music history, for a new approach to the field of folk music, for a practical working knowledge of the musical life of people, which will be equally useful to scholars, professionals and administrators in the field. 4. *Publication*: The projected field work will result in a study intended for publication, jointly edited by Dr. Johnson and his assistants, and by Alan Lomax. [ALC]

On that same day, September 18, Richard S. Hill, Acting Chief, Division of Music at the Library of Congress, accepted Spivacke's recommendation for Alan to return to Fisk University. Alan also heard from Charles Johnson in his letter dated September 18 that Fisk would welcome his arrival in late September.[44]

Alan wrote to his father on September 23:

Enclosed is an amusing note for you from John Hix. I think you still don't understand the Columbia situation. Burl Ives is using your songs only because you have given Columbia permission to let him use them, but he certainly is giving all of our books good advertising in his answers to all the fan mail. He is possibly the most popular folk-song singer on the air now. I think if you are nice and polite to the Columbia people they will be willing to make some kind of adjustment on the songs. I have just received a letter from Mrs. Tartt saying, "If the weather continues good we might record easily until Christmas. If rains set in early however there are several good neighborhoods of congregational singing that we could not make. If date has to be decided on immediately, it might be safer to say spring."

The memo is now ready to go through and I will await your decision by wire as to whether you are willing to undertake the trip at this late date. The decision about the weather in that region is up to you. I apologize for the eternal delay, but I have literally done nothing else for the last ten days but try to get those memos approved in advance. Elizabeth and I are living in a tourist room and both working very hard. We'd like to have news of you and Deanie. How is your book coming? [ALC]

Alan continued in his correspondence with Helen Hartness Flanders on September 19, regarding confusion over control of field recordings between the Library of Congress and local collectors, such as herself:

To prevent recurrences of the mix-up which has further estranged you from the Archive of American Folk Song and which has caused you to write to me and to my Chief extremely unpleasant and, I think, unnecessarily severe letters, I will note on each catalog card of a Vermont songs whether or not it had been previously recorded by you and in what form. That I had not done so beforehand was due, as I thought you might understand, to the lack of staff in the Archive, and to our being tremendously concerned about getting big jobs done. In using a couple of stanzas of Elmer George's *the Foreman Monroe*, the commonest of all the lumberjack ballads, in a recorded radio program, it simply never occurred to me that requesting your permission would be necessary. If I thought about it at all I felt sure that you would be glad for the material to be used, since this did not involve a real, full publication of the song that would conflict with the use that you have already made of it. It seems to me that you should think seriously about the rights of the collector in relation to his folk songs. It is easily possible for a collector to get his just credit when an ordinary phonograph record is published or when the song is published in book form, but at that point I wonder whether collector credit is any longer possible or due. If in order to make material available to teachers and children and interested persons in the United States the Archive must in each case correspond with both the collector and the singer, the situation seems to me to be unworkable. I wish that you could lay down some blanket condition about the use of your records that it would be possible to conform to. If you do not wish them to be used at all for a certain period of time, that too can be considered.

I did not reply to your letter of inquiry early in the summer, but turned it over to Dr. Spivacke just as I was leaving the Library. I did not feel sufficiently collected to reply to it at that time, but I feel that the suggestion implied in your recent letter to Dr. Spivacke about the letters to Sam Henry and Mrs. Parrish is unnecessary. [N-JB]

On October 2, in a memo, apparently to Spivacke, Alan sketched the next steps in the Fisk/Coahoma study:

In accordance with our conference during the week of September 26 to October 1, I revised our understanding with Dr. Johnson of Fisk University about further work on the socio-musical survey in Mississippi, and, in accordance with your recommendation, suggested that the Library loan to them for a period of six weeks to two months its Model Y machine, that it furnish them 75 12-inch discs during the first field period from October 15 to November 15 and 100 16-inch discs during the period from November 15 to December 31; that the Library furnish duplicates of the recordings made in the field for the Fisk folk-song collection. As you will note from the appended revised budget $150.00 is included besides for incidental expenses such as needles, shipping costs, etc.

I was somewhat surprised to learn at Fisk that Dr. Johnson plans to send four people into the field for the entire period of the survey, that two members of the Fisk faculty will act as supervisors and make recurring trips into the field, and that four additional persons will be held in reserve to be used in case there is a prospect of the study not being finished on schedule. The schedule has been revised due to the exigencies of the cotton season in Mississippi. The planters do not want a recording machine to come into the territory until after the cotton is picked on November 15. Therefore Dr. Johnson will send two of his field workers to mouse around between the fifteenth of October and the fifteenth of November, and two more when the recording machine goes on November 15. The revised budget was attached. [F-LC][45]

On October 3 he informed Caroline Joyner in Clarksdale, Mississippi:

I'm sorry, but it looks like I won't be back with the machine. Some of the people from Fisk will. You can make arrangements with them when they come down. [F-LC]

With their differences patched up, Alan wrote a short note to Flanders on October 3:

Thanks for the cordial note, but more for the handsome *Vermont Chap-Book*. I am glad that all of our differences are settled, and delighted to hear that the work of Middletown is going along so rapidly. If you and Miss Olney have recently made any records which will stand public release for the general listener, we might now think seriously about a Vermont album. Could Middletown sponsor such an album, that is, guarantee enough distribution to pay the basic cost? [N-JB]

He supplied more information to his father on October 3:

The Fisk recording job is gong to be done, I believe, more thoroughly and objectively than any that has yet been done in the United States in any field by any recordist. At least, if our outline is followed it will be. Naturally, the Negro looks at the South with different eyes than the white man, but it seems to me that while neither point of view is exactly right, before a decision can be reached in a democracy both sides must be allowed to have their say; and before the Negro will do the job right he perhaps has to get things off his chest. However, this recording project will not be a propaganda means for anyone, but it is complete and well planned. I will send you a copy of the outline sometime soon.

Your suggestion about the book of children's songs is perfectly true, and if I had time for anything else I'd take it. I am forwarding all of your enclosures to Bess, who, I hear by third hand, is having a good time in New York. I'd like very much to hear the story of the trial. The Tartt trip is still nearly pending. Harold is almost impossible to see these days, and so on. I certainly enjoy your eloquent letters. [ALC]

The Lomaxes were anxious for their book to appear, as noted in Alan's letter to Susan Prink, the copy editor at Macmillan, publisher of *Our Singing Country*, on October 3:

Archie MacLeish looked at me as severely as he can look at anybody and said: How did you like my foreword? and I had to admit I'd never seen it. Would you please send me a copy of it right away so that I can speak to him about it? Don't forget that [Clifton] Fadiman expects an advance copy of the book, and I think that if you send one direct to Mr. Luce at *Time* he will give it his personal attention. Mrs. Louise J. DuBose, supervisor of the South Carolina Writers Project, has a folklore manuscript which she wishes to get distributed. If you could lend her for a few days the mailing list that I have prepared for you, I am sure she would find it very useful in preparing for her non-profit folklore release. I am writing her that I have written you about this. [ALC]

On October 6 Alan communicated with Spivacke regarding Charles Todd and Robert Sonkin's previous summer's trip to California:

In completion of the very successful and important recording trip undertaken this summer for the Library by Charles Todd and Robert Sonkin, we find that it will be necessary to make 20 more duplicated than were called for in the original appropriation of $316.00. The additional cost as quoted by Mr. Wiesner will be $30.00. I would greatly appreciate your sending through a quad on this set of records at your earliest convenience, since Messrs. Todd and Sonkin are awaiting their duplicates in New York at this moment. [VFDB]

The following day, October 7, he wrote directly to Charles Todd:

Pare Lorenz is working on a couple of movies for the South American trade, and he wants some records to use, not as sound track or in any commercial fashion, but just to put him in a better mood to work. He has given the Librarian his assurance on this score. Will it be all right for us to go ahead and duplicate some of your stuff for him, and suggest that he get in touch with you about use of it? By the way, when you answer this letter, and I wish you'd make it at once, give us a specific statement of restrictions. Tell Sonkin that Charles Johnson has sent us an M.A. thesis on the life in Gees Bend, done by one of his students. Fisk, I think, would be glad to have copies of some of the Gees Bend records for reference purposes. What's the answer on that? Will you also please let me know on which records you have material—dialog, song, or discussion—which has to do with defense or the war, or how the Okies have been affected in the last six months. P.S. How are the documentary programs coming. [VFDB]

Spivacke received a letter from Alan dated October 7 regarding the Coahoma study, still scheduled to restart in November:

Roy Stryker of the FSA [the Farm Security Administration's photodocumentary project] came in the other day, and said that he was ready for one of his men to go into the field and document the Coahoma study thoroughly. It seems to me that this will be a very fruitful sort of collaboration and will possibly result in further work between the two agencies. If there is any official clearance to be gone through, perhaps it had better be done now. I am going to ask Vance Randolph whether he too would like one of Stryker's boys to come up to Arkansas to work with him for a period. [F-LC]

He updated Charles Johnson at Fisk on October 7:

Thanks for your more than kind letter and for the extremely interesting notes on Coahoma and Gees Bend. I believe that it is out of material of this sort that the development of American music will one day come clearly into focus. May I say again how much I enjoyed my week-end at Fisk, and how much I look forward to further work in your stimulating company. Last week Roy Stryker came in and seemed to feel quite definite about the assignment of one of his photographers to the work in Coahoma County with your people. One of his men will be in the lower South the balance of the winter, and thus, I think, can be more or less on call. I wish you and Lewis Jones would discuss the matter of a photographer coming in before the field work has progressed nearly to the end. Then again, he might be brought in for special occasions like the Baptist Association meeting which Jones told me is shortly to take place. I'd like to hear your reaction to this proposal. Anyway, we may expect the best type of photographic coverage of our material. [F-LC]

That same day, October 7, he also brought Archibald MacLeish into the discussion of the Fisk study:

It has been suggested that McGown of the Rockefeller Committee might be interested in doing a movie on Coahoama County, Mississippi, which would grow out of the extensive field job which the Archive and Fisk University are collaboratively undertaking during the winter. Roy Stryker is going to send one of his field representatives to document our musical study with a still camera, but since the Library recording machine will be making 100 16-inch discs, it occurred to me that these could be used as sound track for a short for South America. If this is desired, some additional arrangements will have to be made before the machine goes to the field. I thought I would let you know in time. [F-LC]

John Lomax received another letter from Alan dated October 9:

My letters must not be getting to you, because I have certainly tried to keep up a correspondence. I think your last note was pretty unfair. I have written Burl Ives a very strong letter, a copy of which is enclosed, and I hope to hear from him soon. The trip has passed its major hurdle, and I think you will hear from Spivacke in the next few days that the machine is on its way. Needless to say, I regret the delay horribly. The enclosed song was left for you by a very charming, white-haired pensioner of the Chicago Public School system who said that they had given her $1700 a year to do what she wanted to do, and what she wanted to do was write lyrics. This is one rejected by the *Harvard Lampoon*! I saw Bess two days ago in New York, and she is very well and working very enthusiastically on the School of the Air. I think you can check her off your list of worries. Enclosed is MacLeish's foreword with a couple of last-minute corrections by me, red-pencilled by MacLeish, which tell their own story. I'm awfully sorry I didn't catch this sooner, but nobody sent me proof, and I didn't think it would be necessary. Miss Prink tells me the book will be out October 24, due to delay over priorities. [ALC]

Alan dashed off a short note to Spivacke on October 10, in reference to Colcord's letter of September 10:[46]

This is a letter which was written before our armistice was declared in September. I thought you might be interested in thinking about it. I have not yet answered Miss Colcord's last letter. She is one of the Archives' best friends and constantly sends me collectors items. [ALC]

On October 16 Alan wrote to Sterling Brown in Washington:

Attached is one of the results of our evening of Negro music at the Library. Father was infuriated by your story about Bessie Smith, and said that he believed he could prove it was untrue. Enclosed are the documents he has collected for his side of the story. I hope you can bring them in personally when you come to see me next week. I am looking forward to it a great deal. [ALC][47]

Alan kept up with Fletcher Collins in North Carolina on October 17:

We are waiting anxiously to hear from you about your recording project, and also about ballad records. I have so many good ballad records which I want to get released and which you people could be the avenue for. Let's do something about that before Christmas. [ALC]

On October 17, always tied down with Library affairs, he wrote to Spivacke:

In process of filling a record order for the University of Texas for 150 of our best Texas records, Mr. Wiesner is making copies of some of our dangerously worn, and at the same time some of our finest originals. Some of these records will, I believe, be constantly in demand for dubbing purposes, and in order to protect them I wish strongly to urge that master dubs be made at the same time as the dubs for Texas are made. This would entail possibly making fifty dubs at an approximate cost of $75.00. I think no more valuable investment could be made, since these records will be constantly in service as orders come in. [ALC]

Still bogged down over the copyright issue with Columbia Records, he contacted Moses Smith on October 21:

I address this letter to you because I know you will appreciate the problem, and feel that I can as a friend entrust the matter to your care. During the last year and a half, I have orally taught Burl Ives a great number of American folk songs. Some of these are to be published for the first time in our forthcoming book, *Our Singing Country*. Some time later he approached me and asked me whether he could record some in this latter category for Columbia, and I told him to go ahead, and to see to it that Columbia got in touch with my father, who, in his dealings with radio companies, recording companies and publishers, insists on reasonable collector's rights in the songs. Burl evidently forgot to tell you people to do this and my father feels rightly that I went further in my friendly relation with Burl than I should have gone. I think it's up to Columbia to get in touch with Mr. Lomax and come to some reasonable settlement.

The legal department has written him to be good enough to send us piano scores of the compositions on which you claim copyright together with complete copyright information, etc. That may be a good way to do legal business but by God it's not a very good way to keep a friendly relationship. I hope if you are ever in Washington you will find time to drop into the Library and listen to some real American music. [ALC]

Concerning mostly a technical matter, he wrote to the ethnomusicologist Laura Boulton[48] on October 21:

Your letter last summer found me in the midst of field work with no mind for it, and I felt sure you'd understand why I delayed so long. I have consulted with Jerome Wiesner of the Recording Laboratory for an answer to your inquiries about recording equipment. Although it's impossible to quote us directly in this matter, Mr. Wiesner says that we have been using Presto recording machines, primarily because they are light in weight and simple to operate. He goes on, however, to add that we are not satisfied with certain features of the Presto machine because of flimsy construction, and that we plan to design special equipment for our own field work in the future. It's impossible to predict when plans for the equipment will be ready. It's my belief that Mr. Wiesner uses both Audiodiscs and Presto discs in the laboratory.

We are discussing various types of lightweight recorders and I believe before the end of the year we will have constructed at least one experimental machine for my use in South America. It will probably be a multiple purpose unit with one turntable that will run by spring and another by alternating current so that recording may be done independently of electricity and easy transportation and in centers where batteries and AC current are available. I'd like very much to hear about your experience in Canada and would be very much pleased to keep in touch with you about your work in Louisiana, since we also are discussing the initiation of a project in that territory. It seems to me that active collectors should keep closely in touch, both in order to avoid duplication and with eventual exchange of materials in mind. Sometime you must stay in Washington long enough to discuss with us the potentialities of some real collaborative work. [ALC]

He sent a short note to Spivacke on October 24:

In regard to Mr. Alistair Cooke's plans, it is my understanding that he will leave with the Library the originals of whatever recordings he makes using our equipment. These records, if they are made following certain suggestions which we have already discussed, will be a worthy addition to our growing file of documentary recordings. I suggest that the Model Y machine be lent to him at least for this first weekend, October 31 to November 2. [ALC]

The same day, October 24, he informed the composer Harry Partch[49] in Chicago:

Your work sounds extremely interesting, and I hope some day to hear you talk about it, face to face. Human speech, particularly as spoken by people rather than poets, is in some ways music richer than our musicians can comprehend. I wish you could hear some of the magnificent human documents on records here in our collection. Somehow, though, it seems to me that for the moment we need songs which are simple and direct and courageous, rather than subtly exploratory. [ALC]

On a much different note, he complained to the jazz reporter Onah Spencer in Chicago on October 24:

I wish to state to you that you grievously misquoted me in the story about Jelly Roll in Down Beat.[50] Even for an inspired writer and folklorist it was an extraordinarily inaccurate quotation. But let that be. I wonder if you would not like to put your Stagolee and other folklore material in the Archive of American Folk Song. There's no particular urgency about this, and we could put any necessary restrictions on it; but this material should be in a safe place, and the safe place for it is in our central folklore depository. I will not soon forget our evening of singing together in Chicago. I hope we can repeat that some time. [ALC]

With new field recordings never far from his mind, Alan connected with Mary Waller Bonelli in Stafford, Virginia, on October 25:

If your friend the Reverend is preaching nowadays, it will be possible for us to come out and record him. I have been out of town on field trips ever since your letter got here, and one attempt to answer it from the field proved abortive. I certainly appreciate your interest and I am anxious to hear the man. If I don't hear from you I will go out to visit him one Sunday anyhow. [ALC]

A much longer piece went out to Louis Chappell in West Virginia on October 25:

I hope you will forgive me for my mistake in addressing you as Lawrence W. Chappell. My recollection of name is often faulty, but I certainly did intend to write the man who is the author of John Henry, and who was active in collecting West Virginia songs. It so happened that Lincoln Thompson came in my office the day before yesterday to demonstrate one of his new machines, and he told me in passing that he thought your records were acoustically as good as any field recordings he had ever heard. That redoubles my concern and my original reason for writing you. We are both aware of the scientific importance of the actual, recorded rendition of the song, which sets forth better than any musical notation could possibly do the stylistic and melodic qualities of the piece. Once a good recording has been made, at the expense and pains that you and I both realize that such recording implies, it seems to me a great pity that the pristine quality of the recording be lost by wear and transcription. It was to prevent this that the Carnegie Corporation gave to the Library of Congress our duplicating laboratory, which was specifically set up to prevent the wearing out of our records, and those in the hands of private individuals, by continual replaying. By means of this duplicating laboratory the original records can be duplicated and while the valuable originals are stored away the duplicates can be used for purposes of transcription. I hope you will seriously consider the possibility of having your records treated in this way before they are, as they will be, worn out in the publication process.

There is another matter which I would like to take up with you. The Library of Congress is making up a set of records for distribution to Latin America, and this set of records will be distributed to all libraries and educational centers by the funds appropriated by the State Department. In view of what Lincoln Thompson said about the acoustic character of your records, I wonder whether you would not be interested in contributing one or two of your best songs to this set. At least, I should like the privilege of auditioning one or two of your most tuneful, best executed pieces for inclusion in this set. In these and all other dealings of the Library of Congress we hold the interest of the local collector paramount and we take the greatest pains that the collector, rather than the institution, receives full credit for his work. I believe that you can consult collectors who have contributed material to our files and find that we are scrupulous in abiding by whatever restrictions are imposed by the collector. In case you should decide to deposit your originals here eventually, or should you wish them to be duplicated in the manner discussed above, you could feel completely secure about the collection. Dr. Harold Spivacke is now the chief of the Music Division, and the Archive is under his supervision. [ALC]

Charles Johnson at Fisk again heard from Alan in this letter of October 25:

I'd like very much to hear what recent developments in the folklore field project have been. I hope that the records left in your hands at Fisk have been useful, and that your workers are already digging away in the field in Mississippi. Let me hear from you. [F-LC]

He updated his father at month's end, on October 29:

On receiving your letter from Austin the other day, I figured you'd already started, so I sent two letters, one care of Gretchen in San Antonio and other care of Railroad Smith. I'll try to repeat as much of what I said as I can remember, and add to that. I suggested that you look up O'Neil Ford, Dave's protegé, who is a practicing architect in San Antonio, and who tells me that he knows a Negro blues singer there of sterling ability. It sounds very good. Perhaps you won't hear from Irene Whitfield. In that case I can make the following suggestions for the Cajun country if you go there. Julien Hoffpauir and family in New Iberia. Joe Segura and family near New Iberia. Sam and Jesse Stafford (who gave us both French and English songs) in Crowley. Joseph Johns and Cleveland Benoit in Jennings (These young fellows sing some remarkable Negro Cajun songs). In the same town we recorded a group of remarkable ring shouts sung by Austin Coleman, Washington Brown, and Samson Brown. I think if you could look into this further you could get some remarkable new material. Irene Whitfield is married and living in Lafayette. She could probably lead you to some good singers.

I'm sorry to hear that the recording isn't good. Why don't you take the machine to the Dallas News radio station and get one of their engineers to tell you what's wrong? They can probably be more helpful than Jerry at this distance. We have sent Brownie McNeil a lot of records to record corridos along the border, and I have suggested that he help Frank Goodwyn record the stuff around Kingsville. You might check with Brownie McNeil to make sure that everything is straight there. Perhaps Goodwyn would prefer to work with you anyway. I didn't send a converter because I didn't think you would want to bother with it. However, we can, if you wire, since we have not sent Mrs. Tartt's to her yet. [ALC][51]

Fletcher Collins in North Carolina received a message from Alan dated November 4:

We are waiting anxiously to hear from you about your recording project. The machine is being held for you, but your project should be initiated this Fall, if possible. The correspondence between Dr. Spivacke and the leadership of your committee seems to be progressing in a satisfactory fashion. I do hope that we can get some ballad records out this year. I have so many on hand that should be published. [ALC]

A short letter to Marie Prince in Cleveland went out on November 6:

I'm awfully sorry that we have missed each other on your trips east. I'm afraid if you come on Christmas week we will be away again, because I am going off to some learned conventions. The Cleveland affair was a frost, because I decided not to go at the last minute. Since you left Washington, the Archive has grown very rapidly, and we are much busier than ever here. I hope you can come in and see me some time. Elizabeth and I often speak of you, and it's nice to hear that you are well and getting along. [ALC]

In a letter to his father, also on November 6, he continued to worry about John's problems with the recording machine, a constant issue:

Jerry [Wiesner] suggests that you do all your recording at 78 RPM, which would probably help things a good deal. Also, watch the needle angle more carefully. If you can't do anything else, be sure and go through San Antonio for the two things I've mentioned there. It's nice to hear that you're record-ing cattle calls in the south Texas brush country. Don't you worry about your radio programs. Just wait until somebody does something better in the next millennium. I have heard indirectly that Bess is working her head off, but probably enjoying her job a good deal. I wouldn't worry for a while yet, any-how. I'll keep in touch with her. Thanks for the pictures, which I prize more than I can tell, especially that of Grandfather, because now I know where I get my evil expression. Mr. Brecker thinks you are one of the great American characters, but wishes that you could break down your inhibitions and get more of yourself into your book. What were some of the wicked things you did on your recording trips?

In regard to the bad news from Mrs. Tartt, my suggestion is that you do what recording you can on that portion of the budget allocated to your trip to Alabama, and that then you return the machine to us. In the spring we can probably arrange for Mrs. Tartt to record in Alabama, and perhaps it will be possible for you to go there and work with her. That will depend on the budget at that time. You know how sorry I am that the situation developed as it did. [ALC][52]

There remained the copyrights issues regarding Burl Ives, as Alan again noted to Moses Smith at Columbia Records on November 6:

Of course, I realized you knew nothing about the whole matter of the record-ing, and my reference to a friendly relationship was to one between myself and the company, rather than between myself and you, for obvious reasons. The difficulty, Moe, lies in the fact that Burl Ives, who in this case was acting as a sort of agent for Columbia, asked me whether it would be all right for him to sing the songs in a book in process of publication, on which no copy-right had yet been obtained. As a favor to Burl Ives and to Columbia, in both of whom I had the greatest confidence, I permitted the issue of these songs before our publication, which takes them really out of the control of our compilation. My father and co-editor, John A. Lomax, very justly has made complaint, and I wonder therefore whether you could ask your legal depart-ment to get in touch with Father and make some equitable and reasonable settlement. [ALC]

Alan also sent a short message to Charles Todd on November 6:

I'm awfully glad you didn't come down last week-end, because the film machine still hadn't come in, and as a matter of fact isn't here now. Don't plan to come down this next week-end until we send you a wire. I presume

Phil has arranged for transportation, etc. You haven't been holding things up at all, but it might be a good idea for you to send your script on this week when you finish it. [VFDB]

Concerning the postponed Lomax-Tartt trip, Alan wrote to Spivacke on November 8:

I have just received word from Mrs. Tartt that the weather has turned out to be so bad in Alabama this early fall that it will be impossible for her to do good work for us until spring. I wish, therefore, to suggest that $150.00 of the $800.00 originally set aside for this trip be allowed for further expenses to Mr. John A. Lomax, who is at present in the field and engaged in work which he wishes to continue. This would make a total of $300.00 allowed to Mr. Lomax and would leave $500.00 for Mrs. Tartt's trip next spring. I think this will probably be ample for that purpose. [ALC]

On November 6, a busy day, Alan also connected with Charles Johnson at Fisk:

I am glad to hear that the field work is going along, and I still hope that perhaps I can come down. I wonder if it would be possible for one of your people on their way to and from the field, preferably Lewis Jones, to stop in and see Son House at Robbinsville, Mississippi, and get from him a long interview about Robert Johnson. It might also be a good idea to interview Robert Johnson's parents, who live nearby, since Mr. Johnson is the most important folk musician that this area has produced. I'd like very much to see what they can get on him, particularly on the subject of his death, which seems to have occurred under mysterious circumstances. [F-LC]

Alan explained the situation to his father, still in Dallas, on November 8:

Dr. Spivacke agrees with my notion that you should go ahead and work until the money allocated for your traveling expenses, i.e. $250, has been exhausted. In the meantime, I shall submit a memo asking that a portion of the funds allocated to the Mrs. Tartt trip be transferred to your budget and that the remainder be held until next spring, when Mrs. Tartt can do the work. We will see then how matters stand. I have written to Mrs. Tartt to this effect. It certainly is too bad that the project has come to a stop. Dr. Spivacke urged me to ask you to, for one thing, record your complete repertory of songs for the Archive, and to take your time to make these good records. If you have any notion where some good cowboy songs could be recorded for the collection, that would perhaps be one more addition. As you know, our cowboy collection is very scattered.

I think Macmillan's attitude in regard to the royalty is pretty cheesy, because the book is about half the size of the first *American Ballads* volume. The first copy came to me a couple of days ago, and I shot it on up to Archie. It's a beautiful book, and it looks like Ruth won nearly all of her arguments, but it certainly isn't $6.00 or even $5.00 worth of book. It's going to hurt sales very much, I'd say. It's still not clear whether or not I'm going to South America, because so many things are developing here in Washington which seem very interesting. Keep me informed of your address, because I want to let you know as soon as I get word myself about whether there will be any additional money available. [ALC]

Alan connected with one of the bluesmen from the Coahoma study, Son House,[53] on November 12:

Don't let my first letter discourage you, because I think some day your blues will bring you a reward. In the meantime I will be glad to send you a copy of one of your records. If you want any additional copies these can be furnished at $1.50 per 12-inch acetate disc. A friend of mine may drop in to see you some time soon. Please give him all the help that you can. [F-LC]

Hazel L. Muller at the American Museum of Natural History in New York heard from Alan on November 12:

Your letter has been referred to me by my chief, Dr. Harold Spivacke, for comment. I am glad to learn of your interest in the recordings made by Mrs. Nicol Smith in Dutch Guiana. These recordings are acoustically extremely fine and represent certain exotic types of music which, I believe, were hitherto unrecorded. Particularly interesting are samples of musical crossings of Dutch, Negro, and East Indian music. Duplicates of these records can be obtained from our recording laboratories at a cost of $2.00 per double-sided twelve-inch record. I feel sure that they will prove to be useful in your work there. The Guiana records form only a small part of our collection of field recordings from the United States, the West Indies and South America. [ALC]

He followed up to John on November 13 regarding copyright matters:

It's going to be a little hard for me to make such an agreement with Columbia until I know what you have agreed to for your other books. Please let me know by return mail what that was. Enclosed is my last communication from the Columbia Recording Company. I am afraid that all I can do is see them when I go to New York next and make what arrangements I can. It seems to me that in regard to the songs in *Our Singing Country*, which are quoted from public domain records in the Library of Congress, you will have a very hard time making your claim good in court. *Peter Grey* is a published song out of the first part of the nineteenth century. *Cotton Eye Joe* was given to us by Margaret Valliant of the National Youth Administration. *Streets of Laredo*, while it is the version published in *Cowboy Songs*, was recorded recently by us for the Library.

Please remember, too, that CBS is not Columbia Recording Company, although the Columbia Recording Company is owned by CBS. The people at Columbia Recording Company are the most honorable people in the field, and they're nice guys. I am not anxious for this relatively small and pretty hard to clinch matter to go into court. It seems to me that your position as curator of the Archive of public domain folk music becomes at this point rather hard to justify. What have you decided about the recording trip? [ALC]

On the same day, November 13, he corresponded with T. J. Brandon of Brandon Films in New York:

Naturally I will be delighted to screen the TALL TALES[54] film. Can you suggest where this can be done? I know very little about the whole matter of movies, and we have no 16 millimeter sound outfit in this building. If you have not so far cleared yourself on your songs, *Strawberry Roan*, *The Grey Goose*, and *John Henry*, I suggest that you do so. The only publication of *Grey Goose* is in *American Ballads and Folk Songs*, copyrighted by John A. Lomax, 7456 San Benito Way, Dallas, Texas. *The Strawberry Roan* is a composed song and belongs to Curly W. Fletcher, published in *Songs of the Sage*, Los Angeles, Frontier Publishing Company, 1931. His copyright on that song appears to be quite secure. *John Henry* is in the public domain. I would be glad to consider the writing of a Foreword for your film, and possible collaboration on other projects. By Foreword, do you mean a spoken foreword or something to be used in the publicity? [ALC]

While Alan was primarily interested in field recordings, he had also demonstrated his (and his father's) fascination with commercial hillbilly and blues recordings from the 1920s and 1930s, as he noted in this long letter to Roger Butterfield, the National Affairs Editor at *Life* magazine, on November 15:

Your pleasure in the Smoky Mountain Melody[55] album certainly delighted me. There is a long story back of that album, and I'd like to tell it to you in brief. The first part is the story of how my father, in the early part of this century, brought American folk songs to the attention of the general public in his lectures and publications. The second part is the founding and growth of the Archive of American Folk Song in the Library of Congress, in the process of which my father and myself and a number of other collectors have brought into the Library 5,000 double-sided 12-in disc recordings of American folk songs, amounting to more than 20,000 items of music, from the South, the Middle West, New England, the Southwest, the West, South America, and so forth; Negro chain gang songs, Negro sermons, the whole range of mountain balladry and dance music, the occupational songs of the cowboy, the lumberjack, the miner and so on, hoodoo songs, folk tales, vaquero ballads, etc. These records are now on file in the Library, and the Carnegie Corporation has given us engineers and equipment so that the records may be dubbed or pressed and made available to the general public.

As a part of our research into the living folk music of the United States on records, we undertook in 1938 and 1939 to make a preliminary survey of American folk music on commercial records. With that in mind I spent a considerable period of time auditioning commercial records in New York, Camden and here. I must have listened to 3,000 odd records, all of which were chosen in advance for interest, and out of these I picked four or five hundred which had special interest. This group I further compressed into a selected list of folk song records which was mimeographed and published by the State Department, and a copy of which you have already seen.

As you undoubtedly know, these records are difficult of access. They go out of print very rapidly, and they once were beneath the notice of the commercial companies. I urged everywhere that a systematic program of release of these recordings be adopted and, I believe, have succeeded in convincing the editors of the companies that this should be done. Victor asked my father to pick out a group of records for them, and to issue them as an album, and I was to do a similar job for Columbia and possibly for Decca. More important things have come in between, but my father has finished his first assignment for Victor in *Smoky Mountain Melodies* [*Smoky Mountain Ballads*] and I must say that even my most sanguine hopes were outstripped in the reaction to the album. This shows, what I have long suspected, that probably the healthiest phase of American folk song is the contemporary "hill billy" development via radio and phonograph, where the performers are paid for their work.

The Victor album does not represent new recording, but only re-issue of chosen material from already recorded commercial records. The individuals on those records sing over the radio every day in the South. The Carter Family, for instance, is a North Carolina group; they are the most popular singers among the Okies of California. They sell transcriptions which advertise everything from patent medicine to false teeth. Uncle Dave Macon broadcasts over the Grand Old Opera in Nashville, Tennessee, and has performed in country vaudeville all over the South. He recently has helped make a movie. The Skillet Lickers were one of the first groups to make commercial records, performing for Black Seal Columbia in years past.

This whole story of folk singers on commercial records is pretty well fresh material. Nobody has ever looked into it, so far as I am aware, but myself during that period of listening to records, and I have never had time since to follow up all the leads which I feel are there to be followed. The Archive of American Folk Song with current expeditions in Alaska, Texas, Old Mexico, New England, Brazil, Tennessee, Mississippi, and Arkansas, with material coming in from Trinidad, Wisconsin, the Okie camps of California, has been too busy to follow up this all-important field.

We are, however, preparing a series of records out of our own files for release, a series of thirty of which will go to all the Latin American republics and then be generally available, and with hundreds more to be issued if we can find a way to do it. I'd like very much to work with you on this story. Will you let me hear from you about your reaction to the additional information contained in this letter. [ALC]

Alan continued to advise his father about copyright issues on November 19:

I don't know if we will ever get straight about Columbia Recording Company and CBS. You complain about Burl's recording your songs and not paying you for it, and then you let CBS take you for a ride on their book contract, when they would never dare to use one of your songs on the air without your express permission. I've been trying to tell you this for a year, but it just doesn't seem to sink in. I am going to follow your suggestion and ask $100.00, but you have established an awfully bad precedent. I am sure your illness was just a temporary thing, and I'm glad to hear you are going so strong. Everybody was perfectly delighted about the book, although Harold agrees with you about the music. Mr. MacLeish I have not seen in a coon's age. Earl Robinson, whom I saw last week-end in New York, thought the music was the best he had ever seen, so there seem to be several opinions.

Christmas I am going to go to the Folklore Convention[56] for the sake of my relations with those people. I wish I could be home for Thanksgiving dinner and a look at those brown leaves. Keep me informed about your whereabouts so that I can let you know about the budget when that comes through. The checklist will be ready for binding at the end of next week. I have just given Macmillans an idea for a book, which I think they will take. I will tell you much more about that later. [ALC]

There was more news and instructions from Alan to Fletcher Collins on November 22:

The machine will be shipped to you today. I thought for a time that I would be able to bring it down myself and give you instructions in its use, but you will have to go by the following information. May I point out that it's very important for you to record these songs as nearly perfect as possible so that they will be useful as recordings. To this end keep experimenting until you get a really silent and satisfactory cut before you begin each recording session. You were correct in telling Mr. Greer that recording for us would not prevent him from making other disposition of his collection. I am sorry that it will be necessary to put any sort of restriction on the collection and I wish you had mentioned this before. However, we are willing to abide by your restrictions as you suggest.

You can keep the machine until the middle of December with welcome. If you happen to have time, you might look up a Negro harmonica player in Durham, North Carolina who is undoubtedly the best harmonica player who ever blown his harp in this or any other portion of the universe. I have jogged Dr. Spivacke about the price costs. P.S. For cataloging purposes would you please submit with the records the following information: Number the records consecutively, labeling the sides A and B and denote each item consecutively on the side. For each song, story, tune, etc., give the title(s), the name of the singer(s), with instruments, the place and the date. Put down below the first line, the first line of the refrain. Go ahead and use your disks liberally for interviews particularly if these interviews are sustained accounts by singers. As you probably are aware, it's best to let people take their own time and you drive them along by conversational devices. The proportion of conversation to song can be as high as one-fifth of the total of the recording without harm. [ALC][57]

A short message to the Management Corporation of America in New York on November 28 dealt with some business matters:

I regret to say that I cannot send a check for the statement you have just submitted to me. My understanding was that my account with you is to be settled as I make lectures under your management. The fact that the payment for my last lecture was not sent to you was due to my forgetfulness, and I will send you a check for that portion of the amount after the first of December. [ALC]

When Alan was in New York, he worked with the Almanac Singers in addition to his radio shows. Formed in early 1941 by Pete Seeger, Millard Lampell, and Lee Hays, the Almanacs were a loose group that at one time or another also included Josh White, Pete and Butch Hawes, Agnes "Sis" Cunningham, Arthur Stern, Woody Guthrie, and Alan's sister Bess. They issued an anti-war album, *Songs For John Doe*, in May 1941, but by the fall they were supporting intervention in the war in Europe. They recorded one album of labor songs, *Talking Union*, in July, and two albums of folk songs. Alan kept in contact with Woody, who had been hired by the Bonneville Power Administration in May to write songs for a film celebrating the building of the Grand Coulee Dam on the Columbia River. On December 2 Alan wrote to Woody, who was back in New York:

I wish you'd write and tell me who in the Department of Interior made the records of your Bonneville Dam songs[58] and what his position is. I want to write and ask permission to copy them and add them to the Archive collection. We're working hard on a couple of swell radio shows about the Okies. [WGA]

Alan dealt with more business issues on December 2 in his note to Mary Jo Wallace at the Columbia Lecture Bureau:

I apologize most heartily for my omission to send you the portion of the fee owing to you from the New Jersey lecture. It was a detail that disappeared under a great rush of work in the office. I am afraid, however, until you remind me what my obligation to you is I have for the moment forgotten. Rest assured I will send you a check immediately on receipt of your reply. [ALC]

Alan had an idea for a new book, as he expressed to James Putnam at the Macmillan Co. on December 2:

I presume the reason I haven't heard from you about the book is that Macmillan is engaged in deciding what the amount of the advance will be?! Nevertheless, I trustfully enclose a few pages of the last chapter, which will be the story of Jelly Roll Morton, as told by himself. It's very rough; it's never even been properly gone over for typographical errors. The order of the book as I now see it will begin with brief sketches and end with the longest story, that of Jelly Roll Morton. Intermediate material will gradually grow in complexity, leading up to the idea of a small biography made up entirely of material from records. Let me know as soon as you can what you think. I have never received the two complimentary copies of the book destined to me. Will you send one of them to me and the other to Herbert Robbins, care of the Mathematics Department, New York University. [ALC][59]

He followed to T. J. Brandon of Brandon Films on December 5:

I judge from a letter from my father that he wishes to be compensated for the use of his song, The Gray Goose, published only in his book, *American Ballads and Folk Songs*. He has authorized me to set a fee for this use. It seems to me, in view of the fact that your film is completely experimental, and for educational distribution only, that a proper figure might be $25.00. I suggest that you mail him a check for this amount. I am still anxious to get the opportunity to review your film here in Washington. [ALC]

Concerning the Archive, he wrote to Captain Thomas Howard Carpenter[60] in Lewes, Delaware, on December 5:

I recently saw a clipping from the Philadelphia Ledger containing a story about your interesting life. It occurred to me that you might possibly have picked up some old-time sea songs and ballads in the course of your travels, particularly material relating to the Delaware Bay. If you know any such material or know where it may be obtained, I would greatly appreciate this information so that we may add these songs to our large collection of American folk songs in the Library of Congress. [ALC]

The following day, December 6, Alan wrote a lengthy letter to his father:

It's fine to know that your trip to southern Texas was such a success, even though you weren't able to get hold of "Explosion!" The Brown Bowen tune, if the story is as well recorded as I heard it in San Antonio, would make a whole radio program by itself, and the Mexican material is just what we need. I think the best thing you could possibly do would be to go to New Mexico with Peter Hurd. You might be interested to know that we have held off our work in New Mexico for a long time because Arthur Campa, Professor of Folk Music at the University of New Mexico, has had a Rockefeller grant to do work in that state. So far, however, having received some funds he has produced zero results, and I see no reason why we should delay further our explorations in that central territory.

I have two additional suggestions: (a) that you get as much cowboy stuff as possible. Ask [J. Frank] Dobie again for contacts in the region, and make as many records of cowboy talk as you feel are important. Our mutual friend Bill Kittrell knows of two or three cowboy singers who he says are very good. I will also send you the names of some of Woody's relatives in the Panhandle area whom you can look up. (b) It would be worth your while,

I think, to get acquainted with a few of the radio performers who work in Dallas and to get from them their versions of American folk song. In the past couple of years I have found some of these people to be extremely good sources for American folk songs. They very seldom sing them on the air, because they are felt to be not commercial, but oftentimes they know good tunes if you will give them a chance to remind themselves of same. One of the best square dance callers I ever heard in my life was the other night over some Dallas radio station. The simplest thing to do is to call on the program managers of the stations in Dallas and Fort Worth and ask them for a list of their local people.

Jerry [Wiesner] will forward you your records today, and I have just received news from the Librarian's office that another $150 has been approved for your further work, bringing the total now to $300 in all. If you foresee that you will need more money I will see what can be done about that. Due to strenuous efforts on the part of myself, my secretary and a large crowd of NYA workers, the Checklist is all collated, six hundred pages of it, and there remains only the binding and mailing to be done. We are about half through our first series of documentary radio programs, in which we will use fragments of interviews, plus music, to build a series of transcriptions along the lines of your Ballad Hunter series. I have definitely decided to go to South America sometime in February, and in the meantime my time will be taken up in preparation for the trip and in selecting the material for our South American albums. I saw Bess last week again, and she is much happier than she was at first, and looks awfully nice. She's going to spend Christmas with us here in Washington, after which I will go to the Modern Language Association and Folklore meetings. [ALC]

Just to clear things up, he informed Mary Jo Wallace at the Columbia Lecture Bureau on December 6:

I enclose check for $25.00 covering the fee for my last engagement. I will forward the $20.00 for the publicity account early in January. [ALC]

Although war had been declared less than a week before, he made no mention of it on December 12 when he wrote to Spivacke:

The opportunity was presented to me in New York to obtain a good copy of an old Victor recording, out of print and unobtainable, which we do not have in our record collection, containing two mountain ballads with authentic banjo accompaniment. This is possibly the most authentic commercial record of American folk song that has been made, to my knowledge. I wish to recommend that we furnish the donor, Woody Guthrie, with an acetate duplicate of this recording in return for his generous gift to the Library of Congress folk song collection. The cost will be $2.00. [ALC]

On December 12 he also contacted Eleanor Stierhem at the *American Magazine* about his current work:

It may be that I will be making a trip into Virginia during the week before Christmas. I will let you know shortly if that is going to happen. There are no pictures in existence of my recording work in the field. Possibly some can be made at this time. Thank you for your interest. [ALC]

The following day, December 13, he again contacted Woody, but now with war news:

I have gotten in touch with the people at the Department of Interior and I think they may decide to pay for the making of a fifteen-minute transcription of your songs about the Bonneville Dam. There will be a fee in it for you, of course. I will let you know when anything develops. I certainly do appreciate your list of informants in West Texas. I've forwarded it on to Father, and I am sure the results will be good. See if you can make these studio people cut their cost for your Pearl Harbor records, since we have practically no money for this project of documenting wartime opinion. I might say that the stuff so far has been very exciting. Nick [Ray] always looks happier outside of New York. I will send his address later. Please hurry the record along, since we will be doing our show over the week end. [WGA]

He kept in touch with T. J. Brandon on December 13:

The other afternoon I saw your excellent film [*Tall Tales*] and enjoyed it a great deal. It seems to me that with the limited resources at your disposal you did a very fine and sensitive piece of work. There is not a trace of artificiality or striving for effect in the whole film. I shall be delighted to write a foreword for your film. I'd like to do this gratis, but at the moment I am somewhat up against it for money, and I wish you would suggest a small fee, whatever you feel you can afford, for the work that I will put in preparing the foreword and the bibliography, etc. I have asked Mr. Nat Lawlor, who is an important person in the MTMA and at this time very much concerned about folk music, to view the film here. I feel sure the results of that will be good too. [ALC]

On December 16 he again updated his father:

I appreciate your efforts in behalf of the documentary series. Your records were extremely interesting and we were able to use one passage from the oil man's speech (which contained some delightful Malapropisms such as phrase for phase and Cardinal Bull for Cordell Hull). Jerry [Wiesner] will send the records off right away. It was my thought that you could go via Pampa on your way to New Mexico. If you need any more records, send me an airmail a few days in advance if possible, and we will ship them to you then. We are getting into our wartime stride up here, and as one of our informants said, we are going to wipe them off the face of the earth. Please return the enclosed reviews after you are through with them. [RRP, AFC, LC][61]

In this letter Alan was partly referring to the expansion of the Radio Research Project on December 8. He had quickly notified fieldworkers in ten places throughout the country to collect man-on-the-street interviews about their reactions to the war. This resulted in over four hours of recordings and a fifteen-minute radio program.[62]

On December 18, Alan expressed to John his concerns over his current recording trip:

It's awfully hard to tell you just what to do about paying informants on your slender budget, but why not go back to our old tack of not paying anybody anything because there ain't no money to pay them with—and then pay the ones that you have to, and we'll try to get the money of out Harold. Be sure to get receipts for all of these items, though, so we won't have any trouble. I know your moans and groans are justified in the past, but maybe this time we can do something about it. I'll tell Jerry [Wiesner] about the cutting needles. Thanks again for the swell records you sent in, and please send Frank Goodwyn's right along so that I can play them over and see whether I should reply favorably to his suggestion about giving him a set of duplicates. I have figured out a complicated scheme there, but I need to hear the records in order to know what to do. [ALC][63]

He wrote a number of letters on December 18 regarding the current Radio Research Project. For example, in one to Robert Allen at Indiana University, he explained how it was going:

I hope you realize how much Jerry, Phil [Cohen] and I appreciate your magnificent response to my request for material, and the material was indeed important. We are going to use a passage from the merchant-isolationist in a fifteen minute transcribed program which will come over the air this week and we'll let you know when that will be. The rest will be stored away as part of our growing archive of contemporary opinion. We got stuff from Texas, Colorado, Massachusetts, New York City, et al., and the total was a priceless expression of the unity of the American people in this time of crisis. It may be that from time to time we will do this again and we hope we can depend on you for your cooperation. We will replace the acetate that was used in the recordings and for this time hope to call it even. [RRP, AFC, LC]

He also fired off a short note to Charles Harrell at radio station WBEN in Buffalo, New York:

Just a note to tell you how much we all appreciated your efforts in behalf of the documentation of American opinion about the war. We have put together a fifteen minute show and it will be out sometime this week on Mutual. We will let you know when that happens. The bill takes its own Government time in being paid. [RRP] Similar letters went to Charles Moore in Cambridge, Massachusetts, Charles Todd at the City College of New York, Leland Coon at the University of Wisconsin, and Duncan Emrich at the University of Denver.

A longer message went to Charles Johnson at Fisk University on December 18:

My hearty thanks for your kind offerings in behalf of the documentation of the war-time opinion. We got material from twelve points scattered broadly over the United States and the whole story is an unforgettable American historical document. The immediate use we made of the material will be in the form of a fifteen minute program on the Mutual Broadcasting System sometime this week. I will let you know the date. As it turned out none of the specific statements you sent were good for the broadcast itself, but that was for internal reasons rather than because of the content of the statements. I hope you express my appreciation to the individuals involved and to Lewis Jones. I am disturbed that I have not heard any more from you about the Mississippi field project. If there has been any delay at your end, perhaps that is just as well for the time being. Our whole perspective is changing, as you can imagine, with extreme rapidity and it might be wise for us to shift the project into something which would relate to the present crisis perhaps more nearly than our present study seems to. I would welcome any suggestions that you and your colleagues have to make in this regard. [RRP]

A detailed letter also went to John Henry Faulk at the University of Texas on December 18:

I can't tell you how much everybody has enjoyed the marvelous field recordings you made for us in Texas. They will go down in history and I am sure some day, will be consulted by all the scholars. In the meantime, however, the American people are going to hear Mr. Brodie and Mrs. Whittaker talk about the war, probably over the Mutual Broadcasting System, as part of the fifteen minute program we have put together out of the material. Your field interviewing was agreed on as certainly the best that was done for us and there may be more of the same coming up in the future although none of us can say now. Our sound engineer is sending you two more batches of recordings right off, and I hope you will ship us the ones that you have finished with so that we can get them copied and get them back to you. You had better hurry because our facilities may possibly be busy with more urgent things at any time now. Your recordings of the interviews had a little too low volume on them. [RRP]

Alan sent a different sort of letter to Annabel Morris Buchanan in Richmond, Virginia, on December 18:

This is a very hard letter to write, because it involves a mistake that is quite difficult to explain. By some mischance in between myself and the printers, no credit was given to you in *Our Singing Country* for the two songs you so generously allowed us to use, "Santy Anna" and "Haul away, my Rosie." I am sending a copy of this letter to Macmillan and insisting that they include your citations in the next edition of the book. I am sure you will understand that this was something that happened somewhere between my office and the final publication of the book, because the citation was in the original copy. With the hope that you can understand and forgive this omission, I remain. [ALC]

As the year was ending, on December 23 he came up with a fresh idea for Moses Smith at Columbia Records:

Remember, a long time ago we talked about an album of repressings of your best old folk song records? I have been thinking about the thing a long time, and have developed an idea for an album of Negro songs which I think will be just about the last word now and for the future. I felt in view of the fact that the album would be one of repressings of records which you'd probably own the full rights to, you could afford to include six records in it and make it a sort of definitive volume of the material. The titles for the album which I suggest are six, out of which you can take your choice: Motherless Children, Troubled in Mind, Singers of the Lonesome Road, John Henry's Children, Just Can't Keep from Cryin', Dark Minstrels.

The album is to contain the best Negro records in your catalogs, all sung by Negro folk singers whom you have recorded for commercial purposes, and musically I feel confident that it would be the most exciting folk song album yet published. There may be some problems in tracing all of the titles and discovering whether or not you have masters of them, but even if you don't have masters, dubbings of these records would be acceptable to ordinary listeners. 1A Last Fair Deal Goin' Down sung with guitar accompaniment by Robert Johnson PE 7-04-60. B Kind-Hearted Woman PE 7-03-56 Master No. SA2580. 2A Travelling River Side Blues (unreleased) Master No. SA2616. B Hell Hound on my Trail VO 03623. Alternate: If I Had Possession of Judgment Day (unreleased) Master no. SA2633. 3A Collector Man Blues, sung and played on piano by Walter Roland PE 0293. B Things about Comin My Way, sung and played on guitar by Tampa Red and Georgia Tom VO 1637.

All these are blues records, and they are absolutely of the first quality. Nothing better has been or ever will be recorded in the line of folk blues. They are poetically strong and musically exciting. The next three records consist of spirituals performed with guitar accompaniment. 4A Dark was the Night, sung and played on guitar by Blind Willie Johnson. B Just Can't Keep from Cryin' CO 4425D. 5A Motherless Children, Blind Willie Johnson with guitar. B Keep your Lamp Trimmed and Burning CO 4425D. 6A I Am the True Vine, sung by Gary PE 5-12-66. B I'll be Rested When the Roll is Called, Blind Roosevelt Graves and his Brother PE 6-11-74 Master no. HAT 11S. In publishing this album there should be an accompanying leaflet containing material about the life of Blind Willie Johnson and that of Robert Johnson, notes about the songs, and the full texts of the records. I wish you'd let me know how you feel about this sometime soon. With very best regards and best wishes for a merry Christmas. [ALC][64]

On December 22 Alan contacted Theodore Finney, a musicologist at the University of Pittsburgh, apparently referring to an upcoming music educators meeting:

It turns out that I am not going to be able to come to the meeting this year, but that Mr. Hill will read my paper. I had planned my session mostly to consist of playing excerpts from recordings, and therefore it doesn't seem advisable to submit a paper at this time. You can obtain from Mr. Hill in Minneapolis a copy of the paper he will read for me. [ALC]

He kept up with Fletcher Collins on December 23:

Harold Spivacke has asked me to obtain from you a *curriculum vitae*, one page in length. By this he means to say that he wants a brief life history, with particular emphasis on how many pounds you weighed when you were a baby and on your career in community recreation work. He says he is quite serious. So, indeed, am I. [ALC]

The next day, December 24, he wrote to the blues musician Son House, whom he had recorded in Mississippi the previous summer:

Would you be interested in coming to New York and playing with a group of singers [the Almanac Singers] who are friends of mine and very nice people? They would be able to keep you while you were in New York and could pay you something for performances with them. They plan to make recordings so that you would be paid your share and also could probably provide you with chances to make recordings on your own. The only thing is that they do not have any money to provide your transportation to and from New York City and the whole thing would be a gamble for you. However, I think that you might get a break and I can assure you that you will be well treated. If you are interested in doing this, let me know and I will put you in touch with them. Merry Christmas and Happy New Year. [F-LC][65]

1942

On January 10 Alan kept John Hammond informed about one of his new projects:

At last the Archive is able to begin to plan the publication of some of our best records. In the next few weeks I hope to be writing a whole group of folk musicians for permission to use their performances in these non-profit pressings, and I find I lack Sonny Terry's address. Can you give it to me? I want to ask him about the use of his *Lost John* and *The Fox Chase*, which you helped me to record some years back. When are you going to visit me in the Archive and hear a few dozen of our really thrilling new acquisitions? [ALC]

The new year started somewhat slowly, as Alan explained in this message to Eleanor Stierham at the *American Magazine* in New York on January 12:

I was called back to Washington suddenly for a date at the White House, and therefore did not stop in Virginia to make records as I had planned. Thank you for your continued interest. I shall be sure to let you know the next time I am going collecting. [ALC]

Parker Wheatley at Northwestern University heard from Alan in a note from January 12 about his upcoming radio discussion:

I will be in Washington on the 31st, and delighted to follow the procedure suggested in your letter. I am a little confused by the second [John T.] Frederick appearance unless he plans to review books at that time. Could you let me know what he's going to say so that I can make my comments make sense after his? The content you suggest seems to me all right. One question: do you want to pick up them from me in Washington at the beginning? That's perfectly all right if that's what you want to do. Thanks for the invite. [ALC][66]

Alan continually advised his father on his collecting trips, as in this letter of January 13:

I am enthusiastic about the recording of the cattle calls and hollers, especially after reading Mr. Matthews' catalog of them. But I don't see why you don't combine the holler trip with a visit to Woody's friends and with the recording of Peter Hurd's Mexicans, which last proposal appeals to me more than the others, perhaps. I'd suggest waiting until warm weather and using what money you have to make a combination trip. However, it's up to you. I wish I could go along, and not stay here in this office. Do you need more needles?

Elizabeth and I have just come back from a superb and restful vacation at Key West, which is as you have always described it. We are both brown and healthy, and I will write you more news as soon as I have caught up. The Men and Books broadcast is scheduled for my birthday, Saturday, January 31. [ALC]

A fascinating letter went out to the artist Thomas Hart Benton in Kansas City, Missouri, also on January 13:

Hear'n tell that you and Father got together the other day and talked about folk songs and that you want to record for us. We'd like to have anything you care to pick up or play. Do you have a machine to do the work, or do you know somebody who will do it for you? We might be able to furnish the acetate if the thing looks good. Better come in to see me, and we'll talk the thing over here if you are ever down this alley. Father told me about your affection for Doc Boggs.[67] He has long been my favorite on commercial records, but you ought to listen, if you haven't, to some of the Mainer Mountaineer stuff on Bluebird, recent. Enclosed is a list of such records of songs which you may not know. I would like to hear from you very much. [ALC]

A week later, January 20, he wrote to Parker Wheatley, Northwestern University's radio director, about his upcoming program:

The sentence might read: Of Men and Books, with John T. Frederick of Northwestern University and his guest, Alan Lomax, Assistant in Charge of the Archive of American Folk Song, Library of Congress. I will try to make my first five minutes general enough so that whatever comes from Frederick next will make plenty of sense, and will put most of the singing into the last five. [ALC]

Alan was continually trying to help Woody, as in this letter to Spivacke on January 20:

Woody Guthrie is living in New York City and is in contact with a number of singers of folk-songs [the Almanac Singers]. He has a recording machine available to him, and he suggested that we send him some blank records and some cutting needles so that he can record for us. He would record material from his own repertory which we do not already have, and a group of new ballads which he has composed within the last year. I believe the material that this group of records would contain would be an important addition to our collection. I therefore recommend that we send to Mr. Guthrie a box of twenty blank records and two sapphire cutting needles. [WGC]

He informed Woody Guthrie on January 21 of the interest in his recordings with the Almanac Singers:

I played the Almanac songs the other day for Mrs. Roosevelt, and she thought they were swell, and asked for copies of the records. She is playing them for her OCD staff, and I think their fame will be spread abroad. Besides, the News and Special Events man from BBC was here, and took a copy of Taking it Easy with the intention of getting it played on their network. He promised to get in touch with you all and get your permission first. The other night I played the stuff for Bobby Strauss, who is Director of Information for OEM, and he was delighted and said he thought that the thing should be used on a broadcast with the only live talent. Something, I am sure, will come of that. I told him that you all could make a new song about any assigned subject at the drop of a banjo.

It's very important, I think, for you to hurry up and change your name, and for heaven's sake make it a good old countrified name like Oklahoma Rangers or something of the sort. Your chief point of contact in America is that of the background of the American soil and American folk songs. Don't become Headline Singers, even though you may be singing the headlines. This all leads up to a request from the Library for the use of one of the songs you recorded for us, namely The Gypsy Davy. We are publishing an album of American ballads for the National Council of Teachers of English. Said album will be used mostly in schools and colleges for teaching purposes, but the individual records will also be available for purchase from the Library to members of the general public. Our fee to singers for permission to use their material is a flat $10.00 per side, which is hereby offered to you with apologies understood. I sincerely believe that this will not compete with your commercial records, even if you decide to record the same song for commercial companies, and I hope you will feel able to tell us to go ahead. If not, I will understand perfectly the reasons why you decided not to. The bill that your commercial recording company sent us from New York is somewhat of a mystery to me. I can't understand the reason for all the items and have so written them; and I might tell you confidentially that the recording stinks. You ought to make a change in your business. I sure would like to hear the news, but even so, all power to your mighty guitars. [WGA][68]

Alan also connected with Lewis Jones at Fisk University on January 21:

I have owed you a letter for a long time, and one of the few letters that I have wanted to write, because I really greatly enjoyed my contact with you last summer and have looked forward to knowing you better and perhaps doing more work with you. As you probably guessed, the tremendous pressure of work in Washington and general hysteria that has existed here has in some measure affected my own work. Most of my time has been spent in developing the documentary program which I discussed with you, a bit fruitlessly, last summer. It is in essence an attempt to develop a genuine approach to history for radio, and what might possibly be termed a democratic type of propaganda in which a free people has the opportunity to explain for itself in its own terms the nature of its own life. This series will be ready within another month, I hope, and you may judge for yourself where we have succeeded and where failed. It's really too bad that there was no opportunity to do an all-Negro program as I had hoped, but if the idea catches on, and I believe it will, we will have that opportunity; and you, who so well know the talent for self-expression which belongs to your people, can best judge how exciting such a program will be.

May I take this opportunity to say that if you have anything to do with further documentary recording at Fisk in relation to war opinion or anything else, it would be very wise to insist that the informants not speak from script but speak in an ad lib fashion, and to pick individuals who not only represent important points of view within the community, but who also are able to speak with charm, eloquence and humor about their problems. You were by far the best of all the people on the records that came to us first, and that was, I judged, [because] you spoke from the bottom of your heart and informally, rather than from a script according to a carefully thought out reaction. I felt, too, that the records did not represent the Nashville community, but only the community of Fisk, probably not even that. However, I am sure that the historians of the future will discover much of interest in the deep current of the belief which those records expressed.

I greatly appreciate your writing to me and letting me know what has happened to our plans for the study of Coahoma County. After thinking the matter over a good deal and worrying about it a good deal, I finally decided that we had better take a tip from John Work and not try to make records there in the cold weather. Rain, and certainly this blizzard, would have held us back a good deal. However, in writing this reaction to Dr. Johnson I certainly did not mean that the program was a closed issue for us, and I have not been able to understand why I have not heard from him about the matter. About two or three weeks ago I wrote him again a letter of inquiry which expressed a feeling of my own that possibly the study we had outlined was a bit utopian in the situation of the present crisis, and asking him whether he thought so, and wondering whether he had better tackle some other job at this moment. Do you feel the same way about it as I do? If so, will you give me Dr. Johnson's reaction and yours about what might best be done. I'd like very much to spend the money which has been set aside for this project for some sort of meaningful study which would be carried on in collaboration with Fisk University. I am very much distressed that I have had no word from Dr. Johnson. It would be a great pleasure to hear from you, and if you ever come our way, please be sure to let us know in advance so that we can arrange to entertain you. Elizabeth sends her best regards, and I, my best wishes for the new year. [F-LC]

He demonstrated his knowledge of French in a letter to Francois J. Brassard in Jonquiere, P.Q., Canada, on January 22, regarding a list of recordings:

Je vous remercie de votre lettre du 7 janvier. Il n'est pas possible de vous donner, tout au moment, la liste que vous voulez. Je vais faire preparer cette information, et vous la recevrez en peu de semaines. S'il y a autre chose dans l'aquelle nous pouvons vous servir, j'espere que vous le demanderez. Je m'interesse beaucoup a vos etudes, et [illegible] en savoir plus. Vous connaissez, sans doute, la collection de Docteur Barbeau dans la Musee Nationale d'Ottawa. Nous sommes au courant de faire copier quelques uns de ses chansons pour notre Archive. Je vous prie d'agreer l'expression de mes sentiments bien distingues. [ALC]

[Translation: I thank you for your letter of January 7. It is not possible to give you, right at this moment, the list that you want. I am going to have this information prepared, and you will receive it in a few weeks. If there is something else with which we can help you, I hope that you will ask for it. I am very interested in your studies and I would like to know more about it. Doubtless you know of the collection of Doctor Barbeau in the National Museum of Ottawa. We are currently having some of his songs copied [for] our Archive. I beg you to accept the expression of my most respectful sentiments.]

Spivacke noted some misgivings regarding Alan's inquiry about Woody, which led to this answer from Alan on January 26:

In response to your note about the project for recording Woody Guthrie's songs, allow me to say that whether or not some of the Guthrie material will be restricted because of his own plans to use it commercially, the continuing documentation of this most unusual of American ballad makers has a very great importance; and no commercial company's release will provide for us the sort of material which will some day make a study of his repertory and his continual production of new songs possible. Also, allow me to say that the group with which Mr. Guthrie is working is continually experimenting with the development and extension of the medium of American folk song, and the record of their experiments will have much historical significance. In answer to your question about the potential usefulness of the records, allow me to say that the only records which have gone from the Archive to Mrs. Roosevelt at her special request were a group made for us by Woody Guthrie and his singers. Copies have also been ordered by O.E.M., and other fragments have been used in the construction of The Ballad Hunter and our current documentary series. Therefore, may I urge again that my first recommendation be passed on favorably. [WGC]

Concerning Library business, Alan again communicated with Hazel Muller at the American Museum of Natural History in New York on January 26, basically a repeat of his letter of November 12:

Your letter has been referred to me by my Chief, Dr. Spivacke, for comment. Through some error in transmission in the Library, your inquiry failed to reach me before, but I now have your original request before me. It is possible for us to make copies of Miss [Nicol] Smith's records at $2.00 per twelve-inch, double-sided record. There are twenty-eight records in the group, almost all of them containing extremely interesting material. The [Dutch] Guiana records form only a small part of our collection of field recordings from the United States, West Indies and South America, and any of these may be copied for your use, with the greatest of pleasure, by us. May I express my regret that the inquiry was not replied to earlier, and assure you that the Archive of American Folk Song will be glad to lend you any service possible in future. [ALC]

Anxious to continue his relationship with some of the bluesmen recorded during the
Delta project, he contacted McKinley Morganfield (Muddy Water[s]) on January 27:

Everyone here in the Library certainly liked your records, because they were
very beautifully performed, and I am sending you under separate cover a
copy of your two best blues. I think that you should keep in practice, because
I feel sure that some time you will get the break that you deserve. I am sorry I
could not write sooner. With very best regards and many thanks. [F-LC]

Alan communicated again with Son House on January 28:

I wrote you in December asking whether you wanted to come to New York
and play and sing with a group of singers whom I know there. They are
friends of mine and very dependable. They need somebody who can make his
own songs and play a good guitar, and who is experienced in Negro music.
They are working all the time and would be able to pay you for your trouble,
although they couldn't pay transportation east. They don't think it is a good
idea for you to plan to move east until you try out with them for a while, but
they would take care of you in New York and pay you for the trouble beside.
They have a good chance now for radio singing and for recording also, and
unless you have some strong reason against it, I would suggest that you consider the matter seriously. Let me know by return air mail what you think,
and I will put them in touch with you at once. But they want to know right
away. [F-LC][69]

He responded to Thomas Hart Benton on January 28:

I am glad to hear about the work you are doing for Decca, and I will write to
Jack Kapp[70] for a couple of pressings of the songs, and I'd like to hear your
new ones when they are done. About the Ozark trip, we have a recording
machine in Galena, Missouri, in the hands of Vance Randolph, and perhaps
he'd be able to record your fiddlers for us if they are somewhere near him. Let
me know if that sounds like a possibility. It would be swell to see you if you
ever get to Washington, and the Seegers [Ruth and Charles] feel the same
way about this. Thanks for writing. [ALC][71]

His father's upcoming recording trip continued to weigh, as in this letter to John on
February 7:

It seems to me that you could add a per diem voucher to the mileage vouchers
you have already sent in. Jerry [Wiesner] is holding those until this voucher

is received. I would still like to have a detailed statement about your planned trip into west Texas, although it seems to me it would be better to wait until it gets a little warmer before you start. In the matter of priorities on tires, we can write you a bang-up letter when you go to the local [tire priorities] board with your request. In the meantime, I am sure you could dig up valuable stuff in and around Dallas, although it's always harder to hunt on your own home grounds, I know. Captain Thompson called up, and I told him that you had gone back to Texas. We agreed to meet later on, however. [ALC]

Two days later, February 9, he communicated with James Putnam at Macmillan Publishing Co.:

Will you please send me the file of review clippings on my book so that I can have them photostated for my files. I will return it intact with great promptness and if you are worried, you can send it by registered mail. . . . I have prepared a long outline on *Listen to our Story* which I will send to you in a couple of days. I am working so hard on the preparation of broadcasts that I have not had time to write any sample commentary but hope that you will take the commentary in good faith in view of the introduction to *Our Singing Country*, the autobiographical section of the *Lead Belly* book and a couple of lengthy articles which I will attach. I am going to have time during the Spring to work on the book and hope that you will make it possible for me to go ahead with it. [ALC][72]

Alan followed on February 10 with a letter to Pete Seeger (who, for political reasons, was going by the name Pete Bowers at the moment):

The two songs you recorded for [Robert] Sonkin are models, it seems to me, for a whole new approach to the basic morale problem in the United States. I can't praise them highly enough and everyone else has felt equally enthusiastic. We are working on the construction of this program, Dear Mr. President, and the plan now is to use your talking blues as part of the weave material all the way through the show. This will necessitate hiring you as part of the cast of the whole program. Attached is a letter from Son Stouse [House] indicating his willingness to go straight up to New York if you will send him the fare. His address, in case you can't decipher it, is Route 1, Box 8, Robinsonville, Mississippi. I will tell him that you are going to get in touch with him. I wish I could help you on this fare but I happen to be very short at the moment. He is worth your while though. [RRP][73]

That same day, February 10, Alan did indeed write to House:

I have written my friends in New York to write you at once and urged them to lend you your fare until you get there. I sure hope the thing will work out. In the meantime, all best wishes to you and your family. [F-LC]

On a quite personal level, Alan wrote to Ethel Lomax Shumaker on February 12:

Thank you for the coat of arms and information about my genealogy. It is my understanding my family goes back to North Carolina and Virginia so I am sure we are related. I am going to send your letter on to my father who will undoubtedly be interested in it. [ALC]

There was more on his father's trip in this letter to John on February 18:

I have sent a letter for Luther Evans' signature about the tire matter, which is enclosed, and have written a memo about the trip you plan to take in west Texas. I hope the memo will be approved this week. I think that your project to document western stuff in west Texas is most important, and I am sure that everyone here will agree with me there. By all means record Harry Stevens' experiences and songs. I think I will request $500 flat for the trip, and I imagine that will take care of the whole thing, since your present expenses amount to about $250 of the $300 originally set aside for your present accomplishment. The more practicing you do at home before you start, to get perfect cuts, the better, because I think Jerry feels that most of your trouble comes not from mechanical defects so much as from sheer failure to hit upon the simple solutions for ordinary recording problems. I enjoyed the enclosures you sent from Johnny and Alice and Frank Goodwyn. The reviews were fine, but they none of them come up to the review in *Modern Music* by Marc Blitzstein. It's by far the best review that's ever been given any of our books. By all means, get a copy. [ALC][74]

Alan had finished his script for Brandon Films, as he explained to T. J. Brandon on February 19:

Attached is a copy of the note on *Tall Tales* with a short bibliography. I hadn't sent it on because I judged that you hadn't liked my introduction to the picture and there was no point in continuing with the other part of my job. I am delighted that you are going to use it and here is my bibliography. [ALC]

On February 21 he gave some advice to Jack Conroy, a writer in Chicago:

I have rather less to do with the OFF than you do, I'm afraid. It's completely separate from the Library and we only feel occasionally a gentle stirring at the foot of the mountain which we presume originates up in that Olympus of big-time publishers and radio production men. I hope you'll have luck in getting a job there but my opinion is that you won't. Sorry. [ALC]

More followed to his father on February 23:

I presume by now that you have received the letter to the Tire Priorities Board and I will wait to hear what they decide before I get you the train travel money. I have sent in a memorandum asking for $700 additional funds for your recording trip across the West and assume I will get approval on it very soon. Last week-end I interviewed the head of Thomas Crowell and Sons who have asked me to write a book on American folk music, the history of the whole field. He was willing to make me an advance of $1,000 which will carry me very comfortable through the next six or eight months and I am prone to accept it. What do you think? I plan an appendix in which we will print 25 to 50 songs. Would you be wiling to let part of these come out of our books without charge or would you want some sort of blanket sum for them? Let me know.

P.S. I think you ought to pay the bills yourself as we have always done in regard to repairs to the machine and send them in with your vouchers at the end of your trips. I don't see why we shall ever have such trouble with any of your accounts as you have had with your last one. There were some special accounting problems there which ought never to arise again unless you have exceeded the sum which has been apportioned for the expedition which, as I said before, is $700 for the next trip. Since there is money left over out of the $300 for the work you have just completed, I would suggest that you pay the two bills and send them in to Gerry for clearance. I'll tell him they're coming. [ALC]

Alan sent a brief message to Frank Luther at Decca Records on February 26:

In reference to your request to include songs from *American Ballads and Folk Songs*, in your forthcoming book,[75] I wish to let you know that my father, John A. Lomax, 7456 San Benito Way, Dallas, Texas, has all permission rights in regard to our books. [ALC]

Library affairs were continually on his mind, as he wrote to Elmer Sulzer at the University of Kentucky, February 26:

As folk-lore consultant on the radio project, I was delighted to read your cordial letter about the documentary series we are about to release. The potentialities of your contacts in the mountains are very great and although it doesn't appear that we can do anything about this material at the moment, I want you to know that I hope to some day. As you are probably aware, the Archive of American Folk Song of which I am in charge, has been documenting sources of regional music and folk lore for some time and your listening post would be ideal starting points for research in the mountain region. Our plans now are to do a little documenting wherever we record folk songs with the hope that perhaps the material will be useful for broadcasting in some way or other. Your letter, therefore, is quite welcome and I hope we can make something positive grown out of this suggestion of yours. [ALC]

He was still trying to assist Hazel Muller at the American Museum of Natural History with South American recordings on February 26:

I think it would be possible to pick out twelve of the recordings for you and at the same time give you a fairly representative idea of the collection. Our charge (subject to change without notice because of the unstable condition of material prices) is $1.85 per record and our practice is that a check made payable to the Library of Congress, be sent in advance before the duplicates are actually made.

We have a collection of 39 records of considerable musical interest, not all of them pure folk song by any means, from Brazil, Argentina, Chile and Peru. A group of these recordings might be of use to you. During this fiscal year, recordings are being made for us in Colombia and Brazil and this material, I am sure, will be of great value. Our North American Indian collection is quite small so far and includes a fine group of records from the Iroquois of northern New York State, a group of Seminole songs from Florida and some material from the Northwest transcribed from dictaphone cylinders. I suppose the last records will not be useful for demonstration purposes. If you would like me to look further into the matter of duplication of either Indian or South American records, I shall be glad to do so. Is it true that the American Museum has a collection of records of primitive songs and folk song and is constantly adding to this collection? I should be greatly pleased to know something about what you have and what your current recording activities are. [ALC]

On a different note, he responded to Arthur Becker at the Star Record Company in New York on February 27:

Neither Jerry [Wiesner] nor I has any ideas about a job. I am sure, however, that it will be easily possible for a trained person like yourself to find

employment in the Navy or Army as a technician if you will make application
to those departments. I know they are looking for people. [ALC]

Alan was involved with Library business and so much else, but he was not through with
the Delta project. John Work and his team at Fisk had been transcribing the recordings and
collecting data from their trip the previous summer. Alan thought that Work would also
record the upcoming Fort Valley Folk Festival, since he could not attend. On February 27 he
wrote to Work:

You evidently misunderstood my telephone conversation because I said that
no expense money from the Government can be paid in advance. We hope
it will be possible to allow you a per diem for five days at a rate of $5.00 per
day counting the fifth of March for travel, the 6, 7 and 8 for recording in
Fort Valley and the ninth for return travel and $15.00 extra for incidental
expenses. If you pay the singers, rent a car or have other expenses out of this
item for more than $1.00, you must turn in a receipt for every item. *Other-
wise, it will not be paid.* The best thing to do is to keep a careful account of
your expenses. When the trip is over, write me a letter sending receipts and a
voucher will be made out, sent to you for your signature and the money will
be paid by the Government Accounting Office. I must warn you there is usually some delay about this because of the amount of the procedure involved. I
am notifying the authorities at Fort Valley that you are coming down to make
records for our use in my place. I have submitted a memo requesting that
$40 be allotted to this project and hope to receive approval for it tomorrow
so that I can notify you definitely by wire. [FVMF][76]

On the same day, February 27, he explained the situation to Harold Spivacke:

On March 6, 7 and 9 of each year at Fort Valley, Georgia, there is given the
only Negro Folk Festival that occurs in America throughout the year, three
days of extremely interesting singing and dancing. We had discussed the
prospect of my going down this year to record the festival and I had definitely
decided to go down when I noticed that John Work who is recording for us
in Nashville was going to be one of the judges of the contest. It occurred to
me that Mr. Work, who has a recording machine and is using our blanks for
field purposes, might do the recording in my place and thus save the Library
a considerable sum of money which would be involved in my traveling there
and back. I have discussed the matter with Mr. Work by telephone and he is
interested in doing the job. May I suggest that the following funds from M.
R. be allocated to this project and approval obtained for it as soon as convenient. 5 days per diem for March 5, 6, 7, 8 and 9 at $5.00 per day. $25.00.

Incidentals, rental of cars, reimbursement to singers, etc. 15.00. Total 40.00. The project should bring us 15 or 20 extremely fine folk song recordings. [FVMF]

Alan informed Miss Caton, his boss's secretary, on March 2 about the previous summer's trips:

In cooperation with the Fisk University Departments of Sociology and Music, the Archive made a trip to Coahoma County, Mississippi, last summer and recorded there about twenty 16-inch slow speed records of Negro music including many items which will eventually be published by the Archive in recorded form. This trip was preparatory to an exhaustive investigation of the folklore of this county by Fisk research workers. On the way back to Washington, according to plan, I stopped to record some of the best ballad singers of the Virginia mountain area, obtaining from them also much material which is being used in our publication of folk songs. [F-LC][77]

He was certainly not done with the Fisk study, as he noted to Charles Johnson also on March 2:

I am very anxious to get the complete transcripts of the field notes taken so far in Coahoma County. If I am not able to review this material during March, I will have no justification for asking that the project be continued and the funds will have to be transferred to some other enterprise. Our fiscal year grows shorter and I wish to be able to make a final decision about this shortly. I hope, therefore, that you will find it convenient to forward me whatever material your field workers have thus far been able to accumulate. We are using one passage from your round table on the OEM show and I hope that subsequently we will be able to use the complete discussion in the form of a 15-minute discussion. [F-LC]

On March 2 he updated Verner Clapp, Chief Administrative Assistant to the Librarian of Congress, of his latest trip:

On February 12, according to instructions from my chief, I went to the University of Florida for the meeting of the Southern Folk Lore Society. There I read a paper on the documentary record as an aid to folklore research and another paper on the ideology of folklore research and participated in a panel on folklore method. These papers were well received and I was able to assist in planning the years activity of the Society through the good offices of the newly-elected president, a close friend of mine, Mr. Fletcher Collins. [ALC]

Three days later, March 5, he was back in touch with Ralph Boggs in Chapel Hill:

The only book I know that comes anywhere close to what you ask is *Singing America* by Augustus Z. Zanzig. C. C. Burchard, Boston, 1940, 128 songs with arrangements, not all folk songs, however, and some of them tampered with. My last book which is, of course, not a pamphlet and which is expensive, is, I feel, a pretty representative selection of songs with only a few weak spots from the point of view of general coverage.

Do you think it would be better to include accompaniments or not? Some people want them. A proportion of 80 imported songs as against 20 indigenous songs seems to me out of kilter. Such a book should rather, I believe, emphasize derivative material and include only examples of the inherited stuff. Maybe I'm wrong but I'm going to take you at your word and do something about the book this Spring. Did you get a copy of my new Regional Bibliography of American Folk Lore?[78] How did you like it? It was swell to see you in North Carolina. [ALC]

He wrote again to Pete Seeger (still going by Bowers) on March 6:

Time is getting rather short and if you don't send the recordings for the square dance soon, it's going to be too late to send it. I am depending on you to do it but if you don't, there's very little that I can do. I wish I had police power in this instance. I also have to know at once whether Woody wants to give us permission to release his Gypsy Davy song. It would be great loss to the album not to use the song but, as I said before, if Woody doesn't feel he can do it, it's perfectly O.K. with me. I understand the reasons but I have got to know within the next few days. I wish you would ask him, please, to write me about this. I understand that you are eating these days and that's good. I hope to see you in New York fairly soon. Let me know at once what you are going to do in these matters. [ALC]

On a different matter, Alan connected with Davidson Taylor at CBS on March 6:

I am sorry I didn't get to see you the other afternoon but I thought perhaps the meeting might last late so I went home. Your remark about Columbia's new policy in regard to playing records late in the evening is the reason for this letter.

As I have told you at various times, we have been working here for the past few months on the development of a new type of radio program constructed entirely from field recordings with connecting narration. We have developed two series of this kind. The first is called, The Ballad Hunter. This is a series of ten fifteen-minute programs with John A. Lomax as narrator (and he has a very remarkable radio personality I think you will feel) with dubbed selections from the field recordings of folk songs he has made for the Archive.[79] The second series, which we have just recently completed, is called, This is History and covers the period from May, 1941, to November, 1941. The actors on the program are the people of various localities discussing their problems, telling stories, singing songs, etc., and the intent of each program is to tell the story of some community or some community activity in the words of the people of that community. By and large, they are quite successful and technically, I believe, acceptable for broadcast. Both these series have gone out in small numbers to local stations, the first last summer, the second currently. It seems to me that they both might fit very nicely into your schedule of late programs and I would like you to audition them and see what you think. Whether or not you decide to use them, I know that you, yourself, will have a lot of fun with the stuff because it's all out of the horse's mouth and pretty damned honest. The final series, particularly, has a very permanent quality and lives up to its title, This is History. It will be just as interesting to broadcast in 1950 as it is now, I believe, and this cannot be said for all radio shows.

Do you think there is any possibility that Columbia might like to use me in a fifteen-minute spot of my own sustaining any time during the day or evening? I would rather like to keep my hands in and I believe I could give you a good show with a lot of entertainment and educational value to reach a good many people. I am sorry we didn't get a chance to talk these things over while you were here but I would be glad to come to New York to discuss either one or both if you think it worth-while. [ALC]

Alan wrote to John Work on March 9 about paying those who had been recorded the previous summer, and he also wondered about his trip to Fort Valley:

Will you please put your name down as witness on these two vouchers and send them back to me in the enclosed air mail envelope. It happens that it wasn't convenient to get the people themselves to sign the vouchers and I signed for them and the Accounting Office wants a witness. Sign below each notion "His mark—witnessed by:". It would be a great favor to me if you could send them right back because the settlement of the trip is waiting for this. By the way, what was your experience at Fort Valley? [ALC][80]

Back to Library business, he contacted Harold Armitage in New York on March 9:

We in the Music Division have done our best to uncover the tune you are in search of, but we have not succeeded, although we have found the references to it in song books containing your song, *Joaquin the Horsethief.* As regards other outlaw songs, you will find several in *American Ballads and Folk Songs,* by John A. Lomax and Alan Lomax. Although some of these describe the final punishment of the individual, I don't know whether they will suit your purpose, since the tendency in folk outlaw ballads is to sympathize rather than to condemn. Please let me know if I can be of further help. [ALC]

Regarding a radio program, Alan wrote to Robert Sonkin on March 10:

The Dear Mr. President show, as it now stands, ends with the sneak recording of the air raid warden. Production was completed last Thursday and we are now faced with the problem of getting it an airing. The very least that will happen will be that it will be sent out in transcription to all local stations but the Lord only knows just what will be. Jerry [Wiesner] and I are very low in our minds at the moment and I can't speak for the rest of Washington. [RRP, AFC, LC]

The Accounting Department at CBS heard from Alan on March 11:

Would you be kind enough to send me a notation of the funds paid me during the current taxable year so that I may give the Bureau of Internal Revenue a proper accounting of my income. A self-addressed, stamped envelope is enclosed. I would appreciate your getting this information to me before Saturday. [ALC]

He then wrote to his father on March 12:

Your advice about the book comes a little late. The publisher has asked me to submit a sample chapter before we mail the contract and right now I don't have the time to bother with it. I've got to scratch around to find some quicker way of earning some money. The Texas-ex banquet was, so far as I was concerned, only a mild success. I was much too tired to go and told them so in advance. I went to bed over the weekend with my first chest ailment of the season. Tom Connelly made a very funny speech. I'm awfully sorry to hear the news about [brother-in-law] Chris [Mansell] and I'll write Shirley at once. I guess everybody will be in the same or other boats pretty soon heading for some foreign shore. It looks like Shirley will stay in Dallas with you where she may be able to earn some money rather than go out to Lovett. Should think you all could console her better than her Dust Bowl friends.

It's good to hear that you're in your natural element again on the lecture platform. I'll call Charles Seeger who has become one of the Silver Burdett managing editors and ask him to write you about that. Bess tells me that she has a regular office and expects to get a regular salary soon from CBS. There's no more news at present about the trip. I'm awfully sorry about that. Will let you know just as soon as it's definite. I'm holding the Emrich letter for my files unless you want it back. I'm going to write and apply for membership in his Board. [ALC][81]

Alan kept up with Charles Johnson at Fisk on March 12:

I am glad to hear that the transcripts are on their way and that you are interested in going ahead with the field project. I would like to plan to leave Washington about the 15th and spend a couple of weeks in Coahoma County and, afterwards, a few days at Fisk working out the details of the publication. I'm going to propose this to Dr. Spivacke this morning in a memorandum and I'll let you know as soon as it's definite. It would be most pleasant to spend at least part of the time in the field with Lewis Jones and/or John Work. [F-LC]

Searching for additional income, Alan contacted Frank Mlakar, assistant editor of *Common Ground* in New York, on March 16:

My father sent me your letter this morning and I wish you would send me a copy of the issue in which Woody Guthrie's article Ear Players appeared with a note about the rate you are able to pay for article in your publication. [ALC][82]

McKinley Morganfield ("Dear Muddy Water") received another letter from Alan dated March 17:

The Library of Congress is going to make pressings of some of its best records for demonstration to the Latin American countries of how much music we have up here in this part of the world. In that series we would like very much to use a record of yours containing on one side the *Country Blues*, and on the other *I Bes Troubled*. Our payment to all people who give us permission to use their records in this fashion is $10.00 per side. The payment to you would be $20.00 for the two sides and we would send you four copies of the record when it is released. I hope you will give us permission to go ahead with this by signing and returning the enclosed form. The record will contain the legend, For non-commercial use only. Your name, of course, will appear on every copy. I think the release of this record will serve to make you known in quarters where greater use might be found for your talent. I hope to hear from you about this soon. [F-LC]

Through the spring Bess was busy working at CBS in New York City, where Alan wrote to her on March 17, before taking his trip to Milwaukee:

The version of John Henry that we're going to use in Milwaukee is the one that Pete knows rather than myself. I'm so tired these days that I can't sing worth a damn anyway so that the choice is obviously Pete's [Seeger] and, besides, I don't want to appear on Carleton's [Smith] show [at the MENC—Music Educators National Conference]. Somewhat surprised that you asked me. About Latin America—there's one pamphlet which is quite pleasant about Latin American dance forms done by Gustavo Duran. It's called "Recordings of Latin American Songs and Dances. An Annotated Selected List of Popular and Folk Music." It's published by the Music Division of the Pan American Union, Music Series No. 3, January, 1942, and sells for thirty cents. You might also look at items 1, 2 and 3 on page 49 of the attached bibliography. I hope it will be of use to you. It sells for 25¢, I think, from the Progressive Education Association and was designed for the laymen.

I'm awfully sorry that you're having commercial constipation. If it's any consolation, remember that everybody connected with radio has it. I hope you can get your foot in the door at CBS, however, because once it's in, you're one of the boys and you can do a hell of a lot of good there. My suggestion would be that you look around for a place where an original script by yourself would get a hearing. The boys, while they have their pat points, are always on the lookout for anybody who can make a pleasant noise over the microphone and there's no reason why you shouldn't compete with Mill [Lampell] and [blank], et al, if his first script is any sample of what he can do. It doesn't look as if I can get to New York or you come to Washington but it does look as if we'll meet in Milwaukee and we can talk everything over out there. You're a darn fool for not getting your application in to Rosenwald [Foundation]. [ALC]

Alan moved forward with commercial releases from the Library of a sample of their field recordings, some destined for South America, as he informed Mr. and Mrs. E. C. Ball on March 18:

We are now beginning to prepare our records for publication and we wish to use two of your songs, *Jennie Jenkins* and *Pretty Polly* which will be contained on one side of a 12-inch record.[83] For this we are able to pay you $15.00 and will send you two copies of the record when it is released. I hope you will give us your permission by signing and returning the enclosed form as soon as possible. The records will carry the legend, For non-commercial use only and your names will appear on every copy. I hope you have been well since Elizabeth and I saw you last. It's been a great pleasure to be reminded of you by listening to your records every once in a while. [ALC]

A different sort of letter went to W. E. Claunch, Guntown, Mississippi, on March 18:

The Archive of American Folk Song is planning to make up a group of the best representative American folk songs to be distributed in Latin America. Among the records we hope to use are your performances of Grub Springs, The Eighth of January, Sally Goodin and Cindy which you recorded for Mr. Herbert Halpert some time ago [May 1939].[84] We will pay you $15.00 for the use of these fiddle tunes and will send you two copies of the record. [ALC]

The payments for the earlier Delta recordings were still on Alan's mind when he corresponded with Charles Johnson at Fisk University on March 20:

About ten days ago I sent John Work a couple of receipts for singers' services out of our last summer's trip on which I needed a witness's signature. He didn't sign them but said he would pass them on to Lewis Jones and Mark Ross for witnessing. It would be a great favor to me if you would ask these gentlemen to send me the receipts by return air mail. The whole darned United States Accounting Office and the war effort are being held up by this procrastination. You will hear from me shortly again. [ALC]

He wrote to Spivacke about payments to Work on March 23:

In my last note about Mr. Work, I didn't mean to imply that I thought we should not pay him. We just make an enemy and the amount isn't worth arguing about even with our present disaster in view. Mr. Work is doing excellent work for us in Nashville and will, I think, do more from time to time. Let's pay him. [FVMF]

On March 23 Alan wrote not only to Spivacke, but also to Charles Johnson:

Last weekend I read over the field notes that you have so far sent me with great interest. Some of the material I felt was extremely valuable and there was an occasional item that was altogether new to me. I was somewhat disappointed, however, to find that at least in so far the interviews I read go, they didn't seem to have followed and developed the field plan of outline which we worked out so carefully. Perhaps there is more material to come which will correspond closely to our original plan but so far as the present batch is concerned, it would not give me much to work with in Coahoma County. Let me urge you, therefore, to send along whatever else you have including especially the detailed life histories. If there is only one copy, don't worry. I won't let them out of my office but I do need the life histories in order to make any sort of intelligent plans about the trip and I do need them at once. Thank you for your continued kindness and interest in this project which we both have so much at heart. [ALC][85]

Alan was always getting letters inquiring about the history of the Archive, which he explained to Irene Carlisle, a journalist in Fayetteville, Arkansas, on March 23:

In response to your note of March 9 the Archive of American Folk Song has been in existence since 1928. It was first under the direction of Dr. Robert Gordon who accumulated a very valuable collection of manuscript and dictaphone cylinders. In 1933, my father, John A. Lomax, was made Curator and since that time practically the entire effort of the Archive has been devoted to field recordings on disks of American folk songs. At the present time we have about 25,000 folk songs and folk tales on records gathered from all over the South, New England, the Middle West and West, the West Indies and now, recently, from South America. Since 1933 [sic] I have been Assistant in Charge of the Archive and have about divided the recording work with my father. Recently we have been in a position to loan our equipment to competent collectors in various parts of the country, such people as Herbert Halpert, Ivan Walton, John Work, Vance Randolph, etc. The entire project is a part of regular Library of Congress activity in the Music Division.

The usefulness of the collection was greatly enhanced two years ago by a Carnegie grant which enabled us to build a very fine recording laboratory and studio in which high quality recording can be done and, best of all, where our field records can be duplicated for the use of students and the pleasure of interested American citizens. Through this laboratory, copies of original field recordings can be purchased and, due to the size of the collection, almost any type of American folk song in English and in a number of foreign languages may be obtained on request.

The accumulation of the material has gone on at such a rapid rate that it has been impossible to make accurate surveys such as the one suggested in your question about Child ballads. I can tell you that we have a great number of Child ballads, somewhat in their due proportion in the community in relation to other types of folk songs. If you are interested, I will send you a copy of our checklist of American folk songs in the Archive which is shortly to be published. I should like very much to have clip sheets of this story when it is published. P.S. You can obtain more information on the Archive by consulting the introduction to *Cowboy Songs* and *American Ballads and Folk Songs* and *Our Singing Country, Negro Folk Songs sung by Lead Belly*, all by John A. and Alan Lomax. [ALC]

Alan wrote very briefly to his father on March 24:

I agree with you about Elie Siegmeister except that I would have used more four-letter words.[86] [ALC]

That same day, March 24, pursuing recording contracts, Alan corresponded with the Warden at the Cummins State Farm in Gould, Arkansas:

Some time ago my father, John A. Lomax, made recordings of the songs of three of the inmates of Cummins State Farm, Kelly Page,[87] Arthur Bell[88] and Irvin Lowry.[89] The Archive of American Folk Song would like to use these records in a group of American folk songs we are preparing to distribute to Latin America. Before we can do so, however, it is necessary that we have the permission of the performers. We would appreciate it very much, therefore, if you would locate these three men and forward the enclosed letters to them. [ALC]

On March 26 Alan wrote again to Frank Mlakar at *Common Ground* about a possible contribution:

The framework of the TVA problem is used by Ledford mostly to set forth his own character among his people in his community. This material is quite objective and quite eloquent, a folk expression without being folksy, and now that I have read your magazine through I think completely appropriate to its format. I judge it might be about twice as long as your usual article. It's the one I would rather do first.[90] [ALC]

Anxious to obtain permissions, he contacted M. P. O. Love, Superintendent of the Mississippi State Penitentiary in Parchman, on April 1:

In reference to your recent letter concerning Frank Jordan[91] and Jeff Webb,[92] I would appreciate it if you would inform me of their counties of residence at the time of their commitment to the Mississippi State Penitentiary. Thank you for your courtesy in this matter. [ALC]

The following day, April 2, Alan made a request to Harry Horlick at Decca Records:

The Library of Congress has a large collection of recordings of folk songs and speech of the people of the United States about contemporary problems. Out of this collection of material, mostly recorded since December 7, we are making an electrical transcription called, Dear Mr. President, in which the people discuss democracy, their local community and the United States at war and address themselves directly to the President of the United States. The Office of Emergency Management is producing this program and distributing it free to local radio stations and schools so that the people of America may hear it. In connection with this educational project, we would like your permission to include part of your arrangement of the Sound of the Guitar (Decca record No. 2116A) in this educational broadcast prepared by the Library of Congress. We understand that you are the copyright owner of this work. I would deem it a great favor to the Library of Congress if you would be so kind as to give us this permission. [RRP]

On April 2 he responded to Carleton Brackett in Newton Highlands, Massachusetts:

A checklist of about 12,000 items in the Archive is about to be published and we shall be glad to send you one should you wish it. However, if you would let me know what type of songs you are interested in, I would be glad to make a representative selection for you and to send you an estimate of their cost. The records which may be obtained through the Archive of American Folk Song are 12-inch, double sided acetate disks which cost $1.75 each. (This price is subject to change without notice because of the changing costs of materials.) I trust this information will be of assistance to you. [ALC]

There was also a brief note to Frank Mlakar at Common Ground on April 2:

I will try to get the Ledford story in to you within the next two weeks. [ALC]

On April 3 he wrote to Wilhelmina Waters of the Harmony Four in Seaford, Delaware. Most of the letter duplicates what he wrote to Harry Horlick the previous day. However, the ending is different:

In connection with this educational project, we should like your permission to include part of the recording of This World Can't Do Me No Harm in this educational broadcast prepared by the Library of Congress. Only a short fragment will be used as cue music. [RRP, AFC, LC]

A much longer letter went out to Eleanor Stierhem at *American Magazine* on April 3:

I wish I could take all the credit for the MENC [National Association for Music Education] conference [in Milwaukee] demonstration but, sadly enough, I can't.[93] The conference itself was very friendly and the committee which sponsored us was headed by Glenn Gildersleeve, State Supervisor of Music, Delaware, which was only one of the activities of his committee which is called American Unity through Music Committee. I wish you could have been there to take pictures of the demonstration itself. Dr. Spivacke talked about the part of the Music Division in pushing folk song collecting and distribution. Peter Bowers [Seeger], a banjo player, and Barbara Bell,[94] a ballad singer, and myself gave an illustrated demonstration of folk songs and then Lilla Belle Pitts[95] of Teachers College, Columbia University, showed how a class of ordinary Milwaukee children reacted to our performance. The whole affair, which lasted two hours, was cheered to the echo by a capacity audience of music educators from all over the country. I think the result will be that the folk songs which we have been collecting for years will be used in large numbers in school text books of all kinds. It should be remarked, however, that we are not anxious to replace European folk songs in the text books so much as to add to them a representative cross section of our own stuff. This cross section will include, I think, many a song in French, Spanish and other minority origins current in the United States.

I think you are right about this being a good story. Perhaps you might come to Washington some time and we could give you an outline of the whole thing and then pick up the other pieces from other parts of the country. I really believe, however, that the movement involves not only the Archive of American Folk Song, but the Pan American Union, the school text book publishers and most of the leaders in music education in America. I will let you know when I go out on my next recording trip. With many thanks for your continued interest in my work. [ALC]

While Alan was distracted by his many professional commitments, the FBI was not through with him; they interviewed him on April 3, mostly about his activism in the early 1930s. A troubled Alan finally asked the agent, "Well, I am perplexed about this, I guess it is just a routine thing. I am perplexed as to why I should be investigated because since 1936 when I first came here to work, I have worked so doggone hard at my job—so many hours a day—that it sort of hurts my feelings a little that I should be investigated because I do know I sure have done my part—as much as I could in my job in the Government which has been a source of some unhappiness to me because this thing has come up. I know it came up once before when I sang at the White House for the King and Queen, and my feelings were hurt a little there, and I thought the thing was settled. Are these investigations repeated all the time."The answer was yes, as he would discover. [Lomax FBI file]

The outbreak of war meant Alan had to contact his local draft board in McLean, Virginia, on April 8:

I have changed my residence from Langley, Virginia, to 3356 M Street, N.W., Washington, D.C. [ALC]

Getting back to the Delta study, Alan wrote a memo on April 8, probably for Spivacke:

Acting on the instructions of the Librarian, on September 26, 1941 I left for Nashville, Tennessee, and arrived in the middle of the day of the 27th. I immediately set in motion a seminar conference in order to acquaint the junior field workers of the Fisk University Department of Sociology with the materials on Negro folk songs. This group of field workers was to document the folk song of Coahoma County, Mississippi, in preparation for a later visit by the Library of Congress sound truck. The project in mind was a functional study of folk song in one community which had been worked out by Dr. Johnson and myself. The conference went on intensively, almost literally night and day, from the 27th to the evening of the 29th. I believe all parties concerned were very well satisfied with the result of our work together. I left Nashville at 9 P.M. September 29 and arrived in Washington, September 30 at 7:40 P.M. [F-LC]

A more personal note went to I. S. Becker at CBS on April 11:

As I stated to you in my previous letter, it will be impossible for me to settle my account except through engagements obtained for me by whatever management corporation has me in tow at the moment. I regret that my financial condition does not enable me to settle the account in any other fashion but I am in the unpleasant position of insisting upon this type of settlement. [ALC]

Another letter to Charles Johnson went out on April 13:

Some time ago I wrote that it might be possible for me to come to Fisk and then go on to Coahoma County for a period of field work about April 15. In view of the fact that the preparatory field work is still somewhat tentative, we thought it would be better to postpone the trip for some time. I would like to either talk to you or correspond with you at length about what we can do to make this project of ours pan out. Yesterday at a folk lore conference I discussed this project publicly and it was received with a great deal of interest. I think it is going to solve a lot of basic problems and I am convinced that we should go ahead.

What do you think of the idea of my taking a couple of your people into the field for about a month's work sometime in the early part of the summer? This might solve some of the problems of their lack of acquaintance with the material of folk lore itself and possibly we could get the whole job done at one time, both the recordings and the social documentations of the background of the recordings. Let me know as soon as possible what you think of this idea. Perhaps you have a better suggestion. At any rate I hope you will keep in mind that I am personally deeply concerned about this study and that I want to follow it through myself as closely as I can. [F-LC]

He again contacted James "Iron Head" Baker in Otey, Texas, on April 14:

On March 20th I wrote you about the use of one of your records by the Library of Congress for pressing purposes. Up until now I haven't heard from you and the release of these records is being delayed by your failure to reply.[96] [ALC]

Searching for former contacts, he wrote to E. E. Moss at the Clemens State Farm in Brazoria, Texas, on April 14:

I have looked in my files and I discover that it is possible that the Smith Cason I wrote you about before is alias for one Roger Gill. If that is so, I would appreciate you passing on the inclosed letter to him. If that doesn't prove to be true, this might serve to refresh your memory about the man. In my father's notes I discovered that Smith Cason had played on the program Behind the Walls on numerous occasions. I hope that through one of these bits of information you will be able to locate Mr. Cason, so that we can release his record and pay him for his services. Thank you in advance. [ALC][97]

Alan also sought permission from Elizabeth Austin in Cat Island, Bahamas, on April 17, using a form letter:

The Archive of American Folk Song is planning to make up a group of the best representative American folk songs to be distributed in Latin America. Among the songs we hope to use is your performance of *Sail Gal* which occupies 1/2 of a 10" record. We will pay you $3.30 for the use of this record and we will send you two copies of it for your own use. I hope you will give us your permission to use this song by signing and returning the enclosed form as soon as possible. All the records will carry the legend, For non-commercial use only and of course, your name will appear on every record. [ALC][98]

On April 18 a letter went out to Fletcher Collins in Burlington, North Carolina:

We are hoping to receive your records any day now. Please send them as soon as possible. I think you understand how important it is that you not use them for transcribing before sending them. The amount of wear involved in transcribing would ruin them for our purposes. It was nice to have you at our conference. As soon as the Utilization Committee begins to work I will get in touch with you. [ALC]

Focusing on the compilation recordings for the South American market, Alan attempted to contact Blind Willie McTell,[99] the blues musician, on April 23:

Some time ago my father, John A. Lomax, recorded some of your songs in Atlanta. They have proved a source of great interest here at the Library of Congress. We are compiling a series of records for distribution to Latin America, and we would like very much to include one of your selections in this group. These records are going to be sent to all the republics of Latin America and will later be generally available to the people in the United States. We are including one of your pieces which I imagine does not have direct potentialities. The song is Delia and it occupies 2/3 of one side of a 12" recording. We are able to pay you a fee of $10.00 for the use of this song, and send you two copies of the record for your own use. I hope that you will be able to grant us the permission to use this record and will fill out the attached form and send it back to us as soon as convenient. All the records will carry the legend, For non-commercial use only and of course, your name will appear on every record. [WMC]

Regarding a recording made in New Mexico, Alan inquired of Richardo Archuleta in Cerro on April 24:

Some time ago you were kind enough to record for Mr. Juan B. Rael some ancient Spanish folk songs. Among them a song entitled "Atencion Senado Ilustre" which occupies less than 1/5 of one side of a 12" record, "O Dulcisimo Jesus," "El Telcolcotito," and "El Mejor Hombre Del Mundo." For the privilege of using these songs we are able to pay you $18.00 and send you two copies of each record for your own use. The Library of Congress is preparing to send some selections from its Archive to various countries in Latin America and it is for this purpose that we wish to use your songs. I hope you will give us your permission to use these songs by signing and returning the enclosed form as soon as possible. All the records will carry the legend, "For non-commercial use only" and of course your name will appear on every record. [ALC]

His father and their work together often preyed on his mind, as he wrote to John on April 25:

I have just received the attached letter from Macmillans and in view of what Jim says I feel that the division of correction costs should follow the line of the division of the royalties: i.e., two- thirds to our side and one-third on Ruth's [Crawford Seeger]. While there is no doubt that you have a legal right to accept the reduction of the royalties for the book it seems to me that you should remember that Ruth, by the same token, had her royalties reduced. Therefore since the reduction was suffered by all the parties concerned equally the residue of text costs should be borne equally by all parties. Ruth might perhaps be willing to pay fifty percent of the music corrections but I don't think she should be asked to. There is no question from the verdict of the reviews that her painstaking work on the music brought her results. One thing I don't understand is why the text corrections cost $405. It seems that we might have been overcharged there. You may be interested to see the enclosed press release. It seems that our documentary programs were finally pressed. [ALC]

Alan's next road trip came up in a letter to Mary Gould Davis at the New York Public Library on April 25:

On June 25 I will be in Bloomington, Indiana teaching at the Summer School of Folk Lore of Indiana University. One of my scheduled classes falls on Thursday so that it looks like it will be impossible for me to come. You might write Stith Thompson, chairman of the English Department in Indiana, and ask him whether it would be possible to arrange for me to come up at that time. If it is I would be glad to come but it has to be up to him. I presume that you plan to take care of my expenses for the trip; otherwise it would be out of the question. I am sorry there are these problems because otherwise I would be delighted to meet with you. [ALC][100]

Alan was getting frustrated with Fletcher Collins at Elon College, as he noted in this letter of April 26:

Will you please send me the records you made for us and send them right away. We need to close our accounts in this matter as soon as possible. Will you please send me the pamphlet copy pronto, if not sooner. The printing problem is going to be a hell of a headache and may delay the whole matter by weeks and weeks. The sooner you act the better. Especially as I shall be away a good deal from now on and shall want to have the album out of the way before I go. I know you're busy as the devil and conquering tougher problems than I have every day, but I'm counting on you for this stuff and I need it at once. Will you accept revisions without submission of copy until the proof stage. The continuing committee meets this Wednesday evening in rump session. I'll let you know what comes of it. In the meantime, my respects to you and yours and your enterprises. [ALC]

Two days later, April 28, he queried folklorist Richard Chase, in Glade Spring, Virginia:

We are including one of Horton Barker's[101] songs—to wit, "The Farmers Curst Wife"—in an album of records intended for distribution to all the Latin American Republics. In introducing his ballad, I wish to give a very brief note about his life and wish to impose on you to the extent of obtaining a few sentences about him from you. Would you be so kind as to write me a brief note about him and in it tell me how long he has been blind, whether or not he is living as a ballad singer, just how famous a singer he is among his own people, etc. [ALC]

Alan dealt with more library business, and his own preferences, on April 28 to Carleton Brackett in Newton Highlands, Massachusetts:

The Checklist will be sent to you in reasonably short time, I hope. When you get it look under Hamilton Ohio for various recordings by Peter Steele, in Hazard Ky. for Justis Begeley, in Salyersville Ky. for records by Ernest Williams, and in Gulfport, Miss. for Thaddeus C. Willingham. These are some of the best banjo singers we have recorded and you will find many others as you look through the catalogue. We will be delighted of course to fill your order for duplicates. You should also look in old record shops for anythings by Doc Boggs and Buell Kazee on the old Columbia label, for commercial records Dave Macon and Wade Mainer on Blue Bird, also the Coon Creek Girls on Okeh. Write to Mary Lee Guard in the State Department and ask for my index of folk songs on commercial records which you might be interested in having. [ALC]

The following day, April 29, he communicated with Robert Wetherald at RCA:

Would you be kind enough to find out for me when your twelve-inch record of "Pretty Polly," Victor No. 35838B, sung by B. F. Shelton,[102] was released? I need this information for preparation of some scholarly notes. Of course, the year would be sufficient for my purposes. I believe you told me once before that this record had been discontinued. By the way, why don't you make a dubbing of it and bring it out on Red Seal. I believe it would sell. It is by far the best folk performance on a commercial record. It would be nice to see you sometime. [ALC]

Having received no reply from his letter to Ricardo Archuleta on April 24, he wrote to Juan Rael at the University of Southern California in Los Angeles on April 30:

Some time ago I wrote to Ricardo Archuleta, Cerro, New Mexico asking for his permission to release in the form of pressings three of his songs. For this privilege we are able to pay him our standard fee and in his case it came to $18.00 These records will be mostly used as you can understand for educational purposes. Their first destination will be the libraries and universities of Latin America. Of course all credit will be given to singers and collectors. Would you be kind enough to help me get in touch with Senior Archuleta. I have so far received no reply from him and I wonder whether the address of Cerro, New Mexico is enough. Please send me word by return Air Mail if it is at all possible. [ALC]

Not having a reply from McTell, Alan followed up with a query to Jack Kapp at Decca Records on May 1:

Some time ago, I wrote asking for the address of Blind Willie McTell in Atlanta, Ga. I wonder if you could have somebody look it up and send it to me. We would appreciate it very much. I have never heard from your assistant in regard to getting the pressings that I need for the preparation of the albums. I left him a long list and I have since been anxiously awaiting the records themselves so that I can go to work on the albums. I wish you would see what has happened. By the way I had a marvelous time playing through your stuff and sometime I will tell you what I think of it and its possibilities. [WMC]

Alan had heard from McKinley Morganfield/Muddy Water(s), and he responded to him on May 2:

I am sorry that you have been disappointed by not getting your payment and your records as soon as you expected them. There is always a certain amount of delay in government payments, and you will just have to be patient. The money will come to you, though, as soon as I can manage it. In the next couple of days you will receive a voucher. When you have signed and returned it the money will be sent to your shortly. This voucher is a form of receipt for the money. [F-LC]¹⁰³

Having no responses from some of his other contacts regarding their recording permissions, Alan wrote to the Postmaster in Jennings, Louisiana, on May 7:

Some time ago I wrote to Cleveland Benoit and Darby Hicks, Joe Washington Brown and Austin Coleman, in your care. As yet I have not heard from these parties and since this is a matter of government business I feel justified in calling on your help to locate these people and try to get their letters to them in case they have moved out of Jennings, La. If their whereabouts are unknown I should like to know that also. I would greatly appreciate hearing from you in this regard by return air mail, since the delay in replying is holding up the whole project. A self addressed air mail envelope is enclosed for your convenience.¹⁰⁴ [ALC]

In the midst of his busy schedule, Lomax did not neglect Helen Hartness Flanders, to whom he wrote on May 8, explaining the Library's policies:

Only a small part of the Archive collection, and this small part includes the restricted Vermont collection, is unavailable to the public. All the rest of our six thousand odd disks may be duplicated on request for anyone. It is made perfectly clear to all applicants for duplicates of any sort that they may well be subject to suit from the singers and, or, the collections. We advise them in case they are interested in using the records for any commercial purposes whatsoever to get in touch with the singers and collectors. Although I am as much concerned about the whole problem of protection of singers as yourself, there is nothing else that the Library can do at this moment except to impose restrictions on parts of its collection such as yours. Even in these cases we feel that this puts a restriction on the natural freedom of movement that is, or should be, the heritage of all folklore. The record of 'King John and the Bishop" was made for Doctor Smith the summer after I came back from Vermont when I had no assistant in the Archive and was quite constantly harassed. I feel sure that such a mistake will not occur again. I have sent your clearance form on to Professor Herrington for his signature and have asked for a reply from him. Hereafter, I shall not duplicate the restricted parts of the Vermont collection unless the specific request is made for these records and unless the person requesting them gets in touch with you directly. [N-JB]

As for John Work's previous ill-fated trip to Fort Valley, Alan explained matters to him on May 8:

I have taken up the matter of reimbursement for your expenses on the Fort Valley trip with my chief and he suggests that the only way in which you can be paid is for you to sell us a couple of recordings. Doctor [Horace Mann] Bond told me that you made a couple in Fort Valley and if this is not correct, purchase three disks from your dealer, fill them with national folk songs and forward them to us with a bill which totals the cost of the disks plus the $11.08 due on the Fort Valley expedition. . . . The collection of records for South America is being delayed because of a few out-standing clearance problems. Among them is the clearance of the Sacred Harp recordings. Will you be willing to sign a clearance for them yourself? Sample attached. If not, please send me in the enclosed air-mail envelope the address of the person who can clear the records. This is a most urgent matter and I shall appreciate an immediate response. I also have to know what progress you have made in your work in Nashville. This project should be completed by June 1st, or at the latest June 15, so that we can make provisions for the work next year. Let me hear from you at once. The records should not be used for the Mississippi trip, by the way, since other provisions have been made for that. [FVMF]

Also on May 8 Alan contacted Suzanne Sylvain-Comhaire (also Comhaire-Sylvain), a Haitian folklorist,[105] who was residing at the International House in New York:

I was fortunate enough to learn from Dr. Metro recently that you were in New York and were considering visiting the Archive. I would be honored by such a visit and delighted to play you our Haitian recordings. We have a collection of 298 aluminum discs of many kinds of Haitian songs; the only type which is not well covered, I believe, is the work song. At the time I was in Haiti I had to work with a slight knowledge of French and therefore decided to take down the titles of the songs in English orthography. I now realize that this was an unfortunate decision, particularly since the Discoteca in Sao Paulo has ordered copies of the entire collection of Haitian discs for their own use. I feel incapable myself of revisiting this list, and I have wondered if you would care to help me. I should think it might require a week of intensive work, but it might be of interest to you, since you could at the same time familiarize yourself with the contents of the Archive. Whether or not this is possible, the Archive would be delighted and honored to receive a visit from you. [ALC]

Alan updated Spivacke on May 9 about his father's proposed trip:

John A. Lomax, who has one of the Archive recording machines in Texas, has decided to devote himself in the early summer to the collection of cowboy songs, cattle hollers, and the stories of old time cattle men in Texas. Strangely enough, although Mr. Lomax's books cover fully the field of western songs, the Archive has very few good field recordings from the West, and this planned trip of his to western Texas, New Mexico and western Oklahoma will help to fill a large geographical gap in our collections. Mr. Lomax plans to go to Austin, San Antonio, Taylorsville, Alpine, Toyah, Abilene, Pampa, on to New Mexico, to Henryetteville, Oklahoma, and back to Dallas, Texas, again. He will probably travel about 6000 miles on this trip. I suggest the following budget: . . . $842.60. [ALC][106]

Charles Johnson received another letter from Alan dated May 13:

I regret that my preoccupation with the recent Paul Robeson concert had prevented my answering your last letter until now. It's also been very difficult for me to see Dr. Spivacke who is occupied with War Department business these days. We have commitment with the Inter-Departmental Committee for Cultural Relations with Latin America to complete a series of phonograph albums and radio transcriptions of folk songs by June 30, 1942. My part in this enterprise will be complete by the first of June and I should be able to leave Washington shortly thereafter for a period of two or three weeks in the field. I hope it will be possible then for me to work with Lewis Jones and to make a complete survey with a recording machine of the field work that has been done up to that time. According to our original plan which, it seems to me, is still good, your people were to make a thorough survey of the county following the field outline agreed on. Of course the fact that they have a recording machine and can take down musical events as they occur will be helpful. Later, I was to come and visit the same people they had documented in the form of notes and reports. My function was to record such portions of their repertoires as seemed significant, to probe deeper into their knowledge of folk songs, and to satisfy myself that the objectives of the study had been fulfilled.

Since Lewis Jones will be in the field during May anyway, I feel confident that the basic field survey will be completed and completed competently by the time I can come. I should like to have as much of the field material as possible before I come down to the county, at least in outline; and I should like Jones to attempt to set up a recording schedule for me. He can use his judgment about how this is best to be done; but if he meets any obstacles in persuading people to work with me for certain set periods of time, I can agree in advance to pay informants a regular hourly rate. The advisability of this device I leave entirely up to him. I should, however, take great pleasure

in working in the field with him for the two week period unless that is absolutely out of the question. Let me know your reactions to this plan, and as
soon as conveniently, so that I can begin to arrange my tire and gasoline
problems. [F-LC]

Alan attracted all sorts of requests, including one from Thomas Anderson in Cleveland,
Ohio, which he answered on May 13:

I regret to say that since I am not connected with a publishing house and
have no experience as an editor, that submission of your manuscript to me
would be somewhat risky on your part. If, however, the material is concerned
with folklore, I would be more than delighted to look at it and give you my
personal opinion of its value. I assure you that this would be no imposition.
[ALC]

Still trying to track down Blind Willie McTell, Alan inquired of the Postmaster in Atlanta
on May 13:

The enclosed letter is addressed to Blind Willie McTell who is a Negro blues
singer and guitar player of your county. As it concerns a matter of government business, I urgently hope that it can be delivered to this party. Have him
sign the enclosed release and return the material to us. I have endeavored to
obtain this man's address from several sources and I have been unsuccessful,
therefore, I am completely dependent upon your good offices in this regard.
I hope that you can let me know within the next two or three days whether it
is possible to reach him and if not please let me hear from you to that effect.
[WMC]

Two days later L. F. Livingston, the Atlanta Postmaster, responded:

In reply to yours of the 13th inclosing a letter addressed to Mr. Willie McTell,
Atlanta, Ga., together with attached form, you are advised I have succeeded
in locating this blind negro blues singer and guitar player, and he states that
he is not willing to grant permission for you to make and sell copies of his
song Delia for the sum of $10.00. In the event you care to communicate with
him further, his address is 142 Clover Lane, N.E., this city. [WMC]

Alan again wrote to Richard Chase on May 15:

Thanks for the information about Horton Barker. I shall incorporate some
of it in the albums. Barker will receive two copies of the records that he is

allowing us to use. I am delighted that your books are going along as swimmingly as they should. I looked over the folk festival program but could not bring myself to attend even one session, since they all looked even worse than they did last year. [ALC][107]

Alan sent a query and some information to Irene Carlisle[108] in Fayetteville, Arkansas, on May 15:

I enjoyed your feature story about Vance Randolph, and am interested to learn that you are yourself a collector. Perhaps you can give me some idea of the work you have already done, and the material that is available to you for recording. We like to keep our files on collectors and material as up to date as possible. The check list is not yet ready for general distribution, but I have put your name on the list and you will be mailed a copy as soon as it is ready. [ALC]

Also on May 15 he contacted Abbott Ferriss in State College, Mississippi:

Dr. [Benjamin] Botkin[109] has shown me your letter of April 27th, and it seems to me you have some interesting ideas. I am coming to Mississippi for field work in June, and if you don't mind I should like to meet you while I am there and have a talk. My work will probably be in the area of Clarksdale, and if you have any suggestions about work in that area, please let me know. [F-LC]

The following day, May 16, he detailed some of his ideas for another book to Gladys Pitcher, Editorial Department at C.C. Birchard and Company, Boston:

The song "The Rattle Sna-wa-wake" was republished out of *American Ballads and Folk Songs,* and for permission to use it as well as "All the Pretty Little Horses" I suggest you write directly to my father, John A. Lomax at 7456 San Benito Way, Dallas Texas. My notion about the "American Songster" is that it be really pocket size, that is, 6 inches by 4 , more or less. It should contain between 150 and 200 songs with melodies and guitar chords indicated. Perhaps it might be wise to publish a separate piano accompaniment book, as in the case of Zanzig's[110] opus. I should hope that a book of that type would sell for 25¢ on the newsstands, just like the pocket novels that are distributed these days, so that it would be available to all kinds of people. I have a notion that if we did a book of this kind quickly enough, we might have the opportunity to bring it into the army camps. At least I can get very good advice about how to bend the book in that direction. We also should have a few engravings like the old time songsters to relieve the monotony of the print.

If you can handle all the permission letters, the editing job should take no more than two months. My general plan is, by the way, to edit the songs for singing, revamping the published tunes whenever necessary so that they will be easy to sing and comparatively understandable at first glance. Most of the material will come out of books already in print, and in the case of songs that come out of Archive records I will give you the address of the singers. You can pay such singers your standard fee for permission to use the songs. I shall have to employ a full time assistant for the period, so I shall have to have an advance. Let me know what you can do about this. [ALC]

Alan responded to Suzanne Comhaire-Sylvain on May 16:

I am delighted to hear that you will be able to come to the Archive and work with us a few days. I will have everything prepared for your coming. It is likely that I will be leaving Washington on a field trip by the 7th of June, so if it would be possible for you to come by the 29th or 30th of May, we would be sure of a few days' work together. I am looking forward to your visit with the greatest of pleasure, I assure you. Of course, you will let me know about when do you plan to come a few days ahead of time. [ALC]

There were always financial matters to handle. Pete Seeger had written wondering where his $50 was for doing the radio performances for The Martins and the Coys and Dear Mr. President. Alan responded to Peter Bowers [Seeger] on May 18:

The money is on its slow, governmental way and is being pricked along as fast as possible. It will arrive; that's about all I can say. Bess says somebody please write her right away about future plans, particularly the Headliners and Detroit, as she has to make up her mind about several things.[111] [ALC]

Having something of a change of plans, he so informed Smith Cason at the Clemens State Farm in Brazoria, Texas, on May 18:

We have decided to use another of your blues in our South American album. This time it's the blues called "Shorty George," and it occupies one-half of a fifteen inch record. The fee for use of this song is $7.50 along with two copies of the record for your own personal use. This, of course, is in addition to the money and records already coming to you from our previous agreement. I trust you will sign the permission which is enclosed and return it to us Air Mail. By the way, I should tell you that copies of the records will not be ready for several weeks. Thanking you for your previous kindness. [ALC]

He shot off a telegram to the Reverend G. S. Rivers in Jackson, Tennessee, on May 21:

Please send word about permission to use songs for South America at once. Wire collect. [ALC]

As Alan prepared for a return to Mississippi, he contacted Lewis Jones on May 25:

Thanks for the swell letter. It would be much more convenient for me to go to Mississippi in July than in June, and if you could work with me at that time, it would make the July trip doubly preferable. What I want to know from you, is whether the material will be sufficiently in hand for me by June 7, in case I cannot come in July. Do you think that from the point of view of availability of people it would be best for me to go in June or July? You know this whole situation much better than I do. How much recording have you already done? How many people are there to be interviewed with a recording machine, more or less? If I come in June will there be one of the field workers to work with me then? If so, is he a person whom it would be profitable for me to train? Please give me your frank opinion about these matters, because from where I sit in Washington it is hard to get a clear notion of what has been done and what is still to be done. I am sending a copy of this letter to Dr. Johnson, so that he can know my state of mind too. [F-LC]

Alan followed up to Charles Johnson on May 26:

I was glad to learn that my continued change of plans did not disrupt the work. I recently received a letter from Lewis Jones in which he says he will be busy in June but possibly will be free to work with me in July. I have written him the attached letter and when I have received his reply, I expect to make my final decision. I am delighted that everything is going along so well, and I am very anxious to talk to you about the planning of more folk lore collecting activity in the South. [F-LC]

He contacted his father in Dallas on May 26:

Bess and I are having a wonderful time working and living together. She now plans to stay on until June 11th, since Jo Schwartz is still sick. We have gotten more done in ten days together than I have done in six months before. Since last Thursday we have been working at home on the pamphlet for the South American Albums, and the job is all but done. I greatly enjoyed the letter from young George Hill. You ought to frame this document, for what he says about your work and influence in this country is quite true. There is no reason for you, as far as your accomplishments are concerned, to be the least bit gloomy. No other American folklorist has come any where close to you in terms of sheer accomplishment, and nobody except [J. Frank] Dobie touches you on the score of bringing folk lore to the American public. When you consider that our folk literature is our most significant contribution so far to world culture, then the significance of your role becomes apparent.

I am glad that you dropped the Clarksville thing for the moment, because I really think that our project might have been hindered by linking the name of Lomax with an investigation of a local chain gang beating. It is impossible to interview the Negroes of the county without the permission of the local plantation owners since we must do all our work on their premises, and I do not want them to have the wrong impression of what I am trying to do. Attached is a letter from Blaine Stubblefield's father to whom Blaine sent an autographed copy of *Our Singing Country* for his birthday. I certainly would like to meet the old gentleman. Attached also is a letter from Jess Norris. You'll be able to see him on your coming trip to West Texas. That little item, by the way, will have been approved by the middle of the week, I am sure. P.S. This is from Bess, the neat and industrious typist of the preceding lines. We're well and happy and doing quite a bit of work. Did you wire Shirley, as I asked in my previous letter? I have a proposition to make to [second page is missing]. [ALC]

As if Alan's life were not busy enough, he now planned a trip for the fall, as noted in this letter of May 27 to Harvey J. Bouck, Chairman of the Lecture Committee at Kalamazoo Teachers Lyceum in Michigan:

I believe it would be possible for me to come some time in October or November to lecture to your audience, and a fee of $150.00 plus travel would be satisfactory. There are a number of things that I might talk about: for one, "Documentary Recording" which would include demonstration of folk song recordings made in various parts of the United States and also documentary records of community life made in the United States. These records cover the period of America's preparation for entry into the war, and include Negro ministers, cowboys, Indians, mountaineers and so on, and well demonstrate the racy eloquence that the people of this country have. Otherwise, I might talk about songs of the American frontier, which is just another way of saying American folk song. Such a talk would briefly and vividly sketch the interconnection of such folk song types as cowboy songs, railroad songs, ballads, spirituals, etc., and it might be called "American Music, Home-Made" or something of that sort. Another perspective on the same body of material would be "America Through a Microphone," the story of collecting folk songs in various parts of the country with illustrative records. I am rather tired of the lectures mentioned on the back of the attached circular, but it gives certain autobiographical material from the press agent's point of view and therefore I thought you might like to have it. [ALC]

On May 28 he responded to L. F. Livingston, the Postmaster in Atlanta:

Thank you for your kind offices in contacting Willie McTell for us. You may inform him that we will not release his record, and we have withdrawn it from the list of pressings. [WMC]

Alan connected with Charles Todd, now the associate manager of the Tulare Migrant Camp in Visalia, California, on May 28:

The documentary records have already been released, and when they are played on local stations is a matter which is up to the station. You can enquire of the nearest representative station on the Don Lee network which, I believe, ordered the records, and see if they can tell you when the programs are scheduled. If that doesn't work, let me know and I think we can lend you a set for a while for your own edification. I shall take up with Dr. Spivacke the matter of furnishing Mr. Beers copies of the Okie programs. He certainly should have them. The Friends of Music Album was a special release for that organization and cannot be purchased, but by June 30th we will have the new release ready—thirty records covering the whole collection—and this will be available on order from the Recording Laboratory. As soon as they are ready we'll send you a circular. The King family money will be held in escrow for them until they turn up—right up to the day before the day of judgment. We don't have an extra machine in the house, nor will we have any funds to send one to you until after the beginning of the fiscal year, if then. It would be swell to get the festival recorded; I bet you could get your local radio station interested in taking it down for you without any trouble at all. I'll call Phil [Philip Cohen, chief of the Radio Research Project] about Sonkin; our trouble is that we don't have any jobs to offer anybody. Sonkin is an awfully nice guy. We sure enjoy your letters; keep them rolling in. [VFDB]

He had a bit of bad news for his father on June 2:

I'm sorry to tell you, but they've just put through a new ruling on me, and you will have to send a one-page report about your last trip before they will pay you for it. It needn't be long or particularly detailed; just get something in, and I swear by the Gods you'll get paid with speed. Your letter to Bess this morning sounded as though you're feeling better. I hope so. The various letters you asked for are coming along under separate cover. [ALC]

As the Mississippi trip approached, Alan updated Charles Johnson on June 8:

I am glad that the development of the Coahoma project has indicated July as the best time to work there, as that suits my plans much better. I will be teaching at the University of Indiana [Indiana University] from June 29th until July 11th. I can meet Lewis in Nashville, have a conference with you then and go down into Mississippi for the remainder of July. It will be fine to see you both. I have many things to talk over with you. Kindest regards to you and your excellent staff. Thank Lewis for his report. [F-LC][112]

He also made plans to stop in West Virginia on his trip west, as he noted to Louis Chappell at the University of West Virginia on June 8:

I am driving out to Indiana on the 27th of this month and I would very much like to drop by for a visit with you at that time. There are a number of things I would like to discuss with you, and you are almost the only active collector in the country that I don't know well. I am very anxious to remedy this situation. Let me know if you will be in town. [ALC]

More on John's trip followed in a letter to his father on June 10:

Your trip to West Texas has been approved. I append the budget. . . . $950.70. Be sure that you don't undertake this necessarily arduous trip unless you feel able to, and if you don't feel like going it alone I am sure that John Brooks or Frank Dobie could dig up a student who would be glad to go with you and help you out. As to payments you can send us a voucher each two weeks if you like, attaching thereto receipts signed by the singers for all such expenses and a short statement of what you have done up until that point. Perhaps even better plan would be for you to sign the enclosed vouchers before a notary after you have filled in the totals for each section of the trip and leave Mary Rogers the job of properly filling in the various items of the total from a statement attached to each voucher. This procedure will, I think, get you paid promptly and without any complications, but don't bother to submit expenses of miscellaneous character without receipts, because they simply won't be paid, and in addition they will delay the whole process by weeks.

With the list of contacts that you already have and with the others that you can develop if you take your time in towns like Alpine and so on, the results of the trip should be extremely valuable. If you are too busy to take notes on the trip, simply turn the machine on and record your impressions at 33 r.p.m. as you go along. Dobie mentioned that Sandy Morris is the greatest of all cowboy singers, but Bess reports that you disagree with him. Cancel that appointment. Write me at once about your needs for records and needles and just for safety purposes have the machine looked at by the Dallas Presto man and get him to bill the Recording Laboratory at the Library of Congress. Bess, to my great sorrow, is about to leave for New York and Detroit. When I said we had all been mistreating her, I meant simply that we had not provided her with enough clothes recently. [ALC]

On June 11 he followed up to Cleveland Bénoit in Jennings, Louisiana:

I realize that it is hard for you to understand why we are paying no more for the use of your song. The reason is this—these are our first records. They are going to be sent to South America to make friends for us there. Then they are going to be used in schools to teach American folk songs. There will be no profit or money made from these records in any sense and, as a matter of fact, the issuance of these records is costing the U.S. Government a considerable amount of money. As a patriotic American I feel that you should participate in this important governmental activity by allowing us to use your song for the purposes as indicated. Yours is the only record which is being held up and you are causing this project a very serious delay.

I hope that you will agree with me that allowing us to use the material will be of sufficient benefit to the welfare of the U.S. that you will sign your release and return it to us at once in the enclosed airmail envelope. This is the first time that American folk songs and particularly American negro folk songs have ever had their real chance to be heard. Please do not do anything to prevent this, and answer me at once. P.S. There must be some mistake about the payment of $10.00. $4.00 is absolutely all we can pay for a song as short as yours. [ALC]

Alan also worried about the future of his father's files, as he wrote to John on June 16:

The blanks and needles for you were shipped today. Next time you are going to need anything, try to wire us in advance so that we won't have to keep you waiting. Miss Rogers has not been in the least involved in the delay of your payment. I would be personally very much embarrassed, and I think it would be an affront direct, if you deposited your valuable folklore manuscripts anywhere else but in the Archive of American Folk Song. It would seem an expression of lack of belief on your part in the Archive which you have created. While Harvard certainly helped you in the early part of your career, there is no question that the Library of Congress ultimately did very much more to make your work known and make you appreciated. I know of your recent unpleasantness abut fiscal matters, but the Library as such is not responsible for that. It's been a matter of pure administrative mixups due to the natural changes that take place when Dr. Putnam retired and a new man stepped in to fill his shoes. I think you might discuss with Dr. Spivacke your obligation to Harvard and inquire whether the Library would be willing to photostat your manuscripts and give a photostatic copy to the Harvard Library. [ALC]

Suzanne Comhaire-Sylvain had visited with Alan at the Library of Congress, and he thanked her in an informative letter on June 16:

I am sure that if you knew what turmoil my life had been in since you left, you would forgive me for not having written you previously. I have often thought of our brief visit together with warm pleasure, and with deep gratitude for the help you gave in straightening out a very thorny catalog matter. You may be sure that what you have done is deeply appreciated by myself and by the Library of Congress, and that if there is anything I can ever do to assist you in any of your many important projects I shall be completely at your service. We lunched with: Charles Seeger, Director of the Music Center of the Pan American Union; Gustavo Duran, Music Center of the Pan American Union; Dr. Donald Doherty, American Council of Learned Societies, 1219 Sixteenth St., N.W.; Benjamin Botkin, Folklore Fellow, Library of Congress. All of these persons are, of course, located in Washington, D.C. Dr. Doherty was much interested in various matters we discussed and I think it would be a very good thing if you were to keep in touch with him.

I am much interested in the notion of your working in the creole area in Louisiana, and I hope that after you have considered the problems involved you will let me know what you think might be fruitful. I believe that I might be able to obtain some material aid for such a project. It might also be desirable for you to consider what further work in the way of recording in Haiti should be done, once you have been able to hear the [Harold] Courlander recordings. I hope to have the opportunity of discussing both of these matters with you in the future. If it is ever possible for you to come back to Washington, we have a little more work to do on the catalog, but there is no great hurry about this. Did you leave a pair of white gloves in my car? I have an extra pair. I'll look for the publications and send them on if I find them. I presume you took my copy of Miss [Katherine] Dunham's thesis with you, and that you will return it when you have had a chance to tear it to pieces sufficiently.[113] [ALC]

The following day, June 17, Alan updated Spivacke in a letter that was, however, not sent:

I have been invited by Dr. Stith Thompson, head of the English Department at the University of Indiana [Indiana University], to give lectures for two weeks at his Summer School of Folklore. The actual time I will have to spend on these lectures is rather slight, and I will have practically full time to devote to collecting in the area. The opportunity to spend two weeks in consultation with Dr. Thompson, Dr. [Ralph] Boggs, and other leading folklorists of the United States will also be of great value to the Archive, I believe. On the way out to Indiana in my car, I am going to stop for a day's conference with L. W. Chappell, of the University of West Virginia. Dr. Chappell is the most active collector of folk songs in any institution outside of the Library of Congress, and he thus far has been chary of cooperative work with the Library. I hope to be able to make him a friend and collaborator in the course of my visit with him. The summer school at Indiana ends on the eleventh. My plans then carry me south to Nashville, where I will meet Lewis Jones of the Fisk Department of Sociology. We are scheduled to spend the remainder of July in Coahoma County, completing the survey of Coahoma County music initiated last summer. This project should require approximately three weeks. At the end of this time I shall take the train home to Dallas for a week's visit with my family. [F-LC]

On June 20 he responded to Harvey Bouck about his proposed trip to Kalamazoo:

I am informed that the cost of a round trip to Kalamazoo, including Pullman berths, is $54.92. Therefore the total fee plus travel would be $204.92. As far as my present plans go, any Tuesday in January would be satisfactory to me. Please let me know which date you select. I am sending you some publicity material under separate cover. The equipment necessary for the lecture on "Documentary Recording" consists of a 16-inch turntable able to play 33 revolutions per minute, with amplifier and speakers. The whole success of the talk will depend on the distinctness with which the illustrative recordings are heard by the audience—and this is up to you. [ALC]

Concerning a different matter, Alan wrote to Samuel Bayard at Harvard University on June 20:

I am beginning to make recommendations for the Archive's work during the next fiscal year. I am wondering whether you are still too engrossed in your work at Harvard that you might not be interested in using one of our machines this summer. Pennsylvania still represents one of the important gaps in our collections, and I hope some work can be done for us there before long. If you are too busy, is there anyone you could recommend who knows the ground there and could do competent work for us? I would be very glad to have your suggestions in making future plans. When are you and I going to get together? [ALC]

A few days later, June 23, he crafted a memo, apparently for Spivacke, about a forth-coming recording at an Army base:

I have arranged with the officials of Camp Belvoir to record a group of singing soldiers from that post on Thursday night at 6:30. I have the following names of the men who definitely intend to come: Ronnie Stringer, Harold Baxer, Ellsworth Moody, and John Reynolds. There will be, at the most, five more people, but it will be impossible now to be definite about these names. These men will come at 6:30 and will be recorded from the stage of the Coolidge Auditorium. The whole operation should be completed at the latest, by 10:00 p.m. It will be necessary to pay taxi fare for these men from Fort Belvoir and return. The taxi costs $3.00 each way for each taxi, making a total of $12.00. They will expect to be reimbursed for this expenditure at the time they come. I don't know whether this is possible, but it would be also nice to provide them with refreshments. [ALC]

His travel plans were now somewhat changing, as Alan informed Louis Chappell in Morgantown, West Virginia, on June 25:

Sudden emergencies will prevent my leaving until Friday morning so that I will have to beg off from your class and will be able to spend only the latter part of the afternoon and evening with you. Terribly sorry. [ALC]

Another memo followed to Benjamin Botkin on June 25:

Yesterday at your request I conferred with Mr. Clapp about the matter of obtaining full clearances for all recordings in the field. I explained to him that this would make for great difficulties in our field work and that in cer-tain respects it was inconsistent with our main purpose. Which is, I judge, scientific. Mr. Clapp thereupon asked me to inspect the records upon my return and write for as many clearances at that time as I judged would ever be necessary. It seems to me that this is the most efficient way to handle this problem. [ALC]

That same day, June 25, he composed a very short, curious memo:

It is requested that the per diem and incidental expenses of $8.00 on the trip from Montreal to Ottawa, Canada in January, 1941, be cancelled. [ALC]

On July 9, a busy correspondence day, he responded to Suzanne Sylvain-Comhaire:

I have tentatively discussed your [knowledge of] Creole with the Rosenwald people and I shall incorporate it into my plan to be submitted to them early in the fall. At that time I'll probably want to have more detail than your letter of June 27 quoted me. I'll be back in Washington by the time you've finished with your work at Columbia and it will give me great pleasure to see you again at that time. I'll do my best to protect you from the savages in civilized garbs. [ALC]

Another letter went to Samuel Bayard in Cambridge on July 9:

Bill Doerflinger[114] is working for Dutton's in New York. As a matter of fact, he has recently done some recording for us there—an old shanty singer. I am very fond of him as I got to know him well while he was in Washington. I am sorry that your draft status makes your future so uncertain. We are all in somewhat the same position I suppose. When I have found out a little more about our budget for the year, I'll try to be more definite about the recording project. My notion would be at the moment that we will send out our sound truck with an engineer for your disposal, say, during the period of a month, and get some good representative examples of the various kinds of folk songs available in the territory that you know so well—a sort of survey trip, so to speak. Another approach would be for you to locate a group of singers and then our sound would come up to do the actual recording. Do you think Harvard would be interested in cooperating in such a project insofar as your services are concerned? Many thanks for your kind words about my book. Having just read your paper on the tunes that Mrs. Voegelin has temporarily in hand, I can be equally effusive.[115] It seems to me somewhat the clearest and wisest statement on tunes that I have seen in English and I should like very much to have a talk with you about it some day. [ALC]

Alan continued to keep in touch with Woody Guthrie, writing to him on July 9:

I spent an afternoon singing your war-time songs to a pretty little gal named Dorothy, and some of her friends. They said they'd like to meet you, and I told them that that could probably be arranged, although you were somewhat tied up at the moment. I have turned awfully long haired for the last two weeks and have been wheeling and dealing with a group of college professors so hard and fast that I wake up in the morning and start to stroke my long grey beard, and I find it warnt [sic] there. On picnics and bear parties the songs that that they've liked the best have been Pretty Boy Floyd and then Pretty Boy Floyd all over again. It's my favorite. I've been bombarding my boss in Washington to get the two song books I talked about, and I think he's going to do something about it. I also sent him your new war songs, and I hope he'll be able to do something bout them, since he's on the Army-Navy Morale committee. The best person to write at Decca is Jack Kapp. Tell him you're a friend of mine and then watch him like a hawk. He likes countrified music and likes to get his hands on it and put it in his pockets. I haven't seen Hitler in the last few days, but the last I heard of him he was getting worried. No changes at this end. P.S. The last time I saw you I decided that you were about the most ornery and unfriendly character I'd ever met, and I decided to avoid you like Hitler does Stalin. The hatchet is buried now, though, and I'm off to Mississippi. [WGA]

He connected on July 9 to Svatava Jakobson, with whom he soon would be working[116]:

I was very greatly interested by the outline of your work you presented to me. As a matter of fact, I discussed it in a seminar here at the University of Indiana [Indiana University] in Field Collecting. Since I am going into the field now for about a month, I have forwarded your letter to Dr. Charles Seeger at the Pan-American Union at his request. At the time you were in Washington, he thought that your project would be of interest to the musicology committee of the American Council of Learned Societies. I hope, too, that if something does come of this project, it will be possible for the Library of Congress to cooperate. If you have not heard from Dr. Seeger within the next few weeks, write me care of the Library. [ALC]

He explained the situation to Charles Seeger on the same day, July 9:

This Folklore Institute has been great fun and very stimulating. I'll tell you all about it when I see you. In the meantime, however, here is the outline of work presented by Mrs. Jakobson, the Czech lady whom we interviewed one afternoon in your library. At the time you said that the anthropology committee might be interested in this project. I have written her that I have sent you her letter for your consideration. I also wish that you would show it to Dr. Spivacke, when it is convenient. [ALC]

Also on July 9, he gave a detailed update to Spivacke:

I deeply appreciate your very kind letter about the efficiency rating. As I wrote you, my long screed, I realize that it could do much to clear up for both of us certain misunderstandings that have been a long time growing. So far as I am concerned, my letter and your kind reply had just that effect for me. Attached is the sheet giving you the answer to the problem of what songs ought to be included on the backs of the South American transcriptions. The songs marked with the simple x should last a minute and a half to two minutes each, and thus provide fourteen minutes of music out of which the local sessions could build programs similar to the transcription on the opposite side of the record. Using the complete songs which generally run three and a half to four and a half minutes would not provide sufficient material for the construction of a program. Therefore I think the sampling technique is much better. Johnny just told me over the telephone that you wanted to use whole songs. Therefore to the left of my xs I have put a row of check marks indicating my preferences if you followed this latter procedure.

Attached is a letter from Sam Bayard with my reply. If there is nothing you can do about it until I return, give it to Jo for filing. Attached also is a letter from Susanne Sylvain-Comhaire. This application I shall take up with the Baltimore people at the proper time. Let Jo have this letter, too, unless you want to take action immediately. Under separate cover I am sending you a group of songs which Woody Guthrie recently handed on to me. I know the tunes to some of them, and some are quite good. Thought perhaps you'd like to look them over. He has written me offering us the chance to make copies of two big manuscript collections of songs in his possession. Botkin's WPA project typed the last collection, but perhaps we could photostat these two. This matter is two or three weeks old and Jo has a copy of the memo I wrote you at that time filed. I have told Woody that he may expect to hear from one or the other of you. I still feel that the Vance Randolph project may as well be continued as long as he cares to go ahead with it, since the cost of the field operation has now dropped to a minimum. I presume that you are following this up as it is practical. I was fully embarrassed about the matter of the test pressings, and I am sorry to have caused the worry. But my whole teaching schedule had been laid out around the use of records, and there was no time to change at that late date. The accidents of life kept occurring as I thought they would, and I was not able to use them entirely until today at noon. I will get them out on the afternoon train.

Here are my suggestions about the USO club activities. (1) Recordings of folk songs particularly hill billy tunes and negro blues and including our own pressings to be available in USO club rooms. I can work up a list of such recordings on very short notice. (2) A guitar, banjo, fiddle and mandolin to be made available in all USO club rooms, along with simple visual instruction books for the use of these instruments. (3) A small library of mainly pamphlet collections of American folk songs, to be made available in the USO club rooms, including such standard books as Sound Off, Cowboy songs, etc. (4) A special regional song book published by the USO containing folk songs according to the regions along the lines that we have already discussed. (5) The encouragement of the composition of new songs by song writer's contests in which the emphasis can be laid on folk and semi-popular material rather than popular material. Devices like a bulletin board for new songs and rhymes or letter boxes for the same to be used in the club rooms themselves. The directors of the club room must make a special point of rounding up fugitive soldier verse and parodies and sending it in to a central office for editing. Certain portions of this material could then be edited and shipped back to the various USO offices in mimeographed form for the use of the men there. (6) In almost any American town now, especially in the South, there are various semi-professional folk musicians, hillbilly performers, or blues singers whose services in entertaining men at the club would, it seems to me, be invaluable. I hope these suggestions are in line with your needs. We are lucky in having Mr. Gainer in that spot, because he is an old-time West Virginia collector who, by the way, has offered his collection to the Library of Congress. Give him my best regards when you see him.

I believe that my visit here has been a successful one. After tomorrow's last lecture, I shall have been on the boards 11 times, mostly for two hours at a stretch, and there are still a few people who are listening to my line of chatter. The only fly in my ointment is this matter of leave. Jo writes me that it has been handed in as annual leave from June 26 to the 11th. My visit to [Louis] Chappell in West Virginia which lost about a day means a good relationship with one of the best, most active and most difficult collectors in the U.S. Since I have been here, I have worked out a couple of tentative plans for work in Nova Scotia and Detroit, which involve for us only the loan of a recording machine. The Nova Scotia woman is Miss Helen Creighton whose work in that field is distinguished and has been asked by John Marshall to submit an application for a grant. The other is with Miss Thelma James, successor to Emelyn Gardner at Wayne University in Detroit. They have what seems to be the most active collecting center in the country with 10 or 12 graduate students working on all sorts of problems in the foreign minority field in Detroit. I have taught these folks how to work the recording machine and have spent a lot of time with them working out details about collecting. Another whole day I devoted to work on the machine which got slightly damaged in transit, and I must have spent at least a day now answering correspondence. I hope that you can get Mr. Rogers or whoever is responsible to change his verdict about taking away my annual leave on this occasion. I feel I have never done a [better] piece of work for the Archive than to spend two weeks with my colleagues at this Institute. I am sorry not to have gotten a note to you sooner, but I have been giving two lectures a day for the past few days, and things have been quite hectic. [ALC]

Alan arrived in Nashville on July 13 and began making plans for a return trip to Coahoma County; he arrived in the Delta on July 17. He would be working with the Fisk music student William Allen and another student, Margaret Just Wormley. On July 15, however, he wrote to Spivacke:

Your letter was naturally a great shock to me. It seems to indicate that we are to have no money for next year, at least no definite amount to plan to record with. It means that LC does not appreciate the magnificent opportunity it has to: 1) Preserve our heritage of pioneer democratic oral music while there is still time. 2) Operate in and through minorities and folk communities in the field of morale. (viz. to assist in the work being done in Detroit through Miss Gardner, et. al.)

I judge, too, that nothing further has developed in our project to record in the army camps. Since you do not mention the Latin American project, I presume nothing has come along that way. We are again poor and looking for money—a great comedown and awfully discouraging—just at the time the rest of the country was looking to us for leadership—just at the time when I had come to a working agreement with a) Chappell, the most active collector in the South-East. b) Miss Helen Creighton, the most active collector in the North East—who will probably get Rockefeller money. c) The Wayne Univ. crowd who have *ten* graduate students operating in the foreign minority field. d) When I was trying to work out a plan for Rosenwald to really cover the South at little expense to us.

I feel that I have made a miserable failure of interesting the LC people in what we were trying to do. I don't even have your backing. Luther Evans doesn't believe in us to go after tire priorities. No one in the Library feels the urgency of collecting folk songs while there is yet time. Every time we plan a trip we will have to make a special appeal to the Librarian—and, if the war is going against us, the general tendency will be for us to feel and him to say, "Better not now." Really, Harold, I think if you had let me go to the mat with Evans, Clapp, Mearns, et al., I could have saved our necks. I am sure you said everything you felt you could honestly say for our benefit and fought like Hell, but then, on the other hand you didn't feel that problem as a problem was as serious as I felt it was. This is not a criticism of you, but an expression of my regret.

Perhaps all this wailing is highly unrealistic, since I shall be sent to the army and there will be no tires, etc., anyhow. Yet, since I have been away, I have felt more than ever that a sturdy and aggressive folk-lore program could become crucial for morale work. This comes out of my recent contacts with P.S. teachers, musicians, Negroes and people in the minority field. Last night T. E. Jones, pres of Fisk kept me up until two thirty telling me how he saw folklore could be used in his program of morale work and adult education to be launched here at Fisk next year. Of course, he is a Quaker and something of a fool, but he says he has access to money and the backing of the General Education board. By the way, he wants me to spend a couple of days on my way back helping the Fisk Jubilee singers and a group of Nashville Negro folk singers get launched in the U.S.O. camp show affairs. Do you want me to cooperate or not? After settling some very nasty difficulties and a lot of talk, I am getting my expedition underway tomorrow morning. Thereafter until my time is up I can be addressed Genl Delivery Clarksdale, Miss. Please write me more in detail about what has happened. Army post tour? Latin America? Can I go?[117] [ALC]

He sent a telegram to Spivacke on July 18:

Please rush very official letter of identification mentioning Fisk field helpers general delivery Clarksdale. [F-LC]

He tied up one more loose end in writing to Casey Smith at the Wynne State Farm in Huntsville, Texas, on July 22:

About a month ago we sent you a voucher to sign. It was addressed to Smith Casey, Wynne State Farm, Huntsville, Texas, because that is the way you signed the original agreement. You have never returned the voucher and we can't pay you until we get it. In case that one was lost, we are sending you a new one. Sign it Smith Casey, because it has to be the same as your signature on the other paper. As soon as we get this voucher back, your check can be sent to you. You will get the money in a very short time after you sign and return the voucher. The records will not be ready until late in August, and that is when we will send your copies. Please send the voucher right away, so you won't have to wait any longer for your money. [ALC]

On July 27, probably from Clarksdale, Alan corresponded with Dr. Raymond C. Archibald, a mathematics instructor at Brown University, who had collected folk songs in Sackville, New Brunswick:

Thank you very much for your comments on our Check-List, and for your information about the Mary Mellish Archibald Memorial Library [at Mount Allison Ladies College in Sackville]. Our supply of copies of the Check-List is very nearly exhausted; nevertheless I expect to send one to that Library when our small final mailing goes out in a few weeks. Our office has had a rush of work in the last month, and I must apologize for the delay in handling your order for ballad records. I am sorry to tell you that six out of the fourteen versions you have asked for are under restriction; that is, we may not duplicate them without express permission of the collectors. If you wish, we will open correspondence to obtain permission, giving full information about the uses to which the records would be put. I presume, however, that you will prefer to avoid this delay, since your purpose is to provide simply a sample of the Archives work.

The cost of duplication for the eight remaining songs will be $[illegible]. This covers the two 12-inch, double-sided disks, and the packing cost, but not the shipping cost; they will be shipped to you express collect. Upon receipt of your check to the Librarian of Congress these records will be sent you without further delay. I imagine you realize that the conditions of our recording work do not produce uniform quality such as may be expected from the records listed in a commercial catalog. For example, of the Lady Isabel versions you will receive number 1736A is complete and certainly sung, and 1746A2 is nearly as good; the others are somewhat marred by incompleteness, acoustical distortion, or extraneous noise. Yet each has its own particular interest.

I am sure you know that our duplicates are released for educational use only; the Memorial Library will, I know, protect them from publication or any commercial use. We have recently arranged to copy a number of French Canadian records from the collection of Marius Barbeau at the National Museum in Ottawa. No doubt you are familiar with his work. I hope you will be pleased with your records, and that we may serve you again in the future. [ALC]

From Clarksdale he updated Spivacke (undated, but apparently July 30):

I have delayed writing you a day in order that when I did write I would know exactly how to plan. 1) The records and films have not come and I have one tire in the shop for vulcanizing. Since I was thus rendered temporarily inactive I decided to leave for Texas one day early. The car will have to stay here. 2) I shall return here next Wednesday and if I obtain an extension would like to remain for about a week more in the area to finish up this job. So much material has been located which I have as yet been unable to record, and much of this material is crucial to the completion of this study. You will be glad to know that we have mapped out the main lines of music in this county and will be able to use our material for recommendations for any type of morale work in the middle South. There are still a good many records and movies to be made, however.

3) Leaving here on the 7th of August I must stop over a day in Nashville and from that point would like to have the opportunity to record a white spiritual session with Jackson on the way home. 4) I suggest, therefore, that you apply for a 10 day extension for my trip—if you deem that wise. Your recent letters have indicated to me that there was nothing pressing on hand for me to do at the moment in Washington. Naturally, if there is something to do there now of importance to our national emergency, I want to drop everything and come straight back. If not, however, I want to stay on a little longer. I am leaving so much which can be useful and that is crucial to our knowledge of American folk song that I want to finish this job up all ship-shape before I leave it. Pardon this hasty note. It is being written a few minutes before train time after an exhausting morning of recording in which the last records were used up. I will write in more detail from Dallas. [ALC]

He had another request sent to Spivacke on August 4:

Mr. Alan Lomax has recommended that funds be provided to enable him to extend his present field trip by two weeks. The purpose of this additional time would be: 1. To continue for one week longer his present recording work in Clarksdale, Mississippi, in connection with the survey undertaken last year in collaboration with Fisk University. Of this work Mr. Lomax says: Much material has been located which I have as yet been unable to record, and much of this material is crucial to the completion of this study. . . . We have mapped out the main outlines of music in this county and will be able to use our material for recommendation for any type of morale work in the middle South. There are still a good many records and movies to be made, however. The Fisk University field workers have been in the county for a number of months, and Mr. Lomax is carrying out work for which they have already prepared the ground.

2. To record the Sacred Harp or white spiritual music of the Southern mountains in collaboration with Dr. George Pullen Jackson[118] of Vanderbilt University. This is a type of music for which the Archive receives constant requests, and Dr. Jackson is the leading collector and authority in the field. The localities visited will be approximately along Mr. Lomax's route from Nashville (where he will wind up the Fisk Project) to Washington. The proposed budget is as follows [with a total of $888.00]. [F-LC]

Alan personally updated Spivacke on August 7 from Dallas, where he was temporarily staying:[119]

When I came to the day to leave home and return to Clarksdale, I just couldn't make it happen. There were things to talk about that hadn't been talked about and I didn't know when I'd see my folks again. So I stayed over a few more hours. For the record my period of leave began on Thursday, July 30, at 12 noon and will end on Saturday, August 8 at twelve noon, by which time I shall be at work in Clarksdale again. That makes nine days. I don't feel that this should be deducted out of my salary as leave without pay, since I accrued enough overtime in the field to make up for it. My working schedule in the field ran from 8 or ten in the morning to twelve midnight and beyond. I hope you can make this adjustment.

Since I have not heard from you here I presume that you have written me in Clarksdale about extension of the trip. I hope the answer was favorable. Even if it wasn't, even if the trip wasn't extended, wouldn't it be all right for me to spend a few extra days in the field without receiving per diem. I would elect to if necessary. I called Louis Jones in Clarksdale yesterday and he says he is wiling to stay on and work with me there until Tuesday or Wednesday so that I can record the material I will need for the final study. Most important item are the children's games which I will film as well as record. I think my contacts will net me forty or fifty of these and they will have immediate use in our educational program. I have so much material that I scarcely dare to try to give you a report on it. It is the best documented body of stuff in the collection, backed by extensive interviews and observations. And it is good for the whole Delta area, not just Coahoma County. I have been able to check much of it with residents of the county who come from other parts of the Delta. Essentially what we will be able to outline: 1) The general growth of folk music in the area over the past eighty years in relation to the social and historical growth of the area itself. 2) The importance of folk song and folk attitudes in the modern Delta community and the implications for education, for morale activity etc.

I have been at work in a territory where the Negroes are not reached by the newspapers or the radio, where the whites are quite defeatist in their point of view, where the Negroes hear about the war 1) Hitler is going to kill all the niggers if he wins. (from the whites). 2) This war is the judgment of God on a wicked world. Only Christianity will win through. Kneel down and pray. (This is message of the Negro church to the religious Negro.) The result is a not surprising apathy on the part of the ordinary Negro to the war effort. If an invasion army were to land in the United States today, the Southern

Negro would *not* volunteer to go and fight the enemy. The whites here know this, sense it rather, and they are tense and nervous. I have had more trouble with local whites on this trip than all the rest put together, because of this tension. It is terribly important that some program be initiated which will offer some solutions for these problems. The best approach to the people is through the Negro church and Negro music and Negro folk attitudes. Such an approach would knit the two groups more closely together emotionally since most of the whites like the folk Negro, and at the same time it is almost the only way that ideas, information and purposeful plans can reach the Negro rural group. When I come back to Washington, I'm going to try to reach people with this idea and I hope you will feel like helping.

Ask Miss Rogers to look up the address of Kelly Page, one of the singers on the South American set of records, and send said address to father. He's going to visit Kelly on the next leg of his trip. I neglected to say that if I stay in Clarksdale until Wednesday of next week I will drive straight on to Washington with only an overnight stop in Nashville. It seems a pity to do that when I have the chance to work a bit with Dr. Jackson and with the head of the music department at the University of Kentucky, but I guess it must stay that way. My best friend in Texas, Johnny Faulk, who has such physical disabilities (vision) that the army won't accept him, has joined the Merchant Marine and will sail this week out of Galveston. He was my last remaining hope as an active folklorist. I guess the thing has died until after the war and of course after the war the best stuff will be gone in this country. His decision has had a great effect on me. If the OCD and other agencies concerned with morale are still as far behind the times as they were when I left town, I am still a bit discouraged. Your last letter offers me a number of opportunities for suggesting projects, and I shall think them over before I come home, but not write them out until I have time to discuss them with you. [ALC][120]

Alan followed up on August 7 with a short letter to Woody:

The Music Division hasn't enough stenographers to typewrite copies of your two books; but if you will donate them, it would be glad to make *photostats* of all the pages for you. The photostat paper is nice and stiff. Send along your MSS and someday, when you are about ninety, we will put them in a big glass case upstairs, beside the Constitution, with two tall guards to prevent people from stealing them. [WGA]

About the same time he wrote an undated memorandum, probably to Spivacke, concerning Woody:

Woody Guthrie, from whom the Archive has received a great number of ballads, left in my possession a manuscript book which contains the background
for these songs. When he asked me to return the manuscript, I first had it
microfilmed, feeling that it was unique and of importance for the Archive
and the Library. The Photoduplication Service has requested that I pay them
the $6.60 owing for this piece of work and I shall be glad to do so if the Music
Division is not able to take care of the bill at this time. [WGC]

Not quite back in Washington by late August, his secretary sent a note to Suzanne Sylvain-Comhaire on August 28:

Mr. Lomax has not yet returned from his field trip. He was scheduled to
arrive tomorrow, but I have not heard from him in more than a week, so I
cannot say for certain whether he may be delayed for several days. I shall call
your letter to his attention as soon as he returns. [ALC]

Once back in his office on August 31, he wrote to Samuel T. Burns in the Department of
Music at Indiana University on September 2:

The project you mention in your letter of August 24th, sounds interesting.
There are, however, several uncertainties in the way and among them the
possibility of my early enlistment. Will you drop me a card with a question
mark sometime about three weeks from now and I shall let you know one
way or another. [ALC][121]

Alan followed up to Suzanne Sylvain-Comhaire on September 2:

I was delighted to learn when I arrived here on Monday that you plan to
come down again. Allow me to suggest that you plan to arrive on Wednesday, September 9th. By that time I should have my affairs sufficiently in order
so that I can spend the time with you that I shall wish to. I look forward to
seeing you again. [ALC]

He was anxious to catch up with his correspondence, as in this follow-up letter on September 3 to Ricardo Archuleta in Cerro, New Mexico:

Before you can be paid for the records you were kind enough to give us permission to release, you will have to sign the voucher that has already been
mailed to you and return it to us. If you have not received this voucher, let
me know promptly and another will be sent to you. The records are not yet
ready, but they will be soon and yours will be sent to you at once. [ALC]

Another plea went to Elizabeth Austin on Cat Island, Bahamas, and to Joe Washington Brown in Lake Arthur, Louisiana, on September 3:

Before you can be paid for the records you were kind enough to give us permission to release, you will have to sign the voucher that has already been mailed to you and return it to us. Please do this at once so we can send you your check for $3.00. If you have not received this voucher, let me know promptly and another will be sent to you. The records are not yet ready, but they will be soon and yours will be sent to you at once. [ALC]

The following day, September 4, Alan communicated to Lonnie Odum in St. Joseph, Tennessee:

Allow me to thank you in behalf of the Library of Congress for the amazingly beautiful collection of records you were so kind as to help me to make. If things go well I plan to suggest that the Library release an entire album of the Sacred Harp pieces recorded in Birmingham so that the general public can become better acquainted with this noble American music. Attached is a complete list of the Sacred Harp pieces recorded by me during the convention, along with an estimate of the cost of duplication of the recordings. Please note that certain ones are recorded in the Court House and others in the studio. Those made in the studio will naturally be of accoustically superior quality. Allow me again to thank you for your fine spirit of co-operation. [ALC]

Another thank you letter went to Turner Jr. Johnson in Como, Mississippi, on September 5:

In behalf of the Library of Congress and its Archive of American Folksong allow me to thank you for your valuable contribution to our collection. The material that you were kind enough to record for me will be preserved in the Library for the pleasure and instruction of American citizens, and will find extensive use for all sorts of educational purposes. Each item recorded by you will be cataloged under your name and to your credit. If you should ever recall further old songs and stories, or if you encounter someone who knows such material, we should appreciate your letting this office know of it. Again, with much appreciation of your kindness and helpful cooperation. [F-LC][122]

Alan sent a similar letter to Son House in Robinsonville, Mississippi, on September 5:

In behalf of the Library of Congress and its Archive of American Folksong allow me to thank you for your valuable contribution to our collection. The material that you were kind enough to record for me will be preserved in the Library for the pleasure and instruction of American citizens, and will find extensive use for all sorts of educational purposes. Each item recorded by you will be cataloged under your name and to your credit. If you should ever recall further old songs and stories or if you encounter someone who knows such material, we should appreciate your letting this office know of it. Again with much appreciation of your kindness and helpful cooperation. [ALC]

Attempting to finalize work on the Coahoma project, Alan contacted President Jones at Fisk on September 8:

I am happy to report that the expedition to Coahoma County was successfully completed, and that plans for a monograph by Lewis Jones and Dr. Work are on the fire. I hope to collaborate, but may be prevented by enrollment in the Navy or something. You may recall that I suggested that you write officially to the Librarian of Congress for continuance of our relationship in regard to more recording by John Work or others on the faculty. This is all the more necessary now, since we are in process of closing up our books on last year's work, and Mr. Work's project represents part of this. Mr. Work still has a number of blank records, and I feel they should be used or sent back, or that the project should be renewed. I wish you would look into this for me. Let me know how your various interesting ideas go forward. [F-LC]

On September 15 he kept in touch with Svatava Jakobson in New Jersey:

Doctor [Charles] Seeger informs me that he submitted your application with extremely favorable comment to the American Council of Learned Societies, but as yet he has received no answer from them. I believe the director, Doctor Leland, has been away on vacation, but you should expect to hear from them sometime very soon. Have you gone forward with your plans for translation of part of your thesis into English? It certainly should be available to American workers in the field of folk lore. I suggest, too, that you do an article on the subject and submit it to Erminie Vogelin, Editor, American Folklore Journal, Bloomington, Indiana. [ALC]

The next day, September 16, Alan, somewhat at loose ends, wrote to Richard Chase:

I am sort of betwixt and between at the moment, but I may be able to be of some help on the USO camp thing later on. Fowler Harper has resigned from the committee. I suggest that you communicate with Doctor Harold Spivacke, Chief of the Music Division, who is on the committee. In the meantime, however, my notion is that you should try to get into work in your own locality and establish yourself there. Best regards to you and Mrs. Chase and Horton Barker. P.S. We have a request from R. C. Archibald who wishes to have all of our versions of the "Wife of Usher's Well" for the Mary Mellish Archibald Memorial Library in the Allison University, Sackville, New Brunswick. Will you be so kind as to drop me a card giving me permission to duplicate your version for him. These records will be used, of course, for purely scholarly purposes. [ALC]

At the same time, September 16, Alan communicated with R. C. Archibald:

I have just returned from a field trip and am interested to find your letters in regard to "Lady Isabel" and "The wife of Usher's well." My secretary is attaching some additional versions that I have found and I shall write to the people who have restricted the versions we are not able to furnish you, for their permission. When these letters have been answered, I shall send you an estimate for the additional records and you can order the whole group at one time if you care to do so. [ALC]

A short note to Mary Bonelli in Stafford, Virginia, followed on September 16:

I am still tied down to Washington, but I am still coming down to visit you some day I hope. Thank you for your continual cordiality and interest. Of course, all recording activity in the field of folklore will be cut down considerably during the war. [ALC]

Vance Randolph[123] also received a letter from Alan dated September 16:

Do you know a Miss Gertie Colvin in Versailles, Missouri? She has asked us for the loan of a recording machine for recording ballads. Do you think it will be possible for you to record her material for her. I can see no point in sending two machines to the same area. I am making some plans for a series of folk song fellowships to be submitted to the Rosenwald Foundation for 1943–44. Would you be interested in continuing your work under the terms of a Rosenwald Fellowship—about $1500.00 plus material costs? My notion would be to cover the whole Ozark area if you have not yet been able to do so. Let me hear from you about this in full. How is your work coming along? [ALC]

The Coahoma study and its outcome were never far from his mind, as he expressed in detail to Larry Morris of the Works Progress Administration in Washington on September 16:

For the past year or more the Library of Congress has been engaged in a collaborative study of folk songs with Fisk University, of Nashville, Tennessee. The location of this study was in Coahoma County and its county seat of Clarksdale, Mississippi. The intent of the study was to integrate folk songs, folklore and folk attitudes into a perspective of the history of the county and the present social scene. The material at hand consists of about fifty hours of musical recordings, plus a similarly large body of interviews, documentation, etc.

A monograph is planned to be executed, largely by the Fisk University staff and myself, which will give a sort of folk history of the county and a history of the folk during the past eighty or ninety years. I believe that the study will be of great importance among studies of the rural Southern Negro. We are naturally anxious to consult as much material as possible that is related to Coahoma County and its environs for the purpose of documenting our findings and conclusions as elaborately as may be. I was told that the Works Progress Administration's Music Project collected a good many folk songs in the territory, and I feel sure that other branches of the Mississippi Arts Projects of the Works Progress Administration have much other valuable material in their files. I should greatly appreciate your looking into the whole matter of making this material available for use in preparation of this study.

Specifically, we should be interested in material which relates to the general history of the Upper Delta Region, the history of Coahoma County and vicinity, the building of the levees in that area, the social life and customs, early and modern, in the territory, the folklore and folk song of the area. Since most of the material we gathered was on the Negro, material on white social history would be all the more valuable as background for our work. I should imagine that the Writers Project, Historical Records Project, the Music Project and possibly the Recreational Project might all have such material. The preparation of the monograph is now in progress at Fisk University. Therefore, I should take it as a great favor if you could look into this matter for me as soon as possible. It is assumed, of course, that if any of said material should be used in the form of quotation or as general background in the study, due credit would be given to the agency or agencies directly involved in its preparation. [F-LC]

On September 18 he wrote a memo to Spivacke supporting a proposal from Thelma James:

Attached are two letters from Miss Thelma James, successor to Emelyn Gardner in her folk-lore work in Wayne University. Miss James took her Ph.D. in folklore under Archie Taylor and is one of the most competent scholars in the field in this country. My contact with her this summer at the Folk-lore Institute convinced me of her executive ability, her capacity for getting work done efficiently and her genuine interest in the field of folk-song. Her proposal should receive your most serious consideration, because I feel that through it a very important job could be done in morale building work in the Detroit area. Perhaps, if the Library does not feel it can back Miss James by furnishing her equipment and disks, you could request the Librarian to take the matter up with one of the foundations. [ALC][124]

Alan had an odd note to Spivacke on September 18:

Ida Hoyt Chamberlain, who says she is an authority on Chinese music, wants to record some of her ancient Chinese music adapted for the Western ballet for our files. Do you want to do it? [ALC]

Another September 18 message went to Lucius Smith in Crenshaw, Mississippi:

I want you to know how much I appreciated the songs you recorded with Sid Hemphill at the picnic on the Fives. We certainly did enjoy your music. I would have written you before to send your money, but I did not get hold of your address until today. Please sign the attached receipt and send it back to me along with some news of yourself. [F-LC]

Louis Chappell in West Virginia again heard from Alan on September 19:

Since I left your delightful home in the early part of the summer, I have been on the run continually, first giving two weeks of lectures at the University of Indiana [Indiana University] with little or no chance to prepare and then plunging into an intensive field period in Mississippi and Tennessee. I have just this moment come back to Washington and begun to get my house in order. I hope you and Mrs. Chappell will accept this apology for not having written before and allow me to express my appreciation for your hospitality and kindness to me.

I should very much like to hear whether in thinking it over you decided to follow out the plans we discussed, whether or not it would now be possible to purchase groups of your records as you conclude their publication. I do not know, since our activities have been reduced due to war-time pressure, whether we can still do this, but I should like to have the opportunity to submit the project for present or future consideration. I am in particular concerned, however, with the matter of the Rosenwald Fellowship we discussed. In the next ten days we plan to set up the whole project and should very much like to include you in it. If you are still interested, give me a notion of how much time you plan to spend in the field during a year beginning in July 1943–1944, what results you would expect such a year to bring in terms of recordings and, roughly, how much you think such a year would cost you in terms of expenses. [ALC]

Alan continued to work with some of the musicians from the Delta, such as in this letter to Charles Berry c/o McKinley Morganfield, Stovall, Mississippi, September 21:

In behalf of the Library of Congress and its Archive of American Folk Song allow me to thank you for your valuable contribution to our collection. The material that you were kind enough to record for me will be preserved in the Library for the pleasure and instruction of American citizens, and will find extensive use for all sorts of educational purposes. Each item recorded by you will be cataloged under your name and to your credit. If you ever recall further old songs and stories, or if you encounter someone who knows such material, we should appreciate your letting this office know of it. Again, with much appreciation of your kindness and helpful cooperation. [ALC]

On a completely different matter, on September 23 he contacted Professor Arthur Posnansky[125] in La Paz, Bolivia:

Doctor Ralph Boggs has informed me that you are trying to arrange to record a folk-drama to be performed in La Joya on December 8th. It may be possible for the Archive of American Folk Song of the Library of Congress to make materials and equipment available for this enterprise. This depends on a number of factors including perhaps most importantly that of transportation of materials to Bolivia in time. I should appreciate your making a formal application to me for the materials you think you will need to record this folk-drama. Specifically, the length of time the recording will take and the number of feet and dimensions of film you will wish to use. If in addition you would be interested in further recording in the region, add your comments about this in as much detail as convenient. Indicate also the official sponsorship for your project and write a paragraph about your background.

There are several questions I want to have answers for. 1) Will the recording take place any where near a source of electricity? If not, could you borrow a reliable portable motor generator delivering 110 volts of alternating current? 2) Is there a portable recording machine available in Bolivia that you could borrow, since the chief difficulty will probably be the shipment of a machine to La Paz? 3) What part of the project could you or your local sponsors finance yourselves? For instance, if we were to furnish the machine and the original disks and film, could you pay for copies of this material for the local collection? Let me hear from you by air mail as soon as convenient. In the meanwhile, I shall look into the matter of transportation. [ALC]

That same day, September 23, he thanked Ralph Boggs:

Thank you for your note about Professor Posnansky. I am working on it and shall let you know if anything comes along. If any more projects like this come to your notice, shoot them on to me. I have not yet heard from Mr. Frank Duffey, although I have written him asking for a brief informal report. Please ask him to write me because I have heard one slightly disturbing report about his activities. [ALC]

Following up with his attempt to help Thelma James, on September 26 he communicated with William Haygood, Director of Fellowships at the Julius Rosenwald Foundation:

When you were in my office a day or so ago you said you had a group of applications for recording fellowships. Would it be feasible to let me examine these projects for a few days while I am in process of making up the set of recommendations I promised to send you? In regard to the group of fellowships for the Library of Congress it might be that I would find a person in your group who would be well suited for the type of work I am particularly interested in. Off the record, does the Rosenwald Foundation consider applications relating to foreign minority work in the United States? I have a proposal on my desk from an excellent person in Wayne University who has developed a very fine center for folklore of the minorities in that city. I wonder whether or not to include it in the fellowship proposal I plan to submit. [ALC]

Suzanne Sylvain-Comhaire again heard from Alan on September 28:

Allow me to thank you once again for your great kindness in revising our catalog of Haitian folk-songs. I have been considerably disturbed for a long time about this catalog and now that you have given it a thorough going-over I feel much better about allowing the general public access to it. The Library is very busy with the Army at present so the estimate for your records will be somewhat delayed. Let me know how soon you want them. As soon as there have been any developments on the Rosenwald project, I shall communicate with you. In the meanwhile let me know what you think about Southern Louisiana. [ALC]

On September 28 he wrote to Fletcher Collins, who was now with Fairchild Aircraft in Hagerstown, Maryland:

Jo has taken leave of absence for six months to have her baby. I am going to be here only a few more days until I go into the Office of War Information [OWI] as a Special Information Consultant. I shall probably be calling on you for help and counsel when I start my new job. In the meanwhile my best to you and Mrs. Why don't you come down for a visit? [ALC]

Anticipating his move to OWI, he continued to take care of business, as in this September 29 note to Mabel Christie in Falmouth, Michigan:

I should very much like to receive from you a list of the old songs and ballads that are traditional in your family. Naturally, I should be delighted to obtain copies of whatever material that you know is truly folk-song. Thank you very much for your letter. [ALC]

A week later, October 8, he sent off a short note to Mr. and Mrs. E. C. Ball in Marion, Virginia:

The Recording Laboratory has not yet completed the records for you. When they are ready they will be sent to you at once. [ALC]

The Coahoma study continued to hang over his head, as in this letter to Fisk President Thomas Jones on October 7:

I am glad to hear that the plans for the Coahoma County study have progressed as far as your letter indicates. On my side, I have gone through the field recordings carefully, culled out the dross and turned the whole batch over to the recording laboratory for duplication. According to our budget for this enterprise you will receive 235 twelve-inch acetate duplicates for your disposition. The first batch is nearly ready and will be shipped to you in the next day or so. After having examined Doctor Work's memorandum, I am still not clear as to what role the Library of Congress is to have in the completion of the study. Our investment in the project was a considerable one and I should be embarrassed to make a report on the basis of the plan attached to your letter of September 22d. It is not clear where the editorial supervision of the project should lie nor how the monograph should be laid out.

In a note to Mr. Lewis Jones and in a personal conference with Mr. William Allen, who was kind enough to make his car available to us last summer, I suggested that the transcription could proceed at once on the duplicates of the records made in the summer of 1941, a large group of which were sent to Doctor Charles Johnson in 1941. It might be well to have a brief report on how many such duplicates were received by Fisk. If any important records in the 1941 series were not duplicated previously, provision might possibly be made for their duplication now. [F-LC]

On October 9, 1942, Alan officially informed Archibald MacLeish, the Librarian of Congress, about his moving to the Bureau of Special Operations, Office of War Information (OWI):

The Office of War Information has requested my services for special work beginning Monday, October 12th. Since this seems to be an excellent opportunity to be of value in the present emergency, I am anxious to enter upon these duties. Therefore, I hereby tender my resignation from the Library of Congress, effective Saturday noon, October 10th, with the request that at the end of the emergency period I may resume my position in the Library. [ALC]

On the same day, October 9, he continued to pursue funding for Svatava Jakobson, in a letter to Homer Rainey, president of the University of Texas:

Some time ago I had the great pleasure to meet a distinguished musicologist and folklorist from Czecho-Slovakia who has made some remarkable studies of both folk song and folk life in the mountains of Moravia. Her name is Mrs. Svatava Jakobson and she is at present continuing her research in Czech folk song in New York City documenting the change and development of this interesting body of material in this country. She discussed with me a plan to study folk music culture of the Czech minority groups in the United States with particular interest in Czech communities of Pennsylvania and Texas. I feel that Mrs. Jakobson would make an important contribution of our own general cultural problems by the work she might do in this field.

This morning I conferred with Doctor [Donald] Goodchild of the American Council of Learned Societies, Doctor [Charles] Seeger of the Pan-American Union and with Mrs. Jakobson. Doctor Goodchild was much interested in the project and suggested that I write you to inquire whether the University of Texas would be interested in her work in the Czech communities of Texas. The use of the University machine and the help of an operator, for instance, would be of considerable value. Or better, perhaps, the University might see its way clear to offering part financial sponsorship to the enterprise. It is possible that the Library may furnish some aid in the project and Doctor Goodchild plans to discuss the matter with one of the Foundations, I believe. I would appreciate greatly to hear from you about this matter with whatever suggestions you find it possible to make. What institute in Pennsylvania do you suppose might be interested in sponsoring Mrs. Jakobson's work there?

Budget for Fellowship of Mrs. Svatava Jakobson. Purpose: A one year survey of Czecho-Slovakian folk song and folklore in three American regions: 1) Metropolitan area of New York City, 2) Miner area in Pennsylvania, 3) Farming area in rural Texas. The study will describe in detail the changes that have occurred in Czech folk song in repertoire and style in the United States and provide material on the assimilation of the Czechs in the life of the United States. . . . Total $2550.00. Note: It is possible that the Library of Congress, if the project proves to be material of national defense interest, would furnish a portable recording machine and field disks for the study. It is estimated that this portion of the budget would amount to approximately $350.00. [ALC]

Also on October 9 he sent brief word to S. T. Burns at Indiana University:

I am being transferred to the Office of War Information to tackle a hell of an assignment next week, so I guess all bets are off. Thanks for the offer and for the reminder. [ALC]

Alan provided additional information to Charles Johnson on October 10 regarding Fisk and other matters:

I am glad to know that the study is proceeding so actively. The first batch of fifty duplicates were shipped to you yesterday and more will be coming to you from time to time. I shall look into the matter of duplication of the remainder of last summer's records although it may be that we shall not have sufficient funds for this. Do you suppose that, since it is likely that this summer's material will exhaust the present budget for duplication, that Fisk University might find the funds for buying what remaining records will be necessary from the 1941 trip? On Monday I expect to transfer to the Office of War Information and for a time will probably be occupied with my new job, but later on I expect to continue the transcription of my field notes and send that material on to you. The first job will be to write up the circumstances of the recording interviews with some remarks that may be of some assistance to Mr. Work and Mr. Jones. I fully expect to take a hand in the final compilation of the monograph and would like to see first draft material as it comes along.

At the moment I am engaged in the preparation of the set of recommendations for the Rosenwald fellowships that I discussed with you last summer. If you have any suggestions about this I should like to have them as soon as possible. Madame Suzanne Sylvain-Comhaire, Haitian folklorist, is one of the people I am most interested in and I would expect her to work in the Creole Negro area of Southern Louisiana. She is not well acquainted with the South and I suggested that she work out of Fisk under your guidance, if that interests you. She will be largely concerned with folk song, folk-lore and language. Willis Lawrence James seems to me to be a good prospect for work in Georgia and I am going to include him in the recommendations. There is another applicant in Washington who has had little training in folk-lore except from book sources, but who last year wanted to come to Fisk for a period of study and then go into the field. I think he would do a good job on a community survey study similar to the Coahoma County study. His name is Myron Higgins and he is a M.A. student under Sterling Brown. Do you know William Harrison Pipes[126] of Ft. Valley, Georgia, who is interested in Negro sermons? Any suggestions about these people or others that you may know of would be very welcome at any early date. [F-LC]

Alan pursued assisting Jakobson in a letter to Donald Goodchild of the American Council of Learned Societies on October 10:

Attached is a tentative budget for Mrs. Jakobson's fellowship. I should appreciate your comment on it. I have asked her to send me material on the exact communities she plans to work in along with a slightly more detailed plan for the fellowship. This should be in your hands early next week. It is a matter of great satisfaction to me that you are interested in this project. Mrs. Jakobson is to me one of the most capable people I have met in the field of folklore. Her point of view is that of a real scientist in her field. Thanking you for your interest. [ALC]

The same day he sent a short note to Charles Seeger at the Pan-American Union about a tentative budget for Jakobson.

Once settled at the OWI, he contacted Helen Creighton from the Bureau of Special Operations on October 27:

It is a matter of great regret to me that your project is still being delayed. Off the record there appear to be complications at the Library of Congress not in regard to your particular project, but of a more general nature which are causing the delay. I feel sure however eventually you will get your machine and records. My successor in the Archives is Ben Botkin former editor of *Folk-Say*, a very nice fellow who will do his best to speed things up for you. I am now working for OWI attempting to utilize folk lore material for wartime education. It looks like it's going to be a lot of fun. The Negro spirituals you have collected all seem to me genuine folk songs, although of course they may have been brought to Nova Scotia by means of printed books. They are definitely worth collecting however if for no other reason than comparison with other Negro music from other parts of the western hemisphere. In a way I envy you your opportunity to get better acquainted with one rich folk lore region. I am sort of spread around all over the map myself. I would greatly appreciate it if you would jot down for me any songs, anecdotes, sayings, etc. which have wartime content or interest. This type of material is being studied here at my office and may well be used later on. [ALC][127]

The same day, October 27, he informed L. W. (Louis Chappell):

There has been some delay in my writing up the Rosenwald project which will include an application for a year's fellowship for your folklore work. I shall ask for only $200 for office help since I am afraid they would not be willing to spend more than that on such an item. Perhaps when you make your own application to them, you might personally put in for more explaining the reasons.

There is one point that I think we should both be clear about from the beginning, and the reason I am writing you is that I want it clear. The records that you make under the terms of the Library project must be deposited in the Archive collection along with what portions of your field notes you are able to work up, by the end of the year. All of this material will be given a publication restriction on request from you, and thereupon will not be used or, I suppose, even played by anyone without your express permission. If, within the collection you make, there should chance to be three or four beautifully sung or performed examples of American folk songs, the Library might request your permission to publish this material in the course of its regular (I hope) release of records. I am going ahead with the preparation of the whole project, but I would like a note from you signifying your willingness to work with the Library on the terms outlined above. Naturally I am delighted that it will be possible for us to work collaboratively. [ALC]

John Vincent in Kentucky, another of the Rosenwald participants, also got a letter from Alan on October 27:

I have not written you because I have just shifted gear and gone into high at the Office of War Information. I have one question to ask you about the Rosenwald Fellowship which I am just preparing. It's quite important that you use your own machine, since the Library machines are going to be spread pretty thin in 1943. Would you be so good as to consult your President or Chief Factotum and let me know for sure that you can use the College's recording machine. I hope Ruth is feeling better by now. [ALC]

Another letter on October 27 went to Homer Rainey, president of the University of Texas, following up on Alan's concerns about Svatava Jakobson:

A short while ago I sent you a letter about a project I felt would be of great interest to the University of Texas. The carbon of this letter is attached, since I suppose the original must have been mislaid. In the meantime further discussion with Dr. Goodchild has resulted in a decision on the approximate budget a copy of which is attached. We have further agreed to request Archibald MacLeish, Librarian of Congress to apply to the Carnegie Foundation for funds sufficient to finance this project for a year. An expression of interest from you and Dr. Dobie would, I am sure, greatly strengthen this application. Since I am about to present the whole matter to the Librarian, I would very much like to know what you think of it. Your suggestions for a sponsor in Pennsylvania would also be extremely helpful. May I expect to hear from you soon. [ALC]

October 27 was indeed a busy day, and this letter went out to Billy (probably William Haygood of the Rosenwald Foundation):

Shortly after your letter came attaching the application I shifted over into OWI, and have since been pretty busy curling up in my little corner of that huge aggregation of thinkers. I'm having a wonderful time at it. The last couple of days however, I have been working on the project discussed with you in September, and I hope to have the whole business ready for your consideration in two or three weeks, signed and sealed by the honorable Librarian. Let me put this bee in your bonnet if you're wearing one this year. Do you think in view of the wartime emergency and in view of the fact that these fellows would be absolutely invaluable to my work here in OWI, that the board might consider launching the whole project sometime say during February? If that is a possibility would a letter from anybody in OWI make it any surer? [ALC]

And yet one more letter went off to Willis James at Spellman College in Atlanta, on October 27:

In answer to your letter of October 2, allow me to say that I am very pleased with your interest in the notion of a collaborative folk song collecting project. I have not answered your letter sooner because I have recently shifted my work to the Office of War Information. In the next few days I hope to prepare the outline of the Southern Collecting Project for the Rosenwald Foundation. In this connection I need from you a brief statement of your academic training and a description of the work you have already done in the field of folk music.

The next question is the projected year's work. Do you have a car of your own, or is one available to you? Are you interested in covering a region in your collecting work or would you prefer to make an intensive study of a small area? Either one of these notions would fit in very well with the whole plan, which envisages three or four Negro collectors scattered through the South from Louisiana to the East Coast. One of these persons is extremely competent in the Negro Creole dialect and will work in southern Louisiana. Another of the fellows will carry out an intensive study of a small community somewhere in the Delta region. My hope is that if you plan to attempt a broad coverage you would choose Georgia, South Carolina, and Florida, or any part of this region.[128] It happens that the Library has very few records from that area, whereas more material has been recorded further west. Since I am considering the applicants just mentioned, along with you, I should like to know definitely what you are interested in doing. Please write me in these various regards as soon as possible. [ALC]

More of his thoughts went to Lyman Bryson and Herbert Hunsaker, Alan's colleagues at the OWI, also on October 27, in a very lengthy memo entitled *Plans for reaching folk groups with war information* (here shortened):

Since this is a people's war, it is essential that, so far as possible, information about the war should be distributed equally to all groups of the people. Again, it is important that the principles and aspirations by and for which the war is won and the peace is decided be those principles and aspirations that the whole people agree upon. Any deviation from this ideal will make this less a people's war, will result in a sense of frustration, neglect and resentment by the groups whose needs are neglected in a war information program, whose special problems are not considered in the war program and whose aspirations do not influence the plans for the peace.

As everyone is aware there is a large body of the American public that is not sufficiently literate or sufficiently accustomed to reading to be reached through the press. This is the same group which either fails to own radios or has special listening interests that puts them beyond the reach of ordinary network radio programs. Many of these people belong to no national organizations and seldom attend public meetings, outside of the church. Lumped together the underprivileged, the undereducated, the isolated and certain of the racial and national minorities, make up what the social scientist, when he is thinking in cultural terms, calls the "folk." The folk have their own traditional ways of self expression, influenced somewhat by industrial civilization, but even today rather different from the means of expression common to our dominant city culture. These means of expression must be adapted to wartime use and must be made to serve as channels of distribution in order that the folk groups may be reached with war information and with the ideals and principles of their people's war. The folk may be thus stimulated to express their own special aspirations, their own reasons for committing themselves to the war program in their own terms. This will establish direct and vital lines of contact and communication between these groups and the rest of the nation and with the government in Washington. The principles of our people's war may also be clarified and vivified when they are crystallized in terms of the needs and problems of the people and expressed in the rich and homely language of the people.

The forms of communication of attitudes and ideas at the folk level are, of course, familiar: songs and tunes, folk tales and humorous stories, folk religious services (including prayers, songs, sermons, etc.), folk talk. All such material is orally transmitted and from being chewed over thoroughly by the group comes to express the group, stylistically as well as ideologically.

The folk have their own artists who create new material or adapt the old within the framework of the folk ways of the group. These singers, talkers, tellers, orators, dance callers, musicians and actors communicate with their audience partly on a face to face basis, partly through national channels such as the phonograph record. It is these folk artists that I hope to be able to motivate. They can assist in distributing war information through the following channels: the phonograph record (in the home and on the juke box), the local radio program, the folk church, the folk theatre (the rep theatre, the medicine show, the Mexican religious play, the foreign minority theatre), the many locales for swapping songs and by-words.

The rest of this very lengthy, expansive report lists various proposed projects. For example:

I want a survey made of the hillbilly and Negro programs already on the air in local stations. . . . Within two weeks, I want to make a field trip to New York, Chicago, Dallas, Shreveport, Nashville, Atlanta and Cincinnati in order to meet the principal singers and composers in these fields, to work out some new songs with them and to leave with them assignments for new songs. [ALC]

Before any of his ideas could be put into practice, he had moved elsewhere.[129]

Three days later, October 30, he wrote to William H. Pipes in Ann Arbor, Michigan, about more of his plans:

I regret that I have been unable to answer your letter about the Rosenwald fellowship sooner. The fact is that I have just changed jobs and have been busy getting oriented in the Office of War Information. My plan is to ask the Rosenwald people for a group of fellowships to be administered out of the Archive of American Folk Songs, Library of Congress, which will cover various regions of the south in the next two years. There are two or three alternative plans of work which I would like to suggest to you that would fit in with the overall plan.

1. An intensive and complete study of the folk music in one rural community in Alabama, Florida, North or South Carolina, this study to relate the folk song and the general musical life of the community to the social history of the community, a kind of folklore history of a rural Negro group. 2. A general survey of the materials of an area such as South Carolina or Alabama. 3. A study of the patterns of folk religion—all the way from the Methodist Episcopal Church to the Holiness Churches in any region you might choose. 4. A study of the Negro Holiness Church in the South.

My reasons for suggesting the geographic areas and the areas of study are strategic in nature. If you have an alternate plan in mind, I wish you would outline it for me. If not, perhaps you could take the trouble to develop one of the suggestions I made in connection with some community or region you are particularly interested in. I leave Georgia out of consideration since I am also in correspondence with Willis James about this same matter. I also tend to steer away from a study of Negro homiletics since we already have in the Library of Congress a good many records of Negro sermons. What we need both for folklore purposes and for crucial wartime use is about the relationship of folklore to life to living social problems. I would appreciate a reply to this letter as soon as possible since I am in process of writing up this whole project for the Librarian. [ALC]

Another letter regarding the Rosenwald application, on October 30, went to Suzanne Sylvain-Comhaire at International House in New York:

I am afraid both the Rosenwald idea and the duplication of your records have been delayed by the fact that I have changed jobs recently going into the Office of War Information. This morning, however, I called the Library to urge them to send your estimate on the records you want duplicated. About the Rosenwald fellowship, I have not been quite sure that you were interested in doing the job in Louisiana we talked over together. Before I formally submit the project, I should like such assurance from you.

Would you suggest a group of Haitian songs, not necessarily folk songs, which symbolize for Haitians the democratic traditions of your country. I wonder whether you would make a few suggestions along this line with comments about songs and their historical background. Are there any Haitian musicians in New York with whom you could work out songs dealing with Ha[i]tian involvement in the war against the Axis? [ALC]

He again wrote to Homer Rainey on November 2, about his interest in Czech folklore and the possibilities for Svatava Jakobson:

I am writing to Mr. [Mody] Boatright asking him to let me see a copy of the thesis on Czech Folk-Lore so that I can make up my mind whether or not it is important for Mrs. Jakobson to come to Texas. In the meantime, I hope you will keep the project in mind. If the University is not able to provide any sort of financial sponsorship, perhaps you would consider giving Mrs. Jakobson your moral support in allowing her to make the University her center of operations while she is in Texas. [ALC]

The same day, November 2, he contacted Mody Boatright[130] at the University of Texas:

A few days ago I learned from Dr. Rainey that a student in the University had done a thesis on the Czech Folklore in Texas.[131] I have written him asking his co-sponsorship of a nationwide survey of Czech Folklore music to be carried out by a Czech Folklore Music Specialist, Mrs. Jakobson. She is a brilliant and extremely competent woman, from all accounts one of the best young people in the whole field of Folklore. Before I proceed to push her project further, however, I should like to know what your student has done in this field. Therefore, I wonder if you could send me a copy of the thesis for a few days so I can decide whether Mrs. Jakobson's work would be duplicating anything that has already been done by your student. I have an idea that her special interest, which is the study of the American Czech Community from the point of view of Folk Music, would not in any way conflict with the work that has already been done. Naturally, this thesis would not leave my hands if you will send it to me. [ALC]

The following day, he explained to Lyman Bryson the need for funding Jakobson's work:

Last Spring I had the great pleasure and good fortune to meet Mrs. Jakobson and to discuss with her the studies she has done in Czecho-Slovakia, and is continuing in this country. Briefly, what she did was to study the musical cultures of several folk villages in the mountains of Moravia in relation to their total culture, to write the histories of these cultures as they have been influenced by social and political developments, and to evaluate all her material in the light of a broad acquaintance with the folk and popular music of Central Europe. She plans to continue her investigation here in this country, studying the assimilation of this same musical tradition into the general culture of the United States.

When she sent me an account of her plan, as I asked her to do, I gave it to Dr. Goodchild, of the American Council of Learned Societies, through the good offices of Dr. Charles Seeger, a member of the ACLS committee on musicological studies. This fall Dr. Seeger, Dr. Goodchild, Mrs. Jakobson and I further discussed the project, and Dr. Goodchild agreed to take the matter of sponsorship up with the ACLS and with the Carnegie Foundation. A tentative budget was prepared by me, and gone over with Dr. Goodchild. He has subsequently decided that the Council cannot undertake so large a project and has suggested that it might be a good idea for the Librarian to apply to the Carnegie Foundation for the funds for a year's fellowship to be administered by the Library.

Naturally, such a project as Mrs. Jakobson's must now be evaluated in terms of its wartime significance. It is in such terms that I wish to discuss it briefly. 1) Our large foreign minorities have tended to be regarded as problems rather than as sources of strength for American cultures. This, I believe, is due to the fact that little serious work has been done in the assessment of the cultural contribution of these minority groups and their assimilation into our national life. Mrs. Jakobson's study would point the way for much valuable work in this field, would provide objective criteria for educators and other social workers interested in these crucial problems, and would, I believe, result in a publication that would vindicate the American way of handling minority problems.

2) In order to reach a minority group with informational material and with propaganda, a very nice sense of the tastes and emotional attitudes of the group is necessary. Mrs. Jakobson, as she visits the three areas of her studies, can provide very valuable suggestions for our informational policy as regards the Czech groups, can report on group attitudes in regard to the war. She has commented that the Czech war production workers in New York area make little connection between their rather dull job, their strong anti-Axis feelings, and their own rich community life. This is a gap which she can advise us how to bridge. 3) She will be able to study the war songs and war humor current among the Czechs, evaluate its usefulness as morale building material, and actually work out with Czech song and joke writers, with Czech folk singers and folk story-tellers material which will be useful for the war effort.

It seems to me, therefore, that in view of Mrs. Jakobson's unusual qualifications, in view of the extreme importance of the whole assimilation problem for the war effort, and for post-war reconstruction, and in view of the actual day-to-day help Mrs. Jakobson can be to this office, to the Bureau of Intelligence, and to the Foreign Language Section to this Bureau, her project might be very seriously considered by both the Librarian and yourself. [ALC]

On November 6 he dictated a short note:

Mr. Elliott of the National War Agency, #7394, has an excellent singer of folk songs He is the head of Government at Harvard [B. F. Wright] and knows two songs. 1. Road to California. 2. He Drove three mules for George McVane. However, he might be reluctant to sing them for you but his wife, who lives in Cambridge, Mass., might sing them. [ALC]

William Pipes soon responded, and Alan answered him on November 12:

I am glad to learn that you are interested in the Negro Holiness church study. That seems to me the most profitable thing that you could do at this time and I shall submit that project as part of the larger plan. [ALC]

Probably sometime in November he outlined in a memo "The Rosenwald Plan" for his proposed southern project:

A. The Mountain Belt. 1) The Ozark Region—Vance Randolph. Ballads and songs, stories, documentaries, philology. 2) Central and Western Ky.—John Vincent. Folk-song & folk music—Negro and white. Emphasis on technical musical aspects—studies of instrumentation and singing styles. 3) West Virginia—Louis Chappell. Completion of a survey of the folk songs and balladry of West Virginia. Preparation of publication. B. The Background of Hillbilly Music—Bess Lomax. A survey of the hillbilly industry in the United States, its relation to its country origin, its commercial aspects, its history, its repertory, its characters. C. The Negro South. [ALC]

At month's end, on November 30, Alan had time to write to his father from the OWI:

I just got a letter this morning from Johnny [John Henry Faulk][132] saying that his local Draft Board has told him that unless I can get an OWI deferment for him, they would draft him, one eye or no. As you know, his vision is very bad and he has to face the prospect of a desk job if they take him in the Army.

Naturally, he doesn't want to risk this. The OWI cannot ask for deferment for him, but something might be done for him locally, I understand. I have written to Frank Dobie asking him to take some action on this and also have written our cousin-in-law, Guyton Morgan, Major in Selective Service in the Tribune Building, Austin, asking whether he thinks anything can be done. There are two other people who are important in the situation. There is Q. C. Taylor, J.A.G., and the other is Captain Huell Nelle, both at the same address as Guyton. Adam Johnson is on the local board. If you know any of these men well enough to call them up and ask them whether they think there is any chance of doing anything, it would sure be a favor.

As you know, Johnny quit his Rosenwald Fellowship to join the Merchant Marine and do something he regarded as important in the war effort. I got him to quit the Merchant Marine to come down and do this job which I believe is the most important thing he could do for the war effort since he can't fight. He's afraid of getting classified as 4-F and getting stuck at a desk job. His only other choice, unless something can be done for him locally, is to go back into the Merchant Marine. If you want more facts on the case before you talk to the local people, you can call Johnny up in Austin. Anyway, do what you can. I am quite well and working hard, right in the middle of a whole lot of projects which are moving along nicely, I hope. I will probably be heading south in about ten days. I hope I can get to come to Dallas for a minute and say hello. [ALC]

Alan followed to Gardiner Cowles[133] on December 4 with a detailed plan to use music in the war effort:

There are a number of groups that are not now reached with war information through the media now extensively used by the OWI. These groups include a majority of Southern Negroes and poor whites, the Spanish Americans of the Southwest, various rural groups all over the United States and rural groups recently transplanted to industrial centers. The importance of developing an understanding of the civilian's proper place in the war effort among these people is clearly demonstrated by reports from the so-called tension areas (Mobile, Baltimore) and by intelligence reports covering topics such as attitudes toward the United Nations.

In wartime, this non-vocal sector of the American people is expected to obey the same complex body of laws and regulations and adjust itself to the same new ways of thinking and behaving as other groups. It is necessary to get wartime information to them, therefore, in something like the same quantity as to other groups. In order to accomplish this, familiar and accustomed channels should be utilized: Topical songs and ballads. Rural church services. The folk theatre. The folk tale. It should be borne in mind that for these people a ballad or a story is more than an entertainment item. It carries information, it sets up important attitudes. In a like sense, the church for many rural people is not merely a place of Sunday worship, but the center of social and intellectual life.

There are a large number of people at the folk level who make the songs, tales, sermons, etc., which are meaningful for these groups. I expect to contact these people, explain to them in simple terms what subjects need to be covered, collect the material and distribute it. This distribution will be accomplished by means of: 1. Two fifteen-minute transcriptions, one consisting of Negro material and one of white material, to go to local radio stations. 2. Records for juke boxes. (From these two sources, other singers will pick up the songs and get ideas for their own compositions.) 3. Through the organized churches which reach these groups, such as the Negro Missionary Baptist Church, the Church of the Nazarene, etc. 4. Through published music and song books, through broadsides. 5. Through the community meetings held by civilian defense groups and others. 6. By the word of mouth—grapevine.

I expect to be able to implement the following general informational campaigns: 1. The nature of the enemy. 2. United Nations Idea. 3. War aims of the Democracies. 4. The story of the war as it develops on all fronts. 5. Rationing. 6. The necessity for community sacrifice and community effort. 7. The necessity for unity of farm and labor groups. In addition, special topical material can be quickly developed for many special campaigns, such as mileage rationing, scrap, salvage, woman-power, etc. I feel sure that my contact with these special groups will be of general usefulness to the Office of War Information and the prosecution of the war.

1) I am planning a correspondence panel of persons in close contact with these groups at the community level to keep us informed about their special informational needs. 2) Much of the material, because of its special color and vitality, will be generally useful for such purposes as community singing, music in schools and colleges, raw material for radio scripts, pamphlets, etc. 3) The broadcast section of the Overseas Branch now uses a great deal of folk stuff for its broadcasts. They are extremely anxious to get more material, specifically about the war, and have indicated their willingness to bear a share of the expense in recording it. 4) The foreign minority section of the Domestic Branch is also interested in using such foreign language material and such foreign language songs and stories as I can collect for them. In the field of the Spanish Southwest, they need Corridos to explain to rural Mexicans such elementary things as the draft regulations. 5) I am developing a pool of the fighting democratic songs of the United Nations, this material to be used for

shortwave and domestic broadcasts in the original languages for community singing, etc.

Perhaps I should add a word of explanation of why I began to work with musical materials. There are several reasons. First, music can be used in so many ways. Second, musical materials can be quickly developed in this field and once the process is begun, will tend to grow by themselves, as needed. Third, songs can be made easily to fit specific informational needs. After this general statement of my program has been passed on, I will develop specific parts of it from time to time, as the need arises. [ALC][134]

While he was still in Washington, and thinking of government projects, he also came up with a new book project, as he detailed to Jim (probably Clarke) on December 6:

I want to tell you that this book we have been discussing is potentially the most wonderful and most exciting book that I have ever been connected with. Here is an outline of it, a sort of table of contents with a running descriptive commentary. Introduction: On December ninth, 1941 we were listening to the radio in the recording room. Three thousand soldiers believed killed at Pearl Harbor, etc., all by courtesy of Tums Stomach Easer. The president was about to come over the wire from the Capitol. The needle of the recording machine was set on the disc to record him. What can we do, we kept saying, What can we here in the Recording Laboratory of the Library of Congress do to make a meaningful contribution in the present emergency?

I. What we did was to send telegrams to field workers in various parts of the country asking them to document in recorded form the opinions of the American people about the Japanese attack and the declaration of war by the President. What they sent us from Nashville, Texas, Denver, Bloomington, Madison, New York, Boston, North Carolina, and what we recorded ourselves here in Washington is the most magnificent expression of spontaneous unity, understanding, and will to win that any people ever gave. . . . We put the material together in a fifteen minute transcribed broadcast, the first documentary broadcast ever to be sent over a radio station in the United States.

II. Various people in agencies over Washington were so much excited about the potentialities of this new kind of broadcast that the Office of Emergency Management has commissioned us to get together the material for a documentary broadcast to be called Dear Mr. President, in which the people will talk directly to the President, tell him about their problems, explain to him what they are doing and what they want to do in this present emergency. The raw material for and the story of this broadcast will be the subject of the second chapter.

III. America in the Summer of 1941. During that summer we sent our
sound truck into the hinterland of the United States to document the life
of the people, their opinions and their problems. We documented an Okie
Folk Festival, the Negro Revival season in Texas, a defense boomtown, the
Tennessee Valley experiment and so on. A.) The first chapter of this section
will be the story of what we recorded at Asheville. The Asheville Folk festival
with its songs, fiddling contests, its folk tales and interviews with the singers backstage. An interview with Thomas Wolfe's mother in whose home we
stayed. A revival service at a local white church with a sermon on Dives and
Lazarus. A day at the home of one of the most important and successful hillbilly singers of our time. B.) We then went to Union County, Georgia, until
recently one of the most isolated and backward counties of the South. There
we documented the effect of the TVA on the life of the people. We recorded
the county editor, the doctor, the farmers, a revival service, the local ballads,
the county agent, a family reunion and a fox-hunt. The interview with the
county doctor is typical of our experience. He was the midwife of the community and also its champion fox-hunter. We went into his kitchen about
seven o'clock one morning and he began to talk right over his morning coffee. You couldn't stop him. Our microphone followed him across the yard
while he fed his dogs, into his little office where he examined his patients and
prescribed for them for the mike. Typical story.

["]In the old days I used to have to get about over this rough country in
the old fashioned buggy—confinement cases, you know, pull you out of bed
at all hours of the night. Well, I was about to start home one night and they
forced a pint of whiskey on me, said it would thaw me out when I got too
cold in the road. When we got along the road about an hour, my driver's
eyes were getting weak on him and I decided to give him a little drink and
my old horse he heard that corn-cob coming out of the jug and by the time
I could get around to him he had his head up high—he was raised down
among the Byersses [sic] and they was great hands to make whiskey. Well,
old Ferd had been raised on still slop and he had learned to drink whiskey
and to know about it. Never would drink more than a half a pint. But his
partner, Old Bess, she was messy about her drinking. She'd slobber it all out
on the ground. I believe she'd just drink to be sociable and then spit it out
when my back was turned.["]

C. Old Man Ledford[135] has a wizened face like a monkey and the wit of an
Irishman. I spent two days with him and recorded his whole story and that
of his friends. The TVA was evacuating all the farmers who lived in his valley
because a new defense dam was being built and the water would cover their
farms. Ledford, one of their best experimental farmers, was now sore as a
boil at the TVA, even though he would admit the necessity of the move. This

section will be presented almost entirely in dialogue form with the story of how this man in two days became a first rate actor for radio. . . . D. Wilmington, North Carolina. In October one of our field men went to Wilmington, which has doubled its population in the past year and talked to the people about what was happening. The story in terms of their own comments is gripping and powerful. The plan here is to make the whole chapter dramatic narrative, a sort of short play in one act. E. There Is a Hell! In Maple Springs Church in Tennessee last summer I recorded a whole Negro revival service, prayers, sermon, spirituals, shouting, mourners' bench and all. The sermon is a magnificent and powerful piece of prose poetry. The whole service is again a dramatic form.

F. Bonneville Dam. The Washington State Section of the Power Division of the Department of Interiors last summer hired Woody Guthrie, Okie poet laureate, as an information Specialist for the summer of 1941. During one month he wrote a series of ballads about the Bonneville Dam and its effect on the land and the people. One about the Jackhammer Man, one about the Columbia River, another about the homeless people coming into the green irrigated land, etc. A cycle of simple and powerful poems that are as interesting and exciting as anything I warrant written during that summer. I propose to make this section a summary of the best of that material.

IV. Fairy Stories from the Fairy Isles. In the summer of 1935 I visited the Bahamas with a recording machine and for the first time in my life discovered that fairy tales were real. I found villages where listening to fairy stories was one of the principal amusements of the people, but, although some of the themes were the same as those in Uncle Remus and Grimm, the stories were elaborate vehicles of the talents of the teller for mimicry, improvisation, singing and low comedy. I recorded these tales and they are uproariously delightful, the only full and elaborate versions of fairy stories that I know of anywhere. I want to make this chapter up of about five or six of the best ones.

V. Aunt Molly Jackson. Aunt Molly Jackson sat with me for two weeks one spring and filled about seventy records full of her songs, philosophy and life history. I shall add to this material additional notes to be obtained from her and make this section the portrait of one of the most remarkable women of our time—midwife for Clay County, Kentucky; ballad singer extraordinary; union organizer; mountain intellectual who joined all the churches in her country one after another searching for the true religion; mountain roughneck who can outdrink, outcuss, outyarn any man of her acquaintance.

VII. Fire Engines! Woody Guthrie has been working for about a year on the story of his life. He has written among many other things a long chapter on his boyhood, called "Fire Engines." It is a picture, as passionate as Thomas Wolfe has written, as penetrating and involuted as Joyce (nearly) about his neighborhood gang, the gang house in the deserted lot, the fist fights in the streets with the whole town watching, the hard and savage life of a boy in a raw Oklahoma dust-bowl town. It ends with the scream of fire engines across the empty lots as his house with his mother in it burns to the ground. (This chapter we will have to buy the rights to.)

VIII. Mister Jelly Lawd! Jelly Roll Morton, recognized as one of the foremost jazzmen of all time, was as fantastic personally as he was fabulous musically. He spent nearly a whole summer with me here in the Library telling me the story of the early days in New Orleans, of how jazz outgrew the town and moved up the river to New Orleans [Chicago]. Charles Smith,[136] the editor of the two most important books in the field, says that this body of manuscript is the most important single document in the history of jazz. I want to present the story of Jelly in his own mad language. It is the story of a man who "ruined his eyes looking for marks on cards under strong lights," who "made a hundred dollars a night in tips at Queenie's place in 1908," "who is the King of jazz and stomps." The burden of the book might be summed up this way. It is our democratic right to speak to the president and we ordinary Americans speak a language as eloquent and beautiful and distinctive and many-colored as any great writer ever wrote. I expect to make the material move out [of] a more or less personal narrative of my own connection with and impressions of these people. And I am going to have time this spring to work on the book. I want to do it very badly. I hope you'll take it. Let me hear from you. [ALC]

On December 9 he followed up to Suzanne Sylvain-Comhaire:

I am delighted to hear that you have been granted a Guggenheim fellowship. Of course, that is much better than the Rosenwald and will give you much more freedom to do what you wish to do. Perhaps you might plan to ask for an extension for next year to do the job we discussed in Louisiana. Now that I am out of the Library, I'll tell you that I did my best to get the set of records sent to you cost free, but discovered that that is entirely against Library policy. I hope that after the war, we can work out further plans for your work in Haiti, in cooperation with the Library. I am sorry to have missed your lecture in New York. I got there about an hour late. Everyone was enthusiastic in their reports of it, you will be glad to know. [ALC]

Mody Boatright sent the thesis Alan had requested in early November, and received this letter from him on December 10:

I very greatly enjoyed reading the thesis on Czech folk lore in Texas. Would you mind if I kept it a little longer as I want Mrs. Jakobson, a Czech musicologist, and a temporary member of my staff, to look it over for what it can suggest to her about wartime work in this country. I agree with you that the work should be published and it might be that Mrs. Jakobson could be of some help in this regard. [ALC]

He wrote two letters regarding his Rosenwald proposal on December 22, one to James Allen, Deputy to the Domestic Branch of the OWI:

As I see my work here in the Office of War Information as advisor on informational problems of special groups, one of the things I most need is field contacts in the South. There are a number of folklorists, sociologists, etc. who know a good deal about the South, but in these times there are few who are in direct contact with the people. For this and other reasons, I have been planning to apply to the Rosenwald Foundation for a project of six fellows to work under the joint sponsorship of the Office of War Information and the Library of Congress. To the Library they will supply records of folk lore and to the Office of War Information they will be able to give invaluable material about the informational problems of special groups.

Only four of the six fellows will need to have gas and tire rationing. These are (1) Professor Willis James of Spellman College, Atlanta, Georgia, who will work in the area of Georgia, Florida and South Carolina. His mileage during the year should not exceed 4,000. (2) James [William] Harrison Pipes, who will be interested in a study of the most important contemporary Negro folk religion, the holiness church. He will work in the deep south, Alabama and Mississippi, and his mileage should not exceed 3,000. (3) Prof. John Vincent, who will work in central and western Kentucky, and his mileage should not exceed 4,000. (4) Vance Randolph, who will work in the Ozark region, and his mileage should not exceed 3,000.

I would greatly appreciate it if you would take this matter up with the Office of Price Administration in order to see whether they would write a letter to the local boards where these individual fellows will make application for their gas and tire rationing exemptions. Since the fellowship plan must be submitted very shortly to the Rosenwald Foundation, anything you can do to obtain a quick reply from OPA would be much appreciated. [ALC]

He conveyed essentially the same information to Herbert Hunsaker, another of his bosses, on the same day:

For some time, I have been discussing with the Rosenwald Foundation a project to collect folklore in the South during 1943–44. This project will involve six fellowships, three to Negroes and three to whites, well distributed throughout the South. These collecting fellows can act as part-time correspondents for the Office of War Information on the informational problems of the regions in which they work and give this office invaluable assistance since they are trained observers. The Library of Congress has indicated its interest in acting as co-sponsor of this project with the Office of War Information. The folklore phase of the project will be administered by the Library of Congress and the war information side by the Bureau of Special Operations.

The six persons for whom I wish to make application to Rosenwald Foundation are Professor Willis James of Spellman College, Atlanta, Georgia, who will work in the region of Georgia, Florida and South Carolina; James [William] Harrison Pipes of the University of Michigan, who will make a study of Negro holiness cults in the deep south; Myron Higgins, who will make a study of folklore in one community in western Tennessee under the direction of Charles Johnson of Fisk University; Vance Randolph, authority on Ozark folklore, who will continue his work in the Ozark region; John Vincent, Director of Music at Western Kentucky State Teachers College, who will work in central Kentucky; and Bess Lomax, who will make a study of the national hillbilly music business at various key broadcasting points throughout the South and Middle West.

The problem of gas and tire rationing comes up at once, of course, and this has been discussed with Mr. Allen, Deputy to the Domestic Branch of the Office of War Information. He has indicated his willingness to take it up with OPA and find out whether they will write a letter to the local rationing boards in the cases of four of these fellows. I should appreciate your consideration of this problem in order that I may take the matter up officially with Mr. Allen. Memorandum to Mr. Allen is attached. [ALC]

Alan composed a fascinating, handwritten, heavily edited, undated memo to William Lewis at OWI about this time, although it was probably never sent:

There is a need, I believe, for regional programming in connection with our informational campaigns. This need is particularly deep running in areas where literacy is low, where race tensions exist, where the cultural background of the people puts them to a greater or lesser extent beyond the reach of most newspapers and national radio programs. It is important for all Americans to feel that this is *their* war and the best way to make them feel this is to put the war issues into *their* language. This does not mean talking down to the people.

The audience I am concerned with here is composed of two parts. 1) The rural Negro and the Negro worker, mainly Southern, but also located in Northern cities such as Chicago, Philadelphia, etc. Our intelligence reports have given an unpleasant picture of the apathy of this group on war issues. I believe this apathy is *in part* due to the fact that the proper kind of informational appeal has not been made to them. This appeal should be made by Negroes, it should be emotional, it should stress the positive side of the picture, it should emphasize the present participation of Negroes in the war effort, it should point to the hope of the post-war period and it should underline the United Nations idea. It should exploit the tremendous power of Negro music since the appeal of this music will cut across Negro class lines and will carry the message to white groups as well.

2) The rural white and the recently urbanized white. This audience is mainly Southern and Southwestern, but, as indicated by the national popularity of the hill billy and western musical programs, is likely to be found anywhere in the U.S. The most complete radio coverage for both groups can be best achieved by utilizing local radio stations. The station managers know best how to program for their local audience and every effort must be made to get their enthusiastic help. I have the following specific suggestions to make and I should like to have the opportunity to discuss these suggestions with the regional representatives at the Dec. 28–Dec. 30th meeting. Their comment and criticism would be invaluable to me in any further development of these plans.

I. *A Local Negro Newscaster on a Southern Station.* It is my belief, and this belief has been confirmed by numerous conferences with others interested in Negro problems in this bureau, that a Negro newscaster on a Southern station would quickly develop a large Negro listening audience. For them he would explain a) the development of the war, b) the nature of the enemy, c) the working of the United Nations plan, d) national political affairs, e) rationing, f) the role of Negroes in the war effort, g) specific government campaigns, as they come along. His language should be simple, his approach objective, his speech pattern a function of his region.

There are obstacles to setting up such a program in the deep South, but I believe it could be done in Virginia where race relations are much better. Norfolk (a defense center) might be an ideal place since Hampton Institute is nearby and through our part-time Negro consultant, William Cooper, who teaches there, the program might be planned and sponsored. Mr. Cooper indicates his willingness to train a commentator, to help him prepare his copy and to help get the program publicity. It is not expected that it will be necessary to pay this commentator. Thus a program will be presented to the local station which will involve no trouble to them and no further expenditure of fund than the allocation of airtime. If successful, there is a good chance that such a show would quickly develop commercial potentialities.

If we can arrange through our regional representative to get such a show on the air in one station under favorable conditions, it will provide an excellent testing situation for the Bureau of Intelligence. From this one station the idea might well spread to other places in the South. I'd like to have the opportunity of discussing this with our Richmond representative.

II. *Transcribed Programs of Wartime Folk Music.* There are a large number of semi-professional and professional musicians in America in the race and hill-billy business who have a tremendous rural and worker following. These singers who reach their audience over local stations and through the juke boxes have a great facility for the composition of topical songs and in these songs and their comment about them express themselves with such natural and homely eloquence. If you want to reach their audience with an information program that will stick you reach them through these people, speaking and singing about the war. I have talked with some of these artists about our campaigns and have attached some material they have developed as a result of these conversations. (See attached songs [attachment is missing].) Much more material along these same lines can be easily accumulated.

I propose to collect songs of this type, performed by the star singers, from key points over the country. This material should then be woven together by a singing commentator who will point up the message to make fifteen minute transcriptions, dealing with both general and special phases of our informational campaigns. These programs sent to local stations and played at the proper times of day will get our message to the special audience I have spoken of. I suggest two programs.

A. *Run, Hitler, Run* (Negro). Once a week for 13 weeks. The master of ceremonies might be Willie Johnson of the Golden Gate Quartette and this quartet, which has a tremendous following both Negro and white, in the South, should provide the linking [of] musical material from week [to week]. Two other Negro singing stars should appear on each show with specially prepared songs or sermons. At a preliminary budget conference it was estimated that this show would cost not more than $3000 for the 13 weeks.

B. *The U.S. Cannonball* (Hillbilly). Once a week for 13 weeks. The master of ceremonies might be Woody Guthrie, who has an amazing facility both as a writer, a singer and a composer of songs. His contribution each week can keep the program up to date. Here again one or two local stars should appear each week with specially composed songs and (or) stories. Here again the budget was estimated at about $3000 for the 13 wks. It might be remarked that this show could well have an almost national use, hill-billy music being popular all over the U.S.

With these two shows I think we could stimulate parallel activity at the local station level all over the country so that after the 13 weeks period this activity would be continued elsewhere. I believe the Bureau of Special Operations would consent to my devoting a lot of my time to the overall project.

III. A possible substitute for this approach comes to mind, which might be a little more complicated, but which might produce similar results. Special scripts might be written along these lines, containing the texts and attaching the lead sheets of the tunes of the songs, and these scripts mailed to a selected list of stations for local production. One advantage here is that more home-town talent would be brought into the picture with the attendant stimulation of local interest and activity in this field. The production disadvantages are obvious.

IV. A second alternative or perhaps addition to the plan lies in the possibility by doing a station by station job. This would involve my going to key stations through the South, working out programs of the type discussed with them, getting the shows started and leaving the job up to the local initiative. Follow up activity in furnishing directions and specially written material, would, of course, be necessary. Some arrangement might be made to have the locally developed material sent to Washington and from that point distributed to other participating stations. The problems here are too obvious to mention. This job should be done in any case, but would be tremendously facilitated if a good series of transcriptions had already been distributed as a model.

In closing I cannot overemphasize the importance of the general approach suggested here. It is one of the few ways that we have of getting at the heart of the Southern situation. It provides the quickest way of getting to an otherwise nearly unreachable group of Americans. I hope it will be possible for me to talk these matters over with the proper people at the regional meeting. In presenting this series of ideas to you, I have the full [space] of Robert Martin and Milton Starr as well as my own Bureau Chief. [ALC]

1943

While busy with his job in the Bureau of Special Operations at the OWI and waiting to be drafted, Alan contacted Vance Randolph on January 9 about the difficulties of obtaining Rosenwald Foundation funding:

I have been staging an uphill and, I am sorry to say, losing fight on the matter of the fellowships. There seems to be no way for me to get the government to ask for an exemption to be made in the gas and tire rationing regulations for the fellowship plan. Since that is true, it looks like the kind of wide-ranging folklore collecting we want to do is out for the duration. If, however, you already have plans in which I could help you, you know I'd back you up to the hilt.[137] [ALC]

That same day, January 9, he explained his concerns to William Pipes in Ann Arbor, Michigan:

I have been much delayed in preparing the fellowship application for Rosenwald because I had first to find out whether gas and tires could be had for your work except by approach to local boards. It appears that I will not be able to arrange for anyone to apply from Washington in behalf of these fellowships and so I have had to revise my plans considerably. It may be that this necessary delay will bring my letter to Rosenwald too late. If that is so, please understand that I have been pushing this whole matter just as hard as I could, but the wheels of government sometimes grind slowly.

I am, by the way, suggesting to Rosenwald that in view of the gas and tire situation, each fellow confine his work to a complete study of the folklore of one county against the background of the social history of the county. From what I have heard from you, that sort of project would interest you a good deal. I figured that you could get around in a rural area without needing to use a car very much, somewhere in Mississippi, Alabama, or Louisiana. What's your reaction? [ALC]

A similar January 9 letter went to John Vincent in Bowling Green, Kentucky:

I've been trying to arrange to get a gas and tire rationing ruling in connection with my application for you to Rosenwald. I was not successful in this. Therefore, I have written Rosenwald Foundation, saying that it looked like my plan in this connection was not a practical one. If, however, I could back up an application you wish to make on your own, you know I would be fully behind you. This hurts me at least as much as it does you, since I had set my heart on having some sort of folklore collecting go on during the war, and since I felt that the people in the field could be of great use to the Office of War Information. If you bump into any local songs or other folklore that has wartime significance, such material would be very useful to me. I hope you're east some time, or I'm west, and we can get together again for a good talkfest. I've seen Jo and she seems to be right peart. [ALC]

Alan repeated to Willis James in Atlanta much of the content of his letters to Pipes and Vincent that same day, but then had some suggestions:

Your comment on the existence of wartime songs and folklore in Georgia interests me a great deal. This type of material, it seems to me, has great importance for the war effort and should be collected. I should like to enlist your voluntary assistance in gathering and sending to me as much of this sort of thing as you can find. It can have a wide variety of uses and I cannot overstress its importance. Would you be willing to do this and to keep up a correspondence with me from time to time about these matters? [ALC]

But on January 23 Alan informed Pipes that there were still some funding possibilities:

I talked to Haygood of the Rosenwald Foundation over the phone the other night and he told me that I could still send in the applications for the two or three fellowships I am still interested in. I will get to this within the next week. Naturally, I am glad that we didn't go past the deadline. [ALC]

From January into March Alan compiled a series of proposals for various government officials regarding his ideas for radio programs to support the war effort. For example, on January 25 he wrote to Louis Cowan, who had initiated *The Quiz Kids* radio show and was now head of the radio program bureau of the Atlantic office of the OWI's overseas branch:

Douglas Meservey[138] called me this morning and asked me to write you in detail about the two transcriptions of American wartime folk songs I am planning. These transcriptions are intended to get war information to poor whites and Negroes all over this country. They will contain topical songs about the enemy, the United Nations, the fighting fronts, rationing, the necessity for sacrifice, etc. These songs will be composed and sung by the leading juke box and Southern radio artists, Negro and White, by Negro ministers, Negro choirs, cowboy singers, etc. They will be recorded in various studies across the country on a commission basis—songs for one week in Nashville, songs for the following week in Dallas, etc. The continuity for each show will be done by a singing commentator, who will tie the songs, sermons, etc., into the theme of the week. These shows will be sent to local stations throughout the country where there is a (1) rural or poor white audience, or (2) a Negro audience.

About half of the finished shows will be useful without change for outpost work, I believe. Perhaps certain of the other shows will not be useful because they will deal with domestic problems. Always, however, a great part of the material I can record in the field will be useable for outpost work. In many instances I will find songs, etc., in the field which will not be pertinent for the domestic shows, but which I can take down for your use. In those songs, stories, sermons, etc., which I will collect, the American people from all over the country will speak their sentiments about the war, they will express their fighting spirit, their will to win and their belief in democratic ideals. In this way the English and Australian audiences will come into direct and warm contact with the people of their country; the troops will learn from the lips of favorite singing stars that their country is behind them with spirit and resolve; the foreign language audience will hear fighting sentiments put in folk form, which because it is simple and old, is one way we can communicate with them directly.

The budget Mr. Meservey has given me breaks down as follows: For two 15-minute transcriptions a week, one using Negro material, the other with folk white: [the total is $7,810.00] . . . These programs should be on the air by the first of March and, therefore, this budget will carry the two shows until the last week of May. I should like then to carry the programs on for 26 more weeks and I hope you will be able to plan accordingly. [ALC][139]

He next gave details to Louis Cowan, Robert Blakely, Douglas Meservey, and Archibald MacLeish about OWI radio programs for overseas broadcasts, on January 25:

After talking with Cellie, with Picard, and with Ferris of your office, I feel I can make some definite suggestions on the subject of musical recordings for the outposts. 1. MUSIC FOR OUTPOSTS ALREADY IN OPERATION. A. *The Near East.* There are a number of good Syrian singers and musicians in Boston and New York who are good enough to be broadcast for the Near Eastern audience. They will probably have to be paid for their work, but they are not accustomed to the American union scale. Mr. Alan who runs the only Syrian recording company in this country, is anxious to work on this project, bring the singers together, and possibly put the best material on commercial records for use in this country and abroad. Perhaps we should help him get foreign distribution since the content of the songs will be pro-Ally and anti-Axis. We can depend upon the material being completely acceptable since a number of the people at the Syrian-Arabian desk are recognized poets in their tongue.

I have hit upon a couple of ideas which will serve to link Syrian music with music of the Western hemisphere. In the first place, their style of violin playing and singing is quite close to our purest, oldest, and most primitive American mountain singing. Records of this type are available in the Library of Congress, and a useful tie-up could be made there. While the Near East does not particularly favor our marches and our most sophisticated jazz, they have been much influenced by modern American popular music, particularly by that from South America. They have many songs in rhumba and tango tempo. Their rumbas and tangoes played in conjunction with our own would point out an additional link between the two worlds.

B. *South Africa.* Josef Marais[140] has expressed great interest in obtaining recordings of Dutch songs performed by Dutch-Americans. He wishes to show how cultural integration proceeds peaceably in our American democracy. Good records of this type can be obtained in various parts of the country and I am working up a list of singers and contacts in this field.

C. *Iceland.* It seems logical to make the point to our Icelandic hosts in Iceland that Icelanders in this country continue to live their own lives in their own way if they want to. This can be done, to a large extent, by the use of Icelandic records made in the United States and Canada. A list of key people in this field is being prepared for potential recording.

D. *French Broadcasts.* Mr. Picard expressed interests in building shows around French folk music recorded in various parts of the United States and Canada. A good deal of this material is already available on records; songs from Quebec, from Michigan, from Illinois, from Louisiana, and the gaps can be filled in easily. According to Mr. Picard, good records of pro-democratic French patriotic music, such as the *Marseillaise* and the *Carmagnole,* are not purchasable. He intimated that he could use records of good French marches, if well performed, along with national songs of this kind. I believe this sort of recording could be easily set up with the Marine Band, or one of the other military musical organizations. E. The material in *English* is covered in the first part of this memorandum.

II. MUSIC FOR OUTPOSTS NOT YET IN OPERATION. In connection with my study of foreign minority music and the music of the United Nations, I am discovering a large number of well qualified singing organizations in this country in all of the European languages. These people can be recorded at various points in the United States singing their old folk songs (to show that we have a truly democratic culture in which every group can follow its own tastes and inclinations), singing pro-democratic anti-Fascist songs, which will, in turn, express the determination of these groups to lick the Nazis, win the war, and bring freedom to their own homelands. Mr. Marrow feels that we should proceed to record a certain amount of this material now, since at any time it may become extremely useful to outpost work. In the meantime, such songs might be of occasional use in very brief excerpts for shortwave.

The idea of my doing recording which will be of use to Domestic or to Overseas or to both, meets with the approval of my Bureau Chief. I should think that with two or three thousand dollars, a good deal of good recording could be done. This sum, however, would serve to keep the project going for six months and is, in addition to the sum covered in the first half of this memorandum. [ALC]

He followed up to Alan Cranston and Lee Falk[141] on February 4 regarding his thoughts on Music for Foreign Language Broadcasts Over Domestic Stations, as part of his work for the Division of Educational Services:

At the risk of reviewing a situation with which you are already familiar, I want to present some of the salient facts on the musical content of domestic foreign language programs. These remarks are based on the [Paul] Lazarfeld study of two years ago, and on a recent series of interviews with the monitors of the Federal Communications Commission. Naturally the following generalizations do not apply to blanket fashion to all languages and to all individual programs, but point out the over-all pattern. Further detailed treatment would be necessary as background for specific action in each language field.

(1) The proportion of time devoted to music on foreign language broadcasts is even greater than on our English language broadcasts: varying from 60 to 90 percent, averaging more than 70 percent. The music is about 85 percent national. Commercial advertisers have therefore found national music the most effective way of reaching and holding the foreign language audience.

(2) The music consists largely of sentimental, nostalgic, popular songs in the foreign language of the broadcast. The general effect of the music with its accompanying announcements is to stir up in the foreign-born listener sentimental and unreal memories of the country of his origin.

(3) By and large there is: (a) No use made of the songs of liberty and the democratic tradition of each country. (b) Little use made of existing anti-Axis songs, pro-Ally songs, or of music which would serve to arouse enthusiasm for the war. (c) Little use made of patriotic American music or of American song in translation. (d) Little use made of Americanized versions of foreign language music. (e) No use made of songs as a means of putting over important slogans and war information.

(4) In the case of Italian and German programs the practices described in (2) and (3) seem to be intentional; in other languages these practices are not consistently followed and seem to be the result of carelessness and lack of resources.

(5) The music is largely recorded and comes from the following sources: (a) Records imported from abroad—little new material has been available for a year. (b) Records manufactured by American companies—very few new records have been released since August and the number continues to be small due to shellac shortages and other production problems. (c) Transcriptions— this business is as yet undeveloped in the foreign language field.

The next result of this program pattern is, very probably, negative, both so far as the war effort and national unity are concerned. The pattern should and must be altered along certain definite lines in order to help to better integrate the foreign groups into the war effort and into our national life. Conferences with many people concerned in the foreign language music field have convinced me that this is a strategic time for action. No new records have been available to the stations for months. The stocks in the recording companies and the record stores are completely exhausted. New records are snapped up as soon as they are ready. *If the OWI can produce or motivate the production of recordings of foreign language records now, we can capture a very great proportion of this broadcast time, because the records and programs will be used over and over. Under the present Petrillo ruling government musical programs are the only ones that can be produced on transcription.* Even when the Petrillo ban is lifted, the planning of such programs and record releases should be followed and guided closely.

Lists of carefully evaluated traditional songs and musical selections are being prepared in each language. There are excellent composers, translators, singers and performers available in each language field for production of new, and adaptation of old, material. The recording companies, the foreign language music publishers and the transcription companies are ready to cooperate, they assure me. I cannot, therefore, too strongly recommend that the Office of War Information launch or motivate the launching of an extensive program in the field of foreign language music to aid in the war effort and as a means of carrying war information to the foreign language groups. Programs should be constructed giving: (1) The songs of freedom and the music associated with the democratic movements of each country. (2) Contemporary anti-Fascist and fighting songs from each country. (3) Topical songs about America and the American war effort in each language. (4) Americanized foreign language music and foreign folk and popular songs made in America. (5) A certain increment of American popular, folk and martial music translated or re-interpreted for the foreign language groups.

These programs can be used to interpret the democratic tradition of each country and its connection with America and our fight against Hitler. The topical songs can carry out the objectives of official OWI wartime campaigns. Additional money must be found for the foreign language section to take care of these programs. If the money is not forthcoming within the OWI, the following possibilities might be fruitfully investigated:

(1) Collaboration with the Treasury Department. They, I understand, are contemplating work in this field. The Department of Justice might also be approached for sponsorship. (2) Application for funds to the Rockefeller Foundation, which, as I understand it, has recently concerned itself much with regional cultural programs. Other foundations, unity councils, etc.,

might be approached. (3) Sponsorship and guidance of program production by the transcription companies. Due to recent material restrictions, and because of the Petrillo ban, they might welcome the opportunity to do government programs for a time. (See attached letters.) (4) With the recording companies, suggesting types of materials for their use. R.C.A. Victor, Continental Records, Columbia, have already asked our advice. Attached is a letter from Mr. Gabor of Continental Records, which represents the first practical step in the direction of the construction of these programs. I hope you will find these proposals important enough to consider them for immediate action. [ALC]

Alan continued his contact with Willis James on February 6:

I have just written a long letter to William Haygood of Rosenwald Foundation, suggesting three fellowships and yours is one of the names included. I sent him copies of excerpts of your letters to me giving your record and your interest in collecting wartime folklore. I have high hopes that something will come of this application. The wartime Negro songs and stories that you are apparently gathering on your own initiative would be of great use to this office and I would be very greatly interested to see them as soon as you could send me copies. In the first place, they will provide interesting material for our survey of Negro folk opinion about the war, and second, some of them may be actually useful for wide distribution over the radio, etc. One way you will make your contribution to the war effort, whether or not these fellowship plans go through, is by continuing to work with my division as a correspondent on Negro wartime folklore. Let me know what you think about this and send me the songs as soon as you can. [ALC]

Also on February 6 he wrote to Joseph Brandt, president of the University of Oklahoma:

Henry Allen was kind enough to send me a manuscript of James [William] Pipes. I read it with great interest and excitement and have sent it on to William Haygood of the Rosenwald Foundation for his inspection. Would you be kind enough to give me Mr. Pipes' address so that I can correspond with him directly. [ALC]

Two days later, February 8, he described his expansive plans to William Haygood at the Rosenwald Foundation:

Wartime restrictions on travel, materials, equipment, etc. have operated to alter completely the plans I discussed with you several months ago for wartime folklore research in the South. Vance Randolph of Arkansas, John Vincent of Kentucky and Lewis Chappell of West Virginia, whom I thought could make contributions in the field of southern white folklore, have been dropped from my list because their projects require a good deal of travel. Bess Lomax is busy at OWI, Overseas Branch. The Library of Congress has greatly restricted its activity. My suggestions for fellowships have, therefore, been narrowed down to three people. Each one of these people can, I believe, operate under wartime conditions, make a valuable scholarly or cultural contribution and be of considerable help in my work in the Office of War Information.

Perhaps I should first say something on this latter point. The Office of War Information has few contacts which enable it to gauge the wartime problems and opinions of folk groups, especially in the South. Folklorists can make a valuable contribution by documenting, as only they are equipped to do, oral opinion on wartime matters. Further than that, wartime songs, stories, and sermons will be useful to me in constructing radio programs and other information bearing material aimed at the South. I am setting up a plan by which folk comment on the war will come to the Office of War Information, play a part in our evaluation of informational problems in general, make a contribution in terms of slogans, songs, etc. to our various information campaigns and go back to the Southern folk group over the radio, through the churches, etc. Thus, the people will help to explain the war and war issues for themselves in the peculiarly eloquent language of which they are past masters.

The fellows I am about to suggest are admirably equipped to assist in this plan. I have, by the way, discussed this approach with [Arthur F.] Raper, Margaret Mead, Lewis Jones and many others interested in the whole question of developing a better understanding of wartime issues among isolated groups of Americans. 1) *William Harrison Pipes*, University of Michigan. . . . Mr. Pipes was recommended to me by President [Horace Mann] Bond of Fort Valley State College. My correspondence with him has encouraged me to believe that he is a competent and intelligent folklorist. He wishes to make a study of the modern Negro Holiness Church in the South. As you know, this group since about 1890 has grown rapidly all over the United States, attracting membership from the more staid Negro congregations, carrying forward and elaborating the traditional patterns of the Negro folk church. In this church or, one might say, galaxy of churches, the members continue to sing old time shouting spirituals, to manifest their conversion by speaking in tongues and by prophecy, etc., to shout in the aisles and to become possessed in the traditional pattern of the West African Negro. Very little, however, is known about the actual structure and history of this religious group, its relationship to other church groups, and its general effect on life in the Negro community. I know, of course, of the excellent WPA study in Chicago. Mr. Pipes' work in the South will supplement this and complete the picture.

Mr. Pipes, by working in Memphis where Elder Mason, the head of the largest of these groups flourishes, and by carrying his investigation out through the Mississippi Valley region will, in a year, be equipped to describe this extremely significant group, which, in a sense, represents the folk Negro's attempt to adjust his oral religious tradition to the needs and pressures of modern living. At the same time, he could be of enormous service to me in collecting wartime folklore and possibly even in contacting church leaders in regard to war information problems. His fellowship might well amount to $2,500 so that he would have funds for recording and a certain amount of travel.

2) *Professor Willis James* . . . has been highly recommended to me by both Sterling Brown and William Bond, and his letters have been full of interesting comments on the folk group of his region. He wishes to carry out a study of wartime folklore in the same region in which he has worked successfully for a number of years, namely, Central and Southern Georgia. This is an area from which we have few recordings of Negro folk songs and such records would make a valuable contribution to the files of the Library of Congress. If Mr. James could come to Washington some time this Spring, he and I could develop a plan which would serve to greatly expand our present knowledge of Southern Negro folk music and aid in the wartime program I have suggested above. His fellowship might amount to $2,500 to cover recording expenses in his area and a certain amount of travel.

3) *Woodrow Wilson Guthrie* is, so far as I know, a unique figure in American literature. First of all, he is a genuine folk poet, the kind of person who created our cowboy and lumberjack ballads. He has written numerous ballads and songs, so completely true to the idiom of the South and Southwest, that they at once become a part of the general tradition of folk literature. About two and a half years ago I encouraged him to write a book about his life. This book has developed into an extremely serious full-length novel, or fictionalized autobiography, which is to be published by Dutton's this month. It has the quality of real greatness about it, both in the broad sweep of its ideas, in the accuracy and incisiveness of its regional detail, and in its truly remarkable rhythmic prose. Mr. Guthrie wants to travel around the south and write a book about what is happening to the migrants in wartime. He has the equipment, I believe, of a major American writer. So far as I am concerned, he could serve as an invaluable informant on folk opinion and wartime folklore among the poor whites of the area. He is a voluminous correspondent, a guitar player who can attract other singers as an equal, and his comments on the war, whether in terms of documentation, ballads, or stories, will be a real contribution to American culture. I strongly suggest that you get in touch with him at once and look at some of his songs and at least a portion of his

new novel. He deserves all the encouragement that anyone can give him. His fellowship might amount to $2,000 which would provide for travel.

Stetson Kennedy,[142] whose plan you sent me for review a few days ago can be of great help to me in gathering wartime folklore. The records, song-manuscripts, etc. gathered by all these individuals should be filed permanently in the Archive of American Folk Song of the Library of Congress. Benjamin Botkin, of the Archive of American Folk Song, could be of great help in advising these fellows and the Library could and, doubtless, will be able to offer assistance in other ways. I am returning to you, herewith, the fellowship forms which you were kind enough to give me some months ago. I shall use these names during the year as sources of information. Enclosed also is a file of material on a Mr. James [William] Pipes, sent to me by Henry Allen Moe of Guggenheim. I thought perhaps you would be interested in looking it over. When you have finished it, would you be so kind as to forward it on to Mr. Moe. If you should like to have additional information on the projects I have covered in my letter, let me know. I hope they meet with favorable consideration of yourself and your Board. [ALC][143]

Alan's attempt to use records in the Southwest hit another snag with the American Federation of Musicians, which was striking against the record companies. He explained the situation to Victor Borella of the Office of the Coordinator of Inter-American Affairs in Washington on February 9:

After the conference at which you, Mr. Siepmann, Mr. Lopez, and I discussed the use of corridos as information carriers in the Southwest to the Spanish-Americans, I contacted the WPB [War Production Board] officials and Mr. Demitriades. The WPB people in charge of rationing shellac said they would be glad to consider an application from Victor for a definitely specified amount of shellac, and would refer this application to yours and Mr. [Alan] Cranston's offices when it came. I thereupon conferred further with Mr. Demitriades and he agreed to record a group of corridos under a number of the suggested titles prepared by Mr. Lopez. He felt sure that the American Federation of Musicians would agree to allow this recording to be done in New York, thus considerably speeding up the whole operation.

Three days later, Mr. Demitriades called me to say that the A.F. of M. had not only refused to allow the recording to be done in New York, but had said that records made in Mexico would be regarded as bootleg by the A.F. of M. if they received commercial distribution in the United States, and that if such records were made and distributed, Victor would be placed on the A.F. of M.'s blacklist.

Perhaps this matter did not come up for consideration with top union officials. Frankly, I doubt if it did. I should think that in view of the wartime necessity for publishing informational corridos on commercial records to reach small-town and rural illiterate Mexicans, that the A.F. of M. might allow these songs to be recorded and used on juke boxes, radio stations, etc. in spite of its general ruling. Perhaps you could look into this phase of the matter. In the meantime, it has occurred to me that we might start the ball rolling by building transcribed radio programs of wartime Mexican songs for distribution in the Southwest and possibly in South America. There are a number of conditions which might make this maneuver extremely successful: (a) since production of commercial phonograph records and commercial transcriptions were stopped by [James] Petrillo in August, local stations are starved for recorded music; and (b) the A.F. of M. will permit music to be recorded for government radio programs. I, therefore, would like to recommend the following two types of shows:

1) A half-hour program to be called *United We Sing*, consisting of anti-Axis songs, pro-democratic songs and military marches from all of the Latin-American countries. These records should be, if possible, recorded in various places in Latin-America, flown to New York and dubbed together with the appropriate commentary. In that way, the final dubbed record could then be distributed to all the Latin-American countries and used heavily over the Southwestern stations. For South America it would be a stirring and emotion arousing presentation of the united front of the western hemisphere. For the Southwest it would be convincing evidence of the progress of the Pan-American idea and would serve, I believe, to greatly hearten Latin-Americans in that area and perhaps, by influence, do the Anglo listeners a lot of good.

2) *Corridos de la Guerra*. This program should be constructed of purely Mexican topical songs dealing with the war effort and taking up wartime problems one by one. Here again, the records could be made in San Antonio, Tucson, Albuquerque, Los Angeles and Mexico City, and present a round-up of Mexican singers in those centers. This would give a feeling of Southwest-wide participation in the program. Through this program the whole Mexican audience would be kept informed, in a style highly acceptable to them, of the week by week necessity of the war effort and of wartime problems.

If possible, this program should be prepared in strip form, that is, with all the songs for one program in strips on one record and the announcements on another disc. In the first presentation of the program, the announcements and songs could be run off to make an entire fifteen-minute program. Later on the songs could be separately used to build other programs in the station, thus providing for the repetition of the best and most pertinent of the material. I would greatly appreciate your taking up these matters with the proper persons in the Coordinator's office. I can assure you of the interest of the Office of War Information in them and our anxiety to see that something is done in this field. [ALC]

The next day, February 10, Alan presented a progress report to his superiors at the Bureau of Special Operations:

1) United Nations Song Collection. a) A large number of critically selected fighting songs, underground songs, freedom songs, etc., from all the United Nations, have been gathered by Mrs. Jakobson and myself. Arrangements have been made with the British Broadcasting Corporation, the Coordinator of Inter-American Affairs and Overseas OWI for this collection to be constantly supplemented as new material is produced abroad. b) A special subcommittee of the Music Educators National Conference has been set up by Lilla Belle Pitts to examine the collection ready by the end of the month. Letters will go to all the music publishers from this committee, recommending the publication of this material. The result, I hope, will be a national songbook or two sponsored by MENC for use in all school and community song work during 1943. c) The collection in my office will form a library invaluable for radio use to OWI, War Department Radio Section, etc.

2) Music for Domestic Language Radio. A survey has been made of the music used on present day foreign language radio programs in this country. Musical programs are perhaps the best way to reach the foreign language audience. A lengthy report with recommendations has been submitted. A foreign language recording company has offered to completely finance three thirteen-week series in Polish, German and Italian, under our direction, and this matter is being investigated. All the commercial recording companies have indicated their willingness to produce special records for juke boxes at our behest, but until the dispute between the American Federation of Musicians and the commercial recording business is settled, nothing can be done.

3) Louis Cowan, director of Outpost work in the Overseas Branch, has expressed interest in recording special wartime music for us through his Overseas facilities. I have sent him a memo at his suggestion on this subject. Note: Mrs. Jakobson has applied for a Guggenheim fellowship and I have high hopes of her getting it. If she does, she will be able to work as full time consultant on foreign language music for OWI.

4) Arrangements have been made with the Radio Bureau to do two fifteen minute transcriptions for them aimed (a) at the folk white, and (b) at the folk Negro. I have assembled a great deal of material for these programs and have made arrangements to obtain more. The Radio Bureau has asked

Overseas for the funds to pay production costs on these programs. We have been promised an answer this week. Even if Overseas does not make these funds available, the Radio Bureau has set aside money for one program and that will be under way at the end of the month.

5) Plans for recording special music (both English and foreign language) for Overseas outpost use have been extensively discussed with the New York staff. I have written Louis Cowan, setting forth my ideas and requesting that the funds for work be put at my disposal. I am told I will have an answer this week.

6) Traveling tent show theaters. A plan for using the traveling rep show theaters (which reach rural and small town groups in the Middle West and Southwest) as distributors of wartime information, is being developed. Contact is being made with writers and managers in this field. A subcommittee to produce special material for these groups and to steer this activity has been set up by the Writers War Board, under the direction of Robert Landry.

7) Several of the American wartime folk songs collected by this office are being used in the Treasury Department's song sheet which will be printed in an edition of a million for community War Bond sings all over the country. The Red Cross has asked us to prepare a booklet of twenty of these songs for use in their overseas recreation activity.

8) I have helped the Special Service Section of the Bureau of Intelligence in preparation of their study of Negro opinion. This collaboration will continue as the work progresses, particularly in regard to radio programs, word of mouth transmission of opinion and the Negro church as agents of moulding Negro opinion. Lewis Jones, who is on the steering committee of this study, was appointed at my suggestion. The radio study was incorporated as a result of my insistence, after I spent considerable time developing a separate study of this medium.

9) I have asked the Radio Bureau to try to get a Negro newscaster on the air in Norfolk, Virginia, as an experiment in building a better informed intelligent Negro opinion on wartime matters. The project has been approved by the Bureau and the possibilities are being investigated by their regional representative. William Cooper has a commentator ready to go to Norfolk.

10) A proposal has been made to the Rosenwald Foundation to put on three special fellows to collect wartime folklore and advise on Southern problems. *PROJECTED ACTIVITIES* All the above mentioned activities will continue during the next three months, at least. In connection with them, I will make trips to New York, one trip to Chicago, one swing through the South. In addition, I hope (1) to be able to launch a campaign in conjunction with Liam O'Connor to use the white and Negro folk churches of the South as information distributing centers; (2) set up a correspondence panel of

folklorists and others who know the folk mind, to advise me on special problems; (3) work out an informational program with Federal Security Agency, department of Agriculture and other agencies dealing with rural people, for better reaching these groups with war information. [ALC]

Alan continued to have hope about the Rosenwald grant, so he had this letter sent by his secretary to William Pipes on February 13:

Enclosed is a set of application blanks which should be filled out and mailed to Rosenwald by air mail *immediately*, as time is very short. I am also enclosing an excerpt of Mr. Lomax's letter to Mr. Haygood, Director for Fellowships, of Rosenwald, for your interest. Mr. Lomax is in the hospital for a few days. He send you his regards and hopes that things will work out well. [ALC][144]

Alan's secretary also sent this message to William Haygood on February 13:

Thank you for your nice letter. The application blanks have gone out to the people concerned with a plea for speed. Mr. Lomax is in the hospital for a few days. He was very happy to see your letter and sends you his best regards. He, too, hopes to get a chance to see you before the army claims you. [ALC]

And yet another was sent on February 13, from Alan to Woody Guthrie:

Enclosed is a copy of all them nice words Alan said about you to Haygood of Rosenwald. Thought you might like to see it. Fill out the enclosed application blanks and mail them air mail *pronto* to Rosenwald Fund, as time is short and of the essence. Alan was glad to see your letter. It was nice, and short, and certainly to the point. Didja ever get my package? Just thought I'd ask. [ALC]

The Rosenwald grant appeared stalled, and so Alan wrote to Willis James on March 3:

A telegram came this morning from the Rosenwald Foundation, saying that they have not yet received your application for a fellowship. I have been somewhat disturbed that you have not written me about this matter and now it seems that if the application is not in to them this week, that it will have come too late. I hope you will see your way to doing something about this at once. I saw Lewis Jones yesterday and he said that he was going down to the [Fort Valley Folk] Festival. I am going to be awfully sorry to miss it. Please give my kindest regards to Dr. Bond. [ALC]

Alan was brimming with ideas but got scant financial support, which fueled his anxiety.
He wrote to William Lewis of the OWI about his concerns on March 12:

Last September you and I discussed the problems of racial tension in the
South and its relation to the war effort. We spoke of the urgent necessity of
reaching rural Negroes and whites with the facts about the war, not only in
order to keep them informed, but also in an attempt to undercut the race
issue by raising the more important issues of the war. We agreed that getting
to these groups at their own level, in their language and through their own
media—local radio programs, rural churches, etc.—was the best way to go
about the job.

On the basis of that conversation and a subsequent conversation with
Lyman Bryson, OWI hired me. It hired me to plan ways of getting information to special groups, isolated by poverty, lack of education, etc. These
groups are special only in the sense that they are not to be reached through
conventional informational channels, but not in the sense that they are small
or unimportant or in any wise a minor part of America. In fact, they make
up the rank and file of industry, agriculture and the armed forces in this
country.

Recently I have heard that you, among others at the head of the Domestic
Branch, have begun to feel that it is not OWI's job to attempt to reach these
special groups with war information. This development has disturbed me
deeply and, if it represents a real tendency, I want to take this opportunity to
speak out strongly against it. We all agree that in order to win this war and
make a decent peace, *all* the people must be kept well informed and must
be made to know that it is their war. The OWI should not, then, fail to reach
those Americans who are isolated by race or nationality or geography or language or lack of education or poverty. To neglect these Americans is not only
undemocratic; in the end it will be dangerous for our country.

The educated and privileged groups, to whom so much of our output is
directed, are in the main so well equipped with dollars and experience that
they will keep themselves informed no matter what we do. But the folks I'm
talking about—an awful lot of the people who build the foundations, plow
the earth, march in the rear rank and raise big families—have fewer sources
of information. Reaching them ought to be one of our biggest jobs, not one
of our smallest. If we don't get to them with the facts, you can feel sure that
they'll get mostly the rumors of war.

These are the folks who listen to anti-Semitic propaganda, who, if we leave
them alone, follow the lead of Negro-baiters, and who are strongly influenced
by Fascist rumors. They make up the rank and file of the Huey Long and

Pass-the-Biscuit-Pappy [W. Lee O'Daniel] movements. They are the people who don't know what the enemy is like and who have little or no understanding of our allies. These people are silent. They sit at the back of the hall and take little part in meetings. Since they are largely unorganized, no one gives an administrative damn about them. If an informational program directed to them gets us into trouble, it can be dropped because no one cared much in the first place. If one or more of these groups is neglected, there will be no repercussions in the press. No radio commentators will discuss the issue. Protesting letters and telegrams will not flood the halls of Congress. But if we don't take the trouble to reach these underprivileged people, the fruits of their ignorance about the issues of this war will continue to ripen.

Under the pressure of wartime problems, these informational blank spots are developing into trouble spots. If we are effective and wise in OWI, we must plan vigorous informational programs for these trouble spots. Like infections in the human body, the trouble in these tension areas cannot be cured by being covered over and forgotten.

Don't leave these vigorous and patriotic Americans out of the picture. Keeping them informed is not a luxury, but a necessity, a privilege and a duty. Their world is changing faster than ours, and, if they are going to play a positive role in the future, they've got to have the background of our times sketched out for them. The effects of our neglect will show up in the way America is able to build for the future.

I'd like to say one thing more. Outside of the yellow press and some Congressmen who wouldn't like us no matter what we did, the OWI is well thought of and respected by the people of the United States. You can go anywhere in the country, as you know, lift up the telephone and introduce yourself as one of Elmer's [Davis] boys and get prompt and friendly assistance on most problems. One of my friends says that people down South react to OWI as if it were a sort of God Voice. That is certainly an extreme opinion, but it points at the truth. The OWI has the confidence of most Americans outside of Washington. It seems to me, therefore, that we should not retreat from positions we hold by conviction.

P.S. I just happened to learn, by chance, that the budget for my Southern transcriptions has been cancelled without anyone having bothered to inform me. After all the sweat and writing that lies behind the acceptance of this show, this seems to be a pretty highhanded and decidedly unfair action. It is also embarrassing. Last week, when the Special Service Section of the Army heard the ballads, they felt strongly that they wanted to record and publish them for all our troops. I agreed to record for them when I went South to record the shows for you people. What'll I tell 'em? [ALC]

He wrote again to Lewis on March 21, expressing his increasing frustration:

I still don't see how you can do the job of reaching underprivileged Americans without (a) budget, (b) planning linked up with the rest of the OWI programs, (c) vigorous administrative backing. Sending out the bulletin you mention to the people whose help we need in reaching these special groups would, I fear, be like throwing into the sea a bottle containing an angry note to Adolf Hitler. In this field one has to work either by example (i.e. transcriptions, church services, etc.) or better, by personal contact. What budgetary considerations seem to have pushed us into is a policy of reaching largely those Americans who are already reached by commercial channels, and of giving them information much of which they'd get anyway. In other words, we are committing ourselves to an information program directed at the middle-class, whereas America is not a middle-class country. Insofar as this is true, we are, for our part, not fighting this war as a people's war nor as humanity's war against tyranny.

My mistake in OWI was that I assume when I was hired that my plans had been approved in advance and that means for immediate action would be provided. This was awfully naïve of me. The failure of my projects has been due as much as anything to my failure to get a hearing for them. I thought that time was too short. I do not now want to continue to feel useless. If there is nothing in OWI for me to do, I want to get out and get closer to the job of killing Fascists. The problems of the South are still there and something might be done if a group of people like Arthur Raper (FSA [Farm Security Administration]), Lewis Jones (OWI), and Don Young (Army Specialist Corps) got together with us and decided on an action program that would get OWI backing. The Southern local station job remains to be tackled, if you can give me the authority to tackle it. But I don't want to just be kept on. If you are convinced nothing can and will be done, let me know, because in that event I want to resign at once. I know you're busy as hell now and I will be too, for about ten days more. Let me hear from you, if possible, by then. [ALC]

Alan's last day at the OWI was April 17, then he was on leave until June 30. He began to devote much of this time to his *Transatlantic Call* CBS/BBC radio programs, as he informed Benjamin Botkin, his successor at the Archive of American Folk Song, in an undated letter sometime in July:

Over Pennsylvania En route, Gallup, N.M. Thanks for your note. The work continues interesting and rewarding, although being away from home hurts. My regards to H[erbert] H[albert]. What is he doing in the army? Let me know how the new records are coming along. And, if any other plans are coming along, I'd always like to hear. About Poppie [John A. Lomax]. He's well worth going after. I don't know that I shall ever stop long enough to see him, but I believe you could work out a co-op recording project with Nick [Ray] at OWI overseas. They need that music for the Caribbean. [ALC][145]

Alan was still shadowed by the FBI. He was described in a report on July 23, 1943 (the last FBI record until 1950):

Neighborhood investigation shows him to be a peculiar individual in that he is only interested in folk lore music, being very temperamental and *ornery*. Moreover: Employee paid his rent when it fell due and enjoyed a reputation of good character. However, he was deemed to be a peculiar individual in that he was always singing peculiar songs of a western or negro type, was always reading books and seemed to be very temperamental, becoming upset at the least provocation and then having an attitude of orneriness and sarcasm. [Lomax FBI file]

He kept in contact with Ben Botkin on November 14:

Would you do me a favor and do something about these letters? I expect to get an advance copy of your book—most anxious to see it. [ALC]

Sometime in November Alan corresponded with Stetson Kennedy, the Florida folklorist and labor organizer, regarding his *Transatlantic Call* radio program recorded in Key West:

My failure to write you hasn't soured you on me, I hope. You will know all when you hear the show. Enough said. Every Conch [worker] walked out on us, the goddam dirty lowdown flopeared [*sic*] crabmannered fascist bastards. Tee Roll [Theodore Rolle] has been drunk for seven days straight. Miss Sawyer turned us down because broadcasting was sinful. And I have spoken to, drunk with, sobered with, shat with, peed with and spat with nine thousand four hundred and eighty-two Conchs by actual count—and got nothing but no for an answer. . . . John is terribly upset, Bacon even is worried, and I am serene, because the Cuban section is as anti-fascist as can be, thanks to a song I dug up—A SECOND FRONT SONG! And CBS has passed it.

Another thing, [Captain John] Singleton tried to rewrite the whole script. And the local newspaper man is spreading wild rumors about us. . . . I wish I could tell you the heartaches and the work we've had to do. Just a bad siege of Conchitis all along. However, I finally caught up with Lije Spencer and he's terrific. Claims to have been drunk for the last 65 years—and sang me songs of the Maine, the Titanic, the lynching of Leo Frank (first anti-Semitic folk

song I've ever heard). . . . I'm going to type up all the notes I got after you left   .
and send them to you. . . . Solidaridad! [ALC][146]

For the remainder of 1943 and into 1944 Alan traveled around the country working on
his radio programs until he joined the Army on April 5, 1944. He was first sent to Camp
Upton on Long Island, then quickly transferred to Camp Crowder, near Neosha, Missouri,
for basic training. By late summer he was transferred to New York and living with Elizabeth
at 67 Perry St. Their daughter, Anne Lyttleton Lomax, was born on November 20. Alan was
back working on radio shows for the Army, including *This Land Is Bright* starting in February 1945, and also shows for the Armed Forces Radio Service (AFRS), beginning with *Bound
for Glory* on January 5, then *Let's Go to Town*, and *Singing Country*. He seemed tired about
doing more folk music shows, feeling the need to go overseas to see the war firsthand, but
also hated to leave his family and safe life in New York.[147]

1945

While absorbed with family and work matters, he remained connected to the Library of
Congress. For example, Private Lomax wrote to Ben Botkin on January 17, 1945:

Have you dropped through a hole in the Washington ice or have you given up
the idea of coming to New York or what? Let us hear—a post card from such
a busy man to such busy folks. News with us is that the baby is a charmer
and married life is really wonderful. You can do me a couple of kindnesses. 1)
Send me all the Jelly Roll material. It's in a couple of binders, maybe in a box,
consists of typewritten transcripts and lots of penciled notes of mine. I'll type
out the penciled notes and send the Library a copy eventually. I'm beginning
to want to do something with that material now. 2) Look around and see if
you can't find bound sets of my School of the Air and Back Where I Come
From scripts for CBS. I'm starting a folk song series for the army and I need
these scripts constantly in this job. The sets on your shelves belong to me,—
when I left them there I just didn't have any place to put them. [ALC][148]

In July he was transferred from his position with the AFRS and his apartment in New
York to Camp Lee, in Virginia. He was back in basic training, then expected to be sent to
Special Service Training, the entertainment branch of the Army, which he thought to have
very low priority among the military brass. He was close enough to New York, however, to
visit with the family each weekend.[149]

With the war now over (as of early August), but still stuck in the Army, Alan began thinking of life as a civilian, as he wrote to Harold Spivacke at the Library of Congress, in early
September:

Thanks for your kind letter. It will be very pleasant to have a full set of AAFS [Archive of American Folk Song] records, if, for no other reason, that they remind me of the many pleasant and fantastic things that went to make up a folklorist's life. I have played through the first group of discs hastily (our phonograph is on the blink) and it struck me that they were not all up to snuff acoustically. As for the selection, I am afraid that Ben didn't know the material too well. Still they are the most interesting group of records published in America in 1945 and should (and will, eventually) be recognized as such.

Perhaps you may be interested to know something about Special Service, since you helped to set it up. The truth is that for some considerable time neither the officers or cadre have tried to do more than keep up appearances. A good deal of attention is paid to certain military formalities; a great deal to getting out of the army—and the classes are a laugh. Usually the instructors are frauds and candid enough to tell us to go to sleep and stay that way till the next period. Nevertheless, the periods, the marching around, the lack of privacy make it difficult (impossible for the most of the boys) to do any work.

As for me, I am spending two to four hours a day, studying music. At the moment I have started from scratch with the guitar—doing scales, exercises, as well as working out accompaniments for my own stuff. Perhaps in six weeks I might be fairly useful as a performer wherever they send me. As soon as the guitar begins to come a bit easier, I shall start to study sight singing. Maybe when they "let go their holts on me," I'll know a little about music.

Apparently men of my age and condition are slated to be in the army from six months to a year and a half more. I have about 30 points and can be shipped overseas. So far as I am concerned, however, the war is over and I want to get out and get back to work. If I can't get clear out right now, I'd like to get into some job as near home or as near my own field of interest as I can. It occurred to me today that you might be able to give me a hand:

a) Have me requested for some sort of higher priority job. b) Have me requisitioned for some kind of job (in uniform) in Washington or New York City. 1) per Major Soltir, whom I have met and who apparently likes me. 2) per Frank (?) ([illegible] asst.). 3) perhaps as some sort of specialist in folk song and documentary records in L.C. There is a lot of cleaning up there in AAFS that I'd like to do on my own and father's stuff—and maybe I could help get the new wartime collections whipped into shape. Well, let me know what you think. After 6 weeks or so it will be goodbye Lomax for quite a stretch. And I really *don't* want that to happen. Regards to the boys and gals. [ALC]

Spivacke responded on September 11:

You may rest assured that I shall bear the matter in mind and if anything turns up let you know at once. [ALC]

By mid-November Alan was back living at 67 Perry Street, but still in the Army.[150] As the year ended, and he remained in the Army, he wrote on December 28 to Duncan Emrich, who had recently replaced Botkin as head of the Archive of American Folk Song:

Just to remind you that I am urgently in need of additional material for my Guggenheim application. To wit: 1) A statistical and briefly descriptive summary of the collections brought into the Archive under my aegis—whether these were duplication jobs like the Barbeau material or field expeditions undertaken for us by other people. 2) The total number of folk song records in the Archive (approximate). The states and countries covered by the present collection. If you do not have the time to prepare this material for me, send me the annual reports covering the years from 1933 to the present and I'll dig out my own information and send the reports back. [ALC]

Although stuck in the Army, he was not forgotten by the mainstream press, as folk music remained of some interest. For example, he was quoted in a *Time* article, "Miserable but Exciting Songs," in late November 1945: "Lomax, now a hefty Army private, disapproves of his own twangy Texas voice, uses it constantly to sell the Archive. . . . When he gets out of the Army he hopes to take American folk songs to Russia, bring back Soviet ballads. The Russians, he says, use folk songs to make their minorities feel better and we should do that too."[151]

Alan was finally released from the Army (and the government) at the beginning of March 1946 and he quickly plunged into various projects, while living in New York. Pete Seeger, Lee Hays, Woody Guthrie, and their friends had launched People's Songs, a progressive musical organization, the last day of 1945, which quickly attracted Alan. He soon began to host their midnight concerts. He received a $3,000 Guggenheim fellowship in April 1946, in order to pursue his writing, and began producing folk music albums for Decca Records. Alan continued to work closely with his father, and they published another song book, *Folk Song: USA*, in 1947. Anxious to return to radio, his Mutual network program, *Your Ballad Man*, began in 1948, featuring a variety of music recordings. Until his move to England in 1950—he would not return until 1958—he continued to be very productive, although he had mostly abandoned any fieldwork. But he would never again be a public employee.[152]

Notes

Letters, 1935–1938

1. An article on John and Alan appeared in the *Austin American*, October 6, 1932: "Following in the footsteps of a father who received three degrees, was a college professor and held numerous positions of importance in literary organizations and publications may be a difficult task, but thus far Allan [*sic*] Lomax, junior student at the university, seems to be measuring his strides to his father's. . . . Allan is at present university correspondent for the Dallas News."

2. Bill Bedell's May 5, 1935, article (newspaper unknown), "Alan Lomax Described Method Of Collecting Primitive Songs," was highly descriptive: "For two years now, Alan, an ex-student of the University who plans to re-enter next year, has traveled the byways of the United States in search of such folk tunes of the negro, cowboy, Cajun, mountaineer, and Mexican. In cooperation with his father, John A. Lomax, widely known cowboy ballad collector, he has plunged into a vast work. . . . And so a University student may become one of America's folk song authorities. Already well initiated into the work while still a boy, soft-drawling Alan Lomax looks forward to a life of song-hunting over the world."

3. For background information see Nolan Porterfield, *Last Cavalier: The Life and Times of John A. Lomax, 1867–1948* (Urbana: University of Illinois Press, 1996); and this first article, "'Sinful' Songs of the Southern Negro," Ronald D. Cohen, ed., *Alan Lomax: Selected Writings, 1934–1997* (New York: Routledge, 2003), 9–31. For Alan's voluminous family correspondence, see the Lomax Papers, Center for American History, University of Texas at Austin, Texas (hereafter cited as LP). See also Zora Neale Hurston to Eslanda Robeson, April 18, 1934; Hurston to Carl Van Vechten, January 5, 1935; and Hurston to John Lomax, January 5, 1935, Carla Kaplin, ed., *Zora Neale Hurston: A Life in Letters* (New York: Doubleday, 2002), 300, 332, 333; Valerie Boyd, *Wrapped in Rainbows: The Life of Zora Neale Hurston* (New York: Scribner, 2003), 275–77.

4. Professor George Herzog, an anthropologist at Yale University, had done the musical transcriptions for *Negro Folk Songs as Sung by Lead Belly*, which would be published in 1936. John Lomax had been appointed Honorary Consultant to the Archive of American Folk Song in 1933, an unpaid title, which spurred his continued southern collecting, lecturing, and other folk music related activities. Ruby Terrill, a Dean at the University of Texas, had married John in 1934. For John's life at this time, see Porterfield, *Last Cavalier*, chapters 21–23.

5. William Oliver Strunk (1901–1980) was appointed chief of the Music Division in 1934.

6. Herbert Halpert (1911–2000) was a folklorist who had studied with Ruth Benedict and George Herzog at Columbia University.

7. See letters from Alan to his father from Mexico in September 1936. [LP, folder 4]

8. On Hurston's trip see Boyd, *Wrapped in Rainbows*, 295–300; and for her letters from Haiti, see Kaplan, ed., *Zora Neale Hurston*, 385–405. She makes no references to Alan, however. For background on Haiti at this time, Matthew J. Smith, *Red and Black in Haiti: Radicalism, Conflict and Political Change, 1934–1957* (Chapel Hill: University of North Carolina Press, 2009). From 1915 to 1934 the United States Marines occupied Haiti.

9. For Alan's Haitian trip, most valuable is *Alan Lomax in Haiti: Recordings for the Library of Congress, 1936–1937* (Harte Recordings, 2009), which includes not only 10 discs but also extensive notes on all of the songs by Gage Averill; see also Ellen Harold, ed., *Haitian Diary: Papers and Correspondence From Alan Lomax's Haitian Journey, 1936–37*. About a week after arriving Alan wrote to his fiancée, Elizabeth Harold, in an undated, partly damaged, letter; see Harold, ed., *Haitian Diary*, 34–39.

10. Herbert Putnam (1861–1955) was the Librarian of Congress from 1899 to 1939, when he was succeeded by Archibald MacLeish.

11. Lincoln Thompson worked for the Sound Specialties Company in Waterbury, Connecticut, which supplied the discs and recording equipment.

12. W. B. Seabrook, *The Magic Island* (New York: Harcourt, Brace, 1929).

13. See also additional letters from Alan to John from Haiti. [LP, folder 4]

14. Printed in Harold, ed., *Haitian Diary*, 56–57.

15. Charles Seeger, a noted composer and ethnomusicologist, was then working for the New Deal's Resettlement Administration as a musical advisor. See Ann M. Pescatello, *Charles Seeger: A Life in American Music* (Pittsburgh: University of Pittsburgh Press, 1992).

16. Printed in Harold, ed., *Haitian Diary*, 87–94. See also Lincoln Thompson to Harold Spivacke, January 18, 1937, and Spivacke to Alan Lomax, January 19, 1937, *ibid.*, 95–96; and Melville Herkovits to Alan Lomax, January 21, 1937, *ibid.*, 115–17.

17. Printed in Harold, ed., *Haitian Diary*, 162-164.

18. *Ibid.*, 165–66. Alan did receive the camera and with Elizabeth's assistance managed to produce six short films, a total of 350 feet; all of the footage can be found on Disc 5 of *The Haiti Recordings*. For Spivacke's reply, see Spivacke to Lomax, April 1, 1937, *ibid.*, 169; and also see Putnam to Lomax, April 1, 1937, *ibid.*, 170.

19. "Haitian Journey—Search for Native Folklore," Cohen, ed., *Alan Lomax*, 32–46. They returned with over fifteen hundred recordings, some fifty hours, along with the moving pictures, all of which were deposited into the Library of Congress.

20. S. H. Reiser was an American expatriate and former ship's pharmacist who ran the Haitian National Insane Asylum.

21. On the history of the Archive, Peter T. Bartis, "A History of the Archive of Folk Song at the Library of Congress: The First Fifty Years," unpublished Ph.D. diss., University of Pennsylvania, 1982. For a glimpse into Lomax's new life, see his letter to his father, July 23, 1937. [LP, folder 4]

22. Suzanne Comhaire-Sylvain, "Creole Tales From Haiti," *Journal of American Folk-Lore*, vol. 50 (1937), 207–95; vol. 51 (1938): 219–346.

23. "Archive of American Folk Song: A History, 1928–1939," Library of Congress Project, Works Projects Administration, 1940, 49–50.

24. Frances Densmore (1867–1957) was an ethnomusicologist who pioneered the recording of Native American music.

25. *Plantation Echoes* was a play written and directed by Rosa Warren Wilson that included spirituals, songs, dance tunes, sermons and prayers performed by black singers and dancers from Wadmalaw Island. Recorded in Hibernian Hall, Charleston, South Carolina, July 1937. (AFS 1047A2-1054; 1304)

26. Strunk had been fired during the summer and replaced by his chief assistant, Harold Spivacke (1904–1977). After studying at New York University, Spivacke received his Ph.D. from the University of Berlin in music. Returning to New York in 1933, he served briefly as a research assistant for the *New York Times* music critic Olin Downes, then joined the Library of Congress's Music Division in 1934. Remarkably, he remained head of the Music Division until his retirement in 1972. Spivacke would soon be inundated by Alan's letters, and proved to be a patient, but somewhat strict, boss.

27. Wyman published, with Howard Brockway, *Lonesome Tunes: Folk Songs from the Kentucky Mountains* (New York: H.W. Gray, 1916) and *Twenty Kentucky Mountain Songs* (Boston: Oliver Ditson, 1920). She died in September 1937.

28. The reference is to Josephine McGill, *Folk-Songs of the Kentucky Mountains* (New York: Boosey, 1917).

29. Josiah Combs, *Folk-Songs Du Midi Etats-Unis* (Paris: Les Presses Universitaires de France, 1925), which was his doctoral dissertation at the University of Paris.

30. Bess Owens was mentioned as a southern collector in the article by Phillips Barry *et al.*, "List of Collectors and Persons Interested in the Ballad and Folk-Song Field," *Southern Folklore Quarterly*, vol. 1, no. 2 (June 1937): 72.

31. See "Recordings of singing by Jenny Devlin in Gloucester, New Jersey, June, 1938. Recorded by Alan Lomax through the courtesy of Kay Dealy of Philadelphia, Pennsylvania, 1938." ALC AFC, LC, AFS 1772–77.

32. "Archive of American Folk Song: A History, 1928–1939," 54–55.

33. See also Alan to John Lomax, October 26, 1937. [LP, folder 4]

34. On Nye, see John Barton and Stephen Winick, "'A Big, Breezy, Wholesome, Smiling Man': Captain Pearl R. Nye," *Folklife Center News*, vol. 28, no. 3 (2007): 13–14.

35. See Paul Brewster to Alan Lomax, January 22, 1938. [ALC]; and Paul Brewster, ed., *Ballads and Songs of Indiana* (Bloomington: Indiana University Publications, Folklore Series no. 1, 1940).

36. See Samuel Preston Bayard, ed., *Hill Country Tunes: Instrumental Folk Music of Southwestern Pennsylvania* (Philadelphia: American Folklore Society, vol. 34, 1944).

37. See Louise Pound, ed., *American Ballads and Songs* (New York: Charles Scribner's Sons, 1922).

38. See H. M. Belden, ed., *Ballads and Songs Collected by the Missouri Folk-Lore Society* (Columbia: University of Missouri Studies, 1940).

39. See Louis W. Chappell, *John Henry: A Folk-Lore Study* (Jena, Germany: Walter Biedermann, 1933); Chappell, *Folk-Songs of the Roanoke and the Albermarle* (Morgantown, WV: Ballad Press, 1939).

40. See John Harrington Cox, ed., *Folk-Songs of the South* (Cambridge: Harvard University Press, 1925); Cox, *Folk-Songs Mainly from West Virginia* (New York: National Service Bureau, 1939); and Cox, *Traditional Ballads, Mainly from West Virginia* (New York: National Service Bureau, 1939).

41. Consult Loyal Jones, *Minstrel of the Appalachians: The Story of Bascom Lamar Lunsford* (Boone, NC: Appalachian Consortium Press, 1984), 70; and Michael Ann

Williams, *Staging Tradition: John Lair and Sarah Gertrude Knott* (Urbana: University of Illinois Press, 2006), 53–54.

42. See John Umble to Lomax, April 7, 1938. [ALC]

43. For the previous letter see, James F. Broussard to Lomax, April 22, 1938. [ALC]

44. Nicholas Ray (1911–1979) worked with the architect Frank Lloyd Wright in Wisconsin before moving to New York, where he became involved with the Theater of Action and the Group Theater. In January 1937, he was put in charge of local theater activities by the Department of Agriculture's Resettlement Administration and moved to Washington. There he met Lomax and somewhat assisted in his southern collecting. They would soon collaborate on radio programs for CBS. Ray would later become an important film director.

45. *Music from the Days of George Washington*. Collected and provided with an introd. by Carl Engel; music edited by W. Oliver Strunk; with a preface by Sol Bloom (Washington: United States George Washington Bicentennial Commission, 1931).

46. Vsevolod Emilevich Meyerhold was a Russian director, actor, and producer who greatly influenced modern theater.

47. Ralph Steele Boggs, *Folklore, an Outline for Individual and Group* Study (Chapel Hill: University of North Carolina Press, 1929); and, a bit later, Ralph Steele Boggs, *Bibliography of Latin American Folklore* (New York: H. W. Wilson, 1940).

48. John A. Lomax and Alan Lomax, *Cowboy Songs and Other Frontier Ballads*, Rev. and Enlarged (New York: Macmillan, 1938); and see Williams, *Staging Tradition*, 63–65. In late May Alan began recording Jelly Roll Morton at the Library of Congress, which lasted into June, then resumed in December. He had also interviewed W. C. Handy just before beginning the Morton recordings.

49. John Szwed, "Doctor Jazz," liner notes to *Jelly Roll Morton: The Complete Library of Congress Recordings by Alan Lomax* (Rounder CD 11661-1888-2 BK01, 2005), 15–17.

50. Seeger, formerly with the Resettlement Administration, from 1938 to 1940 was assistant director of the Federal Music Project of the Works Progress Administration.

51. On Barnicle, Cadle, and Lomax, see Shelly Romalis, *Pistol Packin' Mama: Aunt Molly Jackson and the Politics of Folksong* (Urbana: University of Illinois Press, 1999), 103–5. Barnicle and Cadle were married.

52. Alistair Cooke to Lomax, May 17, 1938, June 1, 1938. [ALC]. Stephen Winick, "Alistair Cooke: A Radio and TV Icon in the Archive of Folk Culture," *Folklife Center News*, vol. 27, nos. 1–2 (Winter/Spring 2005): 6–8.

53. See undated letter, *ca.* June 1938, Esther Peterson to Alan Lomax; and Kay Dealy to Lomax, February 20, 1938. [ALC]

54. Sidney Martin, "Black Diamond Express to Hell," *Down Beat*, vol. 5, no. 6 (June 1938): 3.

55. See Melvin Oathout to Lomax, June 28 and July 7, 1938. [ALC]

56. Theodore Blegen, ed., *Norwegian Emigrant Songs and Ballads* (Minneapolis: University of Minnesota Press, 1936).

57. See Alan Lomax's introduction to Katharine D. Newman, *Never without a Song: The Years and Songs of Jennie Devlin, 1865–1952* (Urbana: University of Illinois Press, 1995).

58. He wrote a similar letter to Dr. Charles Brown at the University of Wisconsin and Director of the Wisconsin State Historical Museum on July 1. On Brown, Robertson, and Lomax's subsequent collecting trip, see James P. Leary, *Polkabilly: How the Goose Island*

Ramblers Redefined American Folk Music (New York: Oxford University Press, 2006), 174–79.

59. Ruth Crawford Seeger was doing the musical transcriptions for John A. and Alan Lomax, *Our Singing Country: A Second Volume of Ballads & Folk Songs* (New York: Macmillan, 1941). See also, Judith Tick, *Ruth Crawford Seeger: A Composer's Search for American Music* (New York: Oxford University Press, 1997).

60. Alan's joking references to Nazis and fascists are connected to the rise of Hitler and fascism in Germany and Italy.

61. Theodore Blegen to Lomax, July 14, 1938. [ALC]

62. See Downes to Spivacke, July 18, 1938, and Spivacke to Downes, July 29, 1938. [ALC]

63. See Spivacke to Lomax, August 4, 1938, in which he thinks there is encouraging news from Downes about Alan participating in the World's Fair. [ALC]

64. Ivan H. Walton was a professor of English at the University of Michigan. His song collecting during the 1930s finally appeared in Walton and Joe Grimm, *Windjammer: Songs of the Great Lakes Sailors* (Detroit: Wayne State University Press, 2002). See also, Joe Grimm, ed., *Songquest: The Journals of Great Lakes Folklorist Ivan H. Walton* (Detroit: Wayne State University Press, 2005).

65. On financial matters, since Alan seemed to be requesting funds that he should already have received as his advance, see Spivacke to Lomax, September 2, 1938. [ALC]

66. For the response, see Spivacke to Lomax, September 16, 1938: "You should plan ahead and play safe. If you find yourself short of money, it is foolish to move very far until you have received some money. . . . You ought to know by now that you cannot expect too much in the way of special service from the government." [ALC]

67. Earl Beck would publish *Songs of the Michigan Lumberjacks* (Ann Arbor: University of Michigan Press, 1941) and *Lore of the Lumber Camps* (Ann Arbor: University of Michigan Press, 1948).

68. Ruth Roark, October 17, 1938. [ALC]

69. "Archive of American Folk Song: A History, 1928–1939," 65–66.

70. The clipping has not been found.

71. Thomas Outram to Lomax, September 18, 1938. [ALC]

72. "Archive of American Folk Song: A History, 1928–1939," 67. Lomax interviewed and recorded the five on December 24 at Havers Studio, including Ammons singing "Dying Mother Blues" accompanied by Pete Johnson on piano, while Lewis did "Honky Tonk Train." Peter J. Silvester, *A Left Hand Like God: A History of Boogie-Woogie Piano* (New York: Da Capo, 1989), 138–44; Christopher Page, *Boogie Woogie Stomp: Albert Ammons & His Music* (Cleveland: Northeast Ohio Jazz Society, 1997); and *The Boogie Woogie Boys: Albert Ammons—Pete Johnson—Meade "Lux" Lewis* (Document Records BDCD-6046).

73. Joseph Arnstein to Lomax, November 29, 1938. [ALC]

Letters, 1939–1940

1. Harold Spivacke, "The Archive of American Folk Song in the Library of Congress in its Relationship to the Folksong Collector," *Southern Folklore Quarterly*, vol. 2, no. 1

(March 1938): 31–35. Also see John Umble to Lomax, December 6, December 12, 1938, January 6, January 21, and March 14, 1939. [ALC]

2. Marc Connelly wrote *The Green Pastures: A Fable Suggested by Roark Bradford's Southern Sketches "Ol' Man Adam an' His Chillun,"* which was first produced in New York at the Mansfield Theatre, February 26, 1930, and made into a film in 1936. Alan is apparently referring to a recent Broadway revival.

3. See Mary LaDame to Alan Lomax, February 11, 1939: "Several of us in the Department of Labor have received very enthusiastic comments on your playing and singing of labor songs. Is there any chance that you may be returning to Washington in the near future? We should like very much to have an opportunity to hear you." On February 27, Alan received two letters from the Department of Labor, one from Secretary Francis Perkins: "It will be appreciated if you can arrange to come to Washington, D.C. on March 3, 1939, for a conference with me and other officials of the Department of Labor on matters pertaining to the work of this Department." The other was from Mary LaDame: "Would it be possible for you to sing some of your songs at Miss Perkins' annual party for the members of the staff of this Department in advance of our reception and dance on Friday evening, March 3? I will explain the situation when you come for your conference in the Secretary's office." [ALC]

4. John Umble to Lomax, March 21, April 4, and June 1, 1939. [ALC]

5. See Paul Hanna to Lomax, March 23, 1939. [ALC]. Also see Hanna, *Youth Serves the Community* (New York: Appleton-Century, 1936), along with his other Social Studies texts.

6. Daniel Wolfert, a music instructor at Brooklyn College, launched Gamut Records in 1937, as a classical music label. It was acquired by the General label in 1946. There is no indication they worked with John Lomax.

7. See Alan Lomax, "Folk Music in the Roosevelt Era," Cohen, ed., *Alan Lomax*, 92–96, for Alan's memories of the White House concert on June 8; and Spivacke to Lomax, June 1, 1939, for his praise of Alan's upcoming performance and encouragement for his proposed radio series. [ALC]

8. "Archive of American Folk Song: A History, 1928–1939," 67. Alan, along with Mary Elizabeth Barnicle, originally recorded Aunt Molly Jackson in 1935, again in 1937, and by himself in May 1939 in New York (AFC 1939/012 [part 1 and part 2]); Romalis, *Pistol Packin' Mama*, 103, 146; *Aunt Molly Jackson* (Rounder Records 1002).

Alan did compile an unpublished twenty-two-page "List of American Folk Songs On Commercial Records," undated but issued by the Library of Congress in 1940: "This list is a reprint, with revisions, of pages 126–146 of the Report of the Committee of the Conference on Inter-American Relations in the Field of Music (September 3, 1940)." Alan wrote in his introduction: "After listening to three thousand odd commercial records of white and negro songs and tunes from the South, I have compiled this list of three hundred and fifty representative titles in order that the interested musician or student of American society may explore this unknown body of Americana with readiness. The choices have been personal and have been made for all sorts of reasons."

9. The grant from the ACLS was for $500, for his graduate work in anthropology and musicological research at Columbia University, and would be administered by the Library of Congress.

10. Andrea Lynn Woody, "'American School of the Air': An Experiment in Music Education and Radio Broadcasting," M.A. thesis, University of Texas, May 2003. Alan's

various CBS shows—"Folk Music of America," "Wellsprings of Music," and "Back Where I Come From"—ran from October 1939 into 1941.

11. Helen Hartness Flanders was an active folk song collector and had published *Vermont Folk-Songs & Ballads* (Brattleboro, VT: Stephen Daye Press, 1932); *A Garland of Green Mountain Song* (Northfield, VT: Vermont Commission on Country Life, 1934); *Country Songs of Vermont* (New York: Schirmer, 1937); and *The New Green Mountain Songster: Traditional Folk Songs of Vermont* (New Haven: Yale University Press, 1939).

12. David Spaziani to Lomax, June 14, 1939. [ALC]

13. See *Columbia's American School of the Air: Teachers Manual and Classroom Guide* (New York: Columbia Broadcasting System, Department of Education, 1939), which does include the sources, all Lomax books except for Joanna C. Colcord, *Roll and Go: Songs of American Sailormen* (New York: W. W. Norton, 1938).

14. Paul G. Brewster, *Ballads and Songs of Indiana* (Bloomington: Indiana University Publications Folklore Series 1, 1940). "The Two Sisters" is no. 6 on his list (Child, No. 10).

15. See Stanton King to Lomax, September 12, 1939. [ALC]

16. See R. P. Wetherald to Lomax, September 14, October 3, 1939. [ALC]

17. Alan's suggestions were not followed; see *Columbia's American School of the Air: Teacher's Manual and Classroom Guide.*

18. See Nelson Sprackling to Lomax, September 16 and September 29, 1939. [ALC] Erick Berry, *Tinmaker Man of New Amsterdam: The Music from an Old Tune Arranged by Nelson Sprackling* (Chicago: John C. Winston, 1941).

19. Franz, Rickaby, ed., *Ballads and Songs of the Shanty-Boy* (Cambridge: Harvard University Press, 1926). In a note on the bottom of Alan's letter, Beck responded: "There is nothing further known of Billy Allen so far as I know. Stewart Holbrook's HOLY OLD MACKINAW is the best lumberjack book I know, and it is fairly authoritative. If you haven't read it, you have missed a treat. Lewis Torrent, Hackley High School, Muskegon, Mich., will be happy to answer any of your questions. He is the youngest son of one of Michigan's pine barons, and he knows the ways of the lumberwoods. Paddy Miles, Big Rapid, Mich., has written something of what you want and it was printed in the newspapers. He probably will send you a clipping. You may use my name when writing to them if you care to. Also, Bill Duchaine, Escanaba Press, Escanaba, Mich., may have some clippings for you."

20. For his father's rather critical feelings about Alan's radio performance, see John Lomax to Alan, October 2, 1939. [ALC]

21. Jean Evans was a writer and later an editor of *Redbook Magazine.* At the time she was married to Nicholas Ray.

22. See Dick to Lomax, November 15, 1939. [ALC] Sheldon Dick was a Farm Security Administration photographer and documentary filmmaker. He filmed working and living conditions in the Tri-State Mining Area of Kansas, Missouri, and Oklahoma in 1939, which resulted in the documentary film *Men and Dust* that premiered in April 1940 in Joplin, Missouri, then opened in New York City in early June. Will Geer was one of the narrators. "There Are Mean Things Happening in This Land" was used at the film's beginning. William Alexander, *Film on the Left: American Documentary Film from 1931 to 1942* (Princeton: Princeton University Press, 1981), 287–93.

23. See Edward P. Jennings to Lomax, November 20, November 28, 1939. [ALC]

24. Bascom Lamar Lunsford (1882–1973) was a North Carolina traditional musician as well as a folk music collector and promoter. See Jones, *Minstrel of the Appalachians.*

25. Harold W. Thompson, *Body, Boots & Britches* (Philadelphia: J. B. Lippincott, 1940).

26. The second concert featured the Golden Gate Quartet, Benny Goodman, Ida Cox, and Big Bill Broonzy; see liner notes to *From Spirituals to Swing: The Legendary 1938 & 1939 Carnegie Hall Concerts* (Vanguard Records 169/71–2, 1999). Charles Smith was a jazz scholar.

27. Pete Seeger, the son of Charles Seeger and four years younger than Alan, worked for him at the Library of Congress for a few months at this time; David King Dunaway, *How Can I Keep from Singing? The Ballad of Pete Seeger* (New York: Villard, 2008), 64–65. Lawrence Gellert, *Negro Songs of Protest* (New York: American Music League, 1936), 6, 7, 14–15; Gellert, *"Me And My Captain": Chain Gang Negro Songs of Protest* (New York: Hours Press, 1939). See Steven Patrick Garabedian, "Reds, Whites, and the Blues: Blues Music, White Scholarship, and American Cultural Politics," unpublished Ph.D. diss., University of Minnesota, 2004. Neither Seeger nor Gellert seems to have been involved with planning the concert, however.

28. See Wetherald to Lomax, December 20, 1939. [ALC]

29. Annabel Morris Buchanan, *Folk Hymns Of America* (New York: J. Fischer and Brother, 1938); and Buchanan, *American Folk Music* (New York: National Federation of Music Clubs, 1939). For a short history of the White Top Folk Festival, see Ronald D. Cohen, *A History of Folk Music Festivals in the United States* (Lanham, MD: Scarecrow, 2008), 10–13; and for more information, David E. Whisnant, *All That Is Native & Fine: The Politics of Culture in an American Region* (Chapel Hill: University of North Carolina Press, 1983), chapter 3.

30. For additional letters from his fans, see CBS.

31. On Gordon, who established the Archive of American Folk Song in 1928, see Debora Kodish, *Good Friends and Bad Enemies: Robert Winslow Gordon and the Study of American Folksong* (Urbana: University of Illinois Press, 1986).

32. After receiving a letter from WNYC's director on January 17, Alan agreed to participate in radio station WNYC's first Annual Festival of American Music, organized by radio personality Henrietta Yurchenco for February. On February 12 Helen Hartness Flanders, now chair of the General Federation of Women's Clubs Committee on Folk Music and Folk Festivals, sent him congratulations on his radio programs: "As I wired, I think your last broadcast was particularly fine. Giving America her folk-music and its applied themes, in orchestration, must be tremendously illuminating. The popularity of your broadcast is certainly nationwide." Ruth Webb, the principal of an elementary school in the nation's capital, was equally positive, as she wrote to CBS on March 30: "I should like to report to your office that we find your weekly broadcasts of Alan Lomax in songs of America and Americans especially fine. We use his program for all kinds of interesting preparatory and follow-up assignments and discussions with the children of my three elementary schools. For example, his songs of the Teamsters some few weeks ago were the basis of a very fine unit of work on the ways in which people express themselves." [ALC]

33. Charles L. Todd studied literature in college and lived in Greenwich Village during the 1930s, where he met Alan Lomax at the Village Vanguard. Robert Sonkin founded the speech clinic, and met Todd when they were both working in the Department of Public Speaking at City College of New York in the late 1930s. During July and August 1940 Todd and Sonkin visited the Arvin, Shafter, Visalia, Firebaugh, Westley, Thornong, and Yuba Farm Security Administration camps in California, making recordings of musicians. They returned in August and September 1941. During June and July 1941

Sonkin recorded African American performers in Shell Pile, near Port Norris, New Jersey, and Gee's Bend and other communities in Alabama.

34. *Dust Bowl Ballads Vol. I* (Victor Records P-27) and *Dust Bowl Ballads Vol. 2* (Victor Records P-28).

35. On Alan and Woody, see Ed Cray, *Ramblin' Man: The Life and Times of Woody Guthrie* (New York: W. W. Norton, 2004), 169–82.

36. "Eleven Cent Cotton and Forty Cent Meat," written by Bob Miller, was early recorded by him and Vernon Dalhart in 1928, as well as Carson Robison in 1929.

37. Alan's collection of protest songs would eventually be published as Alan Lomax, Woody Guthrie, Pete Seeger, *Hard Hitting Songs for Hard-Hit People* (New York: Oak Publications, 1967). Alan wrote in his "Compiler's Postscript" of 1966: "When in the Spring of 1937, I ransacked the files of Columbia, Victor and Decca record companies for anything that had a folk flavor, I found not only the early Blue Grass, not only urban blues tradition, I found scores of songs of protest and social comment by urban and country folk singers. Some of these recorded topical songs praised the New Deal, some damned it; some recited the woes of the poor, some bitterly protested—but, considered as a whole, they proved again that the American topical folk song tradition was live and productive," 366. Most of the songs mentioned in this letter were eventually included in the published volume, for which John Steinbeck wrote a foreword.

38. Irene Whitfield, *Louisiana French Folk Songs* (Baton Rouge: Louisiana State University Press, 1939); and Lomax and Lomax, *Our Singing Country*, 191–93.

39. Alan is referring to the recordings of Lead Belly and the Golden Gate Quartet in New York City on June 15 and 17, 1940, issued as Victor album P50, *Leadbelly and the Golden Gate Quartet with Guitar*. See the original "Artists Letter of Agreement" between Lomax and R.C.A., June 11, 1940. [ALC]

40. In 1942 the Library issued a *Check-list of recorded songs in the English language in the Archive of American Folk Song to July, 1940* (Washington: Music Division, Library of Congress). Alan apparently changed his mind about also listing foreign-language recordings, probably because he could not get the necessary assistance.

41. Archibald MacLeish was appointed Librarian of Congress by President Franklin Roosevelt on July 10, 1939, and served until late 1944. For the 1938–39 academic year the left-wing MacLeish, a noted poet and journalist, was Nieman Curator of Contemporary Journalism at Harvard, where he was a faculty sponsor for the student production of Marc Blitzstein's pro-labor, antiwar musical *The Cradle Will Rock*, staged on May 27, 1939; Drew Massey, "Leonard Bernstein and the Harvard Student Union: In Search of Political Origins," *Journal of the Society American Music*, vol. 3, no. 1 (February 2009): 76. Lomax would have strongly agreed with MacLeish's politics, and MacLeish wrote the introduction to Lomax and Lomax, *Our Singing Country*, vii–viii: "The people 'make' their songs and poems the way the people make a stone stair in an old building of this republic where the treads are worn down and shaped up the way their uses have to have them. The folk songs and the folk poems show the mark of a people on them the way the old silver dollars show the mark of shoving thumbs—but with far more meaning."

42. This is perhaps a reference to John's work on his autobiography, *Adventures of a Ballad Hunter*, finally published in 1947.

43. See, Charles Todd and Robert Sonkin, "Ballads of the Okies," *New York Times*, November 17, 1940.

44. This was surely the Dallas blues pianist Alexander Herman Moore, who had been commercially recorded in 1929 and 1937.

45. Tartt, who lived in Livingston, Alabama, was one of John Lomax's valuable sources; see Porterfield, *Last Cavalier*, 403–5. Tartt introduced Lomax to the performers and cousins Dock Reed and Vera Hall, as well as to various others. Alan later wrote a book partly based on Hall's life, *The Rainbow Sign: A Southern Documentary* (New York: Duell, Sloan and Pearce, 1959).

46. Alan perhaps refers to some older conflicts between John and Lead Belly, although it could be the latter's arrest in New York, on March 5, 1939, for assault. Alan had dropped out of his graduate program at Columbia University to help raise funds for Lead Belly's court costs, including securing a recording contract for him with Musicraft, although John does not seem to have been involved. Lead Belly served eight months in jail. See, Charles Wolfe and Kip Lornell, *The Life and Legend of Leadbelly* (New York: HarperCollins, 1992), 212–14; and Porterfield, *Last Cavalier*, 364–67 and *passim*.

47. His new radio show, *Back Where I Come From*, directed by Nicholas Ray, began in August on CBS, fifteen minutes three evenings a week. Each program had a theme, such as "Nonsense Songs" or "Jails," and would feature Guthrie, Lead Belly, Josh White, Burl Ives, the Golden Gate Quartet, and others. CBS cancelled it in February 1941. For some of Alan's early comments on the show, see an undated letter to his father, apparently written in mid-August. [LP, folder 5]

48. Oscar Sonneck, *The Star Spangled Banner* (Washington: Government Printing Office, 1914); Joseph Muller, *The Star-Spangled Banner: Words and Music Issued between 1814–1864* (New York: G.A. Baker, 1935).

49. For Spivacke's thoughts "considering the ways and means in which the Music Division could be useful to the National Defense Program," see his memos of August 24 and 26, 1940. [ALC]

50. On July 17 Taylor had written to Alan about his upcoming CBS show: "Well, we finally settled on Kip [Clifton] Fadiman as M.C. for 'I'm a Stranger Here Myself.' We still are questioning the title because, as I pointed out, it doesn't quite tell you what the show is about and requires a bit of explaining. Suggestions on that are still in order. We want to make you the offer of $200.00 for your efforts in rewriting and producing this show. . . . I think you should consider carefully what Fadiman says about making himself an integral part of the show." [CBS]. See Woody, "American School of the Air." Fadiman was a journalist who worked for the *New Yorker* at this time, but from May 1938 until June 1948 he also hosted the popular NBC quiz show *Information, Please.*

51. The FBI had been compiling a file on Alan at least since 1939, and as war approached became increasingly nervous.

52. It is not clear which album Alan is referring to, perhaps *Negro Sinful Tunes* (Musicraft 31), recorded in April 1939, or *Leadbelly and the Golden Gate Quartet* (Victor P50), recorded in June 1940.

53. Joseph Mitchell, Profiles, "Lady Olga," *New Yorker*, August 3, 1940, 20.

54. The 1940 White Top festival was cancelled due to flooding, however, and it was never revived.

55. Josh White and his Carolinians, *Chain Gang*, Columbia Records C-22. John Hammond supervised the recording session on June 4, 1940, and the songs can be found on *Songs For Political Action: Folkmusic, Topical Songs and the American Left* (disc 2, Bear Family BCD 15720 JL, 1996).

56. Ray Wood (with a forward by John A. Lomax), *The American Mother Goose* (New York: Frederick A. Stokes, 1940).

57. This probably refers to *Lover's Lament. Kentucky Mountain Folk Melody. Paraphrase by R. Lahmer. Arranged for a cappella Choir, Mixed Voices S.A.T.B., including optional Piano part* (New York: Mills Music, 1941), or *Never said a mumbalin Word. Negro Spiritual arranged by R. Lahmer, a cappella choir, etc.* (New York: Mills Music, 1941).

58. Elie Siegmeister, *A Treasury of American Song* (New York: Howell, Soskin, 1940).

59. On December 5, 1940, the Rockefeller Foundation appropriated $23,320 for the project, which would begin January 1, 1941. See, Alan Gevinson, *"What the Neighbors Say": The Radio Research Project of the Library of Congress* (Washington: Library of Congress, 2002), 95–121.

60. Alan might be referring to a new show he was proposing.

61. Alan is referring to his unpublished twenty-two-page "List of American Folk Songs On Commercial Records," undated but issued by the Library of Congress in 1940: "This list is a reprint, with revisions, of pages 126–146 of the Report of the Committee of the Conference on Inter-American Relations in the Field of Music (September 3, 1940)."

62. For Woody's appearances on *Back Where I Come From*, see Cray, *Ramblin' Man*, 190–91, 195–96, 200, 202. Woody clashed with Ray over the latter's reluctance to have Lead Belly appear on the show. Their differences were temporarily worked out, but Woody finally left the program at the end of the year when he moved to the West Coast.

63. See Spivacke to Lomax, November 18, 1940, for information on recording his School of the Air program from Chicago on December 10 and obtaining local country musicians. [ALC]

64. Doris Willens, *Lonesome Traveler: The Life Of Lee Hays* (New York: W.W. Norton, 1988).

65. For the two articles see Cohen, ed., *Alan Lomax*, 47–55, 56–58. Alan was referring to the Radio Research Project, which would begin in January, and was funded by the Rockefeller Foundation. Jerome Wiesner was the recording engineer, with Philip Cohen as the project chief, Joseph Liss as the script editor, and Alan Lomax as the music and folklore editor. "The intention of this series was to present half-hour dramatized programs based on documentary evidence dealing with contemporary problems faced by different types of American communities." One of the staff was Arthur Miller, the future author. The series lasted through 1941. John Lomax recorded ten fifteen-minute folk music shows for the series *The Ballad Hunter*. Gevinson, *"What the Neighbors Say,"* 100. One of Alan's scripts was later published, "Mister Ledford and the TVA," Erik Barnouw, ed., *Radio Drama in Action: Twenty-Five Plays of a Changing World* (New York: Rinehart, 1945), 51–58, and reprinted in Cohen, ed., *Alan Lomax*, 77–85.

66. Marius Barbeau was a member of the Anthropological (later Human History, then Ethnology) Division of Canada's National Museum (1911–48) who documented the country's folk traditions. *Wellsprings of Music* replaced Alan's *Folk Music of America* CBS radio series in October 1940. Program No. 13, to be broadcast on January 21, 1941, featured "Canadian Folk Songs."

Letters, 1941–1945

1. The banjo player Wade Mainer had joined his brother, J. E. Mainer, in the Crazy Mountaineers, the popular North Carolina string band, by 1935, but had his own band,

Sons of the Mountaineers, by 1941. See Dick Spottswood, *Banjo on the Mountain: Wade Mainer's First Hundred Years* (Jackson: University Press of Mississippi, 2010).

2. Willard Park was an anthropologist at the University of Oklahoma who did research on the Northern Paiute and Great Basin Indians.

3. *Wellsprings of Music* began on October 8, 1940, and lasted until late April 1941, with a total of twenty-five programs. It replaced *Folk Music of America* on CBS's "American School of the Air." The programs included Lomax as well as Burl Ives, Pete Seeger, Lead Belly, the Golden Gate Quartet, and many others. See *The American School of the Air: Teacher's Manual, 1940–41*. Later, Curt Sachs published *The Wellsprings of Music* (The Hague: Martinus Nijhoff, 1962), but there was no connection.

4. He is referring to the Victor album P50, *Leadbelly and the Golden Gate Quartet with Guitar*, recorded on June 15, 1940. Perhaps the song was left out because it contained the words "God damn."

5. He is referring to the "Voyageur Songs" program on his CBS show *Wellsprings of Music* on January 21, 1941, which featured "Boucher," Alouette Quartet, and "Bedard."

6. On January 9, 1941, Horace Mann Bond, President of Fort Valley State College in Georgia, wrote to Alan: "I write to invite you to come to Fort Valley on March 6–9, if possible, to participate in our Second Annual Folk Festival. Last year when we instituted this Folk Festival, we had as our principal guest, Mr W C Handy, the composer of The Saint Louis Blues. We made a special effort to find Negro Folk musicians from the surrounding countryside, in fact, from all over the state of Georgia." Bond responded to Alan's letter of February 4 on February 7: "I am very happy to know that there is a prospect that you may come to be with us during our Folk Festival on March 6th." [FVMF] The Fort Valley State College Festival began in 1940 and lasted until 1955. See Ronald D. Cohen, *A History of Folk Music Festivals in the United States*, 23–25; Bruce Bastin, *Red River Blues: The Blues Tradition in the Southeast* (Urbana: University of Illinois Press, 1986), 72–85.

7. The February 17 performance at the White House included White, the Golden Gate Quartet, Ives, Sailor Dad Hunt, and Wade Mainer. See Alan Lomax, "Folk Music in the Roosevelt Era," Cohen, ed., *Alan Lomax*, 95–96; "Folk Songs in the White House," *Time*, March 3, 1941, 57; and Elijah Wald, *Josh White: Society Blues* (Amherst: University of Massachusetts Press, 2000), 70–71.

8. The Golden Gate Quartet and Josh White appeared on *Wellsprings of Music* on February 18, 1941.

9. Alan sent similar notes to Chaplain Lach at the Arlington Cantonment in Virginia, and Captain Hardison at the Naval Air Base in D.C. on February 20. [ALC]

10. Harold Schmidt was the chairman of the music department at Fisk University in Nashville.

11. The copy in the ALC is heavily marked up, so it is unclear if this letter was ever sent, but even if not it gives a clear indication of Alan's thinking about the Library's coming role, which he would work hard to implement. He calculated a year's budget at a little over $100,000.

12. See Charles Edward Smith, "Music From the Grass Roots," *Christian Science Monitor*, March 8, 1941, 8–9, for Alan's work with Fineschriber on CBS's Folk Music of America series: "In the Folk Music of America series his purpose was to show this grass-roots music growing out of and a part of the life not merely of pioneer America, but of America today. Twenty-five programs were given, including cowboy, teamster, gold rush, courting, love, railroad, poor farmer, play-party songs, British Ballads in America; Negro

spirituals and secular music; blues; and even hobo and outlaw ballads, the latter in the rough-hewn native Robin Hood tradition."

13. Robert Cochran, *Vance Randolph: An Ozark Life* (Urbana: University of Illinois Press, 1985).

14. Cuney was a Harlem poet who collaborated with Josh White on his *Southern Exposure* album for Keynote Records, released in September 1941, a harsh attack on southern racism. Alan might have earlier met Cuney when he wrote the letter supporting his southern trip. See Wald, *Josh White*, 79–80, 87–88.

15. Fisk University planned a seventy-fifth anniversary celebration for April 29, which would feature the Golden Gate Quartet, Joshua White, Sterling Brown from Howard University, and Alan Lomax. See Robert Gordon and Bruce Nemerov, eds., *Lost Delta Found: Rediscovering the Fisk University–Library of Congress Coahoma County Study, 1941–1942* (Nashville: Vanderbilt University Press, 2005), 11–12.

16. Burl Ives, *The Wayfaring Stranger*, Columbia 36733, was reviewed in *Billboard* on October 7, 1944, so it was not issued for a few years.

17. See Porterfield, *Last Cavalier*, 438–39, for a discussion of the problems in publishing; Lomax and Lomax, *Our Singing Country*; Ruth Crawford Seeger, *The Music of American Folk Song and Selected Other Writings on American Folk Music*, ed. Larry Polansky with Judith Tick (Rochester: University of Rochester Press, 2001).

18. Alan created the Library of Congress's Radio Research Project, funded by the Rockefeller Foundation, which began on January 1, 1941. The idea was to produce half-hour documentary radio programs focusing on life in various communities throughout the country. See Gevinson, *"What the Neighbors Say,"* 95—121; Philip H. Cohen, Joseph Liss, Alan Lomax, and Dorothy Allen, "Report of the Radio Research Project The Library of Congress," February 24, 1942. [ALC]

19. For his response, see Carleton Sprague Smith to Alan Lomax, April 25, 1941 [ALC]: "Your idea for Todd and Sonkin is very interesting and I should love to see them begin with Latin American survivals in New York City. I am not quite clear whether you are looking for financial assistance through me or whether you think it could go by itself. I'm all for it, anyway."

20. John Lomax was president of the Texas Folklore Society, which was meeting in San Antonio on May 2.

21. For his response, see Coon to Lomax, June 30, 1941. [H S-T]

22. This is perhaps William Fenton, an expert on the Iroquois, who worked at the Smithsonian Institution at that time.

23. See also John Lomax to Alan, June 30, 1941 [LP, folder 4], where he is concerned about the left-wing politics of Alan and his sister Bess. Indeed, the FBI was keeping tabs on Alan at this time; see Lomax FBI file.

24. Smith responded to Lomax on June 30, 1941, that he was still interested. [ALC]

25. Emrich was a folklorist and professor of English at Columbia University from 1937 to 1940, when he moved to the University of Denver. He would assume Alan's position at the Library of Congress following World War II. In July, John Lomax attended the Western Folklore Conference in Denver, then left with Emrich for the Cheyenne Frontier Days in Wyoming.

26. For the background of the Coahoma County study, see Gordon and Nemerov, *Lost Delta Found*, 1–26.

27. Peter Hurd was a New Mexico artist and collector who released the album *Spanish Folk Songs of New Mexico* on Folkways Records in 1957.

28. Samuel Preston Bayard, *Hill County Tunes: Instrumental Folk Music of Southwestern Pennsylvania* (Philadelphia: American Folklore Society, 1944). Bayard (1908–1997) earned an M.A. from Harvard and taught at Pennsylvania State University, 1945–73.

29. Fletcher Collins was a professor of English at Elon College in North Carolina (1936–42), and the author of *Alamance Play-Party Songs and Singing Games* (1940).

30. See, as a start, Gordon and Nemerov, *Lost Delta Found*, which is generally critical of Lomax's role; and Ted Gioia, *Delta Blues: The Life and Times of the Mississippi Masters Who Revolutionized American Music* (New York: W.W. Norton, 2008), 194–197, who is much more understanding of Lomax. Gordon and Nemerov believe that while Work originally conceived of the project, by July there was "a shift in the control of the project from John Work to Alan Lomax," 12. Lomax's letters, however, demonstrate that while he was distracted by various other projects and Library business at this time, he tried to cooperate with Work as much as possible. For additional criticisms of Gordon and Nemerov. consult the work of Matthew Barton, culturalequity.org\ace\Lost_Delta_Found.pdf.

31. Joanna Colcord to Alan Lomax, September 10, 1941. [ALC]

32. Alan wrote a series of undated letters to his father around this time, probably during the summer and into the fall, with much detail about his life; see LP, folder 4.

33. John W. Work to Lomax, July 24, 1941. [FVMF]

34. See Spivacke to Collins, August 29, 1941. [ALC]

35. Work was planning a recording trip to Ripley, Tennessee, for an annual gospel revival, as well as to Carthage, Mississippi, before the Coahoma study was to begin in late August. Lomax was planning on joining him in Ripley. Gordon and Nemerov, *Lost Delta Found*, 13.

36. See Work to Lomax, August 19, 1941: "I am finding some unique folklore in the Nashville area that I have heretofore been unaware of and which I believe you will be delighted to hear. . . . Helping me as you have, makes me much more interested in collecting this very beautiful music and I am grateful to you for it." [ALC]

37. The trip did not take place, however; see Porterfield, *Last Cavalier*, 438.

38. Gordon and Nemerov argue that Lomax pretty much pushed Work out of the way during this first trip: "John Work—a trained musician and a member of the ethnic group being studied—was kept from the heart of the project, and, after the trip, retired to a room in the social sciences building at Fisk to transcribe the discs," *Lost Delta Found*, 15. Alan's letters do not appear to support this conclusion.

39. See Spivacke to Fletcher Collins, August 29, 1941: "Mr. Alan Lomax, who is on a recording expedition in Mississippi, has asked me to answer your letter of August 7 addressed to him. I regret that I cannot give you the final word about the recording project planned for next October as I have not yet received all the approvals necessary from the various authorities here. I foresee no obstacles, however, and should be able to let you know about this in a short time." [ALC]

40. In September 1941, *Current Biography*, 47, printed a lengthy piece which concluded: "Slight of build, six feet tall, with dark brown eyes, wide forehead and black hair, Alan Lomax has a keen glance, a quick warm smile, and a thoroughly democratic manner. He includes among his friends innumerable folk singers, many of them obscure and impoverished, others, like Woody Guthrie, well known. Such prominent American composers as Earl Robinson, Charles Seeger and Roy Harris are other friends of his. He

works as long as 12 hours a day and when not working he is, like as not, playing his guitar and singing either for friends or for strange audiences. Sometimes, too, he finds time to go sailing, a favorite recreation, or to settle down with a good book for a few hours."

41. Alan had met Estil and Orna Ball at the Galax Fiddlers Convention and would record them in 1941 and again in 1959–60; music.msn.com\music\artist-biography\ec-and-orna-ball.

42. On John's anger over Ives using arrangements of songs published in his books on the radio, and copyright concerns in general, see Porterfield, *Last Cavalier*, 436–37.

43. John Work was not to be part of Alan's return to Coahoma, but in fact the trip had to be postponed until July 1942 because of the advent of war and other matters.

44. Richard S. Hill, memo, September 18, 1941, and Charles S. Johnson to Alan Lomax, September 18, 1941. [ALC]

45. Consult Gordon and Nemerov, *Lost Delta Found*, 14–17.

46. Colcord to Lomax, September 10, 1941: "After the summer hiatus, I turn to your letter of July 19. Your plan for recording folksong in New York City interests me very much. I think one set of people to talk it over with would be the Common Council for American Unity, 222 Fourth Avenue, New York City. They are in touch with all the racial groups here, and are keen on preserving immigrant cultures. . . . Would there be any possibility of getting it done as a New York City WPA project, perhaps sponsored jointly by the Library of Congress and WNYC?" [ALC]

47. Sterling Brown was a professor of African American literature and folklore at Howard University. The controversy was perhaps over the current story that Smith had died in September 1937 near Clarksdale, Mississippi, following a car accident, because she was refused admission at the local white hospital. This has been refuted, and John was correct; see Chris Albertson, *Bessie: Revised and Expanded Edition* (New Haven: Yale University Press, 2005).

48. Laura Boulton, *The Music Hunter: The Autobiography of a Career* (Garden City, NY: Doubleday, 1969).

49. Harry Partch (1901–1974) was an innovative composer and instrument maker; see Bob Gilmore, *Harry Partch: A Biography* (New Haven: Yale University Press, 1998).

50. Alan is certainly referring to Onah Spencer, "Jelly Would Flash That G-Note, Laugh in Your Face," *Down Beat*, vol. 8, no. 15 (August 1, 1941): 4: "One evening last January, Allen (Alan) Lomax, custodian of folk lore at the Library of Congress, Washington, D.C., told me: 'Spencer, I recorded Jelly Roll Morton last week for purely folk musical purposes for the Library of Congress archives and it was the darndest thing you ever heard. One hour and a half of continuous monologue and musical flashes. He would shout "I am the great Jelly Roll Morton" (then he'd play a bit of piano music); then he would shout again "I am the great Jelly Roll" (and intersperse a little more music); then he would holler "I invented jazz, yes I did. I did that," and that record is really something to hear.'" Morton had died on July 10, 1941.

51. See also Alan to John Lomax, October 27, 1941, about similar matters. [LP, folder 4]

52. "All year [John] Lomax had been trying to arrange another field trip that would include a return visit to Mrs. Tartt in Alabama. Aware that she was in dire financial straits, he suggested to Spivacke that the Library supply her with a recording machine, which Lomax would deliver, and pay her a modest sum to collect on her own for a few months. . . . When the arrangement was finally authorized in October, Mrs. Tartt's work with the WPA had ended and she and her husband were subsisting on her last check, but

she told Lomax that it would be a waste to pay her for song collecting at that time of year, when weather conditions would make it difficult to get the sort of material he wanted." Porterfield, *Last Cavalier*, 438.

53. Eddie James "Son" House, Jr. (March 21, 1902–October 19, 1988) recorded for Paramount Records in 1930 and for Alan Lomax from the Library of Congress in 1941 and 1942. He then faded from public view until the country blues revival in the 1960s.

54. *Tall Tales* (American Folk Song Series) was an 11-minute 16mm black-and-white film produced by Brandon in 1941.

55. John Lomax produced the compilation album *Smoky Mountain Ballads* for RCA Victor P-79 in 1941. It included ten commercial recordings by Uncle Dave Macon, the Carter Family, Gid Tanner and His Skillet Lickers, and others. Alan would produce two similar compilations for Brunswick in 1947, *Mountain Frolic* and *Listen to Our Story*.

56. This was the American Folklore Society meeting.

57. He is certainly referring to Sonny Terry as the harmonica player.

58. On Woody's Bonneville Power Administration recordings for Stephen Kahn, May–June 1941, see, Cray, *Ramblin' Man*, 207–12.

59. This was the initial idea for what Alan eventually published as *Mister Jelly Roll: The Fortunes of Jelly Roll Morton, New Orleans Creole and "Inventor of Jazz"* (New York: Duell, Sloan and Pearce, 1950).

60. This was probably Thomas Howard Carpenter, born in 1866, who was a ship's pilot in Delaware.

61. See also Alan to John Lomax, undated but early December 1941. [LP, folder 4]

62. The program was "People Speak to the President"; Gevinson, *"What the Neighbors Say,"* 118.

63. Frank Goodwyn was a distant cousin of J. Frank Dobie, who had grown up on the King Ranch. On John Lomax's late 1941 recording trip with Goodwyn and Dobie, see Porterfield, *Last Cavalier*, 441–44.

64. This compilation album was never issued.

65. Alan Lomax, *Land Where the Blues Began* (New York: Pantheon Books, 1993), 16–20. Although House did not make it to New York City, he moved to Rochester, New York, a year or so later.

66. "Of Men and Books," interview with Alan Lomax, *Northwestern University on the Air*, vol. 1, no. 18, January 31, 1942 (on CBS). In 1942 Alan also wrote the preface to *14 Traditional Spanish Songs from Texas* (Washington: Music Division, Pan American Union, 1942), 1–2, reprinted in Cohen, ed., *Alan Lomax*, 67–68.

67. Dock Boggs (1898–1971) was a coal miner and banjo player from Virginia who recorded briefly for Brunswick Records in the late 1920s, was rediscovered in the early 1960s, and joined the folk revival.

68. In his remark about the Almanacs, he was referring to the just-recorded (although not released until May 1942) album *Dear Mr. President* which included such pro-war songs as Woody's "Reuben James" and "Round and Round Hitler's Grave" (both co-written by Pete Seeger and Millard Lampell). Woody was not on the recording, but Alan's sister Bess joined Seeger, Sis Cunningham, and others. Lomax was also suggesting changing the Almanacs' name to something more folksy, such as the Headline Singers, but this did not happen.

69. See Son House to Alan Lomax, n.d., House to Lomax, March 6, 1942, and Almanac Singers to Son House, February 27, 1942, copies in the Richard A. Reuss Papers,

Indiana University Archives, Bloomington, Indiana; and House to Lomax, October 30, 1941. [F-LC]

70. Kapp (1901–1949), a record company executive first with Brunswick Records, founded Decca in 1934.

71. Decca had recorded the album *Saturday Night at Tom Benton's*. "Saturday night at Tom Benton's became a musical institution. His son, T. P. (for Thomas Piacenza) Benton, took up the recorder. Benton put thumb tacks in the hammers of his piano to give it the proper twang. Friends and musicians began to come around to listen, laugh and join in—among them Singers Frank Luther and Carson Robison, Composers Henry Cowell and Carl Ruggles"; "June Records," *Time*, June 15, 1942.

72. On reactions to *Out Singing Country*, see Porterfield, *Last Cavalier*, 438–40.

73. While Alan's *Dear Mr. President* radio show, including Seeger and Lead Belly, was not aired until May, on February 14 Norman Corwin featured the Almanacs singing "Round and Round Hitler's Grave" on his CBS show *We the People*, with perhaps 30 million in the listening audience. In February 1942 the Almanac Singers recorded six pro-war songs in New York City, which would soon appear as the Keynote album *Dear Mr. President*. In his letter Alan is referring to these recordings, in particular Pete's "Dear Mr. President" talking blues solo.

74. On John's spring trip, see Porterfield, *Last Cavalier*, 446.

75. Frank Luther, *Americans and Their Songs* (New York: Harper & Row, 1942). John charged Luther $25 for the rights.

76. Gordon and Nemerov, *Lost Delta Found, 16–20*.

77. Quoted in Gordon and Nemerov, *Lost Delta Found*, 19. He might have been referring to the three volumes he would publish in 1942, *Check-list of Recorded Songs in the English*, or perhaps the forthcoming albums from the Archive of American Folk Song.

78. Alan Lomax with Sidney Robertson Cowell, *Americana Folk Song and Folk Lore: A Regional Bibliography* (New York: Hinds, Hayden & Eldredge, 1942).

79. Porterfield, *Last Cavalier*, 430.

80. Two days later, March 11, Work responded: "The trip to Fort Valley was not a successful one. At the last moment I found it impossible to persuade anyone here with a car to make the trip. This necessitated the trip by train. . . . But I had just as well not have bought them [the records] inasmuch as I was not able to record anything of worth, due to my inability to bring performers of merit to the campus although arrangements were made to transport twelve. The next day it rained 'cats and dogs.'" [FVMF]

81. For other family letters, see Bess to Alan, March 10 and 14, 1942 [ALC]; Alan to John, March 10 and 13, 1942 [LP, folder 4]; Alan to his brother Johnny, March 21, 1942, and an undated one about the same time [LP, folder 6].

82. Cray, *Ramblin' Man*, 228.

83. Mr. and Mrs. E. C. Ball, "Pretty Polly" and "Jennie Jenkins," appeared on *Anglo-American Ballads*, AAFS 3, and "Jenny Jenkins" appeared on *Anglo-American Shanties, Lyric Songs, Dance Tunes, and Spirituals*, AAFS 8, Division of Music, Library of Congress, 1942. Similar letters went to Smith Cason in Brazoria, Texas, for the use of his songs "The Country Rag" and "The White Horses in a Line," March 19, 1942; James "Ironhead" Baker, still a prisoner in Otey, Texas, for the use of his song "Grey Goose," March 20, 1942; Arthur Ball in Gould, Arkansas, for "John Henry," March 20, 1942. [ALC]

84. W. E. Claunch, "Cindy," "The Eighth of January," and "Grub Springs," *Anglo-American Shanties, Lyric Songs, Dance Tunes, and Spirituals*, AAFS 9.

85. On March 23 Lomax heard from Work: "Enclosed are the vouchers you asked for. You will observe that they are signed by John Ross. In my recent letter to you I explained that these transactions took place before I joined the group. Inasmuch as Mr. Ross was present he consented to sign." [ALC]

86. "Another tempest erupted in March 1942, when Elie Siegmeister, founder of the American Ballad Singers, brought his troupe from New York to Dallas to present their program of 'Native American Music' at Southern Methodist University. Lomax, as the Grand Old Man of American Folk Song, appointed himself to attend and offer his welcome, despite the fact that Siegmeister had earned his wrath by publishing in *A Treasury of American Song* (1941) two pieces from *American Ballads and Folk Songs* without the credit Lomax felt was his due. . . . The program had been all too Broadway slick, sterile, and commercial for his tastes, in his view the work of some Broadway hack ignorant of the true merits of folksong and contemptuous of those who understood it. But, what was worse, he said, Siegmeister had baldly lifted material from the Lomax books." Porterfield, *Last Cavalier*, 447. On the other hand, Alan shared Siegmeister's left-wing politics.

87. Kelley Pace, *et al.*, "Holy Babe," *Negro Religious Songs and Services*, AAFS 49; "Jumpin' Judy," *Afro-American Spirituals, Work Songs, and Ballads*, AAFS 13; "Rock Island Line," *Negro Work Songs and Calls*, AAFS 40.

88. Arthur Bell, "John Henry," *Afro-American Spirituals, Work Songs, and Ballads*, LC 3.

89. Irvin Lowry, "Joe the Grinder," *Afro-American Blues and Game Songs*, AAFS 16.

90. Alan Lomax," Mister Ledford and the TVA," Erik Barnouw, ed., *Radio Drama in Action: Twenty-Five Plays of a Changing World* (New York: Rinehart, 1945), 51–58, and reprinted in Cohen, ed., *Alan Lomax*, 77–85. There is no indication that he ever published in *Common Ground*.

91. Frank Jordan and group, "I'm Going to Leland," *Afro-American Spirituals, Work Songs, and Ballads*, AAFS 14.

92. Jeff Webb and group, "Rosie," *Afro-American Spirituals, Work Songs, and Ballads*, AAFS 14.

93. A newspaper article at the time captured Alan's appearance on March 28 at the Milwaukee conference: "A rangy, boyish looking guitarist came here Saturday to sell the music educators of the nation on the folk songs of their country—the songs that the Texas cowboy chants on the roundup or the Negro cotton picker hum's after the day's work is done. . . . Wisconsin is particularly rich in folk songs, Lomax said Saturday. The Germans, Czechs, Irish and Swedish, Great Lakes sailors, Mississippi river raftsmen and lumberjacks of the state all had something to offer to the collection of typically American songs, he explained." (copy in editor's possession)

94. For unissued Library of Congress recordings of Barbara Bell from Minneapolis, see AFS 1616–1637: twenty-two 12-inch discs of songs performed by Barbara Bell, Ernest Bourne, W. C. Handy, Alan Lomax, Bess Brown Lomax, the Resettlement Administration Singers, the Rindlisbacher Lumberjack Group, Earl Robinson, the Skyline Farm Singers, and Blaine Stubblefield. Recorded primarily in Washington at the Library of Congress, by Alan Lomax, 1937–38; AFS 1631 A5 and 1632 B3: two discs containing two versions of "Contéstame si me amas" (Answer Me If You Love Me), sung by Barbara Bell; AFS 6089-6091: Barbara Bell recorded at the Library of Congress by Alan Lomax and Arthur Semmig, January 1942.

95. Lilla Belle Pitts (1884–1970) was a prominent music educator known for her advocacy of "child-centered" music education and the use of folk and popular music for children.

96. See James "Iron Head" Baker to Alan Lomax, May 4, 1942 [ALC]; Baker and group, "Go Down, Old Hannah" and "Old Rattler," *Negro Work Songs and Calls*, AAFS 38; Baker and group, "The Grey Goose," *Afro-American Spirituals, Work Songs, and Ballads*, AAFS 15.

97. He repeated his request to Moss on April 30, 1942. [ALC]

98. Similar letters went to Carriere Oakdale (a.k.a. Ogdel Carrier), Angola, Louisiana; Cleveland Benoit, Jennings, Louisiana; and Joe Washington Brown, Jennings, Louisiana, April 24, 1942. There were follow-up letters about these men to the warden in Angola, Louisiana, May 9, 1942; the Postmaster in Lake Arthur, Louisiana, May 13, 1942; Joe Washington Brown in Lake Arthur, May 13, 1942; and the Postmaster, Church Point, Louisiana, May 13, 1942. [ALC]

99. Blind Willie McTell (1901–1959) started recording for Victor Records in 1927, for Columbia Records in 1929–1931, and for others until 1936. In 1940 John Lomax recorded him in a hotel room in Atlanta (*Complete Library of Congress Recordings*, Document BDCD-6001, 1990). He returned to commercial recording in 1949.

100. See Mary Gould Davis to Alan Lomax, May 1, 1942. [ALC]

101. Horton Barker, "The Farmer's Cursed Wife," *Anglo-American Ballads, Vol. 1*, AFSL 1, recorded in Virginia in 1939 (originally issued by the Library of Congress in 1941); "Two Sisters" and "Lord Thomas and Fair Ellender," *Anglo-American Ballads, Vol. 2*, AFSL 7 (originally issued by the Library of Congress in 1943). Barker (1889–1973) lived in Virginia, performed at the White Top Folk Festival in 1933, and recorded for the Library of Congress in the 1930s.

102. Banjoist Benjamin Frank Shelton (1902–1963) was recorded performing "Pretty Polly" by Ralph Peer for Victor in Bristol, Tennessee, on July 29, 1927, part of this historic recording session. Charles K. Wolfe and Ted Olson, eds., *The Bristol Sessions: Writings About the Big Bang of Country Music* (Jefferson, N.C.: McFarland, 2005), 49–51.

103. See also Morganfield to Alan Lomax, June 25, 1942 [ALC]. For this whole issue, with much criticism of Lomax, see Robert Gordon, *Can't Be Satisfied: The Life and Times of Muddy Waters* (Boston: Little, Brown, 2002), 35–51.

104. He wrote a similar letter to the Warden at the Louisiana State Penitentiary regarding Oakdale/Ogdel Carrier on May 9; and to the Postmaster in Lake Arthur, Louisiana, concerning Joe Washington Brown, on May 13. [ALC]

105. Suzanne Comhaire-Sylvain, "Creole Tales From Haiti," *The Journal of American Folklore*, no. 197, July 1937.

106. The trip eventually covered three thousand miles in Texas, Oklahoma, and Arkansas, and added about ninety records to the Archive, although John had a difficult time recovering his expenses, which he blamed on Alan and the library's bureaucracy; Porterfield, *Last Cavalier*, 446. See also Alan to John Lomax, May 11, 1942, although he does not mention the upcoming trip. [LP, folder 4]

107. Alan was apparently referring to the National Folk Festival, held in Washington in late March.

108. In February 1942 Vance Randolph recorded Irene Carlisle singing "Adieu to Cold Weather" in Fayetteville, for the Library of Congress. I am not able to locate the article mentioned by Alan.

109. Benjamin A. Botkin (1901–1975) was a folklorist who served as Alan's replacement at the Archive of American Folk Song from 1942–1945. He headed the Folklore Section of the Federal Writers' Project following John Lomax in May 1938. See Susan G. Davis, "Ben Botkin's FBI File," *Journal of American Folklore*, vol. 122, no. 487 (Winter 2010): 3–30.

110. Augustus D. Zanzig, *Singing America: Song and Chorus Book* (Boston: C.C. Birchard, 1940).

111. The Almanac Singers were about to fold in New York, and Bess would move to Detroit with Butch Hawes (they would soon marry). The Headline Singers was a name proposed to replace the Almanac Singers, but Alan was opposed and it did not happen. Pete joined the Army in July 1942. See Pete to Alan, undated but May 1942: "We (also) have not been paid our fifty dollars for the Martins and the Coys and Dear Mr. President, from OEM. Could you phone up or drop a line to the people in charge of that radio program, and sort of stick a pin in the right place to see if they will hurry up on this matter." [ALC]

112. Alan was a visiting lecturer at the Indiana University Folklore Institute in Bloomington, Indiana, June 29–July 11; Thelma James, "Report on Indiana University Folklore Institute," *Journal of American Folklore*, vol. LV (1942): 246–47.

113. Katherine Dunham studied dance in the Caribbean, in particular Haiti, and returned in 1937 to the University of Chicago. Alan refers to her thesis on the dances of Haiti. For Courlander and his collecting in Haiti in 1932, see Nina Jaffe, *A Voice For The People: The Life and Work of Harold Courlander* (New York: Henry Holt, 1997), 19–37.

114. See William Doerflinger, *Shantymen and Shantyboys: Songs of the Sailor and Lumberman (New York: Macmillan, 1951).*

115. Lomax is perhaps referring to Samuel Preston Bayard, "Hill Country Tunes," Memoirs of the American Folklore Society, Vol. 34, 1941.

116. Alan Lomax with Svatava Jakobsonova, "Freedom Songs of the United Nations," Washington: Office of War Information, 1943. Dr. Svatava Pirkova Jakobson, professor, author, folklorist, and musicologist, received her Ph.D. from Charles University in Prague. Along with her husband, she fled to the United States in 1940, and wound up teaching at Columbia, Harvard, M.I.T., and eventually the University of Texas.

117. See Spivacke to Alan Lomax, July 24, 1942: "Your letter from Nashville arrived while I was away from the office on a short vacation and has just come to my attention. I must confess that I was quite surprised at its hysterical tone. There was little in my previous letter to lead you to jump to so many conclusions. Although it is true that no specific allotment has been made for folk song recording during the coming fiscal year, I have worked out an arrangement with the administration whereby we may make recommendations against the Librarian's fund for specific projects. It goes without saying that during this war we must change our basic policy. I am against any business as usual policy and I am sure that you feel the same way. I am perfectly willing to recommend folk song recording expeditions which are directly connected with the war efforts and I feel quite sure that we can obtain the necessary funds for this type of work." [ALC]

118. George Pullen Jackson, *White Spirituals in the Southern Uplands* (Chapel Hill: University of North Carolina Press, 1933).

119. On August 4 the *Dallas Morning News* published an article on Alan's visit: "Alan Lomax, authority on American folklore is currently visiting his father. . . . The work which Mr. Lomax has been doing, that of mapping out a complete history of folklore and music as far back as the memory of the oldest inhabitant goes, has been

concentrated in Coahoma County, Mississippi. . . . He finds that the Negroes of that section listen to only two types of radio program—news and local programs which give their own folk music. . . . Mr. Lomax returns to Mississippi on Wednesday to complete his work after which he'll return to Washington. He expects to be called to the Army within a few months, but will complete the final details of his research before going. Mr. Lomax appeared here last season at McFarlin Auditorium under the auspices of the Community Course, giving a lecture on his work, spiced with vocal demonstrations of the old folk tunes, for which he played his own accompaniment on the guitar."

120. See Spivacke to Lomax, August 1, 1942, August 17, 1942 [ALC]. For more on Alan's activities at this time, see the letter to his father, August 14, 1942, and three others that are undated and very detailed (one mailed from Clarksdale) [LP, folder 4]. In one he mentioned talking to recruiting officers for the military about his options. He was also borrowing money from his father at this time. One very detailed letter written upon his return to Washington noted that Spivacke was encouraging him to enlist at once so as to get a commission, but it turned out he had a health problem, a cyst at the base of his spine. He repeated some of the same information in a letter on September 4 to his brother, Johnny, including his decision to join the Office of War Information (OWI). [LP, folder 6]

121. See S. T. Burns to Alan Lomax, August 24, 1942. [ALC]

122. In September similar letters went to various others in the Delta, including Ulysses Jefferson, Asa Ware, and Charles Berry. [F-LC]

123. Cochran, *Vance Randolph*, 176–77.

124. Thelma James (1899–1988) was a collector and archivist of urban folk traditions, who joined the Wayne State University faculty in 1923. In 1939 she helped established the university's folklore archives.

125. Arthur Posnansky was a Polish engineer, archaeologist, and explorer who lived in Bolivia.

126. Pipes taught at the University of Michigan; William H. Pipes, *Say Amen, Brother! Old-Time Negro Preaching: A Study in American Frustration* (New York: William-Frederick, 1951).

127. Helen Creighton was a prominent Canadian folklorist who published *Songs and Ballads from Nova Scotia* (Toronto: J.M. Dent, 1932).

128. In 1943 James would make recordings at the Fort Valley State College Folk Festival in Georgia.

129. In a fascinating series of undated letters to his father during the fall, he described his new position, health problems, change of jobs, and much else. [LP, folder 4]

130. Mody C. Boatright (1896–1970) was an educator and folklorist who taught at the University of Texas from 1926 to 1968. For years he edited the annual collections of the Texas Folklore Society; see Ernest B. Speck, *Mody C. Boatright* (Austin: Steck-Vaughn, 1971).

131. Olga Julia Pazdral, "Czech Folklore in Texas," M.A. thesis, University of Texas, 1942.

132. Faulk served in the Merchant Marine, the American Red Cross, and the army during the war.

133. Cowles was a liberal Republican and media owner who headed the Domestic Branch of the OWI. He focused on advertising campaigns for various government agencies and programs.

134. See Lomax with Svatava Jakobsonova, "Freedom Songs of the United Nations," n. 116 above.

135. See Lomax, "Mister Ledford and the TVA."

136. Charles Edward Smith *et al.*, *The Jazz Record Book* (New York: Smith & Durrell, 1942); Smith and Frederick Ramsey, eds., *Jazzmen* (New York: Harcourt Brace, 1939).

137. For Alan's feelings at this time, while awaiting his draft status, see a letter to his brother John A. Lomax Jr., January 7, 1943. [LP, folder 6]

138. Douglas Meservey was the Acting Chief of the OWI Radio Bureau. See Howard Blue, *Words at War: World War II Era Radio Drama and the Postwar Broadcasting Industry Blacklist* (Lanham, MD: Scarecrow Press, 2002), chapter 6; Gerd Horten, *Radio Goes to War : The Cultural Politics of Propaganda During World War II* (Berkeley: University of California Press, 2003).

139. While Lomax was not able to launch the radio program here described, he was soon to begin another, *Transatlantic Call: People to People*, which had its first show on April 11, 1943, and lasted to May 1945. There are manuscript copies of the programs in the Alan Lomax Collection at the American Folklife Center, Library of Congress. The program was the product of cooperation between CBS and the British Broadcasting Corporation (BBC), at the initiative of Norman Corwin, and began with citizens of the United States and Great Britain exchanging information about the emergencies of wartime life.

140. Josef Marais (1905–1978) was born in South Africa and moved to the United States during World War II. He worked for the Office of War Information, where he met Rosa de Miranda, and they performed together for many years as a folk duo.

141. Alan Cranston worked for the OWI, as did Lee Falk, who was the head of the foreign language division. Falk also created *Mandrake the Magician* and *The Phantom* for the comics. Cranston would later become a U.S. senator from California. Lomax was apparently referring to Paul F. Lazarfeld, *Radio and the Printed Page* (New York: Duell, Sloan and Pearce, 1940). James C. Petrillo was the head of the American Federation of Musicians, which enforced a recording ban from 1942 to 1944.

142. Stetson Kennedy had headed the Federal Writers' Project Folklore Unit in Florida, starting in December 1938, where he had worked with Alan Lomax. See Margaret Anne Bulger, "Stetson Kennedy: Applied Folklore and Cultural Advocacy," unpublished Ph.D. diss., University of Pennsylvania, 1992.

143. Alan also sent his comments directly to Woody Guthrie on February 13, and asked him to "Fill out the enclosed application blanks and mail them air mail *pronto* to Rosenwald Fund, as time is short and of the essence." [ALC]

144. A similar letter went to Willis James on February 13. [ALC]

145. For details about his life at this time, as he traveled around the country recording for his radio show, see a May 4 telegram to his father, and letters to his father on May 18 and July 20 [LP, folder 5]. Since the beginning of the war Alan had served on the planning committee for the government's Office of Facts and Figures, along with Archibald MacLeish, Jerome Wiesner, Philip Cohen, and Joe Liss, which promoted using radio programs to support the war. In 1943 he would replace Norman Corwin on *Transatlantic Call: People to People*, which first aired on February 7; see, R. LeRoy Bannerman, *On a Note of Triumph: Norman Corwin and the Golden Years of Radio* (New York: Carol Publishing, 1986), 75, 114–16. See also Botkin to Alan, July 21 [LP, folder 5]. He also published the essay "Reels and Work Songs" in *75 Years of Freedom: Commemoration of the 75th Anniversary of the Proclamation of the 13th Amendment to the Constitution of the United States* (Washington: Library of Congress, 1943), reprinted in Cohen, ed., *Alan Lomax*, 69–76 (originally comments at a concert in Washington, December 20, 1940).

146. Quoted in Bulger, "Stetson Kennedy," unpublished Ph.D. diss., 236, including ellipses; original in "Stetson Kennedy Collection," Southern Labor Archives, Georgia State University, Atlanta, 1512/17. The program, *South of the South*, was broadcast on CBS Sunday November 28, 1943, 12:30–1:00 p.m.

147. Alan wrote numerous letters about his radio shows and so much else, including details about his sister Bess's work for the OWI, to his father through 1943, including September 10, October 13, undated but in November 1943, and undated but probably January, and February 6, 1944 [LP, folder 5]. For the earlier history of Camp Upton, Richard Slotkin, *Lost Battalions: The Great War and the Crisis of American Nationality* (New York: Henry Holt, 2005), chapter 4. For his life at Camp Upton see the letter to his father April 5, 1944 [LP, folder 5]. For his life at Camp Crowder and back in New York see various fascinating letters to his father, most undated, but also April 30, late July, December 21, 1944 [LP, folder 5]. Scripts and recordings for the AFRS programs can be found in the Alan Lomax Collection, American Folklife Center, Library of Congress.

148. See Botkin to Lomax, January 20, 1945 [ALC]. On February 12, 1945, he sent off a detailed letter to Hally and John Henry Faulk [JHFP]. And see undated letters to his father around this time, as well as April 22. [LP, folder 5]

149. See Alan to John, July 6 and 31, August 20, and September 5. [LP, folder 5]

150. See also Alan to John, September 18, October 1 and 9, November 19 and 20 [LP, folder 5]; Alan to John Henry Faulk, undated but late 1945. [JHFP]

151. "Miserable but Exciting Songs," *Time*, November 26, 1945, 52.

152. For Alan's writings following the war, discussions of his life, and a complete bibliography, see Cohen, ed., *Alan Lomax*.

Index